NUCLEIC ACIDS

NUCLEIC ACIDS

A Natural Target for Newly Designed Metal Chelate Based Drugs

Edited by

IRSHAD UL HAQ BHAT

University of Bahrain, Bahrain

ZAKIA KHANAM

Aligarh Muslim University, Aligarh, Uttar Pradesh, India

ELSEVIER

ACADEMIC PRESS

An imprint of Elsevier

Academic Press is an imprint of Elsevier
125 London Wall, London EC2Y 5AS, United Kingdom
525 B Street, Suite 1650, San Diego, CA 92101, United States
50 Hampshire Street, 5th Floor, Cambridge, MA 02139, United States
The Boulevard, Langford Lane, Kidlington, Oxford OX5 1GB, United Kingdom

ISBN: 978-0-12-820503-7

For information on all Academic Press publications visit our website at https://www.elsevier.com/books-and-journals

Publisher: Andre G. Wolff
Acquisitions Editor: Linda Versteeg-Buschman
Editorial Project Manager: Susan E. Ikeda
Production Project Manager: Sajana Devasi P. K.
Cover Designer: Miles Hitchen

Typeset by TNQ Technologies

Dedicated to all contributors.

Contents

List of contributors

Sayyed Jaheera Anwar
Faculty of Science and Marine Environment, Universiti Malaysia Terengganu, Kuala Nerus, Terengganu, Malaysia

Masrat Bashir
Department of Chemistry, Aligarh Muslim University, Aligarh, Uttar Pradesh, India

Irshad Ul Haq Bhat
University of Bahrain, Bahrain

Imtiyaz Ahmad Mantoo
Department of Chemistry, Aligarh Muslim University, Aligarh, Uttar Pradesh, India

Shazia Parveen
Chemistry Department, Faculty of Science, Taibah University, Yanbu, Saudi Arabia

Sadiya
Department of Chemistry, Aligarh Muslim University, Aligarh, Uttar Pradesh, India

Imtiyaz Yousuf
Department of Chemistry, Aligarh Muslim University, Aligarh, Uttar Pradesh, India

Hanis Mohd Yusoff
Advance Nano Materials (ANoMa) Research Group, Faculty of Science and Marine Environment, Universiti Malaysia Terengganu, Kuala Nerus, Terengganu, Malaysia

Abbreviations

2mq	2−mercapto−4(3H)−quinazolinone
2TU	2−thiouracil
4-mphen	4-methyl-1,10-phenanthroline
5′-GMP	guanosine 5′-monophosphate
6m2TU	6−methyl−2−thiouracil
8HQ	8-hydroxyquinoline
AFM	Atomic Force Microscopy
Am4Eotaz	N′-(3-ethyl-4-oxothiazolidin-2-ylidene)pyridine-2-carbohydrazonamide Am4Motaz
Arg	Arginine
As	Arsenic
ASC	ascididemin
Asp	Aspartic acid
AT	Adenine−thymine
ATP	Adenosine triphosphate
B	Boron
bb_n	bis[4(4′-methyl-2,2′-bipyridyl)]-1; {n-alkane}
biphy	bipyridine
bipy	2,2′-bipyridine
bipyam	2,2′-dipyridylamine
bpg	4b,5,7,7a−tetrahydro−4b,7a−epiminomethanoimino−6H−imidazo [4,5−f][1,10] phenanthroline−6,13−dione
bpm	2,2′−bipyrimidine
BSA	bovine serum albumin
C	Carbon
CAPIP	(E)−2−(2−(furan−2−yl)vinyl)−1H−imidazo[4,5−f][1,10] phenanthroline
CD	circular dichroism
CEPIP	(E)−2−(4−fluorostyryl)−1H−imidazo[4,5−f][1,10]phenanthroline
CH_2Cl_2	dichloromethane
$CHCl_3$	chloroform
Cl	Chlorine
Cl8HQ	5-chloro-8-hydroxyquinoline
Cp*	pentamethyl cyclopentadienyl
CT DNA	Calf thymus DNA
CT	charge transfer
CV	Cyclic voltammetry
DACH	diaminocyclohexane
DAPI	4′,6-diamidino-2-phenylindole
dicnq	6,7−dicyanodipyrido[2,2-d:2′,3′−f]quinoxaline
dilc	diclofenac
DMF	dimethylformamide

dmp	2,9-dimethyl-1,10-phenanthroline
dmphen	4,7-dimethyl-1,10-phenanthroline
DNA	Deoxyribonucleic acid
Dppb	1,4–bis(diphenylphosphino)butane
Dppf	1,1′-bis(diphenylphosphino)ferrocene
dppz	dipyrido[3,2–a:2′,3′–c]phenazine
Dpq	dipyrido[3,2-f:2′,3′-h]quinoxaline
DpqQX	dipyrido[3,2-f:2′,3′-h]quinoxalino[2,3-b]quinoxaline
EPR	electron paramagnetic resonance
ESI	Electrospray ionization
ESI–MS	Electron spray ionization Mass spectroscopy
Et_2O	diethyl ether
EtBr/EB	ethidium bromide
EtOH	ethanol
ε_{max}	molar extinction coefficient
F	Fluorine
FAMP	2–(4–formylanthryl)imidazo–[4,5–f][1,10]phenanthroline
FES	Fluorescence emission spectroscopy
FID	fluorescent intercalator displacement
fip	2–ferrocenyl–1H–imidazo[4,5–f][1,10]–phenanthroline
FS-DNA	Fish DNA
GC	Guanine–cytosine
Gln	L-glutamine
Gua	guanine
HSA	human serum albumin
HS-DNA	herring sperm DNA
icip	2–(indeno[2,1-b]chromen–6–yl)–1H–imidazo[4,5–f]–[1,10] phenanthroline
IL	intraligand
Im	imidazole
imd	1-methylimidazole
KP1019	indazolium trans–[tetrachlorobis(1H–indazole)ruthenium(III)]
Leu	Leucine
L-Phe	L-phenylalaninate
LysH	protonated L-lysinate
MALDI–MS	matrix–assisted laser desorption–ionization
Me_2bpy	4,4′–dimethyl–2,2′–bipyridine
MeCN	methylcyanine
Mef	mefenamic acid
MeOH	methanol
MG	methyl green
MIm	2-mercapto-1-methylimidazole anion
MLCT	metal-to-ligand charge transfer
mmi	mercapto–1–methyl–imidazole
Mn	Manganese
Mn-SOD	manganese superoxide dismutase
MnTBAP	manganese(iii) 5,10,15,20-tetrakis(4-benzoic acid)-porphyrin

MnTE-2-PyP5+ Mn(III) meso-tetrakis (4-carboxylatophenyl)porphyrin
MnTnBuOE-2-PyP5+ Mn(III) *meso*-tetrakis(*N*-*n*-butylpyridinium-2-yl)porphyrin
MOFs metal-organic frameworks
mpca 6−mercaptopyridine−3−carboxylic acid
MS Mass spectrometry
MSEB (2-(1-(2-hydroxyethyl)-4,5-diphenyl-1H-imidazole-2-yl) (4-bromophenol)
N Nitrogen
N′-(3-methyl-4-oxothiazolidin-2-ylidene)pyridine-2-carbohydrazonamide
NAMI−A imidazolium trans−[tetrachloro−(dimethylsulfoxide)imidazole ruthenium(III)]
nap naproxen
NMR Nuclear magnetic resonance
N-p-NBHA N-p-naphthylbenzohydroxamato
NSAIDs nonsteroidal antiinflammatory drugs
O Oxygen
Oh Octahedral
O-VEDH$_2$ N,N′-bis(O-vanillinidene)ethylenediamine
P Phosphorous
PBIP 2−(4−bromophenyl)imidazo[4,5−f]1,10−phenanthroline
PCS pyridine-2-carboxaldehyde-semicarbazone
phe phenylalanine
PHEHAT 1,10−phenanthrolino[5,6-b]−1,4,5,8,9,12−hexaazatriphenylene
Phen 1,10-phenanthroline
pocl 2−(5−chlorofuran−2−yl)imidazo[4,5−f][1,10]phenanthroline
poi 2−(5−5−iodofuran−2−yl)imidazo[4,5−f][1,10]phenanthroline
poly(A) polyadenylic acid
ppbm 2-(pyridin-2-yl)-1-(pyridin-3-ylmethyl)- 1H-benzo[d]imidazole
PPh$_3$ Triphenylphosphine
ppn 2,4−diaminopyrimido [5,6-b]dipyrido [2,3−f:2′,3′−h] quinoxaline
pta 1,3,5−triaza−7−phosphatricyclo−[3.3.1.1]decane or 1,3,5−triaza−7−phosphaadamantane
py-phen pyrazino[2,3f][1,10]phenanthroline
pytri 2−(1-R−1H−1,2,3−triazol−4−yl)pyridine
pzta pyrazin-2-yl)-1,3,5-triazine-2,4-diamine
RAPTA−C Ru(η^6−p−cymene)Cl_2(pta)
RAPTA−T Ru(η^6−C_6H_5Me) (pta)Cl_2
RNA Ribonucleic acid
ROS reactive oxygen species
rRNA ribosomal RNA
Ru Ruthenium
S Sulfur
SA serum albumin
Salen(tBu)H$_2$ N,N′-bis(3,5-di-t-butylsalicylidene)-1,2-diamino-2-methylpropane
SarGly sarcosine-glycine peptide

Ser	Serine
Si	Silicon
TAP	1,4,5,8−tetraazaphenanthrene
tatp	1,4,8,9−tetra−aza−triphenylene
TEM	Transmission Electron Microscopy
Terp	4′-(3,4,5-trimethoxyphenyl)-2,2′:6′,2′-terpyridine
THF	tetrahydrofuran
Topo I	type I topoisomerases
Topo II	type II topoisomerases
Topo	topoisomerase
TOPRIM	topoisomerase-primase
Tp	terephthalate
tRNA	transfer RNA
trp	L-tryptophan
tzdt	1,3−thiazolidine−2−thione
Uv−vis	Ultraviolet visible
WDLs	water-derived ligands
XAS	X-ray Absorption Spectroscopy
λ_{max}	absorbance maximum

Introduction

The use of a variety of ligands in the chelation process has led to the discovery of thousands of metal-based complexes of biological importance. The nucleic acids are a primary target for these metal complexes and have been immensely studied by scientists. The book chapters from different authors have revealed the importance of metal complexes by compiling the extensive data collected from various search engines. The chemistry of metal, synthetic procedures, and interactive modes of zinc, ruthenium, copper, iron, and magnesium complexes have been compiled. This book can work as a reference material for students as well as researchers at different levels by presenting cutting-edge research for metal-based drug designers to study the interaction of metal complexes with nucleic acids.

CHAPTER 1

Zinc complexes: Their interaction with nucleic acids and other biomolecular targets

Imtiyaz Yousuf, Masrat Bashir, Imtiyaz Ahmad Mantoo and Sadiya
Department of Chemistry, Aligarh Muslim University, Aligarh, Uttar Pradesh, India

1. Chemistry of zinc

Zinc is a transition metal with atomic and mass numbers 30 and 65.38 a.m.u., respectvely, exists in several isotopic forms of masses 66, 67, 68, and 70. Zinc is a malleable, ductile, bluish-white metal element with electronic configuration of [Ar] $4s^2$, $3d^{10}$. Transition metals on account of their distinctive properties, including variable oxidation states, tuneable redox chemistry, lesser toxicity, and target specificity with the biomolecules, offer an excellent platform for the design of therapeutic metallodrugs (Galani et al., 2014; Haghdoost et al., 2018; Santini et al., 2014). Moreover, transition metals form an enormous number of coordination complexes with a diverse range of organic ligands due to a wide range of geometries and coordination numbers that often modulate their kinetic (rates of ligand exchange) and thermodynamic reactivity with the targeted biomolecules (Khare et al., 2021; Psomas & Kessissoglou, 2013). To date, diverse inorganic complexes have been identified as efficient diagnostic and therapeutic agents. Although, the field of metal-based therapy against various diseased states gained momentum after the successful clinical intervention of cisplatin and other platinum dugs against cancer, which opened new prospects for the design of metallodrugs with potential biomedical applications (Mjos & Orvig, 2014). Platinum metallodrugs have shown phenomenal success against various cancers with more than 50% of patients being treated with platinum-based therapy (Olszewski & Hamilton, 2010; Wang & Guo, 2013). However, the issue of systematic toxicity, constrained therapeutic window, and drug resistance exhibited by platinum-based drugs has shifted the focus toward the development of non-platinum complexes (Jung & Lippard, 2007; Wilson & Lippard, 2014). With an aim of achieving lower toxicity, improved selectivity, and better activity, many late 3d-metal

Nucleic Acids
ISBN 978-0-12-820503-7
https://doi.org/10.1016/B978-0-12-820503-7.00002-8

complexes especially Zn(II)-based complexes have been successfully exploited. Zinc is an essential trace element responsible for the development and growth in various forms of life and hence has a considerable therapeutic effect against several diseased states (Maywald & Rink, 2022). Zinc is the most prominent trace metal and has the potential to bind with more than 300 metalloenzymes. It is generally coordinated to sulfur, nitrogen, or oxygen of amino acid residues to facilitate any cellular actions regarding this metal like transport and trafficking, which happen due to uninterrupted exchange of the metal from donor to acceptor ligands (Yaman et al., 2005). The occurrence of zinc is vital for the survival of cells and tissue protection, particularly cellular, production, differentiation, apoptosis, invulnerability, and reproduction (Zhu et al., 2017). It is involved in the synthesis and repair of DNA, as the primary element of binding proteins of DNA has an important function in the genetic message translation and transcription factor purpose, which plays a significant role in examining the cell metabolism and providing protection against oxidation damage (Valko et al., 2016). For an average adult, the regular intake of 8–11 mg is recommended, which regulates its presence of around 3 gm in the individual, mainly confined in muscles, liver, testicles, and brain (Connie & Christine, 2009, p. 151). To avoid the toxic effects caused by the excess or deficiency of metal, the optimum amount of intracellular zinc is mainly controlled by the homeostasis processes depending on the activity of specific transporters like ZIP and ZnT proteins (Wessels et al., 2017). However, zinc imbalance is usual, and its nutritional deficiency can cause breakage in the strands of DNA and oxidative differences that elevate the chances of cancer growth (Skrajnowska & Bobrowska-Korczak, 2019; Ames & Wakimoto, 2002). Unusual variations in the metabolism of Zn may result in neurocognitive disorders and the CNS diseases (Szewczyk et al., 2011), so its leveling is crucial (Davies et al., 2010).

Apart from being an essential cofactor having a catalytic and structural role in an excess of enzymes, its complexes are also employed as drugs (Carrigan & Poulter, 2003). Additionally, it was reported in various literatures that numerous zinc complexes exhibit remarkable biologic activities, viz., anti-Alzheimer (Vasto et al., 2008), anticonvulsant (d'Angelo et al., 2008), antimicrobial (Riduan & Zhang, 2021), antitumor (Pellei et al., 2021), anti-inflammatory (Psomas, 2020), and antidiabetic disease (Chukwuma et al., 2020). It is also found to be beneficial in minimizing cardio- and hepatotoxicity that are triggered by some anticancer drugs (Wang et al., 2022).

Zinc derivatives have advantages over other metal-based drugs in terms of lower toxicity and minimal side effects. The chemical and physical uniqueness of zinc makes it different from the remaining first row transition metals, which is the main reason behind its pervasive occurrence in biologic systems. The redox inactive dicationic Zn^{2+} ion is diamagnetic and a strong Lewis acid (vulnerable to the rapid interchange of ligands), and it stabilizes several coordination geometries (Vallee & Auld, 1990; Suchomski et al., 2012; Chen & Wang, 2020). The charge and steric hindrance of the ligands make it extremely flexible to coordination geometries, which permits the interchange between different coordination geometries, where tetrahedral is the most preferred one in proteins. Being a Lewis acid, the nitrogen binding site of histidine amino acid residue is favored followed by the sulfur of cysteine, oxygen of glutamate/aspartate, and also carbonyl oxygen of glutamate/aspartate, hydroxyl oxygen of tyrosine, and carbonyl oxygen of peptide bond (Haas & Franz, 2009; Barone et al., 2013). On account of possessing diverse geometries and coordination numbers, Zn can coordinate with the binding site of N, O, S, etc., of various ligands (pyridine-based systems and terpyridine, diamine systems and quinoline, and imidazole-based systems, etc.) (Porchia et al., 2020; Banerjee & Chakravarty, 2015). Nevertheless, it forms stable chelates complexes with the ligands of N and O donors (Maret & Li, 2009).

Many studies revealed that the damage of Zn homeostasis leads to its participation in acquiring various cancer diseases. The chelation therapy and the application of ionophore ligands are employed to attain the appropriate zinc concentration in the case of zinc excessiveness and its deficiency respectively (Zhang et al., 2019). Zinc complexes have attracted a lot of attention as potential novel anticancer metal-based drugs compared with other metal (II) complexes. Zinc complexes have been taken into consideration as Zn^{2+} ion is notably nontoxic at heavier doses in comparison with other metals like Hg, Cu, Fe, etc. (Ye et al., 2020). Furthermore, zinc complexes promote the activation of Lewis acid owing to rapid exchange of ligands that lead in playing a role in the hydrolytic catalysis reactions, for example, cleavage and hydrolysis of deoxyribonucleic acid (DNA) possessing anticancer activity (Parkin, 2004). Zinc complexes consist of photosensitive systems, for instance, phthalocyanines, that have been employed as photosensitizer agents in photodynamic therapy. In contrast with other potential metals, zinc is highly coordinated to phthalocyanines, resulting in superior photochemical and chemical properties (Al Mousawi et al., 2017; Yavuz et al., 2018).

2. Interaction of synthesized zinc complexes with nucleic acids

DNA is the prime intracellular target of anticancer drugs that are currently in clinical use or under clinical trials (Skok et al., 2019). DNA consists of four nucleobases, viz., adenine (A), guanine (G), cytosine (C), and thymine (T), which are planar aromatic derivatives of purine (A and G) and pyrimidine (C and T). The phosphodiester bond (which joins 3′ end of one sugar to the 5′ end of another) binds together the adjacent nucleotides in the polymeric chain. As a result, lengthy, single-stranded polyanionic chains with a well-defined directionality (often specified in the 5′ to 3′ direction) are created, and these chains essentially make up the fundamental structure of nucleic acid (Kanvah et al., 2010). Many biologic activities, such as recombination, replication, transcription, and chromosomal segregation during meiosis and mitosis, depend on recognition of specific DNA sequences of various molecules. Similar interactions exist in other processes, including DNA repair, DNA lesions caused by radiation and carcinogens, and the mechanism of action of various antineoplastic agents. Additionally, DNA is typically the main intracellular target of anticancer drugs (Havelka et al., 2007), so it is crucial to understand the various ways how drugs attach to DNA to design novel, effective DNA-targeted medications with solid therapeutic profiles. Furthermore, understanding the chemical reactions that take place between small molecules and DNA is crucial for predicting the potential physiologic and/or therapeutic implications of such interactions (Haq, 2002).

It is generally known that DNA can adopt several conformations that are determined both logically and macroscopically by various structural characteristics rather than existing in a single three-dimensional (3D) structure (Fig. 1.1) (Miyahara et al., 2013). Although both A and B form of double-stranded DNA frequently take a right-handed helical shape, they differ in the sugar conformation (C3′-endo for A-DNA and C2′-endo for B-DNA) and the helical parameters (Ha et al., 2005). It is also found that some DNA sequences are prone to conformational changes that result in the left-handed helical shape known as Z-DNA (Brázda & Fojta, 2019; Zhang et al., 2019).

The negatively charged biopolymer of the human genome known as ribonucleic acid (RNA) controls numerous essential cellular processes. It has been found that RNAs namely, mRNA, tRNA, and rRNA play a crucial role in transcription and translation, spicing, protein synthesis, and retroviral

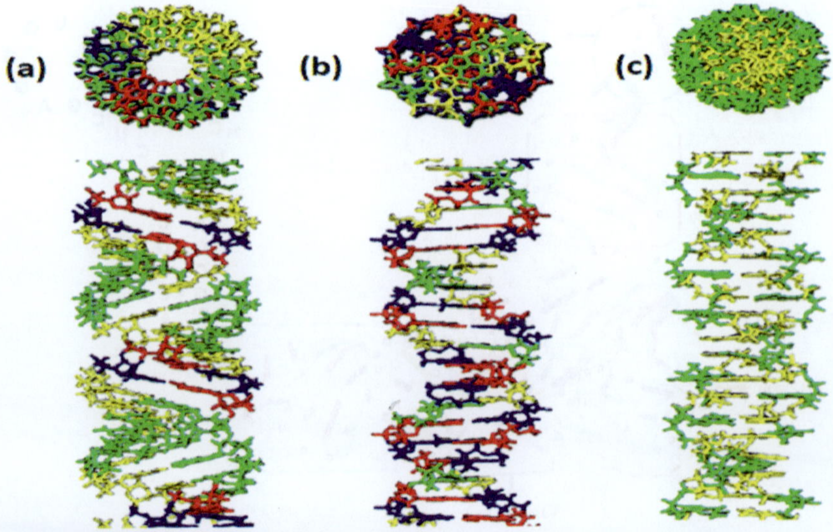

Figure 1.1 Different conformations of DNA (A) A-, (B) B-, and (C) Z-DNA (Brázda & Fojta, 2019).

replication (Arjmand et al., 2019). RNA is predominantly single stranded, but it can fold back on itself to generate base-paired segments between two stretches of complementary sequence that have a significant double-helical nature, akin to A-DNA (Keene et al., 2009). The intervening RNA is looped out from the local regions of the double-helical segment if two stretches of complementary sequences are close to one another by adopting different stem-loop forms, such as hairpin, bulge, or plain loop (Fig. 1.2) (Nagaswamy et al., 2000), thus offering distinctive bingeing and recognition sites for small molecules.

In the past 2 decades, a considerable attention has been drawn toward the study of binding interactions of metal complexes to nucleic acids (Hofstadler & Griffey, 2001). It is generally recognized that metal ions play a key role in nucleic acid chemistry processes such as transcription, translation, DNA replication, DNA denaturation, RNA conformational characteristics, and depolymerization of RNA (Li et al., 2021). Literature reports have revealed that coordination complexes bind with nucleic acids in vivo to exert their anticancer activity (Frezza et al., 2011). Nucleic acids offer three major types of ligating regions to metal centers, viz., the phosphate oxygen of the phosphodiester linkages, the ribose moiety, and the heterocyclic ring nitrogen atoms (Wilner & Willner, 2012).

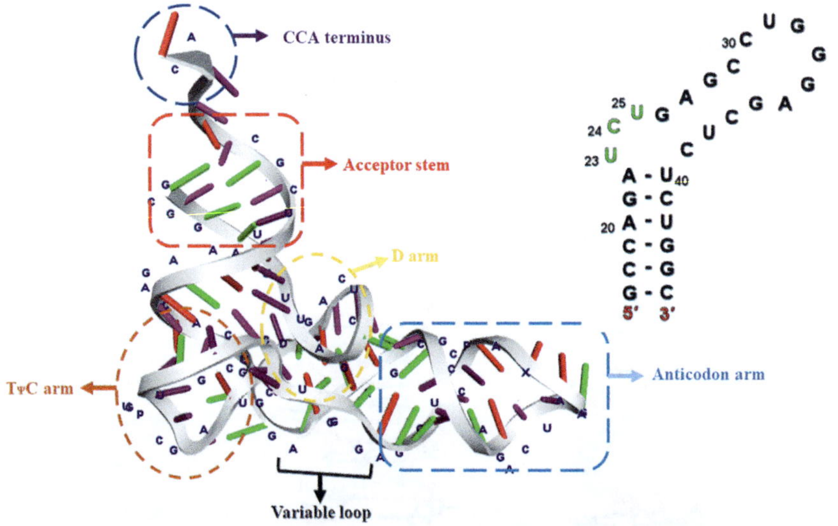

Figure 1.2 3D structure of tRNA (PDB ID: 6TNA).

3. Methods of analysis

There are numerous methods that are used to examine the interaction between metal complexes and nucleic acids including ultraviolet-visible (UV-vis), emission spectroscopy, circular dichroism (CD), viscometry, cyclic voltammetry, nuclear magnetic resonance (NMR), scanning electron microscopy, and transmission electron microscopy. These methods have been efficiently used to examine the binding mode and affinity of metal complexes with nucleic acids and proteins (Misiak et al., 2016). We have focused on some commonly used techniques to characterize the nature of drug–DNA interaction and the effect of metallodrug binding on the structure of DNA.

3.1 Electronic spectroscopy

UV-vis is a simple and sophisticated method to determine the binding mode and strength of zinc complexes when they interact with nucleic acids (Asadi et al., 2004). The changes in the intraligand transition bands of the complexes (either an increase or decrease in intensity, or a shift in wavelength) indicate that complexes interacted with DNA and novel complexes (complex:DNA) were formed (Sirajuddin et al., 2013). The increase in intensity upon increasing concentration of DNA via external contact is called electrostatic mode of interaction. However, if there is considerable decrease in intensity upon progressive addition of DNA, then the possible mode of interaction is intercalation (Paul & Guchhait, 2011). Furthermore, the magnitude of binding strength is quantitatively determined by calculation binding constant values and could be accomplished by observing the alterations observed in absorbance at varied DNA concentrations. Binding constant values are generally determined by Wolfe Shimmer equation (Wolfe et al., 1987). In the metal complex intercalators, binding constant values are generally observed as $>10^5$ M, while the in cases of groove binding and covalent binding mode of interaction, binding constant value is observed to be $<10^5$ M (Barton et al., 1984).

3.2 Fluorescence spectrometry

Fluorescence spectrometry is another important method that reveals better insight about the mode of interaction between nucleic acids and zinc complexes (Fahrni & O'Halloran, 1999). The molecular fluorescence has several advantages over other methods including high sensitivity, a wide linear concentration range, and selectivity. Complexes with aromatic functional groups and low π–π^* transition states exhibit the most intense and useful fluorescence (Fang et al., 2001). However, the complexes containing aliphatic and alicyclic carbonyl structures show small number of transitions in comparison to those of aromatic systems (Jaumot & Gargallo, 2012). The alteration in intensity of the maxima emission band validates the occurrence of interaction between nucleic acids and metal complexes (Gao et al., 2020). The change in intensity is attributed to the penetration of a potential metal complex with the hydrophobic part of nucleic acid especially DNA (Kim et al., 2021). In the case of groove binding agents, hydrogen bonding, hydrophobic, or electrostatic interactions are involved, and the molecules are adjacent to a sugar phosphate backbone, which makes it feasible to see a decrease in fluorescence intensity in the presence of DNA. Moreover, the magnitude of binding affinity is usually calculated by using the Stern–Volmer equation (Hu et al., 2010).

Competitive DNA/RNA binding study is an effective tool to validate the binding mode of interactions between metal complexes and DNA/RNA. Ethidium bromide (EB), acridine orange, and methylene blue are the commonly used compounds that strongly insert themselves between the adjacent base pairs and form stable complexes with nucleic acids (Liu et al., 2009). The emission intensity of EB alone is very weak in aqueous solution, but after forming a complex with DNA, it displays a strong emission band at about 580 nm (Yam & Lo, 1999). However, after gradual addition of strong metallodrug intercalator, a significant decrease in fluorescence intensity was noticed at 580 nm due to effective displacement of EB within the nucleic acid base pairs. Moreover, the mechanism of intercalation is ruled out if the metallodrug showed a weak or no change in fluorescence intensity at 580 nm, thereby indicating that complex would bind via covalent or groove binding mode of interaction. The percent fluorescence intensity decrease is directly related to the extent of DNA/RNA binding (Bonjean et al., 1998).

3.3 Circular dichroism

CD is another crucial method for determining the conformational changes in nucleic acids on interaction with metal complexes (Peng et al., 2020). CD spectral studies provide convincing proof for conformational change in nucleic acid structure on the interaction with a metal complex (Chang et al., 2012). In the case of optically inactive molecules, CD spectra can be used to monitor the asymmetric environment of the complex–nucleic acid adduct, therefore providing important information about the binding mode (Kellett et al., 2019). The B-DNA displays a positive and negative band at 275 and 248 nm, which are assigned to base stacking and right helicity, whereas RNA exhibits four distinctive peaks at 210 and 243 nm (negative) and 225 and 270 nm (positive) (Chang et al., 2012). These bands are quite subtle to demonstrate the changes in the structure of DNA and RNA upon adding concentration of metal complexes (Hofstadler & Griffey, 2001). In comparison to intercalation, which causes large changes in both base stacking and helicity bands and stabilizes right-handed B-DNA, fewer or no alterations are observed in the case of groove or electrostatic mode of binding interaction (Kellett et al., 2019).

3.4 Electrochemical method

The use of electrochemical methods is utilized to supplement the results obtained from spectroscopic techniques (Ganesana et al., 2017). This method is also useful for those complexes whose binding interaction with nucleic acids was not confirmed by UV-vis and fluorescence spectroscopy, either because of weak absorption bands or due to electron transition overlap. Electrochemical analysis is extensively used for the evaluation of exact binding mode and strength of binding interaction (Johnson et al.,

2012). This technique is mostly convenient for metal-based complexes having various accessible redox states. In this experiment, peak current and peak potential of the complex displayed significant change when interacting with nucleic acid. The corresponding change in the peak current and potential can be exploited for the determination of the binding strength and binding mode between metallodrug and nucleic acid (Feng et al., 1997).

3.5 Viscometric studies

Viscometry is a reliable tool to confirm the exact mode of interaction between metal complexes and nucleic acids (Pearlman et al., 2020). Absorption and emission studies provide necessary evidence of interaction but not sufficient clues to conclusively prove how metal complexes interact with nucleic acids. In this study, the binding mode of interaction is usually determined by recording the change in relative viscosity when a fixed concentration of nucleic acid is titrated against concomitant aliquots of metal complexes (Zhang et al., 2011). During intercalative mode of binding, the relative viscosity of nucleic acid increases with increase in concentration of metal complexes due to elongation of nucleic acid by effective separation of base pairs (Anbu et al., 2012). However, in the case of partial intercalation or groove binding of interaction, minimal effect on relative viscosity was observed (Islam et al., 2009). Moreover, electrostatic mode of interaction of the complexes can bend or kink DNA, which results in a decrease in its effective length with a concomitant decrease in its relative viscosity (Yousuf et al., 2022).

4. Interaction of zinc complexes with biomolecules

Metal complexes interact with DNA via different modes, viz., covalent binding, intercalation, and groove binding (Hannon, 2007; Long & Barton, 1990). To recognize and bind DNA molecules, a complex may adopt more than one mode of interaction. These interactions cause the structural alterations in DNA that impair the replication and transcription processes, which in turn causes apoptosis and cell death (Kim, 2005).

The covalent mode of binding of metal complexes with DNA is characterized by hyperchromic effect (an increase in absorption intensity) with small blue shift in wavelength. However, in some cases, a red shift is being observed, which suggests that the complex coordinates with DNA at the N7 site of guanine (Onyido et al., 2004). In the hyperchromic effect, the secondary structure of DNA is disrupted due to strong interaction between the metal complexes and various binding sites offered by phosphate groups (Kasyanenko et al., 1999).

In the intercalative mode of interaction, usually polycyclic aromatic ring metal complexes get precisely inserted within the adjacent base pairs of DNA (Fig. 1.3). The molecule between the adjacent base pairs is stabilized by $\pi-\pi$ stacking interactions with aromatic chromophores, which results in the unwinding of the DNA helix (Monaco, 2010). The strength of binding interaction is totally dependent on the depth of insertion of metal complex within base pairs. The process of intercalation is reversible and stabilized by various interactions, viz., electrostatic, van der Waals, and hydrogen bonding (Pindur et al., 1993; Werner et al., 1996). There are various organic ligand scaffolds that generally act as intercalators including phenanthrolines, acridines, bipyridines, anthraquinones, anthracenes, ellipticines, etc. (Pages et al., 2015). DNA intercalators have been widely employed as anticancer, antimalarial, antineoplastic, antibiotic, and antimicrobial agents (Sundquist et al., 1990).

A reversible intermolecular mode of interaction is generally observed in molecules having crescent-shaped topologies that either interact with DNA via a major or minor groove (Fig. 1.3). Groove binding is dictated by

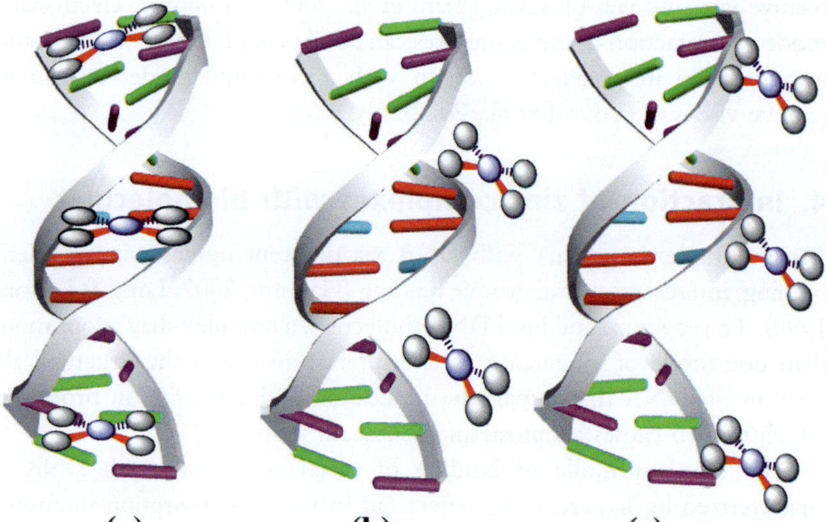

Figure 1.3 Figure illustrating various binding modes of interaction between metal complexes and DNA double helix: (A) intercalation, (B) groove binding, and (C) covalent binding.

intermolecular interactions such as electrostatic and van der Waals attractions; however, groove binding, unlike intercalation, does not significantly alter the conformational changes in DNA and is usually compared with the standard lock-and-key models for ligand–macromolecular binding (Chaires, 1997). Groove binders typically have higher association constants than intercalators and are stabilized by various intramolecular interactions. Additionally, groove binders have demonstrated therapeutic efficacy as antibacterial and anticancer agents (Arya et al., 2001).

Metallodrug interaction with DNA is generally considered a process during which a coordination bond is formed between the metal center and adjacent nucleobase (Timerbaev et al., 2006). The kinetics of metallodrug adduct formation with DNA are often characterized by ligand scaffolds and the geometry of the central metal ion. To investigate the interaction studies of nucleic acids with metallodrugs, it is imperative to understand spectroscopic and analytical methods for investigating drug–DNA interactions (Hartinger et al., 2013).

4.1 Interaction studies of zinc complexes with DNA

Zinc is the second most biologically active trace metal in the human body and holds a special position in the chemistry and biochemistry of nucleic acids (Zhang & Gladyshev, 2009). In contrast to other metal ions, Zn(II) is useful in complete rewinding of DNA, which can be attributed to the balanced affinity of Zn(II) ion for O in phosphodiester group and N in heterocyclic nucleic acid bases (Zamora & Sabat, 2002). Additionally, the functions of Zn(II) ion include DNA synthesis and repair, which are essential for the activity of DNA binding proteins containing Zn fingers. It also plays a remarkable role in translation of the genetic code and transcription factor function, monitoring of cell metabolism, and defense against oxidative damage (Skrajnowska & Bobrowska-Korczak, 2019). Zn is essential for the survival and protection of cells and tissues and in particular for cellular proliferation, differentiation, apoptosis, immunity, and reproduction (Wessels et al., 2017).

Wu et al. reported the synthesis of Zn(II) complex with formulation $[ZnL_2](picrate)_2.2CH_3CN$ (**C1**) from $Zn(picrate)_2$, bis(N-methylbenzimidazol-2-ylmethyl)benzylamines (**L1**), and acetonitrile (Fig. 1.4) (Wu et al., 2012). The authors examined the comparative binding properties of the **L1** and **C1** toward ct-DNA by using absorption titration experiments. The results revealed hypochromism with red shift in absorbance, which is attributable to intercalation and entails a powerful stacking contact between

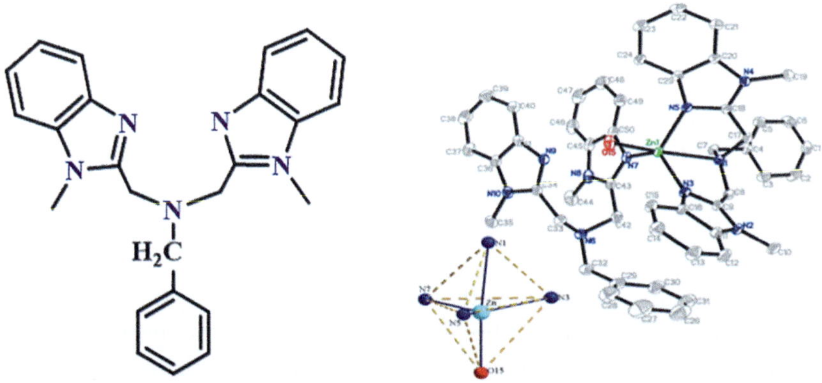

Figure 1.4 Molecular structures of **L1** and **C1.** *(Reprinted with permission from Wu et al. (2012).)*

the DNA base pairs and the aromatic chromophores (Baldini et al., 2004). The hypochromism increased by 17.30% and 38.51% at $\lambda_{max} = 276$ and 272 nm for **L1** and **C1**, respectively, upon incremental additions of concentration of DNA (Liu et al., 2002; Xu et al., 2003). Furthermore, the intrinsic binding constants (K_b) of the **L1** and **C1** to DNA were calculated by observing the change in absorbance with increasing DNA concentration to quantitatively compare the affinity for DNA, which were found to be 7.41×10^3 and 8.04×10^4 $(\text{mol L}^{-1})^{-1}$ respectively. These findings suggested that **C1** binds to DNA more strongly than **L1** (Fig. 1.5) (Wu et al., 2012).

Panja and coworkers synthesized a photoactive bimetallic zinc complex (**C2**) from $Zn(NO_3)_2.6H_2O$ and an azobenzene ligand derived from 4,4′-bis(chloromethyl)azobenzene and (2-pyridylmethyl) (2-pyridylethyl)amine (Panja et al., 2011). The authors reported that **C2** exists in two isomeric forms, viz., *cis* and *trans*, which showed similar binding affinities toward ct-DNA, which was reflected by their K_b values of $4.9 \pm 0.1 \times 10^4\ M^{-1}$ and $4.6 \pm 0.1 \times 10^4\ M^{-1}$ respectively. The computed K_b values were much lower than those reported for typical intercalators, showing that neither *cis* nor *trans* forms of **C2** bind to DNA in an intercalation mode (LePecq & Paoletti, 1967). However, the *trans*-isomer showed very weak DNA cleaving ability in contrast to *cis*-isomer of **C2**. The remarkable binding activity of *cis*-isomer is proportional to the efficient interaction between two Zn centers that are close to each other. Therefore, the authors further examined in detail the comparative DNA and EB binding interactions toward *cis*-isomer of **C2** by using fluorescence spectroscopy. The emission intensity of EB diminished at the outside of the DNA strand due to

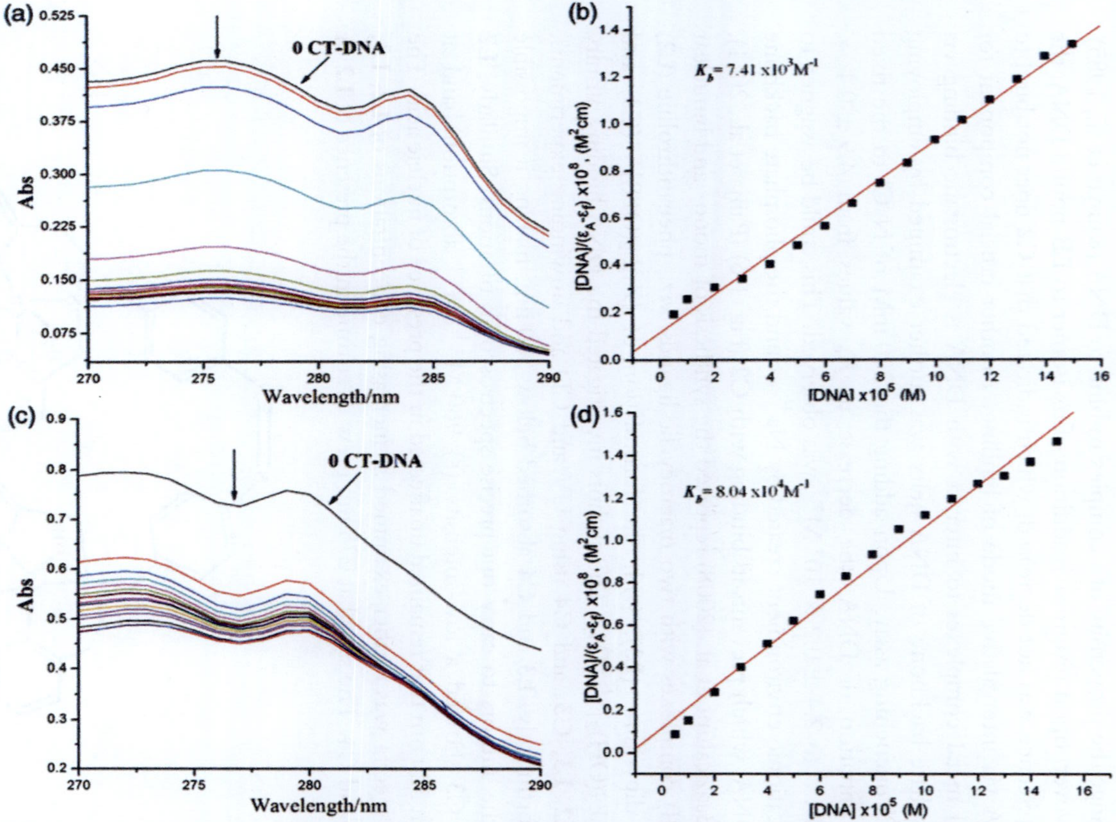

Figure 1.5 Electronic spectra of (A) **L1** and (C) **C1** in Tris–HCl buffer upon addition of CT-DNA showing hypochromic change in absorbance. (B) and (D) represents plots of [DNA]/($\varepsilon_a-\varepsilon_f$) *vs* [DNA]. *(Reprinted with permission from Wu et al. (2012).)*

quenching effect by solvent molecules, whereas it dramatically increased after intercalating to DNA. The emission intensity of EB could be reduced when a complex interacts with EB-bound DNA because EB can be released from the DNA, and the reduction in emission intensity can be used to gauge the propensity of a complex to bind to DNA (Kumar et al., 1985). However, upon progressive addition of *cis*-isomer to EB-bound DNA, the fluorescence was not decreased, which indicated that **C2** does not bind to DNA via intercalative mode of binding. Another crucial component for small metal complexes to interact with DNA is electrostatic binding via phosphate backbone of DNA helix was further examined by employing NaCl quenching assay. Upon adding the 200 mM of NaCl to the fixed concentration of DNA, the decrease in K_b values from $4.9 \pm 0.1 \times 10^4\ M^{-1}$ to $2.4 \pm 0.2 \times 10^4\ M^{-1}$ was observed. This could be assigned to the cationic environment created by Na^+ around the phosphate backbone of DNA, which prevents its binding with **C2** (Fig. 1.6) (Panja et al., 2011).

Bazzicalupi et al. (2008) reported the synthesis of mono- and binuclear Zn(II) complexes with two macrocyclic ligands, viz., phenanthroline (**L2**) and dipyridine (**L3**), with the formulation of $[ZnL_2(OH)]^+$ (**C3**) and $[Zn_2L_3(OH)_2]^{2+}$ (**C4**). The authors investigated the DNA binding affinity of **L2**, **L3**, **C3**, and **C4** using UV and CD and unwinding experiments. Unfortunately, **L3** and **C4** absorbed below 300 nm, making it impossible for the authors to carry out precise spectroscopic titrations. Similarly, **L2** and **C3** showed a low-intensity (ϵ) 960 $M^{-1}\ cm^{-1}$ absorption band at about 320 nm that remained unaffected in the presence of nucleic acid. The CD spectra was further examined at increasing concentrations of **L2**, **L3**, **C3**, and **C4**. The signal at 275 nm grew over time in the presence of **L2** or

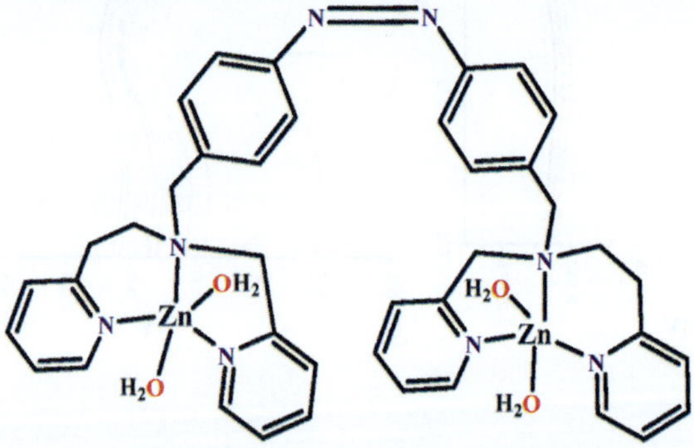

Figure 1.6 Photoactive bimetallic zinc complex (**C2**) derived from 4,4′-bis(chloromethyl)azobenzene and (2-pyridylmethyl) (2-pyridylethyl)amine.

its complex (**C3**), reaching a maximum of 15,000 deg cm^2 $dmol^{-1}$ (mean residue ellipticity) at a complex concentration of 20–30 μM. Further additions of the test complex induced a signal decrease, and a notable decrease in CD intensity was seen in the low micromolar range when **L3** was employed. Parallel studies revealed that DNA solutions containing a concentration of 20 μM caused light scattering. These findings imply that DNA condensation can be successfully induced by **L3**. Because of the presence of an aromatic moiety in the tested ligands, an intercalative mode of binding could be assumed. To evaluate this claim, increasing quantities of the **C3** and **C4** were incubated with supercoiled plasmid in the presence of topoisomerase I. After the ligand is removed, there is no longer a supercoiled form of the plasmid, proving that the complexes are unable to effectively intercalate into DNA (Fig. 1.7) (Bazzicalupi et al., 2008).

Sheng et al. synthesized mono- and bimetallic Zn(II) complexes with ligands 1,4,7-triazacyclononane (**L4**) and 2,6-bis(1-methyl-1,4,7-triazacyclonon-1-yl)pyridine (**L5**) of the type ZnL4 (**C5**) and Zn_2L5 (**C6**) respectively (Fig. 1.8). The authors investigated the DNA binding potential of the synthesized the ligands **L4** and **L5** and **C5** and **C6** using a multitude of spectroscopic techniques including fluorescence and CD spectroscopy. The fluorescence emission intensity of the EB-DNA system after the addition of ligands **L4** and **L5** and **C5** and **C6** was calculated to study the binding of the substances to DNA. The emission intensity decreased (quenching) upon addition of synthesized ligands and complexes to EB-DNA because these complexes replace bound EB, and the K values obtained for ligands **L4** and **L5** and **C5** and **C6** were 0.053 ± 0.01, 0. 157 ± 0.015, 0.259 ± 0.005, and 0.827 ± 0.022, respectively. These results displayed that compared with ligands **L4** and **L5**, complexes **C5** and **C6** have stronger affinity for DNA. Furthermore, the authors calculated the (K_{app}) apparent binding constants,

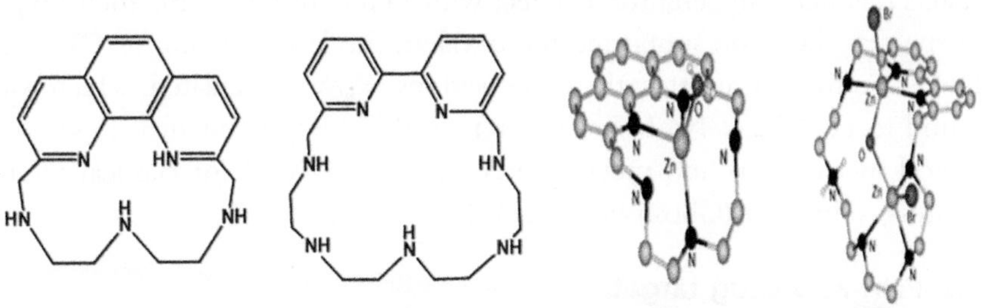

L2 L3 C3 C4

Figure 1.7 Molecular structures of ligands (**L2** and **L3**) and their zinc complexes (**C3** and **C4**). *(Reprinted with permission from Bazzicalupi et al. (2008).)*

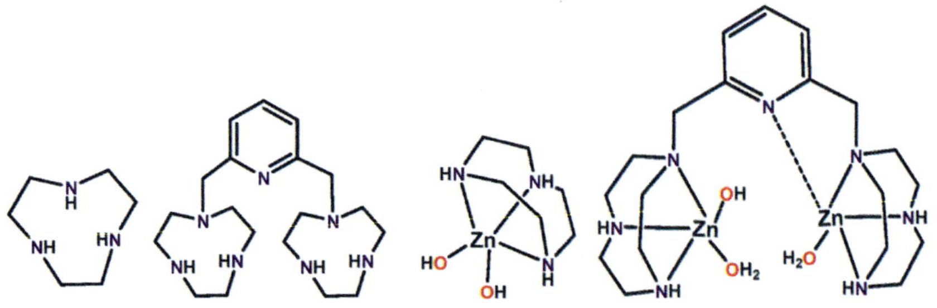

Figure 1.8 Molecular structures of **L4**, **L5**, **C5**, and **C6**.

which were found to be $1.43 \times 10^5\ M^{-1}$ and $3.57 \times 10^6\ M^{-1}$ for **C5** and **C6** respectively. it is noteworthy that bimetallic **C6** possessed 30-fold higher affinity than monometallic **C5**. The authors further investigated binding interactions by CD spectroscopy and observed that upon concomitant addition of **C5** and **C6** to a fixed concentration of DNA, a reduction in the peak intensity of both positive (~275 nm) and negative (~245 nm) bands was observed. However, ligands **L4** and **L5** showed no impact in the shift in bands upon their addition. These results suggested that **C5** and **C6** could unwind the DNA helix and lead to loss of helicity (Pasternack, 2003). In contrast to the other complexes at the same concentration, **C6** significantly reduced the intensity of the CD band. This suggested that **C6** is more effective than **L4**, **L5**, and **C5** at disrupting the secondary structure of DNA. From these findings of fluorescence and CD studies, the authors concluded that the order of the complexes to bind to ct-DNA is **C6** > **C5** > **L4** ≈ **L5** (Sheng et al., 2008).

Ghosh et al. synthesized and demonstrated the binding interactions of Zn(II) complex of the type $[Zn(Pyimpy)(Cl)_2]$ (**C7**) with DNA, where Pyimpy is 2-((2-phenyl-2-(pyridin-2-l)hydrazono)methyl)pyridine. The results revealed a hyperchromic effect with a blue shift of 4 nm. Such a type of spectral alteration supported the covalent mode of binding of **C7** with DNA. To further quantify these interactions, K_b was calculated, which was found to be $1.22 \times 10^3\ M^{-1}$. The reported binding constant is lower for typical intercalators and metallo-intercalators ($10^7\ M^{-1}$ for classical intercalators) (Fig. 1.9) (Ghosh et al., 2011).

4.2 RNA as a drug target

RNA, a nucleic acid having characteristics akin to DNA, is present in all living cells. But unlike DNA, RNA frequently is single stranded and offers

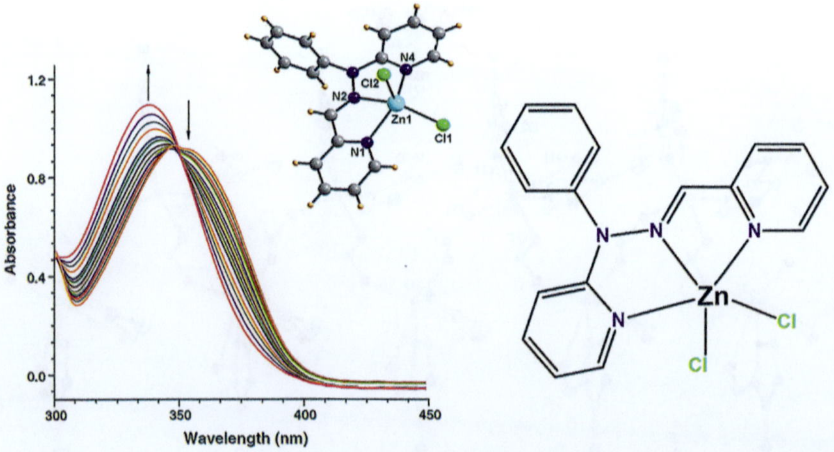

Figure 1.9 Absorption spectrum of groove binder complex **C7** along with its molecular structure. *(Reprinted with permission from Ghosh et al. (2011).)*

far greater structural variations. Its structure is made up of changing the phosphate groups and sugar ribose moieties with a hydroxyl group at the 2′ position. Each sugar moiety has one of the four bases—adenine (A), uracil (U), cytosine (C), or guanine (G)—connected to it (Bayne & Allshire, 2005; Jovanovic & Hengartner, 2006). The structural complexity of RNA is essential for its functioning, the RNA minor groove area is wide and shallow, in contrast to the very deep and tight major groove of DNA. Therefore, in comparison to DNA, RNA grooves are thus less accessible to ligand binding, and nucleobases do not participate in regular base-pairing that could cause double-helical widening and local disruption, which may provide specific binding sites for small molecules like metal complexes (Thomas & Hergenrother, 2008). The positively charged metal complexes generally prefer to bind in the major groove of RNA, as it has been reported in many studies that RNA major groove is highly electronegative as well as more information rich than a minor groove (Chin et al., 1999).

Jana et al. (2014) reported RNA binding of a novel zinc coordination polymer formulated as $[Zn(4\text{-}Me\text{-}5\text{-}CHOIm)_2(HCOO)](ClO_4)$ (**C8**). The molecular structure of **C8** was characterized by Fourier-transform infrared spectroscopy, NMR, and synchrotron X-ray diffraction (sXRD) studies. The authors validated the RNA binding affinity of **C8** by various methods including UV-vis, fluorescence, CD, and isothermal titration calorimetric (ITC) methods. These methods revealed that **C8** binds with RNA via partial intercalative mode of binding with a binding constant value on the

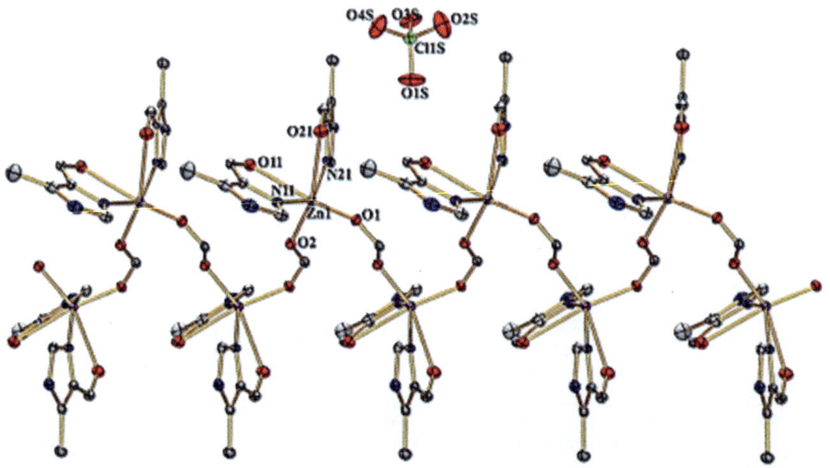

Figure 1.10 Single crystal structure of **C8.** *(Reprinted with permission from Jana et al. (2014).)*

order of 10^5. Moreover, ITC results also validated that the interaction between RNA and **C8** is an exothermic process favored by positive entropy (Fig. 1.10) (Jana et al., 2014).

Arjmand et al. (2019) reported a mixed ligand zinc complex (**C9**) derived from diamino cyclohexane and nalidixic acid and thoroughly characterized by various spectroscopic techniques. The molecular structure of C9 was further confirmed by sXRD studies. The therapeutic potential of **C9** was first examined by comparative in vitro binding studies with biologic targets like DNA and yeast tRNA by using different biophysical techniques, viz., UV-vis, emission spectroscopy, CD, and viscosity. The results obtained from these studies revealed that **C9** binds via electrostatic mode of interaction in the bulge regions of yeast tRNA. Moreover, it has been confirmed from binding constant values that **C9** showed more avid binding with yeast tRNA than DNA. The fact for higher binding affinity for **C9** toward yeast tRNA was attributed to its A form conformation with L-shaped tertiary structure that has a pulled-in narrow major groove and a wide shallow minor groove that allow its base pairs to remain well exposed and accessible for the drug entities. Whereas, **C9** could bind in the bulge region of yeast tRNA, thereby providing a rationale for its higher binding affinity (Fig. 1.11) (Arjmand et al., 2014).

Metalloporphyrin is an essential category of metallodrugs to target RNA because porphyrin–RNA interactions have a significant role in drug design

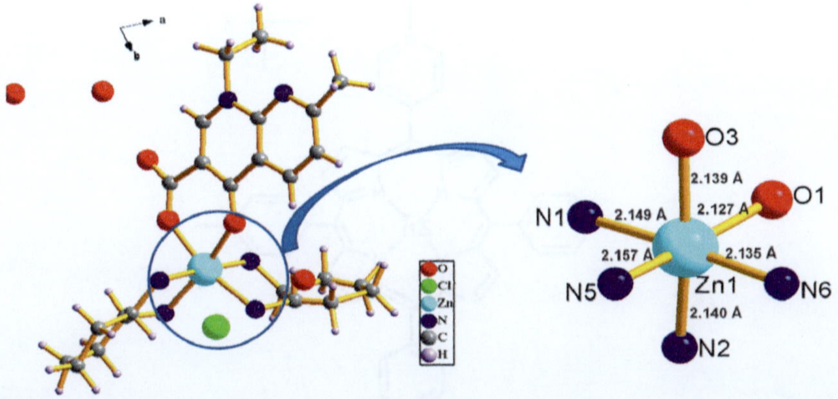

Figure 1.11 Molecular structure of **C9.** *(Reprinted with permission from Arjmand et al. (2014).)*

strategy. Foster and coworkers examined the interactions of yeast tRNA with free porphyrin, T4MPyP (meso-tetrakis(4-N-methylpyridyl) porphyrin), and its Zn(II) complexes (**C12**) (Foster et al., 1988; Duff et al., 1987). A highly specific binding site was discovered in the tertiary region of RNA by employing multispectroscopic methods, viz., UV-vis, CD, NMR, and thermal denaturation, which was later validated by Celander and Nussbaum. They thoroughly characterized these interactions between porphyrin and tRNA and found that porphyrin cations and its analogs recognize hinge areas in RNA where the helices are stacked coaxially. These interactions were improved in absence of stabilizing counterions, which suggested that stack helices are destabilized and provide a more advantageous environment for binding the porphyrin molecule. As a result, porphyrin cations could be highly useful for monitoring RNA folding interactions such as coaxial stacking of helices (Fig. 1.12) (Celander & Nussbaum, 1996).

4.3 Interaction of zinc complexes with albumin proteins

Serum albumin is most prevalent protein in blood and cerebral fluid (Bellomo et al., 2019). It is essential for the transportation of several metabolites, hormones, drugs, metal ions, and metal complexes via the bloodstream (Bal et al., 2013). Therefore, the biological features of the original drug may be diminished or improved, or there may be novel routes for drug delivery, as a result of binding of metal ions and metallodrug complexes to the albumins. It is believed that albumin is the main zinc

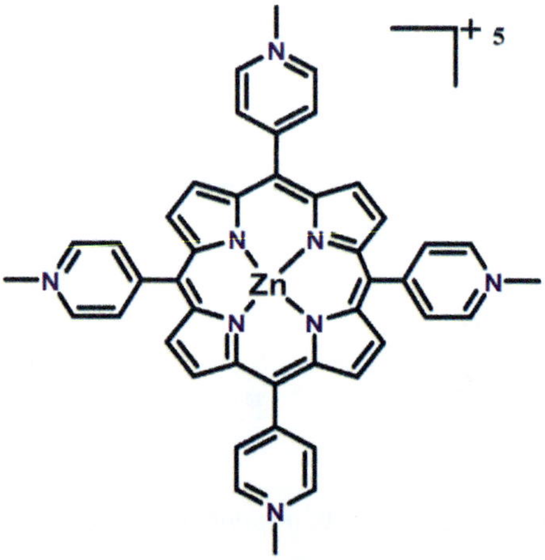

Figure 1.12 Structural representation of **C12**.

transporter in plasma (Lu et al., 2008), and it typically binds about 80% of all plasma (Foote & Delves, 1984). Numerous researches have also shown that albumin regulates the absorption of zinc into cells (Pattison & Cousins, 1986; Gálvez et al., 2001). Some studies also suggested that albumin-bound zinc uptake could occur via a receptor-mediated endocytosis route (Rowe & Bobilya, 2000), and albumins could also be involved in the cotransport of zinc across endothelia (Tibaduiza & Bobilya, 1996; Liu & Chen, 2016). Furthermore, some cases of familial hypozincemia appear to be due to increased zinc binding to albumin (Lu et al., 2008).

Human serum albumin (HSA) is the main plasma protein in bloodstream that significantly increase the reversible binding and serves as a carrier for a variety of endogenous and exogenous drug entities. Drug–HSA interactions are therefore essential because they offer a deeper understanding of the ADME (absorption, transportation, distribution, metabolism, and excretion) characteristics of a drug. As a result, they are recognized as a critical step in evaluating the therapeutic effectiveness and pharmacologic response of a drug in a body (Han et al., 2012). However, a very high affinity to HSA is undesirable for potential drugs because of their lower dissociation constant values at the target site. Therefore, examining the binding phenomena will be crucial in providing fundamental information on the pharmacological activities, bio-transformation, and bio-distribution. The most commonly used drugs that bind with HSA/bovine serum albumin (BSA) at one of the two primary sites located in subdomains IIA and

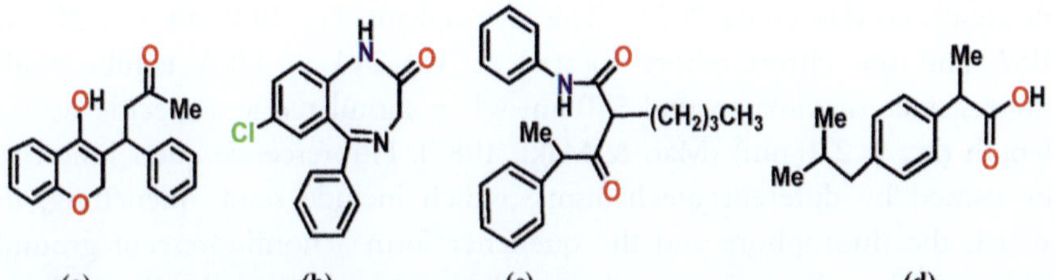

Figure 1.13 Molecular structures of a few potential HSA-binding drugs. (A) warfarin, (B) diazepam, (C) phenylbutazone, and (D) ibuprofen.

IIIA were determined by X-ray crystallography (Fig. 1.13) (Lacroix et al., 2017; Ramezani & Rafii-Tabar, 2015).

HSA and its structural equivalent, BSA, are the most thoroughly examined serum albumins to support the therapeutic potential of metal complexes (Moriyama & Takeda, 1999). The interaction mechanism of HSA/BSA with metal complexes is essential to understand the pharmacodynamics and pharmacokinetic profiles of metallodrugs. Interaction of metal complexes with HSA/BSA has been usually investigated by utilizing electron absorption, fluorescence quenching, and CD studies (Voicescu et al., 2012).

The absorption spectrum of albumin proteins displayed two distinctive spectral bands at 220 and 280 nm, respectively, which could be attributed to the α-helix structure and aromatic amino acid residues, respectively (Zhao et al., 2010). In the electronic absorption studies, a fixed concentration of HSA/BSA has been titrated upon increasing aliquots of metal complexes, and their respective absorbances were recorded at 280 nm (Pan et al., 2007; Jisha et al., 2010). The increase in absorbance at this particular wavelength validates the interaction between zinc complexes and albumin protein (Zhang et al., 2012). The binding strength was wholly dependent on the geometry and structure of the ligand moieties attached with the zinc ion. Moreover, the magnitude of binding strength is ascertained by evaluating intrinsic binding constant values (Satterfield & Brodbelt, 2001).

Fluorescence spectroscopy is a very simple, sensitive, and effective approach to investigate the interactions between drug molecule and serum albumin (Maurya et al., 2019). Serum albumin has shown luminous capabilities and emits highly intense emission maxima upon excitation, and three amino acid residues, viz., tryptophan, tyrosine, and phenylalanine, found in the structure of serum albumin are responsible for its intrinsic fluorescence (De et al., 2021). The tryptophans Trp-134 and Trp-212 in BSA and the chromophore located at Trp-214 in HSA exhibit high fluorescence maxima around 340 nm when stimulated at a specific wavelength ($\lambda_{ex} = 270$ nm) (Mao & Maki, 1987). Fluorescence quenching can be caused by different mechanisms, which include static quenching, in which the fluorophore and the quencher form a nonfluorescent ground state complex, dynamic quenching, which occurs, when the fluorophore and the quencher interact during the transient existence of the excited state, or a simultaneous static and dynamic quenching (Zhang et al., 2011). Various parameters have been employed to define and evaluate the binding interactions between drug moieties and serum albumin. Such an interaction can be quantified by calculated K_b values by using Stern–Volmer equation (Zhao et al., 2010). High values of binding constant determine the effective host–guest binding interactions between the HAS/BSA and corresponding zinc complexes (Kuan et al., 2018).

CD is a powerful and sensitive tool to elucidate the alterations of the secondary structure of albumin proteins when they interact with metallodrug molecules (Bashir et al., 2022). CD spectra of native protein exhibited two signature bands in the UV region at 208 and 222 nm attributed to π-π^* and n-π^* transitions, respectively, and these two bands represent the characteristic α-helical structure in a protein (Zsila, 2022). The results of CD were expressed in terms of the mean residue ellipticity (Provencher & Gloeckner, 1981).

Butkus et al. synthesized eight water soluble zinc complexes (**C11–C18**) and characterized their molecular structures by different spectroscopic methods. In this work, authors reported the interaction studies of these complexes with BSA, HSA, lysosome, and free tryptophan by employing steady-state fluorescence spectroscopy. The results demonstrated that upon titrating a fixed concentration of albumin by zinc complexes, intrinsic fluorescence quenching was noticed, which suggested occurrence of an interaction between albumin and zinc complexes. However, the authors further concluded that strong quenching was observed in zinc complexes having planar aromatic chromophores. Moreover, temperature-dependent emission studies were also performed, and the calculated thermodynamic parameters revealed that binding of zinc complexes with albumin proteins is a spontaneous process, and the process is static rather than dynamic. The results obtained from binding constant values also suggested that complexes having planar aromatic ligand scaffolds bind more efficiently than other complexes (Fig. 1.14) (Butkus et al., 2016).

Parseka et al. reported a new mononuclear zinc complex formulated as [Zn(HL) (o-phen) (H_2O)](OAc)·H_2O (**C19**). The complex was

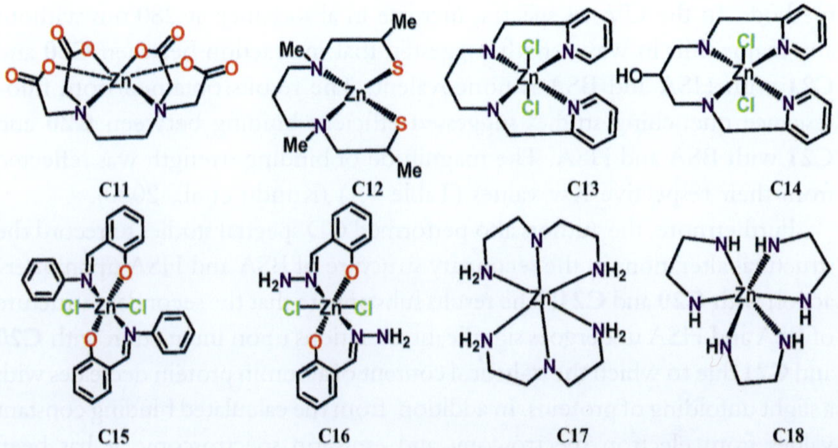

Figure 1.14 Molecular structures of zinc complexes (**C11–C18**) with different types of ligands.

characterized by various spectroscopic methods, and then its therapeutic potential was validated by various interaction studies with HSA by employing electronic absorption and emission studies. In the electronic spectra, a significant increase in absorbance at 280 nm upon cumulative addition of **C19** indicating binding between **C19** and BSA occurs via noncovalent interaction. Furthermore, in the emission studies, strong quenching noticed upon gradual addition of **C19** validates avid binding interaction of **C19** within the hydrophobic pocket of HSA. In addition, the authors also reported docking studies, and the results showed that **C19** was located in the subdomain IIA of HSA, which were also found to be consistent with spectroscopic results (Fig. 1.15) (Parsekar et al., 2020).

Kundu et al. synthesized two novel hemi-salen based Schiff base zinc complexes (**C20–C21**) with different nuclearity. In this work, the authors first elucidated the biological significance of complexes **C20** and **C21** by preliminary DNA and BSA/HSA binding studies by spectroscopic

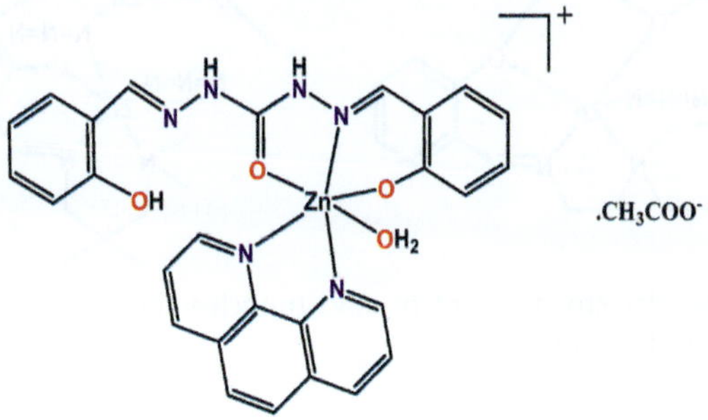

Figure 1.15 Molecular structure of zinc complex (**C19**).

methods. In the UV-vis spectra, increase in absorbance at 280 nm without any major shift in wavelength suggested that interaction between **C20** and **C21** with HSA and BSA is noncovalent. The results obtained from fluorescence quenching studies suggested efficient binding between **C20** and **C21** with BSA and HSA. The magnitude of binding strength was reflected from their respective Ksv values (Table 1.1) (Kundu et al., 2020).

Furthermore, the authors also performed CD spectral studies to record the structural alterations in the secondary structure of BSA and HSA upon interaction with **C20** and **C21**. The results substantiate that the secondary structure of BSA and HSA undergoes significant alterations upon interaction with **C20** and **C21** due to which the α-helical content of albumin protein decreases with a slight unfolding of proteins. In addition, from the calculated binding constant values from electron spectroscopy and emission spectroscopy, it has been concluded that trinuclear zinc complex (**C21**) showed higher binding affinity than dinuclear zinc complex (**C20**) (Fig. 1.16).

Guo et al. (2022) synthesized a new zinc complex derived from imidazole and tetrazole type derivates formulated as $[Zn(H_2tmidc)_2(H_2O)_2]\cdot$

Table 1.1 Binding constant values of complexes **C20** and **C21** with BSA and HSA.

System	K_{SV} (M^{-1})	Kq ($M^{-1}S^{-1}$)
C20-BSA	5.14 (±0.04) × 10^3	8.2 × 10^{11}
C20-HSA	4.28 (±0.22) × 10^3	6.7 × 10^{11}
C21-BSA	6.38 (±0.64) × 10^4	1.0 × 10^{13}
C21-HSA	4.68 (±0.04) × 10^4	7.4 × 10^{12}

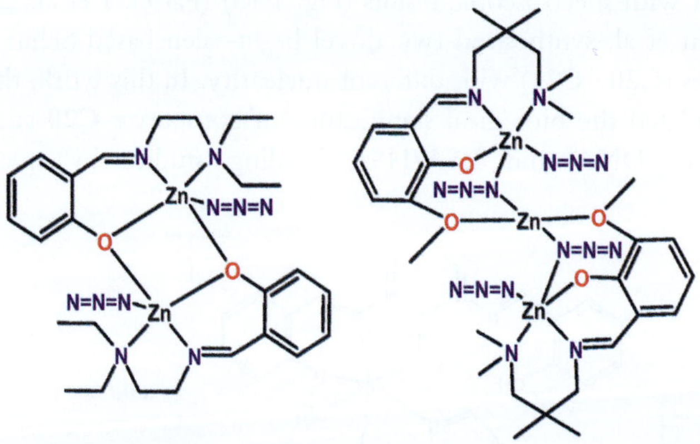

Figure 1.16 Molecular structures of di- and trinuclear hemi-salen based zinc Schiff base complexes **(C20 and C21)**.

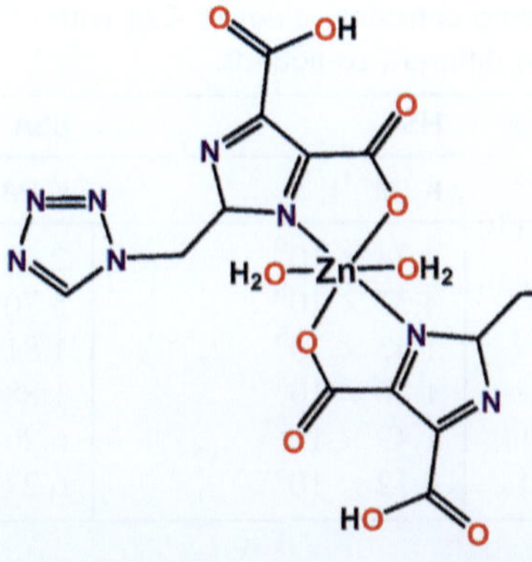

Figure 1.17 Molecular structure of complex **C22**.

$2H_2O$ (**C22**). The molecular structure of **C22** was initially characterized by spectroscopic methods and then validated by single-crystal diffraction studies. The authors investigated in vitro protein binding studies of **C22** by employing fluorescence quenching studies. The results revealed that **C22** interacts with both HSA and BSA via static quenching mechanism. The authors further substantiates from the negative value of thermodynamic parameters (ΔH and ΔS) that van der Waals forces and hydrogen bonding play a significant role in the binding of proteins with **C22** (Fig. 1.17) (Guo et al., 2022).

Tarushi et al. (2014) synthesized a zinc complex (**C23)** derived from nonsteroidal anti-inflammatory drug tolfenamic acid and 2,2′-dipyridylketoneoxime formulated as $[Zn(tolf\text{-}O)_2(Hpko\ N,N')_2]\cdot MeOH$ (Fig. 1.18). The molecular structure of **C23** was confirmed by spectroscopic and single-crystal X-ray diffraction studies.

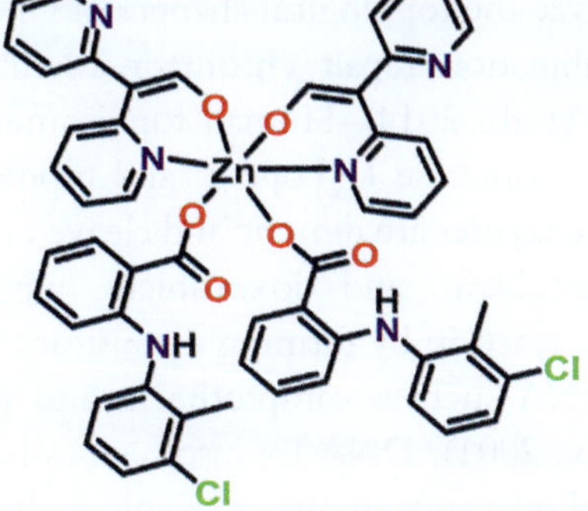

Figure 1.18 Molecular structure of zinc tolfenamate complex (**C23**) with 2,2′-dipyridylketoneoxime as co-ligand.

Table 1.2 Comparison of binding constant values of **C23** with other similar zinc tolfenamate complexes having different co-ligands.

	HSA	BSA
Complexes	**K (M^{-1})**	**K (M^{-1})**
$[Zn(tolf)_2(Hpko)_2]$ **(C23)**	4.74×10^5	2.40×10^6
[Zn(tolf) (phen)Cl] **(C24)**	4.37×10^5	5.70×10^4
[Zn(tolf) (bipy)Cl] **(C25)**	1.43×10^5	1.81×10^5
$[Zn(tolf)_2(phen)]$ **(C26)**	1.36×10^5	1.88×10^5
$[Zn(tolf)_2(bipy)]$ **(C27)**	1.49×10^5	6.20×10^4
$[Zn_3(tolf)_6(CH_3OH)_2]$ **(C28)**	4.12×10^5	6.27×10^5

The biological evaluation of the complex was first validated by interaction studies with albumin proteins and CT-DNA by using absorption and emission methods. The authors reported that in the emission studies, **C23** exhibited high fluorescence quenching ability, BSA and HSA fluorescence, and efficient binding strength with these proteins providing relatively high binding constants that are in the optimal range to allow the binding, the transfer, and the release upon reaching the targets. Furthermore, the authors also compare the binding strength of **C23** with similar reported zinc tolfenamate complexes (**C24**—**C28**) (Table 1.2). From the results, it is quite evident that the presence of an ancillary ligand or co-ligand coordinated with zinc ion has a significant effect on the biologic activity of zinc complexes (Tarushi et al., 2012).

4.4 Interaction studies of zinc complexes with topoisomerase enzymes

Topoisomerases are common enzymes that trigger, break, and re-join the DNA strand to catalyze the topological changes of DNA during replication, transcription, recombination, repair, chromatin assembly, and chromosome segregation (Katkar et al., 2014). Human topoisomerase enzymes exist in two types, viz., topoisomerase I (Topo I) and topoisomerase I (Topo II) (Fig. 1.19). Topo II enzymes are dimeric and cleave both DNA strands such as etoposide, daunorubicin, and doxorubicin, while Topo I enzymes mediate the catalytic reaction by forming a transitory single-strand break in the backbone of DNA such as camptothecin and its corresponding derivatives (Champoux, 2001). DNA topoisomerases have proved to possess extraordinary clinical relevance in cancer oncology, being one of the highly expressed enzymes in the cancerous cells (Leppard & Champoux, 2005). Topo II is considered a validated drug target for most of the promising

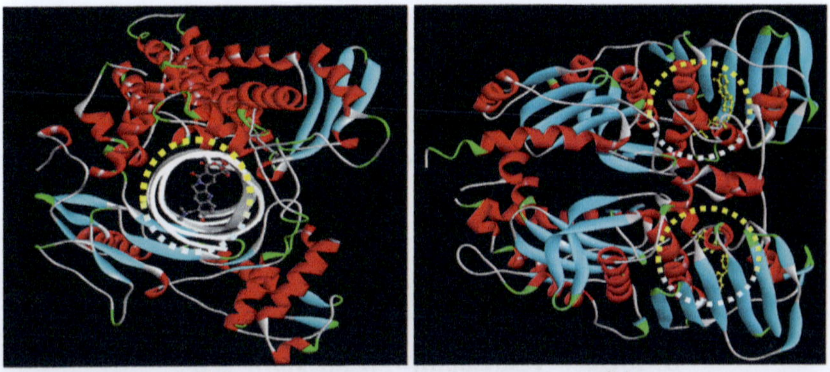

(a) (b)

Figure 1.19 Crystal structures of human topoisomerase enzyme: (A) Topo I and (B) Topo II. Dotted regions illustrate active domains of topoisomerase enzymes.

chemotherapeutic drugs, viz., acridines, anthracyclines, epipodophyllotoxins, and quinoline antibacterial agents. The mechanism of topoisomerase inhibition could involve the formation of topoisomerase poisons, which reversibly bind to the DNA—enzyme cleavage complex and consequently prevent DNA strand relegation. On the other hand, catalytic inhibitors prevent the binding of topoisomerase to DNA or inhibit the cleavage reaction of the enzyme (Pommier, 2009; Pommier, 2013). Since the ability of the metal to modulate the coordination geometry can be significantly exploited to improve interactions with the topoisomerase enzyme at various levels of the catalytic mechanism, different metal-based complexes have been designed to target this ubiquitous enzyme, especially Au, Pt, Cu, and Zn complexes.

Several zinc-based metal complexes including essential and nonessential metals were found to target topoisomerases with efficient ability to inhibit both cleavage and relegation. A. Desideri et al. reported topoisomerase activity of zinc complex derived from oxindolimine (isapn) and formulated as $[Zn(isapn)]^+$ (**C29**) (Fig. 1.20) by analyzing the different steps of the enzyme catalytic cycle.

In this work, the authors claimed that **C29** complex significantly inhibited the human topoisomerase activity and slowed down the relaxation process in a concentration-dependent manner. **C29** demonstrated a complete inhibition of the relaxing activity during the first minutes even when a significant excess of the drug (150 μM) was employed independently. However, if the substance was gradually added or it was preincubated with the enzyme, it showed that under both circumstances, the action was reversible (Fig. 1.21) (Katkar et al., 2014).

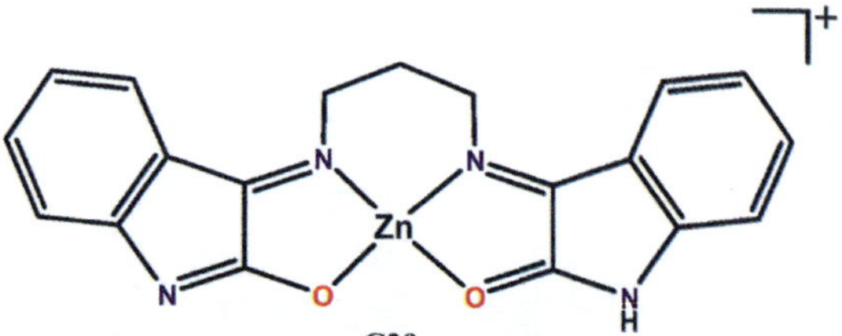

C29

Figure 1.20 Structural representation of **C29**.

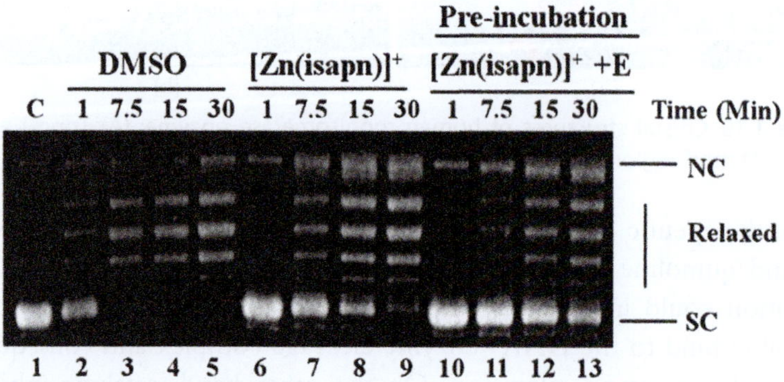

Figure 1.21 Relaxation of negative supercoiled plasmid DNA in a time course experiment with DMSO (lanes 2–5), in the presence of 150 μM **C29** (lanes 6–9), after preincubation of 150 μM **C29** with the enzyme for 5 min at 37°C (lanes 10–13). *(Reprinted with permission from Arjmand et al. (2014).)*

Similarly, Arjmand et al. reported a zinc complex derived from first-generation nalidixic acid and investigated Topo II inhibition activity of Zn complex (**C9**) in a dose-dependent manner by using enzyme-mediated supercoiled pBR322 DNA relaxation assay. The results obtained by the authors reveal that at lower concentration (5 μM), **C9** showed partial inhibitory effect. However, upon increasing concentration (10–30 μM), **C9** significantly inhibited the relaxation activity of Topo II. Thus, the authors claimed that **C9** effectively binds to the ATPase domain of Topo II due to the formation of hydrogen bonds, which results in higher binding affinity and significantly enhances its Topo II catalytic inhibitory activity (Arjmand et al., 2014).

Smolková et al. (2018) reported a series of zinc complexes derived from nonsteroidal anti-inflammatory drug fenamic acid (fen) formulated as $[Zn_3(fen)_6(MeOH)_2]$ (**C30**), $[Zn(fen)_2(tmen)]$ (**C31**), [Zn(bapen)(fen)]fen (**C32**), and $[Zn(cyclam)\ (fen)_2]$ (**C33**) (Fig. 1.22). Where, fen is fenamic acid, tmen represents N,N,N′,N′-tetramethylene diamine, bapen represents

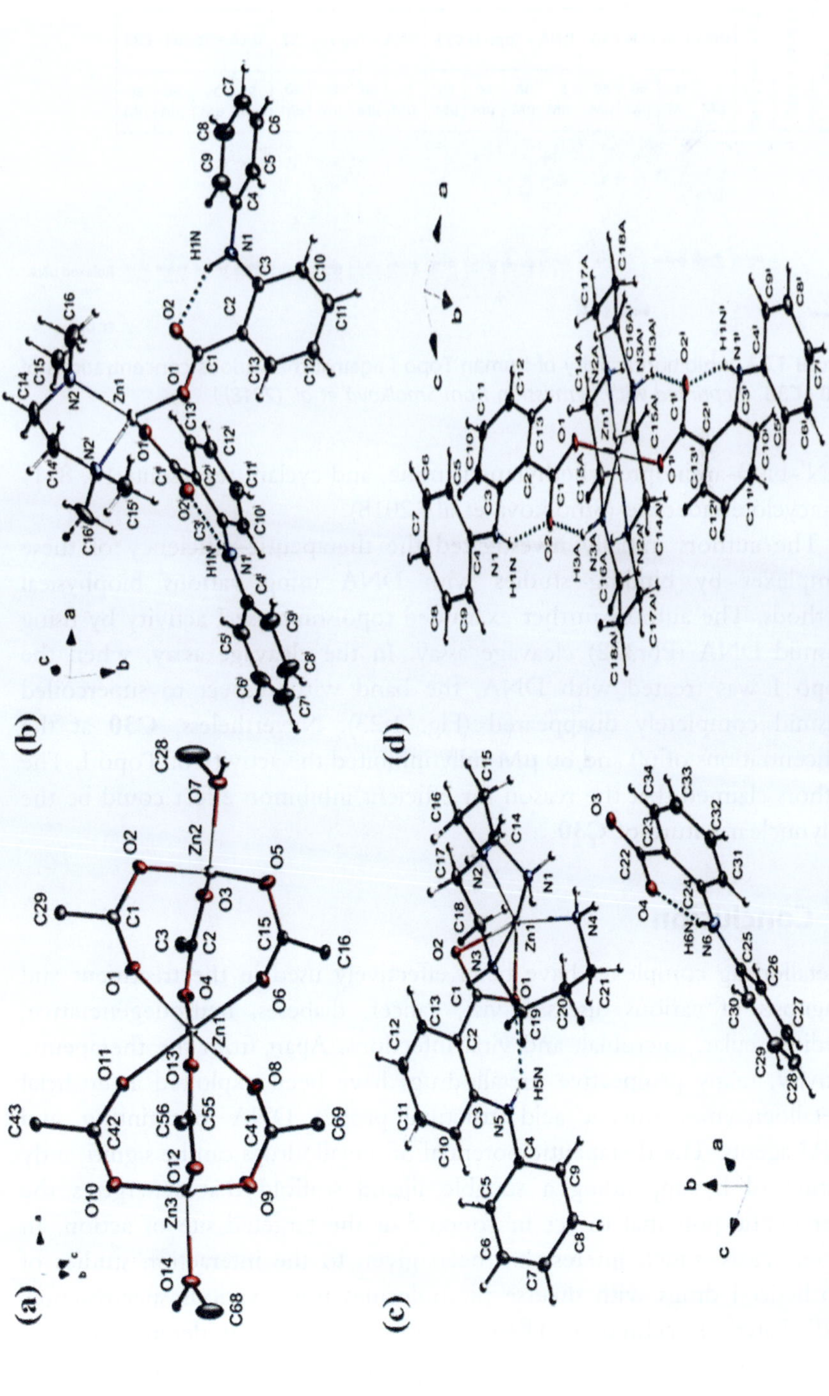

Figure 1.22 (A), (B), (C), and (D) Represent the molecular structures of complexes **C30–C33**. *(Reprinted with permission from Smolková et al. (2018).)*

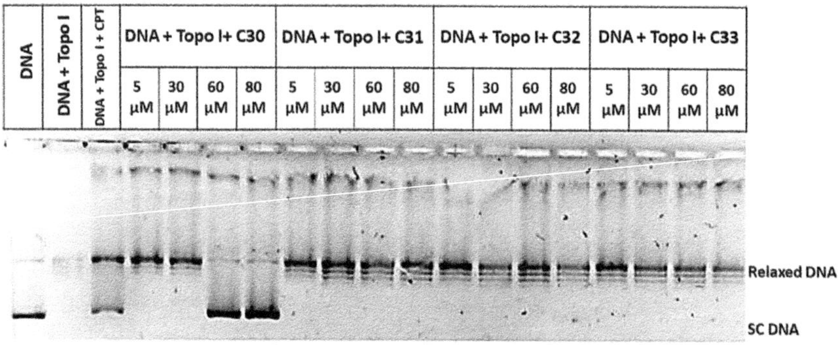

Figure 1.23 Inhibition activity of human Topo I against the various concentrations of **C30**–**C33**. *(Reprinted with permission from Smolková et al. (2018).)*

N,N′-bis(3-aminopropyl)ethylenediamine, and cyclam represents 14, 811-tetracyclotetradecane (Smolková et al., 2018).

The authors initially investigated the therapeutic efficiency of these complexes by binding studies with DNA using various biophysical methods. The authors further examined topoisomerase I activity by using plasmid DNA (Pbr322) cleavage assay. In the cleavage assay, when the Topo I was treated with DNA, the band with respect to supercoiled plasmid completely disappeared (Fig. 1.23). Nevertheless, **C30** at the concentrations of 60 and 80 μM fully inhibited the activity of Topo I. The authors claimed that the reason for efficient inhibition effect could be the polynuclear nature of **C30**.

5. Conclusion

Metallodrug complexes have been effectively used in the treatment and diagnosis of various diseases, viz., cancer, diabetes, neurodegenerative, cardiovascular, microbial, and viral infections. Apart from the therapeutic activity, many prospective metallodrugs have been exploited as artificial metalloenzymes, nucleic acid structural probes, DNA footprinting, and MRI agents. The therapeutic potential of metallodrugs can be significantly optimized by appending a suitable ligand scaffold that synergizes the therapeutic potential to act in concord at the targeted site of action. In recent years, much interest has been given to the interaction studies of synthesized drugs with diverse biomolecules using various spectroscopic and analytical technique. These studies are crucial in determining the mechanistic pathway and a consequent therapeutic potential of a prospective drug. Nucleic acids (DNA and RNA) serve as prime targets for most anticancer agents, and their binding interaction often dictates their chemotherapeutic potential. Interaction of drug molecules with DNA can often result in damage or perturbation in its configuration that eventually leads to cancer cell death or inhibition of cancer cell growth. Plasma proteins (HSA and BSA) are principal carrier proteins, and their binding interaction essentially evaluates the ADMET, which has direct implication on the pharmacokinetics/dynamics of a prospective drug. Given the immense scope of transition metal complexes as therapeutic agents, in this book chapter, a detailed discussion on the potential of Zn(II) complexes in the development of therapeutic and diagnostic metallodrugs has been provided. Zn(II) complexes on account of their low toxicity and specificity have been successfully exploited against many disease conditions. Many Zn(II) complexes with diverse ligand scaffolds have exhibited promising biologic properties and have been the preferred choice for the design of therapeutic metallodrugs. A detailed overview of the interaction studies of numerous Zn(II) complexes with nucleic acids, proteins, and enzymes has been described.

References

Al Mousawi, A., Poriel, C., Dumur, F., Toufaily, J., Hamieh, T., Fouassier, J. P., & Lalevée, J. (2017). Zinc tetraphenylporphyrin as high performance visible light photoinitiator of cationic photosensitive resins for LED projector 3D printing applications. *Macromolecules, 50*, 746–753. https://doi.org/10.1021/acs.macromol.6b02596

Ames, B. N., & Wakimoto, P. (2002). Are vitamin and mineral deficiencies a major cancer risk? *Nature Reviews Cancer, 2*, 694–704. https://doi.org/10.1038/nrc886

Anbu, S., Kamalraj, S., Varghese, B., Muthumary, J., & Kandaswamy, M. (2012). A series of oxyimine-based macrocyclic dinuclear zinc (II) complexes enhances phosphate ester hydrolysis, DNA binding, DNA hydrolysis, and lactate dehydrogenase inhibition and induces apoptosis. *Inorganic Chemistry, 51*, 5580–5592. https://doi.org/10.1021/ic202451e

Arjmand, F., Afsan, Z., Sharma, S., Parveen, S., Yousuf, I., Sartaj, S., Siddique, H. R., & Tabassum, S. (2019). Recent advances in metallodrug-like molecules targeting non-coding RNAs in cancer chemotherapy. *Coordination Chemistry Reviews, 387*, 47–59. https://doi.org/10.1016/j.ccr.2019.02.015

Arjmand, F., Yousuf, I., Afzal, M., & Toupet, L. (2014). Design and synthesis of new Zn (II) nalidixic acid–DACH based Topo-II inhibiting molecular entity: Chemotherapeutic potential validated by its in vitro binding profile, pBR322 cleavage activity and molecular docking studies with DNA and RNA molecular targets. *Inorganica Chimica Acta, 421*, 26–37. https://doi.org/10.1016/j.ica.2014.05.015

Arya, D. P., Coffee, R. L., Willis, B., & Abramovitch, A. I. (2001). Aminoglycoside–nucleic acid interactions: Remarkable stabilization of DNA and RNA triple helices by neomycin. *Journal of the American Chemical Society, 123*, 5385–5395. https://doi.org/10.1021/ja003052x

Asadi, M., Safaei, E., Ranjbar, B., & Hasani, L. (2004). Thermodynamic and spectroscopic study on the binding of cationic Zn (II) and Co (II) tetrapyridinoporphyrazines to calf thymus DNA: The role of the central metal in binding parameters. *New Journal of Chemistry, 28*, 1227–1234. https://doi.org/10.1039/B404068F

Baldini, M., Belicchi-Ferrari, M., Bisceglie, F., Dall'Aglio, P. P., Pelosi, G., Pinelli, S., & Tarasconi, P. (2004). Copper (II) complexes with substituted thiosemicarbazones of α-ketoglutaric acid: Synthesis, X-ray structures, DNA binding studies, and nuclease and biological activity. *I*norganic Chemistry, *43*, 7170–7179. https://doi.org/10.1021/ic049883b

Bal, W., Sokołowska, M., Kurowska, E., & Faller, P. (2013). Binding of transition metal ions to albumin: Sites, affinities and rates. *Biochimica et Biophysica Acta (BBA)-General Subjects, 1830*, 5444–5455. https://doi.org/10.1016/j.bbagen.2013.06.018

Banerjee, S., & Chakravarty, A. R. (2015). Metal complexes of curcumin for cellular imaging, targeting, and photoinduced anticancer activity. *A*ccounts of Chemical Research, *48*, 2075–2083. https://doi.org/10.1021/acs.accounts.5b00127

Barone, G., Terenzi, A., Lauria, A., Almerico, A. M., Leal, J. M., Busto, N., & Garcia, B. (2013). DNA-binding of nickel (II), copper (II) and zinc (II) complexes: Structure–affinity relationships. *Coordination Chemistry Reviews, 257*, 2848–2862. https://doi.org/10.1016/j.ccr.2013.02.023

Barton, J. K., Danishefsky, A., & Goldberg, J. (1984). Tris (phenanthroline) ruthenium (II): Stereoselectivity in binding to DNA. *J*ournal of the American Chemical Society, *106*, 2172–2176. https://doi.org/10.1021/ja00319a043

Bashir, M., Yousuf, I., & Prasad, C. P. (2022). Mixed Ni (II) and Co (II) complexes of nalidixic acid drug: Synthesis, characterization, DNA/BSA binding profile and in vitro cytotoxic evaluation against MDA-MB-231 and HepG2 cancer cell lines. *Spectrochimica Acta A: Molecular and Biomolecular Spectroscopy, 271*, 120910. https://doi.org/10.1016/j.saa.2022.120910

Bayne, E. H., & Allshire, R. C. (2005). RNA-directed transcriptional gene silencing in mammals. *Trends in Genetics, 21*, 370–373. https://doi.org/10.1016/j.tig.2005.05.007

Bazzicalupi, C., Bencini, A., Bonaccini, C., Giorgi, C., Gratteri, P., Moro, S., Palumbo, M., Simionato, A., Sgrignani, J., Sissi, C., & Valtancoli, B. (2008). Tuning the activity of Zn (II) complexes in DNA cleavage: Clues for design of new efficient metallo- hydrolases. *I*norganic Chemistry, *47*, 5473–5484. https://doi.org/10.1021/ic800085n

Bellomo, G., Bologna, S., Cerofolini, L., Paciotti, S., Gatticchi, L., Ravera, E., Parnetti, L., Fragai, M., & Luchinat, C. (2019). Dissecting the interactions between human serum albumin and α-synuclein: New insights on the factors influencing α-synuclein aggregation in biological fluids. *The Journal of Physical Chemistry B, 123*, 4380–4386. https://doi.org/10.1021/acs.jpcb.9b02381

Bonjean, K., De Pauw-Gillet, M. C., Defresne, M. P., Colson, P., Houssier, C., Dassonneville, L., Bailly, C., Greimers, R., Wright, C., Quetin-Leclercq, J., & Tits, M. (1998). The DNA intercalating alkaloid cryptolepine interferes with topoisomerase II and inhibits primarily DNA synthesis in B16 melanoma cells. *B*iochemistry, *37*, 5136–5146. https://doi.org/10.1021/bi972927q

Brázda, V., & Fojta, M. (2019). The rich world of p53 DNA binding targets: The role of DNA structure. *International Journal of Molecular Sciences, 20*(22), 5605. https://doi.org/10.3390/ijms20225605

Butkus, J. M., O'Riley, S., Chohan, B. S., & Basu, S. (2016). Interaction of small zinc complexes with globular proteins and free tryptophan. *International Journal of Spectroscopy*, 1–12. https://doi.org/10.1155/2016/1378680

Carrigan, C. N., & Poulter, C. D. (2003). Zinc is an essential cofactor for type I isopentenyl diphosphate: Dimethylallyl diphosphate isomerase. *Journal of the American Chemical Society, 125*, 9008–9009. https://doi.org/10.1021/ja0350381

Celander, D. W., & Nussbaum, J. M. (1996). Efficient modification of RNA by porphyrin cation photochemistry: Monitoring the folding of coaxially stacked RNA helices in tRNAPhe and the human immunodeficiency virus type 1 rev response element RNA. *Biochemistry, 35*, 12061–12069. https://doi.org/10.1021/bi960557k

Chaires, J. B. (1997). Energetics of drug–DNA interactions. Biopolymers: Original Research on Biomolecules, *44*, 201–215. https://doi.org/10.1002/(SICI)1097-0282(1997)44:3

Champoux, J. J. (2001). DNA topoisomerases: Structure, function, and mechanism. *Annual Review of Biochemistry, 70*, 369–413.

Chang, Y. M., Chen, C. K. M., & Hou, M. H. (2012). Conformational changes in DNA upon ligand binding monitored by circular dichroism. International Journal of Molecular Sciences, *13*, 3394–3413. https://doi.org/10.3390/ijms13033394

Chen, Q., & Wang, H. (2020). Tunable optical linear&nonlinear, magnetic and Faraday rotation properties: Comparison of ZnO based DMSs alloys in diamagnetic solid matrix. Journal of Alloys and Compounds, *846*, 156394. https://doi.org/10.1016/j.jallcom.2020.156394

Chin, K., Sharp, K. A., Honig, B., & Pyle, A. M. (1999). Calculating the electrostatic properties of RNA provides new insights into molecular interactions and function. Nature Structural Biology, *6*, 1055–1061. https://doi.org/10.1038/14940

Chukwuma, C. I., Mashele, S. S., Eze, K. C., Matowane, G. R., Islam, S. M., Bonnet, S. L., Noreljaleel, A. E., & Ramorobi, L. M. (2020). A comprehensive review on zinc (II) complexes as anti-diabetic agents: The advances, scientific gaps and prospects. Pharmacological Research, *155*, 104744. https://doi.org/10.1016/j.phrs.2020.104744

Connie, W. B., & Christine, S. R. (2009). *Handbook of clinical nutrition and aging*. New York: Springer.

Davies, N. W., Guillemin, G., & Brew, B. J. (2010). Tryptophan, neurodegeneration and HIV-associated neurocognitive disorder. International Journal of Tryptophan Research, *3*. https://doi.org/10.4137/IJTR.S4321. IJTR-S4321.

d'Angelo, J., Morgant, G., Ghermani, N. E., Desmaële, D., Fraisse, B., Bonhomme, F., Dichi, E., Sghaier, M., Li, Y., Journaux, Y., & Sorenson, J. R. (2008). Crystal structures and physico-chemical properties of Zn (II) and Co (II) tetraaqua (3-nitro-4- hydroxybenzoato) complexes: Their anticonvulsant activities as well as related (5- nitro-salicylato)–metal complexes. Polyhedron, *27*, 537–546. https://doi.org/10.1016/j.poly.2007.10.006

De, S. K., Maity, A., & Chakraborty, A. (2021). Underlying mechanisms for the modulation of self-assembly and the intrinsic fluorescent properties of amino acid- functionalized gold nanoparticles. *Langmuir, 37*, 5022–5033. https://doi.org/10.1021/acs.langmuir.1c00431

Duff, G. A., Yeager, S. A., Singhal, A. K., Pestel, B. C., Ressner, J. M., & Foster, N. (1987). Separation of metalloporphyrins from metallation reactions by liquid chromatography and electrophoresis. *Journal of Chromatography B: Biomedical Sciences and Applications, 416*, 71–80. https://doi.org/10.1016/0378-4347(87)80486-3

Fahrni, C. J., & O'Halloran, T. V. (1999). Aqueous coordination chemistry of quinoline-based fluorescence probes for the biological chemistry of zinc. Journal of the American Chemical Society, *121*, 11448–11458. https://doi.org/10.1021/ja992709f

Fang, X., Cao, Z., Beck, T., & Tan, W. (2001). Molecular aptamer for real-time onco-protein platelet-derived growth factor monitoring by fluorescence anisotropy. *Analytical Chemistry, 73*, 5752–5757. https://doi.org/10.1021/ac010703e

Feng, Q., Li, N. Q., & Jiang, Y. Y. (1997). Electrochemical studies of porphyrin interacting with DNA and determination of DNA. Analytica Chimica Acta, *344*, 97–104. https://doi.org/10.1016/S0003-2670(97)00008-1

Foote, J. W., & Delves, H. T. (1984). Albumin bound and alpha 2-macroglobulin bound zinc concentrations in the sera of healthy adults. *Journal of Clinical Pathology, 37*, 1050–1054. https://doi.org/10.1136/jcp.37.9.1050

Foster, N., Singhal, A. K., Smith, M. W., Marcos, N. G., & Schray, K. J. (1988). Interactions of porphyrins and transfer RNA. Biochimica et Biophysica Acta (BBA)- Gene Structure and Expression, 950, 118–131. https://doi.org/10.1016/0167-4781(88)90004-8

Frezza, M., Dou, Q. P., Xiao, Y., Samouei, H., Rashidi, M., Samari, F., & Hemmateenejad, B. (2011). In vitro and in vivo antitumor activities and DNA binding mode of five coordinated cyclometalated organoplatinum (II) complexes containing biphosphine ligands. Journal of Medicinal Chemistry, 54(18), 6166–6176. https://doi.org/10.1021/jm2006832

Galani, A., Efthimiadou, E. K., Theodosiou, T., Kordas, G., & Karaliota, A. (2014). Novel levofloxacin zinc (II) complexes with N-donor heterocyclic ligands, as potential fluorescent probes for cell imaging: Synthesis, structural characterization and in vitro cytotoxicity. *Inorganica Chimica Acta, 423*, 52–59. https://doi.org/10.1016/j.ica.2014.09.034

Gálvez, M., Moreno, J. A., Elósegui, L., & Escanero, J. F. (2001). Zinc uptake by human erythrocytes with and without serum albumins in the medium. *Biological Trace Element Research, 84*, 45–56. https://doi.org/10.1385/BTER:84:1-3:045

Ganesana, M., Lee, S. T., Wang, Y., & Venton, B. J. (2017). Analytical techniques in neuroscience: Recent advances in imaging, separation, and electrochemical methods. Analytical Chemistry, 89, 314–341. https://doi.org/10.1021/acs.analchem.6b04278

Gao, T., Xing, S., Xu, M., Fu, P., Yao, J., Zhang, X., Zhao, Y., & Zhao, C. (2020). A peptide nucleic acid–regulated fluorescence resonance energy transfer DNA assay based on the use of carbon dots and gold nanoparticles. Microchimica Acta, *375*. https://doi.org/10.1007/s00604-020-04357-w

Ghosh, K., Kumar, P., & Tyagi, N. (2011). Synthesis, crystal structure and DNA interaction studies on mononuclear zinc complexes. Inorganica Chimica Acta, 375, 77–83. https://doi.org/10.1016/j.ica.2011.04.035

Guo, J. L., Liu, G. Y., Wang, R. Y., & Sun, S. X. (2022). Synthesis and structure elucidation of two essential metal complexes: In-vitro studies of their BSA/HSA- binding properties, docking simulations, and anticancer activities. *Molecules*, 27, 1886. https://doi.org/10.3390/molecules27061886

Haas, K. L., & Franz, K. J. (2009). Application of metal coordination chemistry to explore and manipulate cell biology. Chemical Reviews, 109, 4921–4960. https://doi.org/10.1021/cr900134a

Haghdoost, M. M., Guard, J., Golbaghi, G., & Castonguay, A. (2018). Anticancer activity and catalytic potential of ruthenium (II)–arene complexes with N, O- donor ligands. *Inorganic Chemistry, 57*, 7558–7567. https://doi.org/10.1021/acs.inorgchem.8b00346

Ha, S. C., Lowenhaupt, K., Rich, A., Kim, Y. G., & Kim, K. K. (2005). Crystal structure of a junction between B-DNA and Z-DNA reveals two extruded bases. Nature, 437, 1183–1186. https://doi.org/10.1038/nature04088

Han, X., Nabb, D. L., Russell, M. H., Kennedy, G. L., & Rickard, R. W. (2012). Renal elimination of perfluorocarboxylates (PFCAs). *Chemical Research in Toxicology, 25*, 35–46. https://doi.org/10.1021/tx200363w

Hannon, M. J. (2007). Supramolecular DNA recognition. Chemical Society Reviews, 36, 280–295. https://doi.org/10.1039/B606046N

Haq, I. (2002). Thermodynamics of drug–DNA interactions. Archives of Biochemistry and Biophysics, 403, 1–15. https://doi.org/10.1016/S0003-9861(02)00202-3

Hartinger, C. G., Groessl, M., Meier, S. M., Casini, A., & Dyson, P. J. (2013). Application of mass spectrometric techniques to delineate the modes-of-action of anticancer metallodrugs. Chemical Society Reviews, 42, 6186–6199. https://doi.org/10.1039/C3CS35532B

Havelka, A. M., Berndtsson, M., Olofsson, M. H., Shoshan, M. C., & Linder, S. (2007). Mechanisms of action of DNA-damaging anticancer drugs in treatment of carcinomas: Is acute apoptosis an "off-target" effect? *Mini Reviews in Medicinal Chemistry, 7*, 1035–1039. https://doi.org/10.2174/138955707782110196

Hofstadler, S. A., & Griffey, R. H. (2001). Analysis of noncovalent complexes of DNA and RNA by mass spectrometry. Chemical Reviews, 101, 377–390. https://doi.org/10.1021/cr990105o

Hu, Y. J., Ou-Yang, Y., Dai, C. M., Liu, Y., & Xiao, X. H. (2010). Site-selective binding of human serum albumin by palmatine: Spectroscopic approach. Biomacromolecules, 11, 106–112. https://doi.org/10.1021/bm900961e

Islam, M. M., Chowdhury, S. R., & Kumar, G. S. (2009). Spectroscopic and calorimetric studies on the binding of alkaloids berberine, palmatine and coralyne to double stranded RNA polynucleotides. The Journal of Physical Chemistry B, 113, 1210–1224. https://doi.org/10.1021/jp806597w

Jana, S. K., Seth, S. K., Puschmann, H., Hossain, M., & Dalai, S. (2014). Synthesis and X-ray structure of a new zinc (II) coordination polymer: Interaction with DNA and double stranded RNA and elucidation of the molecular aspects of the binding to bovine serum albumin. RSC Advances, 4, 57855–57868. https://doi.org/10.1039/C4RA06588C

Jaumot, J., & Gargallo, R. (2012). Experimental methods for studying the interactions between G-quadruplex structures and ligands. *Current Pharmaceutical Design, 18*, 1900–1916. https://doi.org/10.2174/138161212799958486

Jisha, V. S., Arun, K. T., Hariharan, M., & Ramaiah, D. (2010). Site-selective interactions: Squaraine dye– serum albumin complexes with enhanced fluorescence and triplet yields. *The Journal of Physical Chemistry B, 114*, 5912–5919. https://doi.org/10.1021/jp100369x

Johnson, R. P., Richardson, J. A., Brown, T., & Bartlett, P. N. (2012). A label-free, electrochemical SERS-based assay for detection of DNA hybridization and discrimination of mutations. Journal of the American Chemical Society, 134, 14099–14107. https://doi.org/10.1021/ja304663t

Jovanovic, M., & Hengartner, M. O. (2006). miRNAs and apoptosis: RNAs to die for. *Oncogene, 25*, 6176–6187. https://doi.org/10.1038/sj.onc.1209912

Jung, Y., & Lippard, S. J. (2007). Direct cellular responses to platinum-induced DNA damage. *Chemical Reviews, 107*, 1387–1407. https://doi.org/10.1021/cr068207j

Kanvah, S., Joseph, J., Schuster, G. B., Barnett, R. N., Cleveland, C. L., & Landman, U. Z. I. (2010). Oxidation of DNA: Damage to nucleobases. *Accounts of Chemical Research, 43*, 280–287. https://doi.org/10.1021/ar900175a

Kasyanenko, N. A., Zanina, A. V., Nazarova, O. V., & Panarin, E. F. (1999). DNA interaction with complex ions in solution. Langmuir, 15, 7912–7917. https://doi.org/10.1021/la980980p

Katkar, P., Coletta, A., Castelli, S., Sabino, G. L., Couto, R. A. A., da Costa Ferreira, A. M., & Desideri, A. (2014). Effect of oxindolimine copper (II) and zinc (II) complexes on human topoisomerase I activity. Metallomics, 6, 117–125. https://doi.org/10.1039/c3mt00099k

Keene, F. R., Smith, J. A., & Collins, J. G. (2009). Metal complexes as structure- selective binding agents for nucleic acids. Coordination Chemistry Reviews, 253(15–16), 2021–2035. https://doi.org/10.1016/j.ccr.2009.01.004

Kellett, A., Molphy, Z., Slator, C., McKee, V., & Farrell, N. P. (2019). Molecular methods for assessment of non-covalent metallodrug–DNA interactions. Chemical Society Reviews, 48, 971–988. https://doi.org/10.1039/C8CS00157J

Khare, E., Holten-Andersen, N., & Buehler, M. J. (2021). Transition-metal coordinate bonds for bioinspired macromolecules with tunable mechanical properties. *Nature Reviews Materials, 6*, 421–436. https://doi.org/10.1038/s41578-020-00270-z

Kim, R. (2005). Recent advances in understanding the cell death pathways activated by anticancer therapy. Cancer: Interdisciplinary International Journal of the American Cancer Society, *103*, 1551–1560. https://doi.org/10.1002/cncr.20947

Kim, Y. H., Lee, K., & Li, S. (2021). Nucleic acids based polyelectrolyte complexes: Their complexation mechanism, morphology, and stability. Chemistry of Materials, *33*, 7923–7943. https://doi.org/10.1021/acs.chemmater.1c01832

Kuan, S. L., Bergamini, F. R., & Weil, T. (2018). Functional protein nanostructures: A chemical toolbox. *Chemical Society Reviews, 47*, 9069–9105. https://doi.org/10.1039/C8CS00590G

Kumar, C. V., Barton, J. K., & Turro, N. J. (1985). Photophysics of ruthenium complexes bound to double helical DNA. *Journal of the American Chemical Society, 107*, 5518–5523. https://doi.org/10.1021/ja00305a032

Kundu, B. K., Mobin, S. M., & Mukhopadhyay, S. (2020). Studies on the influence of the nuclearity of zinc (ii) hemi-salen complexes on some pivotal biological applications. *Dalton Transactions, 49*, 15481–15503. https://doi.org/10.1039/D0DT02941F

Lacroix, A., Edwardson, T. G., Hancock, M. A., Dore, M. D., & Sleiman, H. F. (2017). Development of DNA nanostructures for high-affinity binding to human serum albumin. *Journal of the American Chemical Society, 139*, 7355–7362. https://doi.org/10.1021/jacs.7b02917

LePecq, J. B., & Paoletti, C. (1967). A fluorescent complex between ethidium bromide and nucleic acids: Physical—chemical characterization. *Journal of Molecular Biology, 27*, 87–106. https://doi.org/10.1016/0022-2836(67)90353-1

Leppard, J. B., & Champoux, J. J. (2005). Human DNA topoisomerase I: Relaxation, roles, and damage control. *Chromosoma, 114*, 75–85. https://doi.org/10.1007/s00412-005-0345-5

Liu, J., Cao, Z., & Lu, Y. (2009). Functional nucleic acid sensors. Chemical Reviews, *109*, 1948–1998. https://doi.org/10.1021/cr030183i

Liu, Z., & Chen, X. (2016). Simple bioconjugate chemistry serves great clinical advances: Albumin as a versatile platform for diagnosis and precision therapy. *Chemical Society Reviews, 45*, 1432–1456. https://doi.org/10.1039/C5CS00158G

Liu, J., Zhang, T., Lu, T., Qu, L., Zhou, H., Zhang, Q., & Ji, L. (2002). DNA-binding and cleavage studies of macrocyclic copper (II) complexes. *Journal of Inorganic Biochemistry, 91*, 269–276. https://doi.org/10.1016/S0162-0134(02)00441-5

Li, M., Yin, F., Song, L., Mao, X., Li, F., Fan, C., Zuo, X., & Xia, Q. (2021). Nucleic acid tests for clinical translation. Chemical Reviews, *121*, *1*0469–10558. https://doi.org/10.1021/acs.chemrev.1c00241

Long, E. C., & Barton, J. K. (1990). On demonstrating DNA intercalation. *A*ccounts of Chemical Research, *23*, 271–273. https://doi.org/10.1021/ar00177a001

Lu, J., Stewart, A. J., Sadler, P. J., Pinheiro, T. J., & Blindauer, C. A. (2008). Albumin as a zinc carrier: Properties of its high-affinity zinc-binding site. *Biochemical Society Transactions, 36*, 1317–1321. https://doi.org/10.1042/BST0361317

Mao, S. Y., & Maki, A. H. (1987). Comparative phosphorescence and optically detected magnetic resonance studies of fatty acid binding to serum albumin. *Biochemistry, 26*, 3576–3582. https://doi.org/10.1021/bi00386a049

Maret, W., & Li, Y. (2009). Coordination dynamics of zinc in proteins. *Chemical Reviews, 109*, 4682–4707. https://doi.org/10.1021/cr800556u

Maurya, N., Maurya, J. K., Singh, U. K., Dohare, R., Zafaryab, M., Moshahid, A. R.,M., Kumari, M., & Patel, R. (2019). In vitro cytotoxicity and interaction of noscapine with

human serum albumin: Effect on structure and esterase activity of HSA. *Molecular Pharmaceutics, 16*, 952–966. https://doi.org/10.1021/acs.molpharmaceut.8b00864
Maywald, M., & Rink, L. (2022). Zinc in human health and infectious diseases. *Biomolecules, 12*, 1748. https://doi.org/10.3390/biom12121748
Misiak, M., Mantegazza, F., & L Beretta, G. (2016). Methods for elucidation of DNA-anticancer drug interactions and their applications in the development of new drugs. Current Pharmaceutical Design, *22*, 6596–6611.
Miyahara, T., Nakatsuji, H., & Sugiyama, H. (2013). Helical structure and circular dichroism spectra of DNA: A theoretical study. *T*he Journal of Physical Chemistry A, *1*17, 42–55. https://doi.org/10.1021/jp3085556
Mjos, K. D., & Orvig, C. (2014). Metallodrugs in medicinal inorganic chemistry. *Chemical Reviews, 114*, 4540–4563. https://doi.org/10.1021/cr400460s
Monaco, R. R. (2010). Capture of a transition state using molecular dynamics: Creation of an intercalation site in dsDNA with ethidium cation. *J*ournal of Nucleic Acids, 702317. https://doi.org/10.4061/2010/702317, 2010.
Moriyama, Y., & Takeda, K. (1999). Re-formation of the helical structure of human serum albumin by the addition of small amounts of sodium dodecyl sulfate after the disruption of the structure by urea. A comparison with bovine serum albumin. *Langmuir, 15*, 2003–2008. https://doi.org/10.1021/la981442f
Nagaswamy, U., Voss, N., Zhang, Z., & Fox, G. E. (2000). Database of non-canonical base pairs found in known RNA structures. *N*ucleic Acids Research, *2*8, 375–376. https://doi.org/10.1093/nar/28.1.375
Olszewski, U., & Hamilton, G. (2010). A better platinum-based anticancer drug yet to come? *A*nti-Cancer Agents in Medicinal Chemistry (Formerly Current Medicinal Chemistry-Anti-Cancer Agents), *1*0, 293–301. https://doi.org/10.2174/187152010791162306
Onyido, I., Norris, A. R., & Buncel, E. (2004). Biomolecule– mercury interactions: Modalities of DNA base–mercury binding mechanisms. remediation strategies. *C*hemical Reviews, *1*04, 5911–5930. https://doi.org/10.1021/cr030443w
Pages, B. J., Ang, D. L., Wright, E. P., & Aldrich-Wright, J. R. (2015). Metal complex interactions with DNA. *Dalton Transactions, 44*, 3505–3526. https://doi.org/10.1039/C4DT02700K
Panja, A., Matsuo, T., Nagao, S., & Hirota, S. (2011). DNA cleavage by the photo-controlled cooperation of ZnII centers in an azobenzene-linked dizinc complex. *I*norganic Chemistry, *5*0, 11437–11445. https://doi.org/10.1021/ic201244y
Pan, H. C., Liang, F. P., Mao, C. J., Zhu, J. J., & Chen, H. Y. (2007). Highly luminescent zinc (II)–Bis (8-hydroxyquinoline) complex nanorods: Sonochemical synthesis, characterizations, and protein sensing. *The Journal of Physical Chemistry B, 111*, 5767–5772. https://doi.org/10.1021/jp0703049
Parkin, G. (2004). Synthetic analogues relevant to the structure and function of zinc enzymes. *C*hemical Reviews, *1*04, 699–768. https://doi.org/10.1021/cr0206263
Parsekar, S. U., Velankanni, P., Sridhar, S., Haldar, P., Mate, N. A., Banerjee, A., Antharjanam, P. S., Koley, A. P., & Kumar, M. (2020). Protein binding studies with human serum albumin, molecular docking and in vitro cytotoxicity studies using HeLa cervical carcinoma cells of Cu (II)/Zn (II) complexes containing a carbohydrazone ligand. *Dalton Transactions, 49*, 2947–2965. https://doi.org/10.1039/C9DT04656A
Pasternack, R. F. (2003). Circular dichroism and the interactions of water soluble porphyrins with DNA—a minireview. *Chirality, 15*, 329–332. https://doi.org/10.1002/chir.10206
Pattison, S. E., & Cousins, R. J. (1986). Zinc uptake and metabolism by hepatocytes. In *Federation proceedings* (Vol 45, pp. 2805–2809).

Paul, B. K., & Guchhait, N. (2011). Exploring the strength, mode, dynamics, and kinetics of binding interaction of a cationic biological photosensitizer with DNA: Implication on dissociation of the drug–DNA complex via detergent sequestration. *The Journal of Physical Chemistry B, 115*, 11938–11949. https://doi.org/10.1021/jp206589e

Pearlman, S. I., Leelawong, M., Richardson, K. A., Adams, N. M., Russ, P. K., Pask, M. E., Wolfe, A. E., Wessely, C., & Haselton, F. R. (2020). Low-resource nucleic acid extraction method enabled by high-gradient magnetic separation. *ACS Applied Materials and Interfaces, 12*, 12457–12467. https://doi.org/10.1021/acsami.9b21564

Pellei, M., Del Bello, F., Porchia, M., & Santini, C. (2021). Zinc coordination complexes as anticancer agents. Coordination Chemistry Reviews, 445, 214088. https://doi.org/10.1016/j.ccr.2021.214088

Peng, S., Bie, B., Jia, H., Tang, H., Zhang, X., Sun, Y., Wei, Q., Wu, F., Yuan, Y., Deng, H., & Zhou, X. (2020). Efficient separation of nucleic acids with different secondary structures by metal–organic frameworks. Journal of the American Chemical Society, 142, 5049–5059. https://doi.org/10.1021/jacs.9b10936

Pindur, U., Haber, M., & Sattler, K. (1993). Antitumor active drugs as intercalators of deoxyribonucleic acid: Molecular models of intercalation complexes. Journal of Chemical Education, 70, 263. https://doi.org/10.1021/ed070p263

Pommier, Y. (2009). DNA topoisomerase I inhibitors: Chemistry, biology, and interfacial inhibition. *Chemical Reviews, 109*, 2894–2902. https://doi.org/10.1021/cr900097c

Pommier, Y. (2013). Drugging topoisomerases: Lessons and challenges. *ACS Chemical Biology, 8*, 82–95. https://doi.org/10.1021/cb300648v

Porchia, M., Pellei, M., Del Bello, F., & Santini, C. (2020). Zinc complexes with nitrogen donor ligands as anticancer agents. Molecules, 25, 5814. https://doi.org/10.3390/molecules25245814

Provencher, S. W., & Gloeckner, J. (1981). Estimation of globular protein secondary structure from circular dichroism. *Biochemistry, 20*, 33–37. https://doi.org/10.1021/bi00504a006

Psomas, G. (2020). Copper (II) and zinc (II) coordination compounds of non-steroidal anti-inflammatory drugs: Structural features and antioxidant activity. *Coordination Chemistry Reviews, 412*, 213259. https://doi.org/10.1016/j.ccr.2020.213259

Psomas, G., & Kessissoglou, D. P. (2013). Quinolones and non-steroidal anti- inflammatory drugs interacting with copper (II), nickel (II), cobalt (II) and zinc (II): Structural features, biological evaluation and perspectives. *Dalton Transactions, 42*, 6252–6276. https://doi.org/10.1039/C3DT50268F

Ramezani, F., & Rafii-Tabar, H. (2015). An in-depth view of human serum albumin corona on gold nanoparticles. *Molecular BioSystems, 11*, 454–462. https://doi.org/10.1039/C4MB00591K

Riduan, S. N., & Zhang, Y. (2021). Recent advances of zinc-based antimicrobial materials. Chemistry–An Asian Journal, 16, 2588–2595. https://doi.org/10.1002/asia.202100656

Rowe, D. J., & Bobilya, D. J. (2000). Albumin facilitates zinc acquisition by endothelial cells. *Proceedings of the Society for Experimental Biology and Medicine, 224*, 178–186. https://doi.org/10.1111/j.1525-1373.2000.22418.x

Santini, C., Pellei, M., Gandin, V., Porchia, M., Tisato, F., & Marzano, C. (2014). Advances in copper complexes as anticancer agents. *Chemical Reviews, 114*, 815–862. https://doi.org/10.1021/cr400135x

Satterfield, M., & Brodbelt, J. S. (2001). Relative binding energies of gas-phase pyridyl ligand/metal complexes by energy-variable collisionally activated dissociation in a quadrupole ion trap. Inorganic Chemistry, 40, 5393–5400. https://doi.org/10.1021/ic010356r

Sheng, X., Guo, X., Lu, X. M., Lu, G. Y., Shao, Y., Liu, F., & Xu, Q. (2008). DNA binding, cleavage, and cytotoxic activity of the preorganized dinuclear zinc (II) complex of triazacyclononane derivatives. *Bioconjugate Chemistry, 19*, 490–498. https://doi.org/10.1021/bc700322w

Sirajuddin, M., Ali, S., & Badshah, A. (2013). Drug–DNA interactions and their study by UV–Visible, fluorescence spectroscopies and cyclic voltametry. *Journal of Photochemistry and Photobiology B: Biology, 124*, 1–19. https://doi.org/10.1016/j.jphotobiol.2013.03.013

Skok, Z., Zidar, N., Kikelj, D., & Ilaš, J. (2019). Dual inhibitors of human DNA topoisomerase II and other cancer-related targets. *Journal of Medicinal Chemistry, 63*, 884–904. https://doi.org/10.1021/acs.jmedchem.9b00726

Skrajnowska, D., & Bobrowska-Korczak, B. (2019). Role of zinc in immune system and anti-cancer defense mechanisms. *Nutrients, 11*, 2273. https://doi.org/10.3390/nu11102273

Smolková, R., Zeleňák, V., Gyepes, R., Sabolová, D., Imrichová, N., Hudecová, D., & Smolko, L. (2018). Synthesis, characterization, DNA binding, topoisomerase I inhibition and antimicrobial activity of four novel zinc (II) fenamates. *Polyhedron, 141*, 230–238. https://doi.org/10.1016/j.poly.2017.11.052

Suchomski, C., Reitz, C., Brezesinski, K., Tavares de Sousa, C., Rohnke, M., Iimura, K. I., Esteves de Araujo, J. P., & Brezesinski, T. (2012). Structural, optical, and magnetic properties of highly ordered mesoporous MCr2O4 and MCr2−x Fe x O4 (M= Co, Zn) spinel thin films with uniform 15 nm diameter pores and tunable nanocrystalline domain sizes. *Chemistry of Materials, 24*, 155–165. https://doi.org/10.1021/cm2026043

Sundquist, W. I., Bancroft, D. P., & Lippard, S. J. (1990). Synthesis, characterization, and biological activity of cis-diammineplatinum (II) complexes of the DNA intercalators 9-aminoacridine and chloroquine. *Journal of the American Chemical Society, 112*, 1590–1596. https://doi.org/10.1021/ja00160a044

Szewczyk, B., Kubera, M., & Nowak, G. (2011). The role of zinc in neurodegenerative inflammatory pathways in depression. *Progress in Neuro-Psychopharmacology and Biological Psychiatry, 35*, 693–701. https://doi.org/10.1016/j.pnpbp.2010.02.010

Tarushi, A., Totta, X., Papadopoulos, A., Kljun, J., Turel, I., Kessissoglou, D. P., & Psomas, G. (2014). Antioxidant activity and interaction with DNA and albumins of zinc–tolfenamato complexes. Crystal structure of [Zn (tolfenamato) 2 (2, 2′- dipyridylketoneoxime) 2]. *European Journal of Medicinal Chemistry, 74*, 187–198. https://doi.org/10.1016/j.ejmech.2013.12.019

Tarushi, A., Totta, X., Raptopoulou, C. P., Psycharis, V., Psomas, G., & Kessissoglou, D. P. (2012). Structural features of mono-and tri-nuclear Zn (II) complexes with a non-steroidal anti-inflammatory drug as ligand. *Dalton Transactions, 41*, 7082–7091. https://doi.org/10.1039/C2DT30547J

Thomas, J. R., & Hergenrother, P. J. (2008). Targeting RNA with small molecules. *Chemical Reviews, 108*, 1171–1224. https://doi.org/10.1021/cr0681546

Tibaduiza, E. C., & Bobilya, D. J. (1996). Zinc transport across an endothelium includes vesicular cotransport with albumin. *Journal of Cellular Physiology, 167*, 539–547. https://doi.org/10.1002/(SICI)1097-4652(199606)167:3

Timerbaev, A. R., Hartinger, C. G., Aleksenko, S. S., & Keppler, B. K. (2006). Interactions of antitumor metallodrugs with serum proteins: Advances in characterization using modern analytical methodology. *Chemical Reviews, 106*, 2224–2248. https://doi.org/10.1021/cr040704h

Valko, M., Jomova, K., Rhodes, C. J., Kuča, K., & Musílek, K. (2016). Redox-and non-redox-metal-induced formation of free radicals and their role in human disease. *Archives of Toxicology, 90*, 1–37. https://doi.org/10.1007/s00204-015-1579-5

Vallee, B. L., & Auld, D. S. (1990). Zinc coordination, function, and structure of zinc enzymes and other proteins. *Biochemistry, 29*, 5647–5659. https://doi.org/10.1021/bi00476a001

Vasto, S., Candore, G., Listì, F., Balistreri, C. R., Colonna-Romano, G., Malavolta, M., Lio, D., Nuzzo, D., Mocchegiani, E., Di Bona, D., & Caruso, C. (2008). Inflammation, genes and zinc in Alzheimer's disease. Brain Research Reviews, 58, 96–105. https://doi.org/10.1016/j.brainresrev.2007.12.001

Voicescu, M., Ionescu, S., & Angelescu, D. G. (2012). Spectroscopic and coarse- grained simulation studies of the BSA and HSA protein adsorption on silver nanoparticles. *Journal of Nanoparticle Research, 14*, 1–13. https://doi.org/10.1007/s11051-012-1174-0

Wang, S., Fan, X., Gao, Y., Zuo, L., Hong, M., & Xu, Y. (2022). The relationship between zinc deficiency and hepatocellular carcinoma associated with hepatitis B liver cirrhosis: A 10-year follow-up study. *Biological Trace Element Research*, 1–7. https://doi.org/10.1007/s12011-022-03156-z

Wang, X., & Guo, Z. (2013). Targeting and delivery of platinum-based anticancer drugs. *Chemical Society Reviews, 42*, 202–224. https://doi.org/10.1039/C2CS35259A

Werner, M. H., Gronenborn, A. M., & Clore, G. M. (1996). Intercalation, DNA kinking, and the control of transcription. *Science, 271*, 778–784. https://doi.org/10.1126/science.271.5250.778

Wessels, I., Maywald, M., & Rink, L. (2017). Zinc as a gatekeeper of immune function. Nutrients, 9, 1286. https://doi.org/10.3390/nu9121286

Wilner, O. I., & Willner, I. (2012). Functionalized DNA nanostructures. Chemical Reviews, 112, 2528–2556. https://doi.org/10.1021/cr200104q

Wilson, J. J., & Lippard, S. J. (2014). Synthetic methods for the preparation of platinum anticancer complexes. Chemical Reviews, 114, 4470–4495. https://doi.org/10.1021/cr4004314

Wolfe, A., Shimer, G. H., Jr., & Meehan, T. (1987). Polycyclic aromatic hydrocarbons physically intercalate into duplex regions of denatured DNA. Biochemistry, 26, 6392–6396. https://doi.org/10.1021/bi00394a013

Wu, H., Yuan, J., Bai, Y., Pan, G., Wang, H., Shao, J., Gao, J., & Wang, Y. (2012). Synthesis, crystal structure, DNA-binding properties, and antioxidant activity of a V-shaped ligand bis (N-methylbenzimidazol-2-ylmethyl) benzylamine and its zinc (II) complex. *Journal of Coordination Chemistry, 65*, 4327–4341. https://doi.org/10.1080/00958972.2012.741229

Xu, H., Zheng, K. C., Chen, Y., Li, Y. Z., Lin, L. J., Li, H., Zhang, P. X., & Ji, L. N. (2003). Effects of ligand planarity on the interaction of polypyridyl Ru (II) complexes with DNA. Dalton Transactions, 11, 2260–2268. https://doi.org/10.1039/B300353A

Yaman, M., Atici, D., Bakırdere, S., & Akdeniz, I. (2005). Comparison of trace metal concentrations in malign and benign human prostate. *Journal of Medicinal Chemistry, 48*, 630–634. https://doi.org/10.1021/jm0494568

Yam, V. W. W., & Lo, K. K. W. (1999). Luminescent polynuclear d 10 metal complexes. Chemical Society Reviews, 28, 323–334. https://doi.org/10.1039/A804249G

Yavuz, O., Alcay, Y., Kaya, K., Sezen, M., Kirlangic Atasen, S., Yildirim, M. S., Ozkilic, Y., Tuzun, N. S., & Yilmaz, I. (2018). Superior sensor for Be2+ ion recognition via the unprecedented octahedral crystal structure of a one-dimensional coordination polymer of crown Fused Zinc Phthalocyanine. Inorganic Chemistry, 58, 909–923. https://doi.org/10.1021/acs.inorgchem.8b03038

Ye, R., Tan, C., Chen, B., Li, R., & Mao, Z. (2020). Zinc-containing metalloenzymes: Inhibition by metal-based anticancer agents. *Frontiers in Chemistry, 8*, 402. https://doi.org/10.3389/fchem.2020.00402

Yousuf, I., Mantoo, I. A., Bashir, M., & Bhat, S. A. (2022). Structure elucidation of a bimetallic μ-hydroxo-bridged Cu (II)-flufenamate-bpy complex and cytotoxic evaluation against MDA-MB-231 and A549 carcinoma cell lines. *Applied Organometallic Chemistry, 36*, 6906. https://doi.org/10.1002/aoc.6906

Zamora, F., & Sabat, M. (2002). Simultaneous N7, O6-binding of guanine to two zinc centers and its possible biological significance. *Inorganic Chemistry, 41*, 4976–4977. https://doi.org/10.1021/ic0258532

Zhang, Y., Cui, Y., An, R., Liang, X., Li, Q., Wang, H., Wang, H., Fan, Y., Dong, P., Li, J., & Cheng, K. (2019). Topologically constrained formation of stable Z-DNA from normal sequence under physiological conditions. *Journal of the American Chemical Society, 141* 7758–7764. https://doi.org/10.1021/jacs.8b13855

Zhang, G., Fu, P., Wang, L., & Hu, M. (2011). Molecular spectroscopic studies of farrerol interaction with calf thymus DNA. *Journal of Agricultural and Food Chemistry, 59*, 8944–8952. https://doi.org/10.1021/jf2019006

Zhang, Y., & Gladyshev, V. N. (2009). Comparative genomics of trace elements: Emerging dynamic view of trace element utilization and function. *Chemical Reviews, 109*, 4828–4861. https://doi.org/10.1021/cr800557s

Zhang, G., Wang, L., & Pan, J. (2012). Probing the binding of the flavonoid diosmetin to human serum albumin by multispectroscopic techniques. *Journal of Agricultural and Food Chemistry, 60*, 2721–2729. https://doi.org/10.1021/jf205260g

Zhang, D., Zhang, T., Liu, J., Chen, J., Li, Y., Ning, G., Huo, N., Tian, W., & Ma, H. (2019). Zn supplement-antagonized cadmium-induced cytotoxicity in macrophages in vitro: Involvement of cadmium bioaccumulation and metallothioneins regulation. *Journal of Agricultural and Food Chemistry, 67*, 4611–4622.

Zhao, X., Liu, R., Chi, Z., Teng, Y., & Qin, P. (2010). New insights into the behavior of bovine serum albumin adsorbed onto carbon nanotubes: Comprehensive spectroscopic studies. *The Journal of Physical Chemistry B, 114*, 5625–5631. https://doi.org/10.1021/jp100903x

Zhu, D., Su, Y., Young, M. L., Ma, J., Zheng, Y., & Tang, L. (2017). Biological responses and mechanisms of human bone marrow mesenchymal stem cells to Zn and Mg biomaterials. *ACS Applied Materials & Interfaces, 9*, 27453–27461. https://doi.org/10.1021/acsami.7b06654

Zsila, F. (2022). Far-UV circular dichroism signatures indicate fluorophore labeling induced conformational changes of penetratin. *Amino Acids*, 1–5. https://doi.org/10.1007/s00726-022-03149-1

CHAPTER 2

Ruthenium complexes: An insight into their interactions with nucleic acids and biomolecules

Shazia Parveen
Chemistry Department, Faculty of Science, Taibah University, Yanbu, Saudi Arabia

1. Chemistry of ruthenium

Ruthenium (Ru) was originally discovered in 1807 by the Polish chemist Sniadecki, but the claim was not accepted by a Paris commission and had to be withdrawn. Later in the year 1844, another Russian chemist Karl Karlovich Klaus succeeded in providing the proof about the new element 44 extracted from platinum ores. He named it "ruthenium" after the name Ruthenia (Latin name for Russia) (Krebs, 2006).

Ruthenium, a silvery whitish, shiny, lustrous hard metal, is also one of the rare metals in the earth's crust (0.0004 ppm). The atomic number is 44, relative atomic mass is 101.07 u ± 0.02 u, and electronic configuration is $1s^2\ 2s^2\ 2p^6\ 3s^2\ 3p^6\ 4s^2\ 3d^{10}\ 4p^6\ 5s^1\ 4d^7$. It is placed in group 8 of the periodic table along with Fe, Os, and Hs. Of the several isotopes of Ru, only seven are stable. The key isotopes include ^{101}Ru, ^{102}Ru, and ^{104}Ru. Ru is unreactive but paramagnetic at room temperature (Valente et al., 2014). It is oxidized upon reaction with oxygen at higher temperature, ~800°C (Singh et al., 2014). It is an inert metal insoluble in most of the acids or mixtures of acids, e.g., aqua regia (Singh et al., 2014; Valente et al., 2014). Ru possess high melting and boiling points of 2334°C and 4150°C, respectively.

It undergoes oxidation reaction to form ruthenium oxide, which upon further oxidation in the presence of sodium metaperiodate gives ruthenium tetraoxide (RuO_4) (Singh et al., 2014). At lower oxidation states such as +2 or +3, Ru does not undergo oxidation, whereas it reacts with hydroxide ions to achieve higher coordination number (Miyada et al., 2014). The

Nucleic Acids
ISBN 978-0-12-820503-7
https://doi.org/10.1016/B978-0-12-820503-7.00003-X

ability of Ru to exist in many oxidation states is an important property of this rare element, which plays an important part in its applications.

A wide range of applications of Ru in industry include its uses in (i) manufacturing of electronic chips (Daxiong et al., 2004), (ii) as anodes for production of chlorine in electrochemical cells (Gunanathan et al., 2014), (iii) as a hardener when mixed with other metals to form alloy, in making of palladium jewelry (Ang et al., 2006), (iv) to form an alloy with titanium to improve corrosion resistant property, (v) and its alloys are used in manufacturing of jet engine turbines. Apart from these applications, ^{106}Ru is used in radiotherapy of malignant cells of the eye, determination of blood calcitonin level, etc. Ru demonstrates DNA binding ability inhibiting its replication and protein synthesis.

Ru possesses unique properties, viz., slow ligand exchange kinetics, various available oxidation states, and iron mimicking ability in binding to certain biologic molecules, making it theoretically suitable for chemotherapeutic use. Some Ru(III) complexes bind to Fe(III) sites of lactoferrin and transferrin proteins (Smith et al., 1996), while Ru(III) delivery to cancer cells is supposed to be facilitated by transferrin, where its uptake proceeds via receptor-mediated endocytosis (Frasca et al., 1996). Furthermore, these proteins solubilize and are involved in the transport iron in blood plasma. There is a requirement of iron in rapidly dividing cells, including cancerous cells, resulting in the accumulation of transferrin receptors on the cell surface, thereby sequestering more circulating iron-loaded transferrin. The in vivo reduction of Ru(III) to Ru(II) is a significant step in the mechanism of action of Ru(III) complexes, where Ru(II) is kinetically more reactive.

Generally, the Ru center is mostly hexacoordinate exhibiting octahedral geometry. Metabolically, cancer results in comparison to healthy cells exhibit (i) a reductive environment, i.e., a low concentration of oxygen, (ii) elevated glutathione concentration, and (iii) a lower pH (Schluga et al., 2006). Redox potential of Ru can be altered to improve drug selectivity to reduce harm to healthy cells and to increase the entry of Ru metal in cancer cells. They are administered as inert prodrug Ru(III) complexes, which are then activated by reduction in the tumor tissues. Theoretically, the active Ru(II) complexes are converted back to inert Ru(III) compounds upon leaving the low-oxygen environment by a variety of biologic oxidants.

Two Ru agents that are entering in phase II of human clinical trials are NAMI-A and KP1019 (Pieper et al., 1999; Sava et al., 1999). While an organometallic species, [Ru(η^6-toluene)Cl_2(pta)] (pta = 1,3,5-triaza-7-phosphatricyclo-[3.3.1.1] decane or 1,3,5-triaza-7-phosphaadamantane),

RAPTA-T exhibited in vitro and in vivo effects, specifically the selectivity toward metastatic tumors, demonstrating low overall toxicity, apparently reducing the side effects related to chemotherapy (Wu et al., 2011). Another Ru(II)-arene lead compound is RAPTA-C, which is found to exhibit low in vitro cytotoxicity (Ang et al., 2006) but relevant anti-metastatic (Bergamo et al., 2012) and antiangiogenic (Sliwinska et al., 2011) in vivo properties. RAPTA-C is also known to diminish the growth of primary tumors in preclinical models for ovarian and colorectal carcinomas via an antiangiogenesis (Weiss et al., 2014). The structures of all four Ru complexes are shown in Fig. 2.1.

2. Methods of synthesis

The modes of binding, location, and affinities could be altered by the modifying the ligands, which could lead to subtle or even significant changes, opening the field of prospects to explore countless valued site-specific or conformation-specific probes of DNA and potential

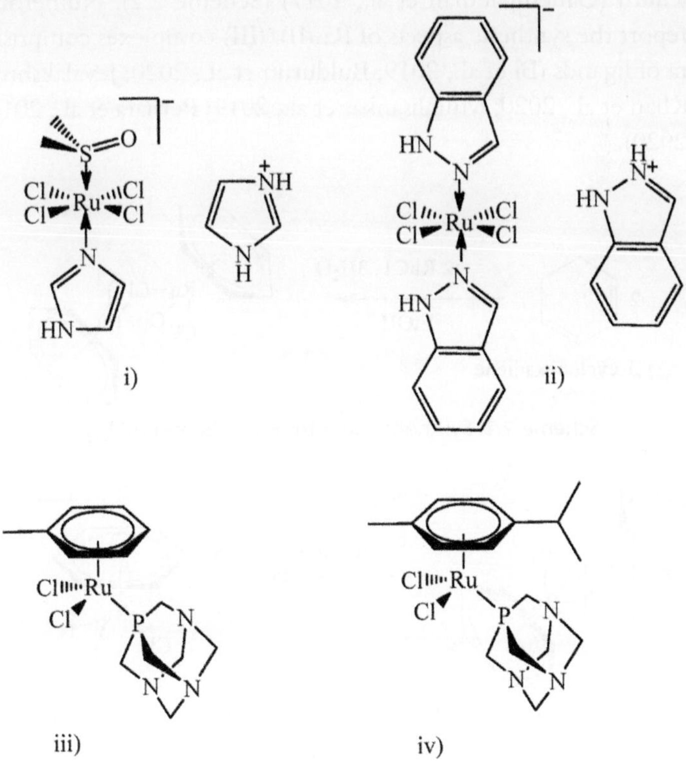

Figure 2.1 i) NAMI-A, ii) KP1909, iii) RAPTA-T, and iv) RAPTA-C.

therapeutic agents. The general synthetic methodologies toward the design of Ru(II) complexes incorporating a variety of ligands can be broadly classified as Ru-arene, homoleptic, heteroleptic, and dinuclear complexes.

2.1 Organometallic Ru(II)-arene complexes

The starting material for Ru(II)-arene complex, $[Ru(\eta^6\text{-benzene})Cl_2]_2$ was prepared by Zelonka and Baird in 1972 according to the procedure described (Zelonka et al., 1972). Ru(II)-arene complex was yielded by adding 1,3-cyclohexadiene to a solution of $RuCl_3$. The dimer was obtained, which was soluble in water after refluxed for several hours at desired temperature. The resulting red precipitate was then collected in high yields, washed with EtOH, and dried in a vacuum (Scheme 2.1).

The general method of synthesis of Ru(II)-arene-diimine complexes of the type $[Ru(\eta^6\text{-benzene})(diamine)Cl](PF_6)$ was proceeded by adding a methanolic solution of diimine to a solution of $[Ru(\eta^6\text{-benzene})Cl_2]_2$ in methanol with stirring at room temperature; then the solution was filtered and NH_4PF_6 was added. The desired solid complex was collected by suction filtration, washed with water, methanol, and diethyl ether and dried in a vacuum (Ganeshpandian et al., 2017) (Scheme 2.2). Numerous literatures report the synthetic aspects of Ru(II)/(III) complexes comprising of a plethora of ligands (Bi et al., 2019; Buldurun et al., 2020; Jeyalakshmi et al., 2019; Khan et al., 2020; Muralisankar et al., 2019; Pernara et al., 2019; Vyas et al., 2020).

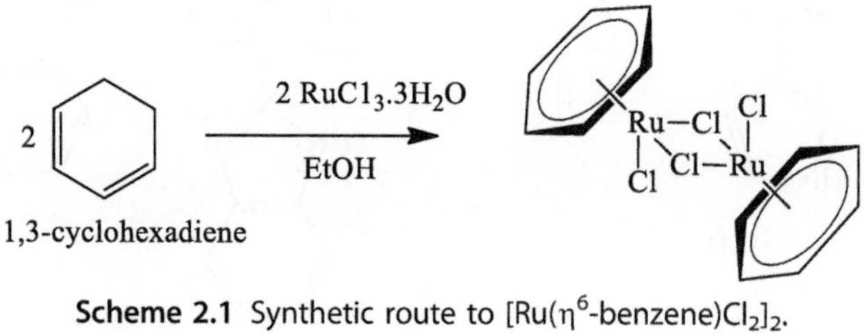

Scheme 2.1 Synthetic route to $[Ru(\eta^6\text{-benzene})Cl_2]_2$.

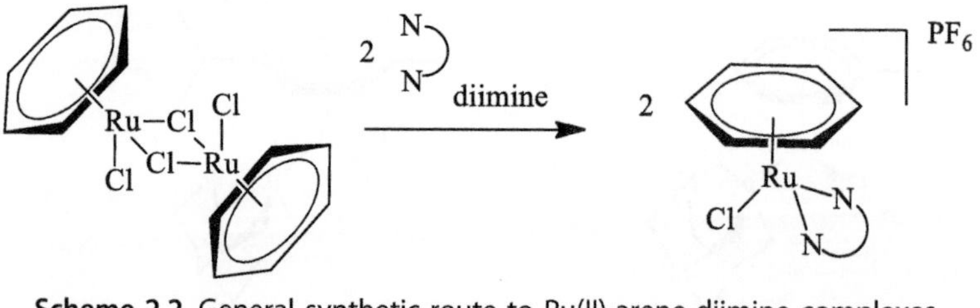

Scheme 2.2 General synthetic route to Ru(II)-arene-diimine complexes.

In an another synthetic protocol, to a methanolic solution of $[RuCl(PPh_3)_2(\eta^5\text{-}C_5H_5)]$, methanolic solution of ligand, HL^{1-4} (HL^1 = acetophenonethiosemicarbazone/HL^2 = acetophenone-4(N)-methylthiosemicarbazone/HL^3 = acetophenone-4(N)-ethylthiosemicarbazone/ HL^4 = acetophenone-4(N)-phenylthiosemicarbazone) was added in 1:1 ratio, and the resulting mixture was refluxed for 5 h. The reddish-orange suspension gradually turned red. The solvent was then removed on a rotary evaporator until a red solid formed, which was washed thrice with petroleum ether to remove any traces of unreacted PPh_3 (Scheme 2.3) (Devagi et al., 2018).

2.2 Homoleptic Ru(II) complexes of the type $[Ru(L)_3]^{2+}$

Homoleptic Ru(II) complexes having general formula of $[RuL_3]Cl_2$ where L = bidendate ligand, e.g., bpy, phen, tatp, dppz, ppn, were synthesized by following a simple procedure (Lin et al., 1976) (Scheme 2.4). Potassium aquopentachlororuthenate(III) was dissolved in hot water with one drop of

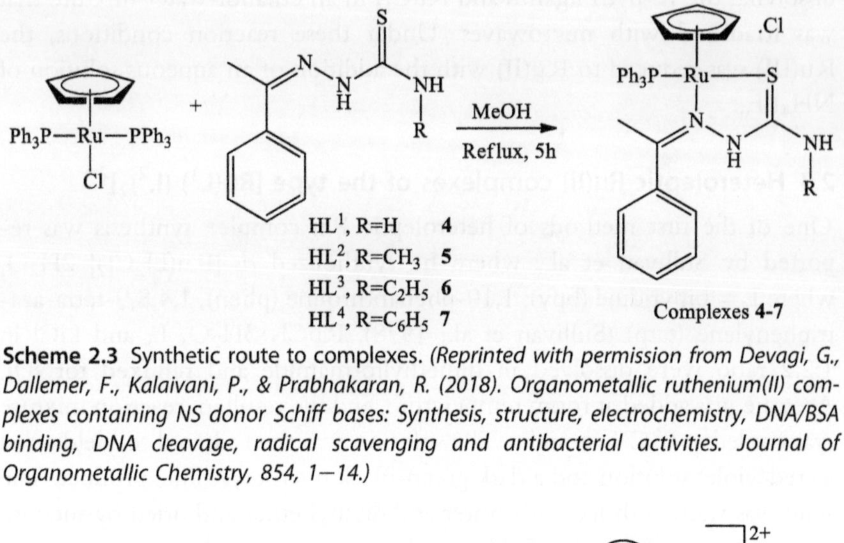

Scheme 2.3 Synthetic route to complexes. *(Reprinted with permission from Devagi, G., Dallemer, F., Kalaivani, P., & Prabhakaran, R. (2018). Organometallic ruthenium(II) complexes containing NS donor Schiff bases: Synthesis, structure, electrochemistry, DNA/BSA binding, DNA cleavage, radical scavenging and antibacterial activities. Journal of Organometallic Chemistry, 854, 1–14.)*

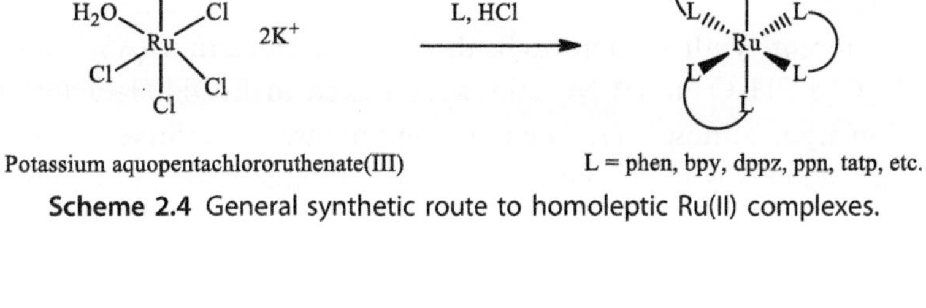

Scheme 2.4 General synthetic route to homoleptic Ru(II) complexes.

6N hydrochloric acid, and a stoichiometric amount of the ligand, L, was slowly added with continuous stirring. The mixture was boiled for 10–20 min, followed by the addition of hypophosphorous acid (H_3PO_2) neutralized with sodium hydroxide, and the resultant mixture was refluxed 15–30 min until change in color was observed, followed by filteration and crystallization.

Homoleptic Ru(II) complex, $[RuL_3]$-$(PF_6)_2$ (where L = 4,4′,6,6′-tetramethyl-2,2′-bipyridine), was synthesized upon suspension of $RuCl_3$ and L in ethylene glycol and irradiated with microwaves (Kohler et al., 2017). This was followed by the addition of ammonium hexafluorophosphate (NH_4PF_6), to yield the product. The mixture was filtered and the product was washed with water and diethyl ether, and finally dried.

Kumar et al. synthesized a series of tris(homoleptic) Ru(II) complexes of the type $[Ru(R\text{-pytri})_3]^{2+}(X^-)_2$ (where X = PF_6 or Cl^-) by "click" ligands (R-pytri) {(R = butyl, hexyl, octyl, dodecyl, and hexdecyl) and aromatic (R = phenyl and benzyl) substituents} by microwave-enhanced conditions in good yields (Kumar et al., 2016). The procedure involved dissolving the R-pytri ligands and $RuCl_3$ in an ethanol-water mixture that was irradiated with microwaves. Under these reaction conditions, the Ru(III) was reduced to Ru(II) with the addition of an aqueous solution of NH_4PF_6.

2.3 Heteroleptic Ru(II) complexes of the type $[Ru(L^1)(L^2)_2]^{2+}$

One of the first methods of heteroleptic Ru complex synthesis was reported by Sullivan et al., where he synthesized *cis*-$[Ru(L)_2Cl_2]\cdot 2H_2O$, where L = bipyridine (bpy), 1,10-phenanthroline (phen), 1,4,8,9-tetra-aza-triphenylene (tatp) (Sullivan et al., 1978). $RuCl_3\cdot 3H_2O$, L, and LiCl in 1:2:2 ratio were dissolved in dimethylformamide and refluxed for 8 h. Acetone was added at room temperature, and the resultant reaction mixture was cooled at 0°C overnight. The solution was then filtered to yield a red to red-violet solution and a dark green-black microcrystalline product. The solid was washed thrice with water and diethyl ether and dried by suction. Yields ranged from 65–70% based on starting ruthenium derivative (Scheme 2.5).

In a recent synthetic approach, the ligand ascididemin (ASC) and *cis*-$[Ru(L)_2Cl_2]\cdot 2H_2O$ in 1:1 M ratio were mixed in EtOH:H_2O (6:1 v/v) under an argon atmosphere. The resulting mixture was refluxed for 6–8 h, to which water was added and the solution was filtered to remove any solid

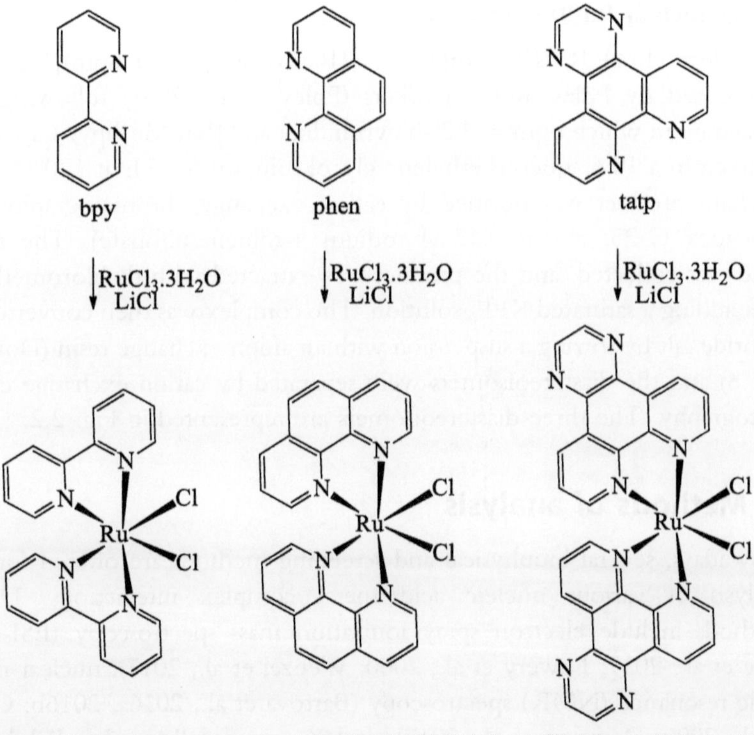

Scheme 2.5 Synthetic route to *cis*-[Ru(bpy)$_2$Cl$_2$]·2H$_2$O, *cis*-[Ru(phen)$_2$Cl$_2$]·2H$_2$O, and *cis*-[Ru(tatp)$_2$Cl$_2$]·2H$_2$O.

impurities, followed by the addition of concentrated aqueous solution of NH_4PF_6. The crude product was filtered, dried, and dissolved in MeCN and purified by silica chromatography using eluent (MeCN:H_2O:$NaNO_3$) in the proportion of (40:4:1) with high yields (Wumaier et al., 2019).

Li et al. reported the synthesis of a variety of heteroleptic complexes of the type $[Ru(L^1)(L^2)_2]^{2+}$ following a similar procedure (Li et al., 2016). Other studies reported the similar synthetic procedures for Ru(II) polypyridyl complexes, $[Ru(bpy)_2(ppn)]^{2+}$ and $[Ru(phen)_2(ppn)]^{2+}$, Ru(II) cyano complexes, $[Ru(phen)_2dicnq]^{2+}$ and $[Ru(bpy)_2dicnq]^{2+}$, chiral Ru(II) complexes, Δ- and Λ-$[Ru(bpy)_2dppz]^{2+}$, using phen or bpy (phen = 1,10-phenanthroline, bpy = 2,2′-bipyridine) as ancillary ligands and ppn or dicnq or dppz (ppn = 2,4-diaminopyrimido [5,6-b] dipyrido [2,3-f:2′,3′-h]quinoxaline, dicnq = 6,7-dicyanodipyrido[2,2-*d*:2′,3′-*f*]quinoxaline, dppz = dipyrido[3,2-**a**:2′,3′-**c**]phenazine) as the main ligand (Li et al., 2016; Ma et al., 2019).

2.4 Dinuclear Ru(II) complexes

Dinuclear chiral Ru(II) complexes, $[\{Ru(Me_2bpy)_2\}_2(\mu\text{-}bpm)]^{4+}$, were synthesized by Foley and coworkers (Foley et al., 2001) following the procedure in which bpm = 2,2′-bipyrimidine and $[Ru(Me_2bpy)_2Cl_2]$ were refluxed in a 10% aqueous ethylene glycol solution for 5 h at 120°C. The resultant product was purified by cation exchange chromatography (SP Sephadex C-25; eluent 0.15 M sodium 4-toluenesulfonate). The main band was collected, and the product was extracted with dichloromethane after adding a saturated KPF_6 solution. The complex was then converted to chloride salt by stirring a suspension with an anion exchange resin (Dowex; 1 × 8) and the diastereoisomers were separated by cation exchange chromatography. The three diastereoisomers are represented in Fig. 2.2.

3. Methods of analysis

Nowadays, several biophysical and screening methods are offered for the analysis of various nucleic acid–metal complex interactions. Direct methods include electron spray ionization mass spectroscopy (ESI-MS) (Lee et al., 2017; Lowery et al., 2000; Wenzel et al., 2017), nuclear magnetic resonance (NMR) spectroscopy (Bartova et al., 2016a, 2016b; Chen et al., 2000; Dagenais et al., 2017), and X-ray crystallography. While indirect methods are UV-vis spectroscopy, fluorescence spectroscopy (Arjmand et al., 2019), circular dichroism, and electrophoresis-based techniques. In recent years, a significant effort has been made to determine the interaction of metal-based drug molecules with nucleic acids, resulting in the development of a number of compatible molecular methods

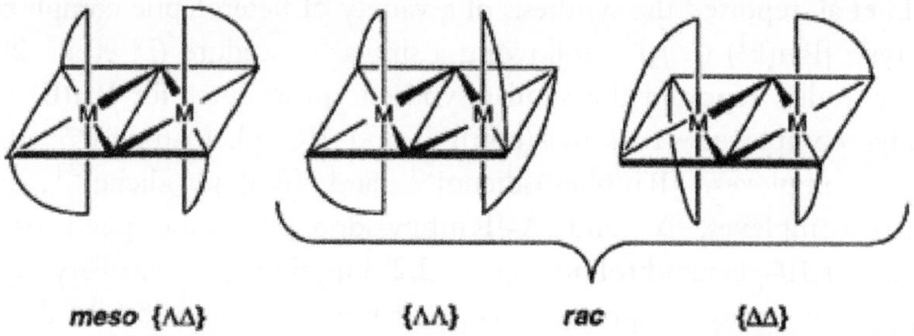

Figure 2.2 Representation of diastereoisomers of $[\{Ru(Me_2bpy)_2\}_2(\mu\text{-}bpm)]^{4+}$. *(Reprinted with permission from Foley, F. M., Keene, F. R., & Collins, J. G. (2001). The DNA binding of the ΔΔ-, ΔΛ- and ΛΛ-stereoisomers of [{Ru(Me2bpy)2}2(μ-bpm)]4+. Dalton Transactions, 2968—2974.)*

probing reversible and nonreversible interactions. However, these binding modes are being supported by the shape- and charge-dependent structural factors of the complex.

3.1 Mass spectroscopy

ESI-MS is a crucial method for probing the interactions between metal complex nucleic acids (Chen et al., 2019). Instrumental developments and advances in ionization techniques have resulted in an increased range of mass and decreased requirement of the sample. Due to which, mass spectroscopy is being progressively used for analyzing noncovalent complexes. This is because strong noncovalent interactions involved in noncovalent binding modes (viz., electrostatic interactions, hydrogen bonding, and intercalative binding) can be transferred to the gas phase without disruption. Studies of single-stranded, double-stranded, and G-quadruplex DNA and TAR RNA and the Tat−TAR complexes, have been carried out, and mass spectra in combination with other techniques can provide information on binding sites and binding strength (Arjmand et al., 2019).

3.2 NMR spectroscopy

NMR is regarded as one of the most established consistent techniques for nucleic acid-targeted drug discovery depending on the shifts of the chemical values. NMR studies further supplement the solid-state structures, providing further detailed information to the varied conformations in solution. This technique has been benefitted considerably from the advances in strength of the magnetic field, magnetic shielding, and cryogenic probes. NMR detection methods are based on one of the three approaches: (i) observing the preassociation, strong noncovalent binding kinetics of DNA, (ii) detecting small molecules in both free and bound DNA/RNA macromolecules (Blakeley et al., 2012), or (iii) by detecting the changes in chemical shift of the target molecule upon DNA/RNA binding. Recent reports detail the usage of NMR methods for screening nucleic acid-targeted drug moieties (Bartova et al., 2016a, 2016b; Chen et al., 2000; Dagenais et al., 2017; Kellett et al., 2019). NMR spectroscopy was successful in determining the structural domains of RNA, their intramolecular dynamics, and also their interaction with metal complexes. However, the approaches based upon the detection of the complex are found to be more rational compared with the ones based on detection of target, since they include no size limitations and require a relatively low concentration while being highly sensitive owing to the slow relaxation of the detected small molecules. While on the other hand, changes in the chemical shift values of ^{15}N or ^{13}C upon binding to the target molecule are detected by the target-detected NMR screening method.

3.3 X-ray crystallography

Single crystals of nucleic acids, viz., DNA, oligonucleotides, ternary RNA structure, and their complexes with drug molecules, are studied by X-ray crystallography. This technique provides a decisive visualization of coordination binding modes and quality data that reveals a detailed atomic-level structural information. 3D maps of electron density obtained from the experimental results determine the atomic positions. Once these atomic positions are known, other geometrical data including bond lengths and bond angles can be easily calculated, further enabling the exploration and illustration of the structure employing various graphics programs available. Franklin, in 1953, for the first time, published photos of B-DNA, demonstrating its helical nature using single X-ray crystallography (Franklin et al., 1953). Nowadays, crystallographic studies of most biologic macromolecules are being carried out at high-end research facilities that meet the required criteria such as (i) the availability of high intensity X-ray sources that can be tuned accordingly and (ii) fast, sensitive detectors that enable the study of even minute crystals with higher resolutions (Garman, 2014; Helliwell et al., 2015).

The foremost disadvantage in using crystallographic technique is to be able to grow crystals of good quality and appropriate size, which would require a considerable amount of pure complex, as well as analyzing a wide range of extensive conditions until an appropriate set is found, which could be quite expensive and time-consuming.

3.4 Absorption spectroscopic techniques

UV-visible spectroscopy of DNA/RNA could be controlled by the absorptions of the nucleobases due to the fact that these nucleobases are of low symmetry and consist of many lone pairs on the heteroatom. A single, strong, broad absorption spectrum for the full nucleic acid is observed with λ_{max} (absorbance maximum) in the range of 250–280 nm, since the transitions for individual nucleobases overlap. The maximum absorbance (λ_{max}) of nucleic acids depends on the amount of AT and GC bases. Whereas, the molar extinction coefficient (ϵ_{max}) of the nucleic acid depends on the composition of the nucleobase and the preferred 2-degree structure.

In this method, the absorption titrations are performed on a UV-vis spectrophotometer with a fixed concentration of complexes and varying the DNA/RNA concentration, keeping the total volume constant. The absorbance is then recorded after successive titrations upon addition of DNA/RNA solution. The changes in the absorbance give an idea of the type of binding mode. Hypochromism has been attributed to changes in DNA due to the intercalation of Ru(II) complexes, while hyperchromism is due to the contraction of DNA in the helix axis due to external binding (Fig. 2.3).

The corresponding binding constant, K_b value, is calculated using the Wolfe–Shimer equation (Eq. 2.1), and Gibb's free energy values for complexes are calculated from Eq. 2.2 (Wolfe et al., 1987).

$$[\text{DNA or RNA}]/\ \epsilon_a - \epsilon_f = [\text{DNA or RNA}]/\ \epsilon_b - \epsilon_f + 1/K_b\ (\epsilon_b - \epsilon_f) \quad (2.1)$$

where [DNA or RNA] is the concentration of nucleic acid, and ε_a, ε_f, and ε_b are apparent (A_{abs}/[complex]), free and bound complex extinction coefficients, respectively. In a plot of [DNA or RNA]/$\epsilon_a - \epsilon_f$ versus [DNA/RNA] with a slope of $1/(\epsilon_b - \epsilon_f)$ and intercept of $1/K_b\ (\epsilon_b - \epsilon_f)$, K_b values were obtained by the ratio of slope to intercept.

$$\Delta G = -RT \ln K_b \quad (2.2)$$

where ΔG is the change in Gibb's free energy, R is the gas constant, 8.314 $JK^{-1}mol^{-1}$, T is temperature, 298 K, and K_b is the binding constant.

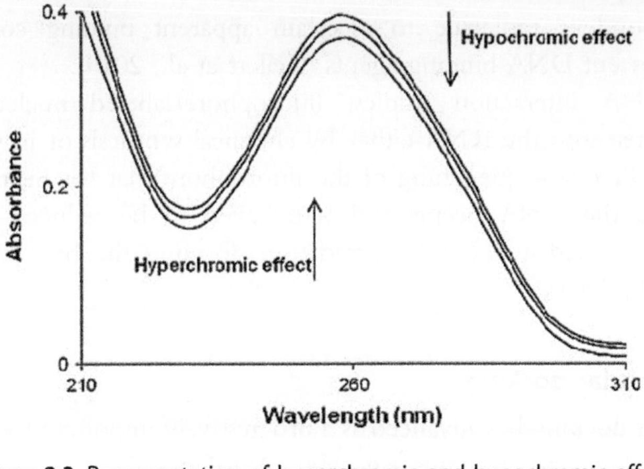

Figure 2.3 Representation of hyperchromic and hypochromic effect.

3.5 Fluorescence spectroscopy

While absorbance spectroscopy is based on absorbance measurements, fluorescence spectroscopy is believed to be most beneficial and vigorous method based on emission used to detect nucleic acid—complex interactions. The advantages of fluorescence methods are that they (i) are highly sensitive, (ii) are easily applicable to highly efficient screening, and (iii) are relatively cheaper. Since the fluorescence study of bio-macromolecules, viz., nucleic acids, proteins, lipids, and membranes, needs extensive fluorescent labeling, the most common methodology is the labeling of the nucleic acid/ligand with a suitable fluorophore, e.g., blue fluorescent AT-specific minor groove binder DAPI, the green fluorescent protein, organic dyes, fluorescein, or ethidium bromide. Fluorescence quenching assays carried out with excess DNA treated with limited bound fluorophore allow us to identify the preferential DNA binding sites. Depending on the mode of interaction, the fluorescent probe molecules can be varied, e.g., EtBr intercalator or Hoechst 33,258 minor groove binder, but then again, one could even vary the duplex DNA target (Molphy et al., 2014). This technique is particularly useful for structurally related metallodrug moieties and within oligomers of changing sequence by comparing quenching, Q, values. The quenching constant, K_{sv}, values are achieved by using the Stern—Volmer equation (Eq. 2.3) (Ghosh et al., 1989).

$$I_o / I = 1 + K_{sv} [Q], \tag{2.3}$$

where I_o and I are the fluorescence intensities in the absence and presence of the test complex respectively, and [Q] is the quencher concentration. Fig. 2.4 depicts an indirect fluorescence displacement assay using EtBr as a correspondent molecule to ascertain apparent binding constants of nonfluorescent DNA binding agents (Kellett et al., 2019).

In RNA interaction studies, fluorophore-labeled nucleotides are incorporated into the RNA either by chemical synthesis or in vitro transcription. Frequent quenching of the fluorophore that has been incorporated into the RNA occurs and is believed to be reduced upon the ribonuclease-mediated RNA degradation, forming the basis of an assay (Rist et al., 2001).

3.6 Molecular docking

Molecular docking has advanced as a progressively important tool for drug discovery. Docking programs, e.g., Hex, AutoDock, Vina, etc., are utilized for calculating the binding sites and the affinities of drug candidates

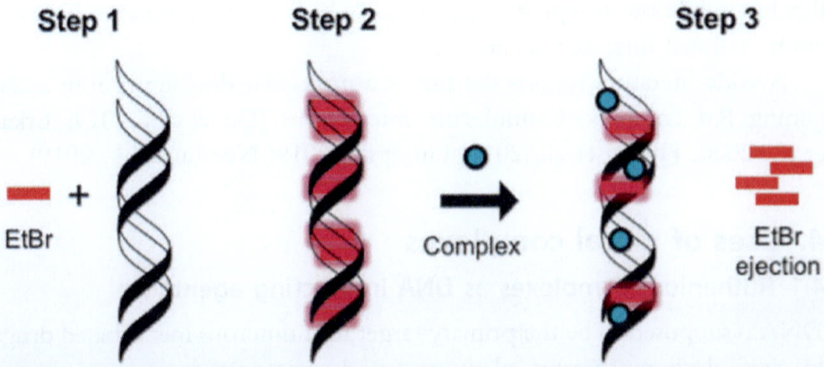

Figure 2.4 Indirect fluorescence displacement assay using EtBr. *(Reprinted with permission from Kellett, A., Molphy, Z., Slator, C., McKee, V., & Farrell, N. P. (2019). Molecular methods for assessment of non-covalent metallodrug-DNA interactions. Chemical Society Reviews, 48(4), 971–988.)*

theoretically and also are advantageous in designing novel therapeutic agents (Roy, 2019). The molecular docking methodology could provide a basis for atomic-level modeling of the interaction between a complex and a protein or nucleic acid, allowing us to illustrate the complex behavior in the binding site of target receptor molecules and also to find out principal biochemical processes (Torres et al., 2019). The molecular docking technique involves two steps: (i) the prediction of the complex conformation as well as its position and orientation within the binding sites of target molecules and (ii) the calculation of the binding affinity. Moreover, various other different parameters including hydrogen bonding, van der Waals interactions, and exposed surface area reduction can easily be derived by means of molecular docking approaches.

When both complex and the receptor (target molecule) are rigid, it limits the search space, allowing only three each rotational and translational degrees of freedom. In this case, the issues of complex flexibility could be overcome by designing and using a precomputed set of conformations, or by allowing for a degree of atom–atom overlap between the protein (receptor) and ligand/complex. Quite the reverse, for the systems whose behavior follows the induced fit prototype (Guedes et al., 2014), it is of utmost importance to consider the flexibilities of both the complex and the receptor, since in that case to form a minimum energy perfectly fitting complex, both the complex and the receptor alter their conformations. Thus the common approach during docking is to treat the complex as flexible, while the receptor is kept rigid, which creates a synergy between computational time and accuracy.

A wide literature reports the use of a molecular docking tool in ascertaining Ru complex–biomolecule interactions (De et al., 2019; Erkan et al., 2020; Huang et al., 2019; Liu et al., 2019; Neethu et al., 2019).

4. Uses of metal complexes

4.1 Ruthenium complexes as DNA interacting agents

DNA is supposed to be the primary target for numerous metal-based drugs. In classical chemotherapy, platinum-based anticancer drugs form specific lesions on DNA inducing apoptosis (Pieter et al., 2008).

A majority of the reported ruthenium complexes are DNA interacting agents via apoptosis (DNA damage of cancerous cells). Although, the DNA interaction mode differs based upon the complex structure and could involve intercalation, cross-linking, and ionic interactions (Brabec & Kasparkova, 2018) (Fig. 2.5). A range of specific DNA-interacting ruthenium complexes have been designed (Ang et al., 2006).

Wumaier et al. reported three new Ru(II) polypyridyl complexes **1–3** containing ascididemin (ASC) (Fig. 2.6) (Wumaier et al., 2019). Their interactions with G-quadruplex sequences of DNA were studied and compared with the free ligand, ASC employing various spectroscopic

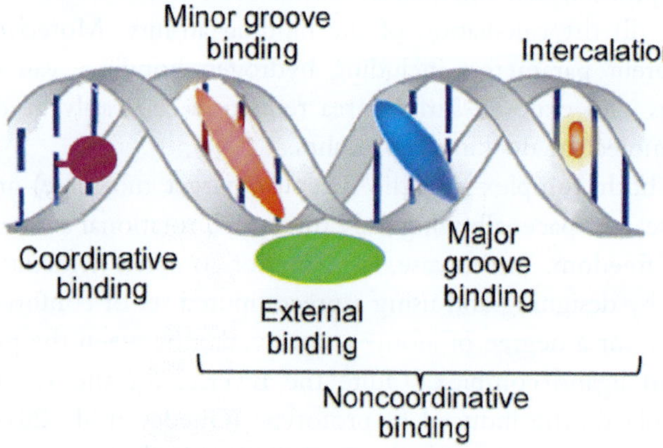

Figure 2.5 DNA binding modes of ruthenium complexes. *(Reprinted with permission from Brabec, V., & Kasparkova, J. (2018). Ruthenium coordination compounds of biological and biomedical significance. DNA binding agents. Coordination Chemistry Reviews, 376, 75–94.)*

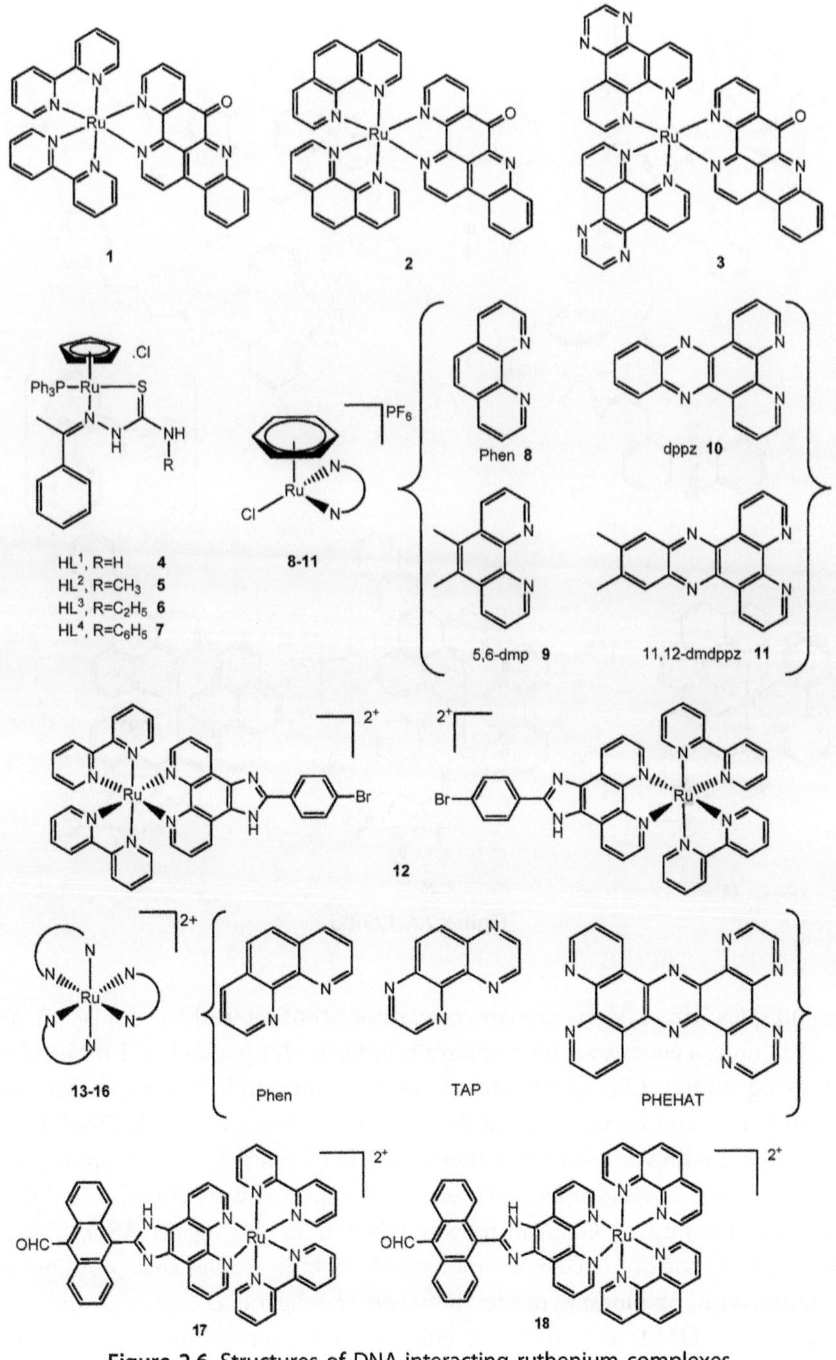

Figure 2.6 Structures of DNA-interacting ruthenium complexes.

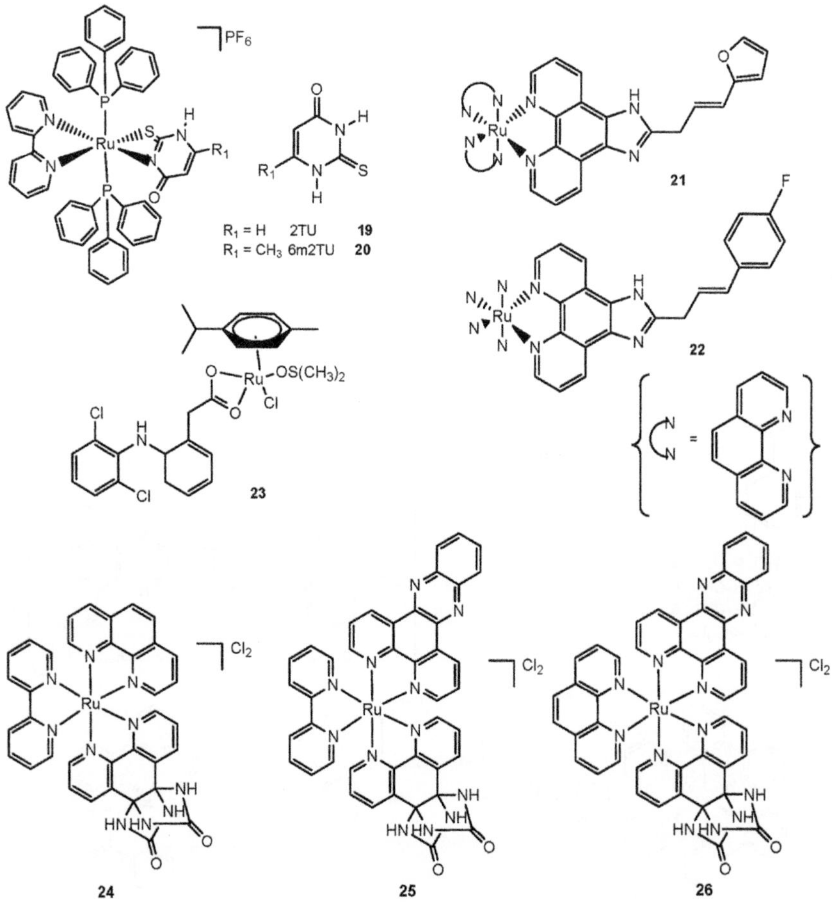

Figure 2.6 Cont'd

techniques (viz., UV-vis spectroscopy, fluorescent intercalator displacement assay, fluorescence resonance energy transfer melting assay) and molecular docking studies. UV-vis absorption spectroscopic studies revealed that the ligand ASC and complex **3** exhibited strong interactions with DNA base pairs along with π−π stacking interactions between the aromatic moiety of complex and G-quadruplex quartet. Ru complexes were found to exhibit stronger binding to G-quadruplexes DNA than the ligand ASC. These results well corroborated with molecular docking studies that indicated a combination of binding modes between the ligand/complex **3** and G-quadruplex DNA, viz., (i) π−π end stacking interactions between ASC and G-quartet, (ii) electrostatic interactions between Ru and DNA's backbone, and (iii) hydrophobic effects (Fig. 2.7). The positive charges of Ru complex favor the binding to G-quadruplexes, which in turn provides a stronger binding of Ru with DNA.

Devagi et al. reported four new cyclopentadienyl Ru(II)-acetophenone-4(N)-substituted thiosemicarbazone complexes **4–7** with the formula $[Ru(\eta^5\text{-}C_5H_5)$ (H-Aptsc)$PPh_3]$.Cl (**4**), $[Ru(\eta^5\text{-}C_5H_5)$ (H-Apmtsc)$PPh_3]$.Cl (**5**), $[Ru(\eta^5\text{-}C_5H_5)$ (H-Ap-etsc)$PPh_3]$.Cl (**6**), and $[Ru(\eta^5\text{-}C_5H_5)$ (H-Ap-ptsc)$PPh_3]$.Cl (**7**) were synthesized and characterized (Scheme 2.3, Fig. 2.6) (Devagi et al., 2018). The ligands (HL^1–HL^4) and the complexes (**4–7**) were titrated with CT DNA and observed by

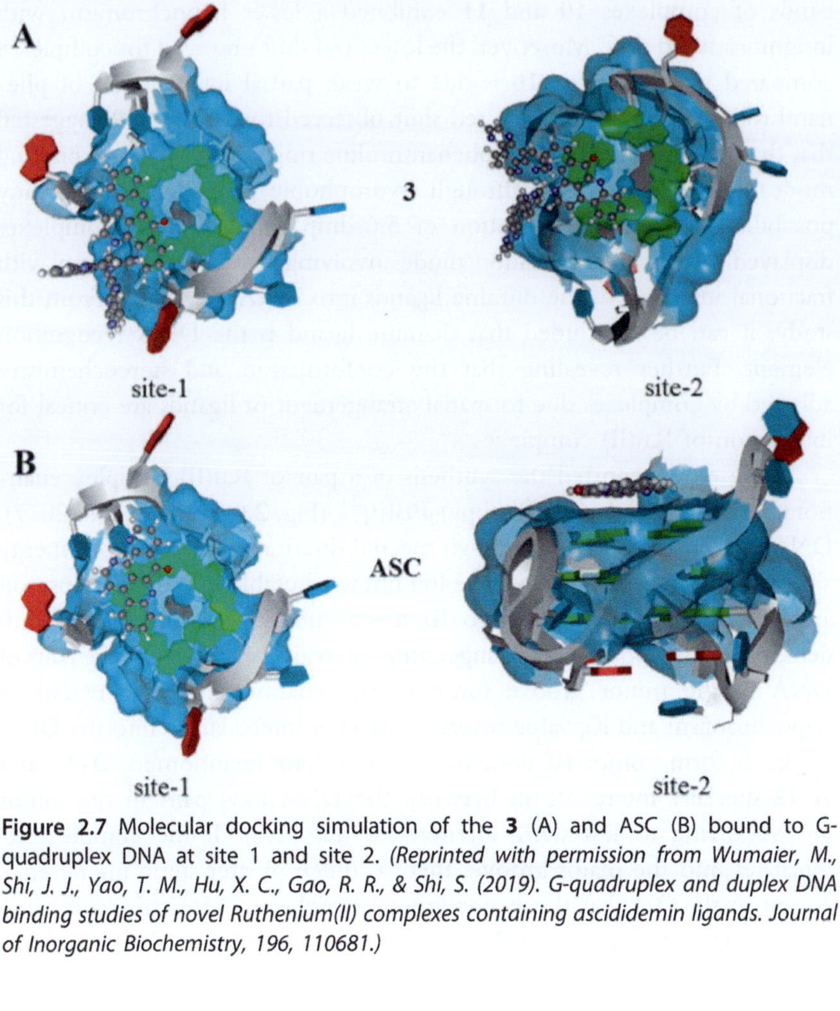

Figure 2.7 Molecular docking simulation of the **3** (A) and ASC (B) bound to G-quadruplex DNA at site 1 and site 2. *(Reprinted with permission from Wumaier, M., Shi, J. J., Yao, T. M., Hu, X. C., Gao, R. R., & Shi, S. (2019). G-quadruplex and duplex DNA binding studies of novel Ruthenium(II) complexes containing ascididemin ligands. Journal of Inorganic Biochemistry, 196, 110681.)*

UV-vis spectrophotometer. The hyperchromic effect (a subsequent increase in absorption) with a blue and red shift in the intraligand (IL) band observed. From these results, it could be inferred that the interaction of Ru(II) complexes with CT DNA was by an external contact, probably via electrostatic mode of binding.

Ganeshpandian and coworkers report the synthesis of four half-sandwich Ru(II)-arene complexes, viz., [Ru(η^6-benzene)(diimine) Cl](PF_6) (**8–11**) (Fig. 2.6) (Ganeshpandian et al., 2017). UV-vis absorption spectral measurements demonstrated that the ligand-centered $\pi \rightarrow \pi^*$ absorption bands exhibited hypochromism (decrease in molar absorptivity) with red shifts suggesting deep insertion of the coordinated dppz ring into the DNA base pairs. However, the metal-to-ligand charge transfer (MLCT) bands of complexes **10** and **11** exhibited a lesser hypochromism with insignificant red shift. Moreover, the lower red shift observed for complex **8** compared with complex **10** is due to weak partial intercalation of phenanthroline. The insignificant red shift observed for complex **9** suggested that the methyl groups on the phenanthroline ring bind via groove binding mode with DNA surface through hydrophobic forces, ruling out any possibility of partial intercalation of 5,6-dmp ring. All four complexes displayed a similar coordination mode involving partial intercalation with fractional insertion of the diimine ligands into DNA base pairs. From this study, it can be concluded that diamine ligand is the DNA recognition element. Further revealing that the conformation and stereochemistry adhered by complexes due to spatial arrangement of ligands are critical for interaction of Ru(II) complexes.

Hong et al. reported the synthesis of a pair of Ru(II) complex enantiomers, **Δ-12** and **Λ-12,** $[Ru(bpy)_2PBIP]^{2+}$ (Fig. 2.6) (Hong et al., 2017). DNA binding studies using UV-vis spectral titrations revealed a low energy absorption band centered at 458–469 nm attributable to MLCT transition and another at 285–291 nm to IL $\pi-\pi^*$ transition. Both these bands demonstrated hypochromism, suggesting intercalation between base pairs of DNA in the minor groove for both the enantiomers. The extent of hypochromism and K_b value revealed a deeper intercalation into the DNA of the Δ form compared with the Λ form. The enantiomers, **Δ-12** and **Λ-12** specially intercalate in between the DNA base pairs in the minor groove owing to less steric interference (Fig. 2.8). If the complex intercalates into the major groove, there is much greater steric interference owing to the fact that the major groove is richer in base pairs compared with the minor groove, and also the extended orientation of the base pairs

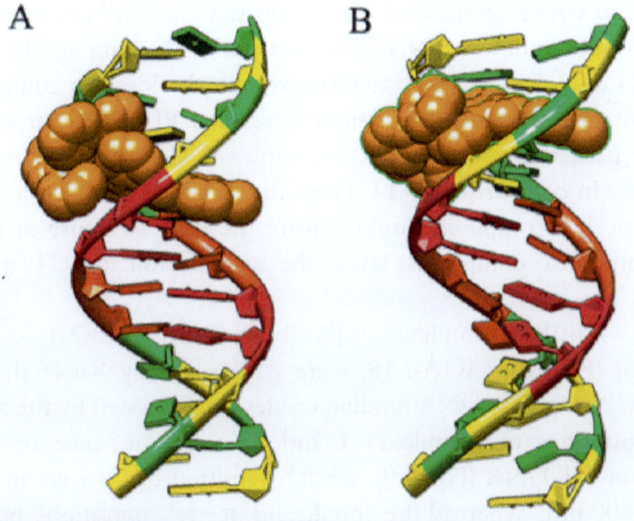

Figure 2.8 Molecular docking of DNA (PDB ID: 1BNA) with **Δ-12** (A) and **Λ-12** (B). *(Reprinted with permission from Hong W. X., Huang, F., Huan, T., Xu, X., Han, Q., Wang, G., Xu, H., Duan, S., Duan, Y., Long, X., Liu, Y., & Hu, Z. (2017). Comparative studies on DNA-binding and in vitro antitumor activity of enantiomeric ruthenium(II) complexes. Journal of Inorganic Biochemistry, 180, 54–60.)*

faces the major groove. Owing to apt steric matching of the **Δ-12**, with right-handed B-DNA forming a two-pole complementary complex compatible to its molecular symmetry, it therefore exhibits strong electrostatic interactions, resulting in a deeper and stronger intercalative DNA binding.

In a recent study, Magnieto et al. reported a comprehensive study of the selective binding modes of a series of Ru complexes with DNA G4 (human telomeric sequence) in various solution conditions (with K^+ and Na^+). The complexes studied were two homoleptic complexes, $[Ru(TAP)_3]^{2+}$ **13** and $[Ru(phen)_3]^{2+}$ **14**, and two heteroleptic complexes, $[Ru(phen)_2PHEHAT]^{2+}$ **15** and $[(phen)_2RuPHEHATRu(phen)_2]^{4+}$ **16** (Fig. 2.6) (Magnieto et al., 2018). Luminescence lifetime and melting temperature measurements revealed that both the homoleptic Ru complexes were found to interact weakly with G4 ($d[AG_3(T_2AG_3)_3]$). Further, molecular docking studies of **14** were performed, and the results revealed distinctive binding modes interaction to G4, viz., top, bottom, and groove modes, deforming the G4 structure, particularly for the hybrid G4 in K^+. On the other hand, two heteroleptic Ru complexes demonstrated G4 stabilization, where **15** showed a large selectivity toward G4 in comparison to the double-stranded DNA. The molecular docking results of **15** to hybrid G4 demonstrated the interactions with the loops in addition to the π-type interactions between adenine bases and PHEHAT strongly stabilizing the partial intercalation of the complex in G4, with a greater binding free energy in comparison to **14**. From the results, it could be inferred that homoleptic Ru complexes could deform the basic structure of G4, while heteroleptic Ru complexes favor the stabilization of G4 quadruplex structure.

Two Ru(II) complexes, $[Ru(bpy)_2(FAMP)](ClO_4)_2$, **17**, and $[Ru(phen)_2(FAMP)](ClO_4)_2$, **18**, were synthesized by Xu et al. (Fig. 2.6) (Xu et al., 2014). The DNA binding modes were assessed by the absorption spectral titrations of complexes **1** and **2** in the presence of increasing amounts of CT DNA (Fig. 2.9). π−π* transition bands were in the range of 300−400 nm, whereas the intraligand π−π* transitions bands were below 300 nm. Upon increasing concentrations of CT DNA, both the complexes exhibited hypochromism suggesting DNA intercalation, involving a strong π−π stacking interaction between the aromatic chromophore and DNA base pairs. Comparatively, a larger K_b value of complex **18** reflected its higher binding affinity and deeper intercalation than complex **17**.

Carvalho et al. synthesized 2-thiouracil (2TU and 6m2TU)-derived Ru(II)-based complexes *trans*-$[Ru(2TU)(PPh_3)_2(bpy)]PF_6$ **19** and *trans*-$[Ru(6m2TU)\text{-}(PPh_3)_2(bpy)]PF_6$ **20** (Fig. 2.6) (Carvalho et al., 2020). The results of DNA binding experiments carried out by absorption spectroscopy revealed the K_b values of 5×10^3 and $3 \times 10^3\ M^{-1}$, respectively, for complexes **19** and **20**. From the K_b values it could be inferred that the weak binding takes place between the complexes and DNA, since the complexes lack the ability to form hydrogen bonds. An intercalative binding mode depending upon the structural aspects of complexes **19** and **20** could contribute to the biologic activity.

Jiang et al., in 2019, reported two Ru(II) polypyridyl complexes, viz., $[Ru(dmp)_2(CAPIP)](ClO_4)_2$ **21** and $[Ru(dmp)_2(CEPIP)](ClO_4)_2$ **22** (Fig. 2.6) (Jiang et al., 2019). Upon interaction of these two complexes with CT DNA, it was found that MLCT bands displayed hyperchromism with bathochromic shift and bonded through intercalative mode of binding. The K_b values of Ru(II) complexes **21** and **22** were calculated to be $6.12 \times 10^5\ M^{-1}$ and $5.07 \times 10^5\ M^{-1}$, respectively. The degree of the hypochromism in a UV-vis band is constant with the strength of the

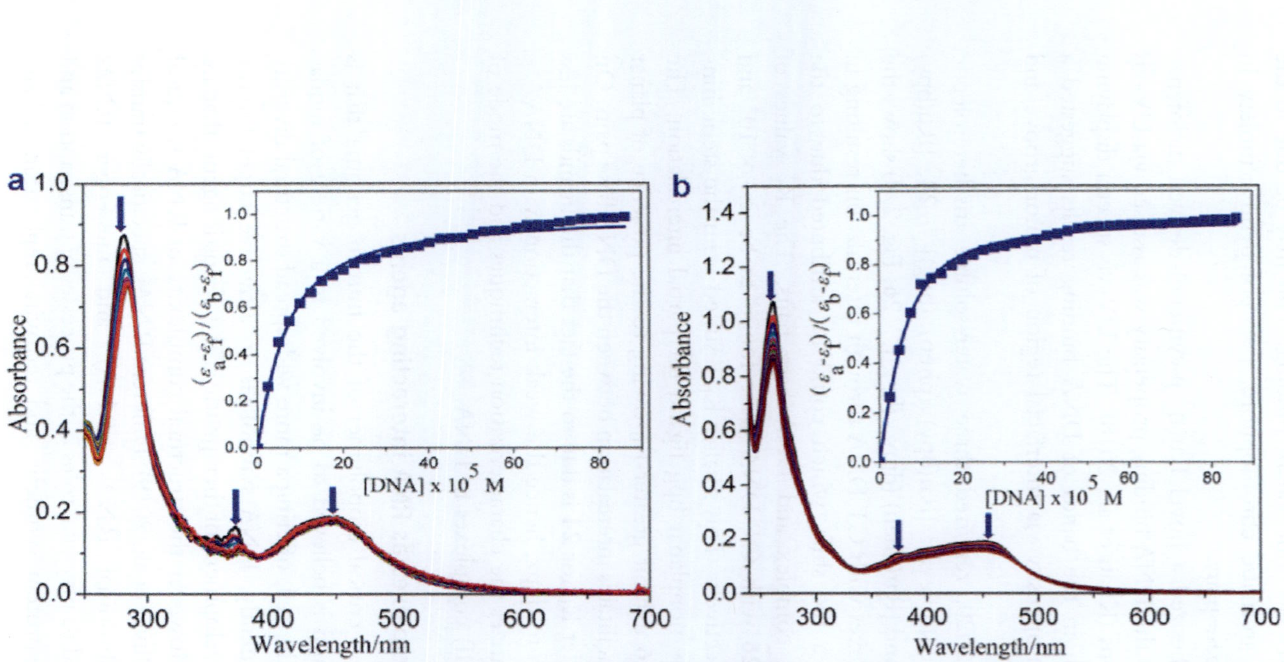

Figure 2.9 Absorption spectra of complexes in Tris–HCl buffer upon addition of CT DNA in presence of complexes A) **17** and B) **18**. Arrows show the absorbance change. Plots of $(\epsilon_a-\epsilon_f)/(\epsilon_b-\epsilon_f)$ versus [DNA]. *(Reprinted with permission from Xu, L., Zhong, N. J., Xie, Y. Y., Huang, H. L., Jiang, G. B., & Liu, Y. J. (2014). Synthesis, characterization, In vitro cytotoxicity, and apoptosis–inducing properties of ruthenium(II) complexes. PLoS ONE, 9(5), e96082.)*

interaction. Usually Ru(II) polypyridyl complexes are broadly documented to interact with DNA via noncovalent binding. This may be due to the intercalation of the aromatic chromophore, i.e., polypyridyl moiety in between the DNA base pairs.

Khan et al. synthesized a novel Ru(η^6-*p*-cymene)-derived diclofenac complex **23**. Further the DNA binding propensity was assessed via UV-vis spectroscopic titrations (Khan et al., 2018). The UV-vis spectra displaying slight hypochromism in the bands of DNA binding results suggested a significant binding propensity via interfacial region of minor groove and intercalation site.

Bhat et al., in 2020, reported three water-soluble tris-heteroleptic Ru(II) polypyridyl complexes: $[Ru(bpy)\ (phen)\ (bpg)]^{2+}$ **24**, $[Ru(bpy)\ (dppz)\ (bpg)]^{2+}$ **25**, and $[Ru(phen)\ (dppz)\ (bpg)]^{2+}$ **26**. Fig. 2.10 shows the interaction of complexes with CT DNA through intercalation resulting in hypochromism and a red shift, which could be attributed due to the interaction between complex and DNA base pairs. The K_b values of complexes **25** and **26** with CT DNA were found to be 2.3×10^4 and $6.8 \times 10^4\ M^{-1}$, respectively. This smaller K_b resulted from the steric hindrance caused by the nonplanar bpg ligand for partial intercalation. The complexes **25** and **26** exhibit greater K_b owing to the presence of planar dppz ligand, which facilitates intercalation between the DNA base pairs. On the other hand, smaller K_b for **24** is due to the fact that the ligands are less planar in comparison to dppz, hence the weak interaction with DNA.

Table 2.1 summarizes the characterization techniques and the mode of binding of Ru(II)/(III) complexes to DNA.

4.2 Ruthenium complexes as RNA interacting agents

RNA is considered a critical biopolymer of the human genome that is negatively charged and is believed to be involved in a variety of fundamental functions in the cell, offering a more widespread structural diversity than DNA. Consequently, RNA symbolizes an attractive target for the designing and the development of therapeutic and diagnostic agents that are structure selective. However the structural complexity of RNA is critical for its functioning (Oliver et al., 2019). Different RNAs, specifically transfer RNAs (tRNA), ribosomal RNAs (rRNA), and messenger RNAs (mRNA), were found to play vital roles in the processes of transcription and translation, splicing, protein synthesis, and retroviral replication (Zhang et al., 2018).

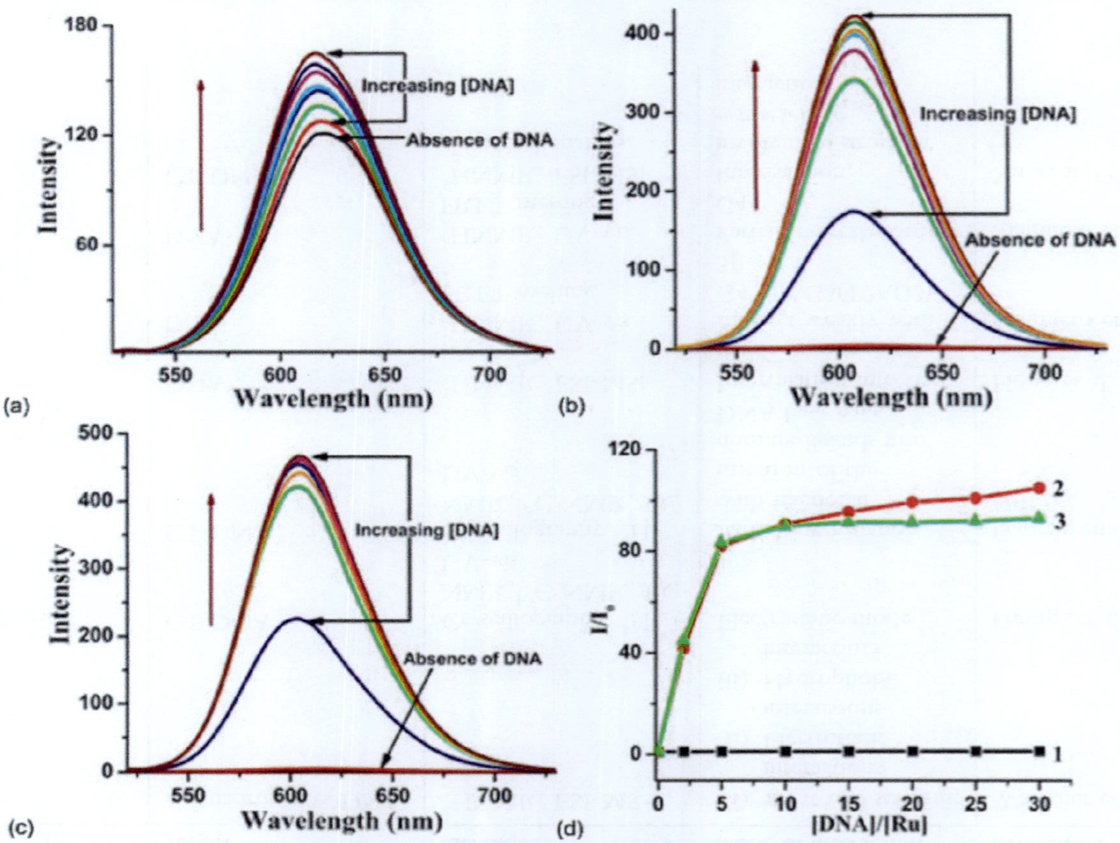

Figure 2.10 Emission spectra of complexes (A) **24**, (B) **25**, (C) **26**, 20 μM in phosphate buffer, pH 7.2, at 298 K with increasing [CT DNA]/[Ru] ratio 0–30, (D) plot of relative integrated emission intensity versus [CT DNA]/[Ru] for the complexes **24**, **25,** and **26**. *(Reprinted with permission from Bhat, S. S., Kumbhar, A. S., Purandare, N., Khan, A., Grampp, G., Lönnecke, P., Dixite, E. H. R., & Vanka, K. (2020). Tris-heteroleptic ruthenium(II) polypyridyl complexes: Synthesis, structural characterization, photophysical, electrochemistry and biological properties. Journal of Inorganic Biochemistry, 203, 110903.)*

Table 2.1 Summary of the modes of DNA interaction of ruthenium complexes.

Complex	Target	Characterization techniques	Mode of interaction	References
1–3	G-quadruplexes DNA	^{1}HNMR, ESI-MS	**i)** $\pi-\pi$ end stacking interactions **ii)** Electrostatic interactions **iii)** Hydrophobic interactions	Wumaier et al. (2019)
4–7	CT DNA	Crystallography, ^{1}H NMR, ^{13}C NMR, IR, UV-vis	Electrostatic mode	Devagi et al. (2018)
8–11	CT DNA	Crystallography, ^{1}H NMR, ^{13}C NMR, IR, UV-vis	Partial intercalation with fractional insertion of the diimine ligands into DNA base pairs	Ganeshpandian et al. (2017)
Δ/Λ–12	DNA	^{1}HNMR, ESI-MS, IR	Intercalation into the major groove	Hong et al. (2017)
13, 14	DNA	^{1}HNMR, UV-vis, FRET melting	Interact weakly with G4 (d[AG3(T2AG3)3])	Magnieto et al. (2018)
15, 16	DNA	^{1}HNMR, UV-vis, FRET melting	Partial intercalation in G4	Magnieto et al. (2018)
17, 18	CT DNA	^{1}HNMR, ESI-MS, elemental analysis,	Intercalation, involving a strong $\pi-\pi$ stacking interaction	Xu et al. (2014)

19, 20	CT DNA	Crystallography' ^{1}HNMR, ESI-MS, UV–vis, IR, elemental analysis	Weak intercalative binding mode	Carvalho et al. (2020)
21, 22	CT DNA	^{1}HNMR, HR MS, elemental analysis	Noncovalent binding	Jiang et al. (2019)
23	CT DNA	^{1}HNMR, ESI-MS, FTIR, UV-vis,	Interfacial region of minor groove and intercalation site	Khan et al. (2018)
24, 25, 26	CT DNA	^{1}HNMR, ESI-MS, elemental analysis	Intercalation	Bhat et al. (2020)

Metal complexes binding to RNA could be achieved by both covalent and noncovalent manner. In covalent binding, the metal center directly binds to an atom of the nucleobases, as observed for platinum drugs, and the metal complex binds to the N atom of the nucleobase. Alternatively, noncovalent interactions depend upon the nature of the organic ligands attached to the metal center and can be accomplished by a variety of modes, viz., groove binding via hydrophobic interactions, electrostatic interaction, intercalation, hydrogen bonding, insertion, or a combination of these (Dominguez et al., 2018; Pages et al., 2015; Ramanathan et al., 2019).

RNA nonduplex structures offer an attractive framework for supramolecular recognition. One such structure is the triple-helical structure of RNA that has been found playing vital roles in metabolism of DNA and gene functioning, RNA processing, and regulation of transcription. They can be used as tools in molecular biology and gene therapy. In the triple-helical structures of RNA, a third strand is bound to the double helix via Hoogsteen base pairing. Stable RNA triplexes, although weaker in stability compared with that of the Watson−Crick base pairing duplex strand, play fundamental roles in several biologic processes, which could be attributable to the electrostatic repulsion among three polyanionic strands (Fig. 2.11) (Zhu et al., 2017). Significant efforts has been made to develop agents that could recognize, bind, and stabilize these triplexes of RNA (Arya et al., 2011; Li et al., 2016; Ma et al., 2019; Peng et al., 2017; Spillane et al., 2007; Zhao et al., 2012).

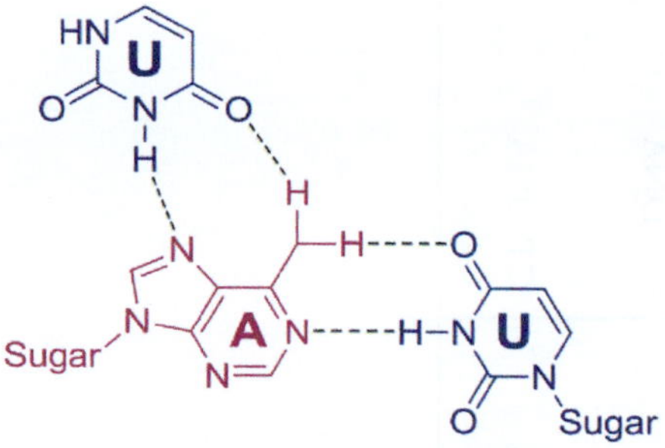

Figure 2.11 The base pairing scheme in RNA triplex. *(Reprinted with permission from Zhu, Z., Peng, M., Zhang, J., & Tan, L. (2017). Interaction of octahedral ruthenium(II) polypyridyl complex [Ru(bpy)2(PIP)]2+ with poly(U)·poly(A)*poly(U) triplex: Increasing third-strand stabilization of the triplex without affecting the stability of the duplex. Journal of Inorganic Biochemistry, 169, 44−49.)*

Peng and coworkers reported two chiral Ru(II) complexes **Δ-** and **Λ-**$[Ru(bpy)_2dppz]^{2+}$ **27** and their interaction with triplex RNA poly(U)·poly(A)*poly(U) (Fig. 2.12) (Peng et al., 2017). The binding of the enantiomers to the triplex RNA revealed hypochromism with no significant red shifts of both MLCT and π−π* IL transitions of the intercalating ligands. The binding constant, K_b, for Δ-enantiomer was found to be

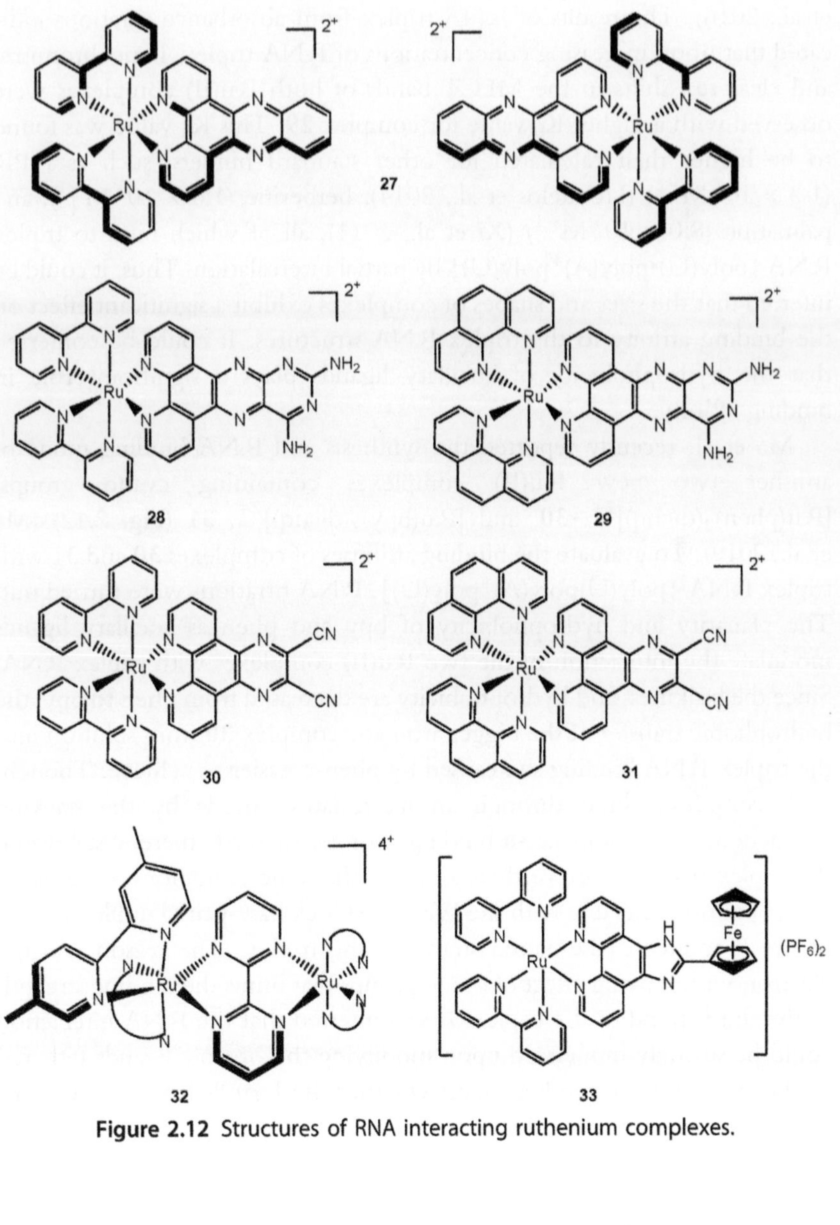

Figure 2.12 Structures of RNA interacting ruthenium complexes.

significantly higher than for Λ-enantiomer, suggesting a strong intermolecular interaction for Λ-enantiomer involving an effective overlap of the π-electron clouds with the base triplets. These RNA binding results suggested that chirality plays a significant role in the mode and extent of binding of complexes to the nucleobases.

In another study, Li et al. reported the binding of two Ru(II) complexes, $[Ru(bpy)_2(ppn)]^{2+}$, **28** and $[Ru(phen)_2(ppn)]^{2+}$, **29** (Fig. 2.12) (Li et al., 2016). The results of RNA triplex from absorbance titrations indicated that upon increasing concentrations of RNA triplex, hypochromisms and clear red shifts in the MLCT bands of both Ru(II) complexes were observed with a higher K_b value for complex **29**. This K_b value was found to be higher than calculated for other standard binders, such as PtPR ($1.3 \times 10^4\ M^{-1}$) (Hoyuelos et al., 2014), berberine ($1.6 \times 10^5\ M^{-1}$), and palmatine ($8.0 \times 10^5\ M^{-1}$) (Xi et al., 2011), all of which bind to triplex RNA {poly(U)•poly(A)*poly(U)} by partial intercalation. Thus, it could be inferred that the sizes and shapes of complexes exhibit a significant effect on the binding affinity to the triplex RNA structures. It could be conferred that the hydrophobicity of ancillary ligands plays a significant role in binding affinity.

Ma et al. recently reported the synthesis and RNA binding mode of another two new Ru(II) complexes containing cyano groups, $[Ru(phen)_2(dicnq)]^{2+}$, **30**, and $[Ru(bpy)_2(dicnq)]^{2+}$, **31** (Fig. 2.12) (Ma et al., 2019). To evaluate the binding affinities of complexes **30** and **31** with triplex RNA {poly(U)poly(A)*poly(U)}, RNA titrations were carried out. The planarity and hydrophobicity of bpy and phen as ancillary ligands modulate the interaction of the two Ru(II) complexes with triplex RNA. Since the bulkiness and hydrophobicity are decreased from phen to bpy, the hydrophobic transfer of the bigger aromatic complex **30** from solution into the triplex RNA binding site caused by phen is easier to achieve. Though, both complexes bind through an intercalation mode by the stacking interaction, with complex **30** binding stronger than **31**, thereby stabilizing the triplex structure. Nevertheless, under the same conditions, both complexes bound preferably with the Watson–Crick base-paired duplex instead of the Hoogsteen base-paired strand of the triplex. The reason was the electron-withdrawing effect of cyano groups that limits the binding strength of the third strand of the triplex. It was inferred that the RNA interaction could be strongly influenced upon modifying the organic ligands tethered to the Ru center depending upon whether the ligands have an electron-releasing or electron-withdrawing group.

Spillane et al. reported the use of ^1H NMR spectroscopy and molecular modeling for investigation of binding modes of **ΔΔ**- and **ΛΛ**-enantiomers of the dinuclear Ru(II) complex $[\{Ru(Me_2bpy)_2\}_2(\mu\text{-bpm})]^{4+}$, **32**, to an RNA tridecanucleotide duplex containing a single-base bulge $\{r(CCGAGAAUUCCGG)_2]\}$, and the corresponding control dodecanucleotide $\{r(CCGGAAUUCCGG)_2\}$ (Spillane et al., 2007) (Figs. 2.12 and 2.13). The binding was measured by the changes in the chemical shift value of NMR spectra. From upfield shifts of the Ru(II) complex, H3 and H3′ protons throughout the titration of the control dodecanucleotide with the **ΔΔ-32** complex bound the bulge-containing RNA with a significantly greater affinity ($6 \times 10^4\ M^{-1}$) than the nonbulge control RNA duplex. Whereas, upon addition of the **ΛΛ-32** to the control dodecanucleotide, no significant changes in chemical shift were observed for either the Ru(II) complex or RNA protons. Further, addition of **ΔΔ-32** to the bulge-containing tridecanucleotide induced selective changes in chemical shift for the base H8 and sugar H1' resonances from the adenine bulge residue and resonances from nucleotide residues adjacent to the bulge site. These primary binding modes, corroborant with the NMR binding results, exhibited that the Ru complex could effectively associate in the RNA minor groove at the bulge site (Fig. 2.14). The competitive binding experiments indicated that the **ΛΛ-32** bound the tridecanucleotide with similar affinity to the **ΔΔ-32**.

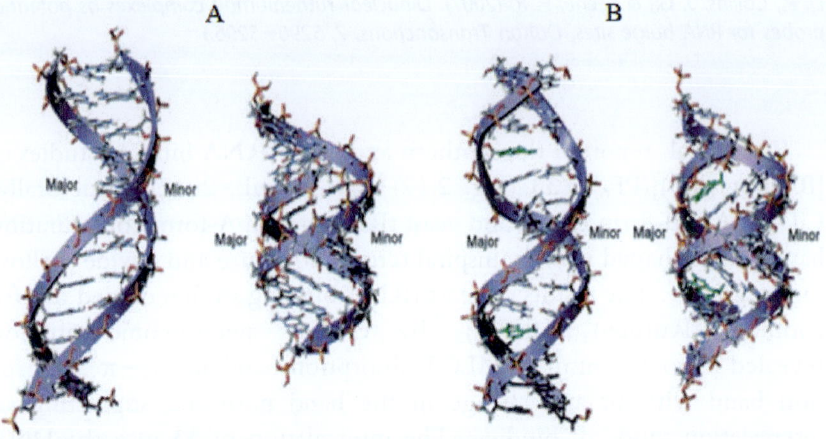

Figure 2.13 Comparative models of the control (A) and bulge (B) oligonucleotides used in this study (left = DNA; right = RNA). *(Reprinted with permission from Spillane, C. B., Smith, J. A., Buck, D. P., Collins, J. G., & Keene, F. R. (2007). Dinuclear ruthenium(II) complexes as potential probes for RNA bulge sites. Dalton Transanctions, 7, 5290–5296.)*

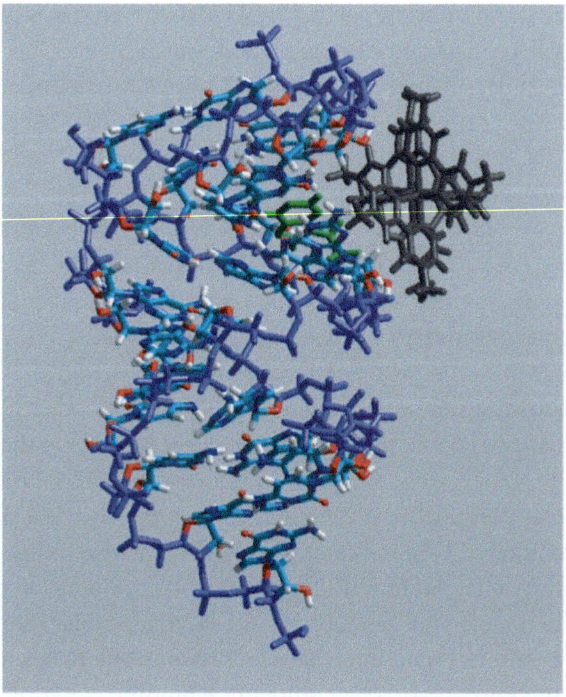

Figure 2.14 The RNA tridecanucleotide duplex with ΔΔ-**32** bound, rendered using tubes, and viewed looking down the minor groove at the binding site. The atoms of the RNA backbones are shown in purple, the unpaired adenine base is green, and the metal complex is black. *(Reprinted with permission from Spillane, C. B., Smith, J. A., Buck, D. P., Collins, J. G., & Keene, F. R. (2007). Dinuclear ruthenium(II) complexes as potential probes for RNA bulge sites. Dalton Transanctions, 7, 5290–5296.)*

Zhao et al. reported the synthesis and yeast tRNA binding studies of $[Ru(bpy)_2(fip)](PF_6)_2$, **33** (Fig. 2.12) (Zhao et al., 2012). Structurally, CT DNA is B-form DNA, and yeast tRNA has an A-form configuration having an L-shaped mainly unspiral tertiary structure and a wide shallow minor groove. The results of yeast tRNA binding studies carried out for complex $[Ru(bpy)_2(fip)](PF_6)_2$ by UV-vis spectroscopic titration revealed hypochromism in MLCT absorption band and $\pi-\pi^*$ absorption band without any change in the band positions, suggesting an intercalation mode of binding. The intercalation of **33** into the DNA was the dominant binding mode with larger binding affinity to the DNA $\{K_b=(5.37 \pm 0.35)\times10^5\ M^{-1}\}$ compared with the RNA $\{K_b=(2.16 \pm 0.23)\times10^5\ M^{-1}\}$.

Table 2.2 summarizes the characterization techniques and the mode of binding of Ru(II)/(III) complexes to RNA.

4.3 Ruthenium complexes as other biomolecule interacting agents

4.3.1 DNA topoisomerases

DNA topoisomerases are crucial enzymes required for various processes, viz., (i) recombination of DNA and (ii) chromosomal segregation and relaxation of DNA during replication and transcription (Cuya et al., 2017). Topoisomerase I (Topo I) and topoisomerase II (Topo II) are the two types of DNA topoisomerases. Topo I is essential in catalyzing superhelical DNA relaxation by producing a transient single-strand nick in the DNA duplex during cleavage and religation cycles (Chowdhury et al., 2019). On the other hand, Topo II generates coordinated nicks in both strands of the DNA duplex, mediated by ATP-dependent induction (Wang, 2002). Topoisomerases are recognized as pharmacologic targets for several clinically prescribed drugs since Topo inhibitors can be exploited as a useful strategy for anticancers, antibiotics, and in other therapeutics (Bansal et al., 2017; Delgado et al., 2018; Ketron et al., 2014; Pommier, 2013; Skok et al., 2019). Ru complexes present rich photochemical properties and have gained a significant attention as possible topoisomerase inhibitors (Brabec & Kasparkova, 2018).

Qian et al. reported four new chiral Ru(II) complexes bearing furan ligands, Δ/Λ-$[Ru(bpy)_2(pocl)]^{2+}$ **(Δ/Λ-34)** and Δ/Λ-$[Ru(bpy)_2(poi)]^{2+}$ **(Δ/Λ-35)** (Fig. 2.15) (Qian et al., 2016). DNA Topo IIα enzyme was selected to perform the cleavage experiments to ascertain the DNA damaging capability of the Ru complex. It was evident from the results of cleavage experiments that **Δ-35** acted as Topo IIα poison/inhibitor causing DNA double-strand damage eventually leading to apoptosis. The specific binding mode with the DNA–Topo II complex for **Δ-35** was further ascertained by molecular docking. As evident from the results shown in Fig. 2.16, **Δ-35** was lodged into Glu596, Glu614, Ser709, Glu712, Asp541, and Asp543 binding pockets. Upon interaction from the binding of **Δ-35** inducing the reorientation in the active site, **Δ-35** displays significant Topo inhibition, leading to enzyme inactivation. Whereas, **Λ-35** compared with **Δ-35** exhibited a lower binding score due to the smaller lipophilic contribution. Hence the entry of the L-form of bpy into the binding pocket (Glu544, Leu592, and Arg672) was prevented, thus posing to be a selective factor for the chirality.

Table 2.2 Summary of the modes of RNA interaction of ruthenium complexes.

Complex	Target	Characterization techniques	Mode of interaction	References
Δ/Λ-27	Triplex RNA poly(U)·poly(A)* poly(U)	–	Interaction by effective overlap of the π–electron clouds with the base triplets.	Peng et al. (2017)
28, 29	Triplex RNA poly(U)·poly(A)* poly(U)	–	Partial intercalation	Li et al. (2016)
30, 31	Triplex RNA poly(U)·poly(A)* poly(U)	^{1}HNMR, MALDI-TOF-MS, elemental analysis, UV-vis,	Intercalation mode by the stacking interaction	Ma et al. (2019)
ΔΔ/ΛΛ-32	RNA	^{1}HNMR, NOESY spectra, DQFCOSY, MS	RNA minor groove at the bulge site	Spillane et al. (2007)
33	Yeast tRNA	–	Intercalation mode	Zhao et al. (2012)

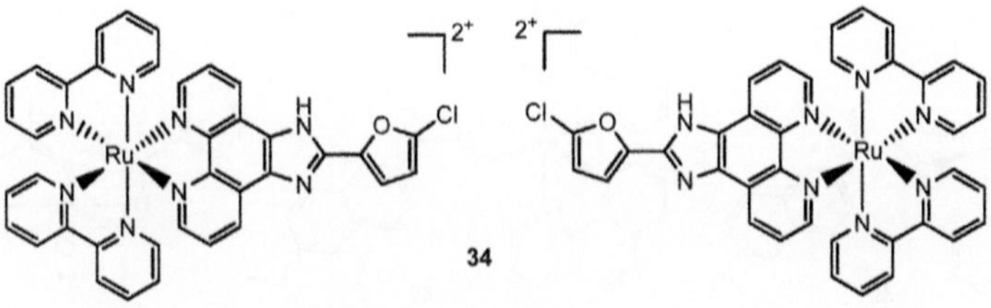

34

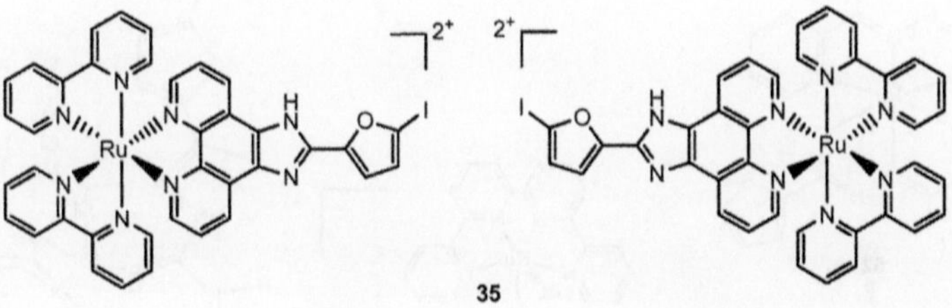

35

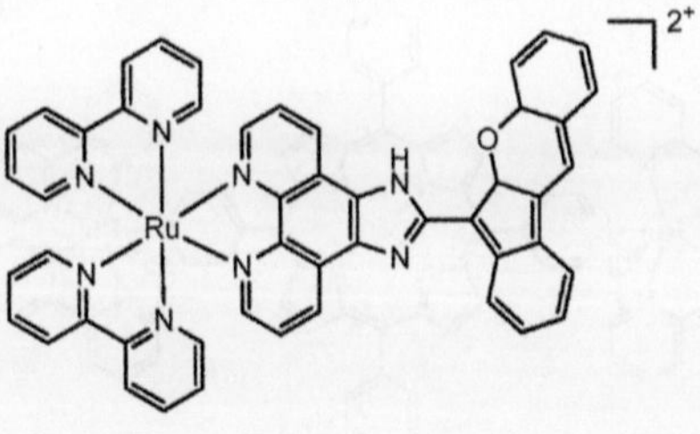

36

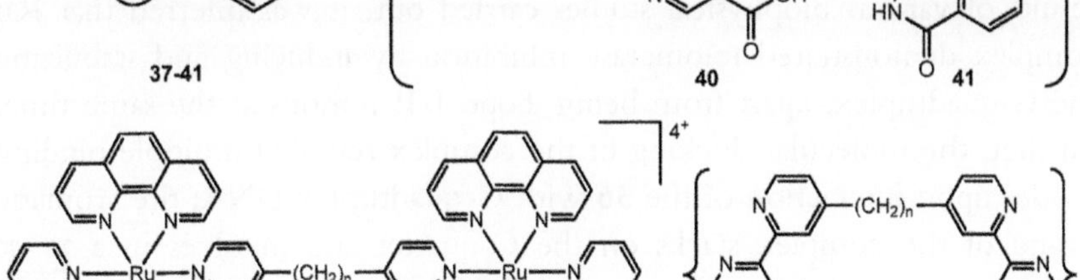

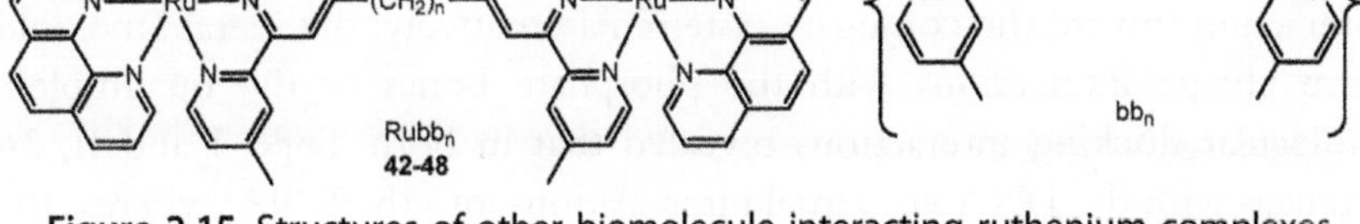

Figure 2.15 Structures of other biomolecule interacting ruthenium complexes.

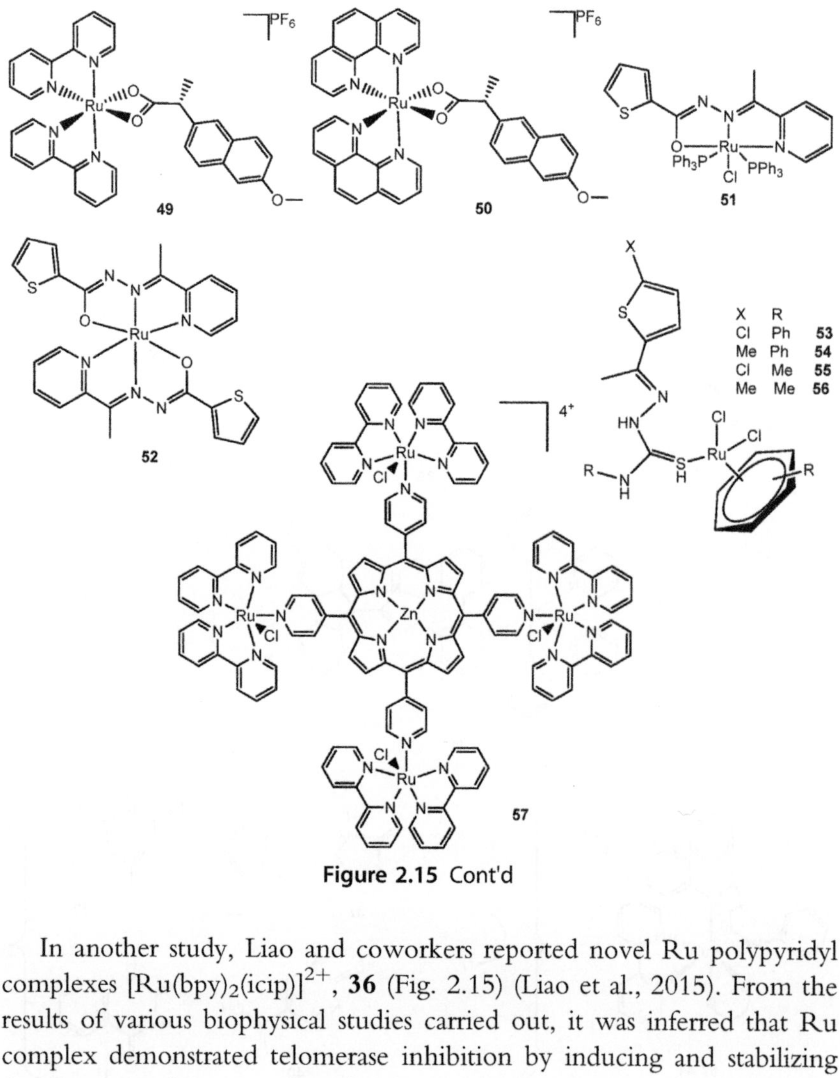

Figure 2.15 Cont'd

In another study, Liao and coworkers reported novel Ru polypyridyl complexes $[Ru(bpy)_2(icip)]^{2+}$, **36** (Fig. 2.15) (Liao et al., 2015). From the results of various biophysical studies carried out, it was inferred that Ru complex demonstrated telomerase inhibition by inducing and stabilizing the G-quadruplex, apart from being Topo I/II poisons at the same time. Further, the molecular docking of the complex revealed multiple binding modes upon interaction of the **36** with G-quadruplex DNA; the aromatic ligand of the complex stacks on the G-quartet and involves in a π−π interaction toward the conjugate system. Alternatively, the metal ion could form charge interactions with the phosphate bones of the quadruplex. Molecular docking interactions revealed that in both Topo I and II, **36** interacts with the DNA via partial intercalations into the DNA, whereas the remaining part of **36** is exposed and binds with amino acid residues of the

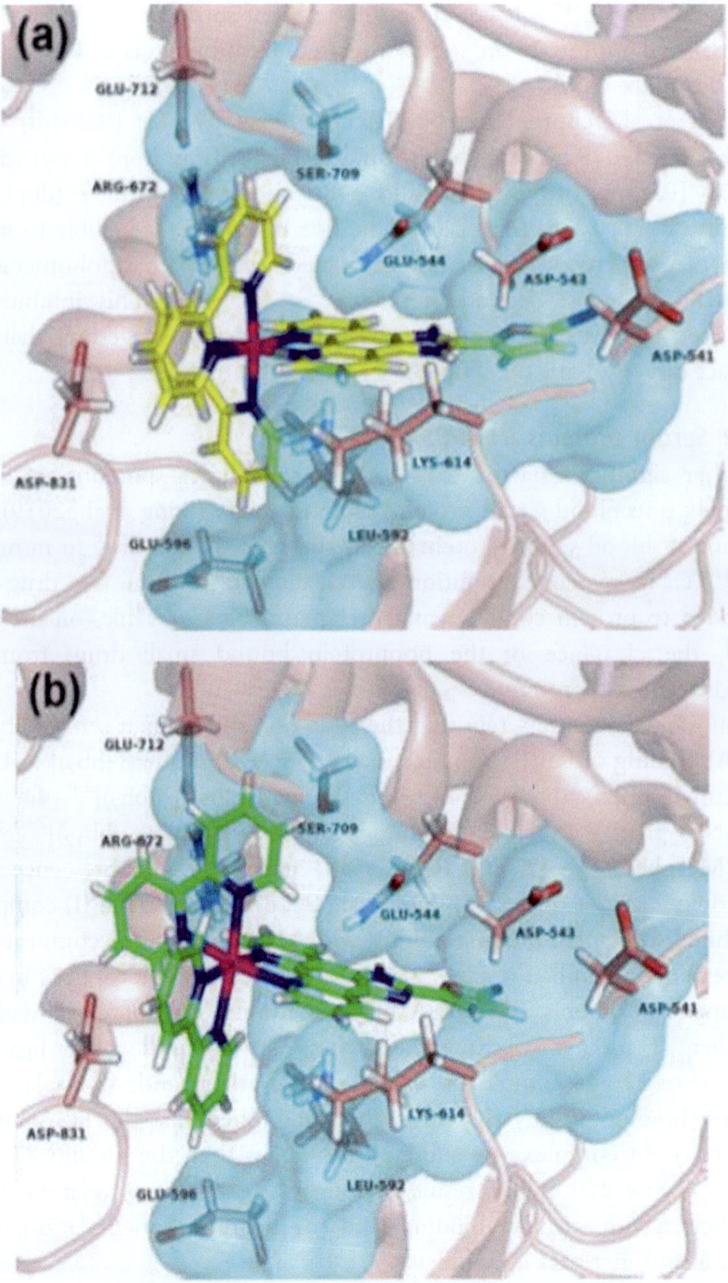

Figure 2.16 Binding mode of (A) **Δ-35** and (B) **Λ-35** with human-Topo IIα. *(Reprinted with permission from Qian, C., Wu, J., Ji, L., & Chao, H. (2016). Topoisomerase IIα poisoning and DNA double-stand breaking by chiral ruthenium(II) complexes containing 2-furanyl-imidazo[4,5-f][1,10]phenanthroline derivatives. Dalton Transanctions, 45(26), 10546–10555.)*

Topo I/II (Fig. 2.17). It could be inferred that some DNA-binding complexes also demonstrate the topoisomerase inhibition effect or interact with G-quadruplex DNA.

Silva et al. reported five Ru(II) complexes **37–41**: [Ru(tzdt) (bipy) (dppb)]PF_6 **37**, [Ru(mmi) (bipy) (dppb)]PF_6 **38**, [Ru(dmp) (bipy) (dppb)] PF_6 **39**, [Ru(mpca) (bipy) (dppb)]PF_6 **40**, and [Ru(2mq) (bipy) (dppb)]PF_6 **41** (Silva et al., 2019) (Fig. 2.15). The five complexes were able to inhibit the DNA supercoiled relaxation mediated by human topoisomerase IB (TopIB) in a dose-dependent manner at 25.0 μM. This inhibition is enhanced upon its preincubation with the enzyme, suggesting that they interact directly with the TopIB.

4.3.2 Serum proteins (HSA/BSA)

Another significant factor that governs the clinical potential of a Ru complex is its blood serum proteins binding ability (Song et al., 2019). The binding of blood serum protein affects the ADME of a drug in numerous ways (i.e., its overall distribution and clearance); only the free drug nonbounded to protein could act as a therapeutic agent. While, on the other hand, the clearance of the nonprotein bound small drugs from the bloodstream is more rapid.

Sun and coworkers reported the synthesis and human serum albumin (HSA) binding of Ru(II) complexes, viz., {*cis*-α-[Ru(phen) $(bb_7)]^{2+}$ **42**, *cis*-α-[Ru(Me_2phen) $(bb_7)]^{2+}$ **43**, *cis*-α-[Ru(Me_4-phen) $(bb_7)]^{2+}$ **44**, *cis*-α-[Ru(NO_2phen) $(bb_7)]^{2+}$ **45**, *cis*-α-[Ru(phen) $(bb_{12})]^{2+}$ **46**, $[Ru(Me_4phen)_3]^{2+}$ **47**, and $Rubb_{12}$ **48**} utilizing the fluorescence spectroscopic methods (Fig. 2.15) (Sun et al., 2018). All these Ru(II) complexes exhibited substantial binding affinity with HSA, since HSA comprises one fluorescent tryptophan residue that could be used as a fluorophore in drug-binding experiments. The HSA binding affinity was increased with the number of methyl substituents on the 1,10-phenanthroline ligand in the case of **42–44** complexes. While, on the other hand, **45** displayed the highest binding affinity. It was further established that the HSA binding affinity of **44** complex was substantially higher than the **46** and **47** complexes (Table 2.3). These results are suggestive of the correlation of lipophilicity, with stronger binding, and the degree of methylation of the phen ligand increases lipophilicity.

Srivastava et al. reported two Ru(II) complexes $[Ru(bpy)_2(nap)][PF_6]$ **49** and $[Ru(phen)_2(nap)][PF_6]$ **50** that are coordinated bidentately to Ru(II) center through carboxylato oxygen atoms ($-COO^-$) (Fig. 2.15)

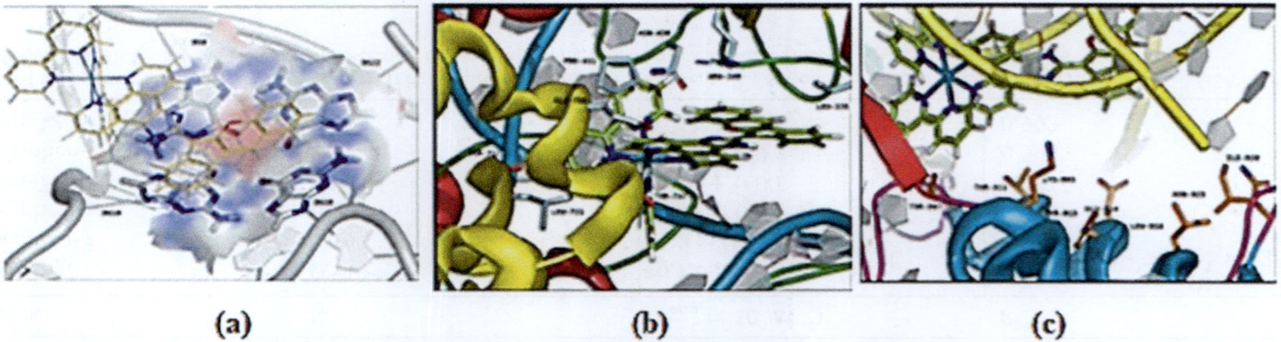

Figure 2.17 Molecular docking between the Ru(II) complex, **36**, and G-quadruplex (A), Topo I (B), and Topo II (C). *(Reprinted with permission from Liao, G., Chen, X., Wu, J., Qian, C., Wang, Y., Ji, L., & Chao, H. (2015). Ruthenium(II) polypyridyl complexes as dual inhibitors of telomerase and topoisomerase. Dalton Transanctions, 44(34), 15145–15156.)*

Table 2.3 K_{app} (HSA binding constant) and n (binding numbers) for the ruthenium complexes at [Ru]/[HSA] ratio from 0 to 2.4.

Complex	N	K_{app} (x 10^5 M^{-1})	R^2
$(Me_4phen)_3$	0.81	0.12 ± 0.03	0.98
α-Me_4phen-7	1.14	4.6 ± 0.90	0.996
α-Me_2phen-7	0.91	0.29 ± 0.13	0.984
α-phen-7	0.80	0.10 ± 0.00	0.991
α-NO_2phen-7	1.27	23.5 ± 4.9	0.998
α-phen-12	0.95	0.43 ± 0.17	0.993

Reprinted with permission from Sun, B., Musgrave, I. F., Day, A. I., Heimann, K., Keene, F. R., & Collins, J. G. (2018). Eukaryotic cell toxicity and HSA binding of [Ru(Me4phen)(bb7)]2+ and the effect of encapsulation in cucurbit[10]uril. Frontiers in Chemistry, 6(595), 1−12.

(Srivastava et al., 2020). The protein interaction studies were performed in the presence of the complexes by employing intrinsic tryptophan fluorescence quenching of BSA (bovine serum albumin). Upon the addition of the complexes, quenching of the emission intensity of BSA at 354 nm was observed, owing to the modifications that occur in the 2-degree structure of protein, resulting in efficient stronger binding with the complexes (Fig. 2.18). The K_{sv} values were calculated to be $1.06 \pm 0.04 \times 10^5\ M^{-1}$ and $0.91 \pm 0.04 \times 10^5\ M^{-1}$ for complexes **50** and **51** respectively.

Eswaran et al. reported the synthesis and BSA binding of two Ru(II) complexes $[Ru^{II}Cl(PPh_3)_2(L)]$ **51** and $[Ru^{II}(L)_2]$ **52**, where L = thiophene-2-carboxylic acid (1-pyridine-2-yl-ethylidene)-hydrazide (Eswaran et al., 2018) (Fig. 2.15). The fluorescence quenching experiments were performed with BSA. An enhancement in the absorption intensity of BSA followed by a blue shift was observed when the complexes were added. Scatchard binding constants (K) corresponding to the complexes **51** and **52** were calculated to be $2.04 \times 10^5\ M^{-1}$ and $1.86 \times 10^6\ M^{-1}$, respectively. A larger K value for complex **52** represents stronger binding with tryptophan residues than tyrosine residues in BSA compared with complex **51** via

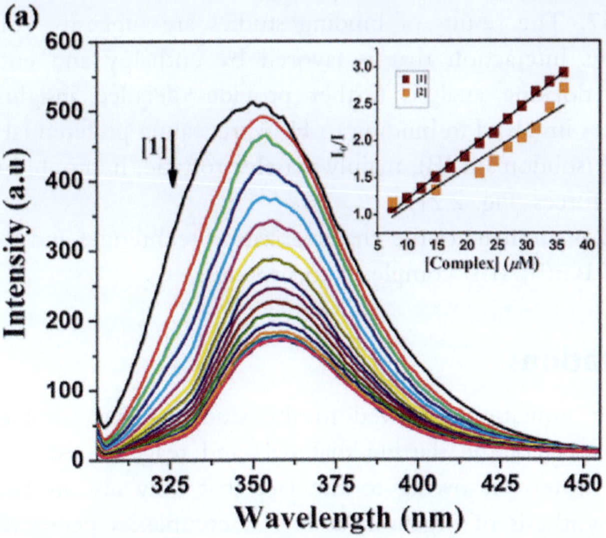

Figure 2.18 Emission spectral traces of BSA (7 μM) in the presence of **49** in tris buffer. Inset: (a) (I_0/I) versus [**49**] (μM). *(Reprinted with permission from Srivastava, P., Mishra, R., Verma, M., Sivakumar, S., & Patra, A. K. (2020). Cytotoxic ruthenium(II) polypyridyl complexes with naproxen as NSAID: Synthesis, biological interactions and antioxidant activity. Polyhedron, 172, 132–140.)*

hydrophobic interactions. This larger value of complex **51** in comparison with complex **52** can be attributed to the presence of two hydrazone ligands in the former.

Subasi et al. reported four new thiosemicarbazone-based organoruthenium(II)-arene complexes **53–56** and their BSA binding affinity by using fluorescence spectra (Subasi et al., 2020) (Fig. 2.15). Upon increasing concentrations of complexes, fluorescence intensity decreases for all complexes exhibited a slight blue shift;, suggesting that van der Waals contacts or hydrogen bonds may have formed during interaction with BSA (Fig. 2.19). The binding constant K_b values of complexes with BSA were found to be 5.5×10^2, 0.03×10^2, 15×10^2, and $0.42 \times 10^2\ M^{-1}$ respectively for complexes **53–56**. The Kb values though lower were in the order **55** > **53** > **56** > **54**, suggesting that presence of Cl group increases the affinity toward BSA binding.

Chaves et al. reported the interaction of a Ru(II)-porphyrin complex, **57**, previously reported (Toma et al., 2000) with HSA employing a variety of spectroscopic techniques, viz., steady-state, time-resolved, circular dichroism, synchronous, and 3D fluorescence and molecular docking (Fig. 2.15) (Chaves et al., 2019). Fig. 2.20 depicts the steady-state fluorescence emission of HSA in the presence and absence of successive additions of **57**. The results of binding studies are suggestive of moderate spontaneous interaction that is favored by enthalpy and entropy. The molecular docking analysis further provides detailed insights into the binding sites involved in binding to HSA, revealing preferential binding in the site III (subdomain IB), mainly via electrostatic, hydrophobic, and van der Waals forces (Fig. 2.21).

Table 2.4 summarizes the characterization techniques and the mode of binding of Ru(II)/(III) complexes to proteins.

5. Limitations

The major limitation involved in the study of Ru complexes is the expensive costs of the starting materials and reagents required for their synthesis. Moreover, owing to the fact that they are air and moisture sensitive, synthesis of organometallic Ru complexes necessarily requires inert atmosphere, Schlenk lines, and glove boxes. In spite of this perception, they are still believed to be crucial to life and several drugs comprising M–C (metal–carbon) bonds are in therapeutic use for a wide-ranging spectrum of diseases. Moreover, the yields of the final product being low

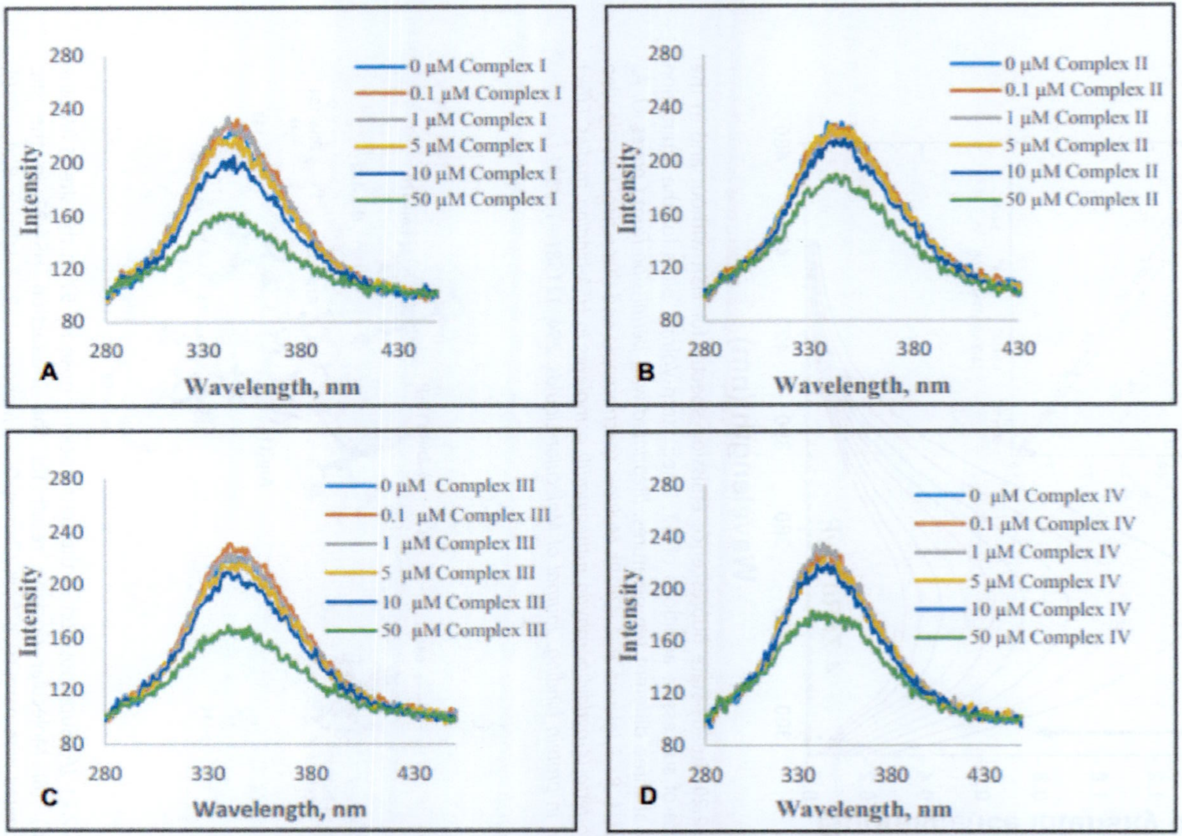

Figure 2.19 Emission spectra of **53** µM BSA in complex **53** (A), **54** (B), **55** (C), and **56** (D). *(Reprinted with permission from Subasi, E., Atalay, E. B., Erdogan, D., Sen, B., Pakyapan, B., & Kayali, H. A. (2020). Synthesis and characterization of thiosemicarbazone-functionalized organo-ruthenium (II)-arene complexes: Investigation of antitumor characteristics in colorectal cancer cell lines. Materials Science & Engineering C, 106, 110152.)*

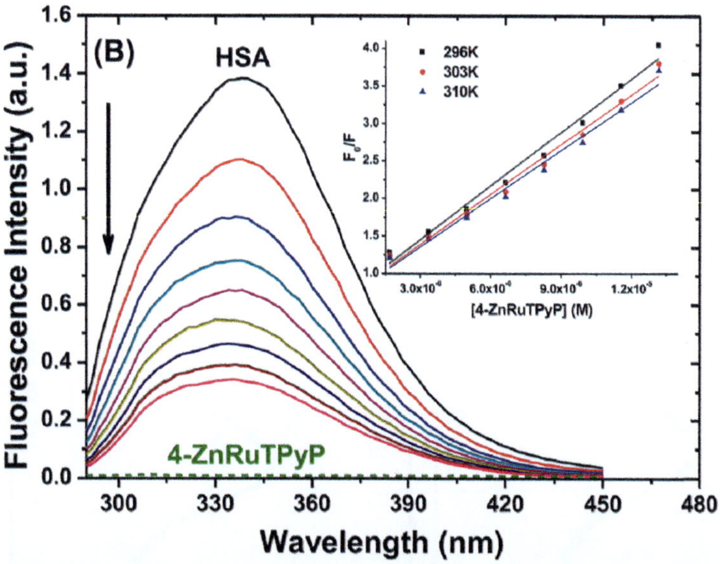

Figure 2.20 Steady-state fluorescence emission spectra for HSA without and in the presence of successive additions of **57**. Inset: Stern-Volmer plots for the interaction HSA:**57** at three different temperatures. *(Reprinted with permission from Chaves, O. A., Menezes, L. B., & Iglesias, B. A. (2019). Multiple spectroscopic and theoretical investigation of meso-tetra-(4-pyridyl)porphyrin ruthenium(II) complexes in HSA-binding studies. Effect of Zn(II) in protein binding. Journal of Molecular Liquids, 294, 111581–111591.)*

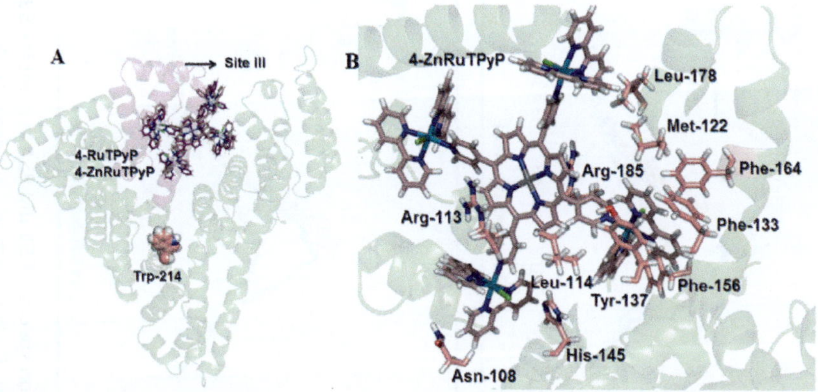

Figure 2.21 (A) Superposition of the best docking pose for **57** in the site III (in pink cartoon). (B) Molecular docking result for the interaction HSA:**57** in the site III. *(Reprinted with permission from Chaves, O. A., Menezes, L. B., & Iglesias, B. A. (2019). Multiple spectroscopic and theoretical investigation of meso-tetra-(4-pyridyl)porphyrin ruthenium(II) complexes in HSA-binding studies. Effect of Zn(II) in protein binding. Journal of Molecular Liquids, 294, 111581–111591.)*

Table 2.4 Summary of the modes of ruthenium complexes interacting with other biomolecules (proteins).

Complex	Target	Characterization techniques	Mode of interaction	References
Δ/Λ-34, Δ/Λ-35	DNA Topo IIα	^{1}HNMR, ESI-MS, elemental analysis	Inhibition	Qian et al. (2016)
36	Topo I/II	^{1}HNMR, ESI-MS, elemental analysis	Inhibition	Liao et al. (2015)
37–41	Topo IB	Crystallography, ^{1}HNMR, COZY, HSQC, IR, elemental analysis, UV-vis	Inhibition	Silva et al. (2019)
42–48	HSA	^{1}HNMR, MS, elemental analysis	Stronger binding in domains of HSA	Sun et al. (2018)
49, 50	HSA	^{1}HNMR, ESI-MS, elemental analysis, UV-vis	Hydrophobic interactions	Srivastava et al. (2020)
51, 52	BSA	Crystallography, ^{1}NMR, ESI-MS, elemental analysis, FTIR, UV-vis	Hydrophobic interactions	Eswaran et al. (2018)
53–56	BSA	Crystallography, ^{1}HNMR, ^{13}CNMR, ESI-MS, elemental analysis, FTIR	Van der Waals contacts or hydrogen bonds	Subasi et al. (2020
57	HSA	–	Binding in the site III (subdomain IB), mainly via electrostatic, hydrophobic, and van der Waals forces	Chaves et al. (2019)

limits the opportunity to study the underlying mechanisms of these Ru-based drugs.

The literature recapitulates the anticancer effects of Ru complexes, though less attention is being paid to decipher the underlying molecular mechanisms. Ru complexes are easily transported into the cells and initially bind to cellular DNA in the same manner as that of cisplatin, but their mode of DNA binding is dissimilar. Similarly, there are many other reports of numerous instances of synergy between different noncovalent DNA binding interactions of Ru complexes and their cytotoxic effects. Up till now, amidst various applications of Ru complexes, only some accounts are focusing on their covalent bonding interaction with nucleic acids.

6. Future prospects

Though it can be proposed that N7 of guanine is the preliminary DNA binding site of several Ru complexes, which is same as that of conventional Pt-based drugs, e.g., cisplatin and their analogs, the binding mode of Ru complexes to DNA is different, leading to different cytotoxic effects. This connection explains well the toxic effects of some Ru complexes in the cisplatin-resistant cancer cell lines. NAMI, a Ru compound in clinical trials, is known to exhibit its antimetastatic activity, which is independent of DNA interaction, possibly depending on matrix proteinase regulation. In that case, a better understanding of transferrin-mediated transport of Ru to the tumor site could deliver more effective and less toxic agents. The covalent bonding between Ru complexes and nucleic acids permits the direct use of their inherent properties in probing DNA, in detecting mismatches in vivo, serving as gene silencing agents, or stabilizing DNA structures by intercalation. With the development of light switches, probes to study thermal stability or kinetics in DNA or the interpretation of several electron transfer mechanisms, the interpretation of underlying different mechanisms involved in DNA binding of Ru complexes has been made possible.

The future development of clinical Ru-based drugs depends on the results of combination trials, where a specific Ru complex is administered in combination with a standard drug, topoisomerase I/II inhibitor, or an antimetabolite. However, it becomes essential to evaluate the balance between Ru complexes and classical chemotherapeutic agents in cancer cell lines and preclinical animal models. Once a preclinical rationale comes into existence, the trail from lab to clinic could be accelerated.

Undoubtedly, this further accentuates that currently there are a number of possible in cellulo or in vivo applications of Ru complexes in medicinal chemistry, and they are likely to emerge as potential therapeutic agents more effective than those in clinical use, only after addressing the issues in selective binding and uptake. In this context, it is important to acknowledge that even though if the investigated therapeutic agent is capable of modifying the properties of a specific bio-macromolecule, it cannot be mechanistically meant that this bio-macromolecule could be the cellular target of the Ru complex pertaining to its biologic effect.

7. Conclusions

This chapter highlights various modes of binding with nucleic acids (viz., DNA/RNA) of biologically or bio-medically important Ru complexes, and also how these complexes target various DNA/RNA conformations. Since DNA is the pharmacologic target of *cis*-platinum and its analogs, the most successful anticancer metallodrugs in the clinical use, the understanding of DNA interactions has become important for Ru complexes. Ru(II) complexes exhibit cytotoxicity and antimetastatic properties combined with low overall toxicity and overcoming cisplatin resistance. This is attributed to the various unique properties of Ru, viz., rate of ligand exchange, variable oxidation states, and the Fe mimicking ability in binding. Thus, to have a clear understanding of the underlying mechanisms of the biologic effects of Ru(II) complexes and their use clinical applications, in addition to anticancer properties, the identification of their pharmacologic target associated to their biologic effects and applications is of ultimate importance. Recently, transition metal complexes have netted an extensive revolution in DNA binding and potential application-related spectral properties of interest, viz., chemical and stereoselective DNA probes. These Ru complexes are believed to bind to nucleotides, through various modes including both covalent and noncovalent interactions. In general, in covalent interaction, it is the complex coordinate to guanine N7 of DNA. While noncovalent binding modes include (i) electrostatic binding, (ii) intercalation and partial intercalation, and (iii) groove binding.

Thus, the versatile chemistry of Ru permits a series of complexes incorporating a plethora of ligands providing a library of therapeutic complexes. It was found that many factors, in addition to the electronic effects, can affect the binding to nucleic acid and spectral properties of Ru(II) complexes. Using Ru complexes in drug development comes with a variety of advantages that include reliable synthetic protocols of stable complexes with expected geometries that are able to modify accordingly the rates of electron transfer and substitution, ligand affinities, and reduction potentials. Most of the Ru complexes bind to cellular DNA by penetrating the tumors.

Apparently, Ru complexes are postplatinum second-generation transition metal chemotherapeutics possessing exclusive properties that render them an enhanced selective entry into the cancer cells exhibiting less toxicity to noncancerous cells in preclinical trials. Consequently, Ru complexes that either interact with nucleic acids or moderate their mode of function have established diverse uses as therapeutic agents.

References

Ang, W. H., Daldini, E., Scolaro, C., Scopelliti, R., Jeannerat, J. L., & Dyson, P. J. (2006). Development of organometallic ruthenium arene anticancer drugs that resist hydrolysis. *Inorganic Chemistry, 45*, 9006–9013.

Arjmand, F., Afsan, Z., Sharma, S., Parveen, S., Yousuf, I., Sartaj, S., Siddique, H. R., & Tabassum, S. (2019). Recent advances in metallodrug–like molecules targeting non–coding RNAs in cancer chemotherapy. *Coordination Chemistry Reviews, 387*, 47–59.

Arya, D. P. (2011). New approaches toward recognition of nucleic acid triple helices. *Accounts of Chemical Research, 44*(2), 134–146.

Bansal, S., Bajaj, P., Pandey, S., & Tandon, V. (2017). Topoisomerases: Resistance versus sensitivity, how far we can go? *Medicinal Research Reviews, 37*, 404–438.

Bartova, S., Alberti, E., Sigel, R. K. O., & Donghi, D. (2016a). Metal ion binding to an RNA internal loop. *Inorganica Chimica Acta, 452*, 104–110.

Bartova, S., Pechlaner, M., Donghi, D., & Sigel, R. K. O. (2016b). Studying metal ion binding properties of a three–way junction RNA by heteronuclear NMR. *Journal of Biological Inorganic Chemistry, 21*, 319–328.

Bergamo, A., Gaiddon, C., Schellens, J. H. M., Beijnen, J. H., & Sava, G. (2012). Approaching tumour therapy beyond platinum drugs: Status of the art and perspectives of ruthenium drug candidates. *Journal of Inorganic Biochemistry, 106*, 90–99.

Bhat, S. S., Kumbhar, A. S., Purandare, N., Khan, A., Grampp, G., Lönnecke, P., Dixite, E. H. R., & Vanka, K. (2020). Tris–heteroleptic ruthenium(II) polypyridyl complexes: Synthesis, structural characterization, photophysical, electrochemistry and biological properties. *Journal of Inorganic Biochemistry, 203*, 110903.

Bi, J., Pay, T., Wong, Z. X., Khong, Y. Y., Kueh, M. X., Ng, K. J., Lee, P. F. P., & Tan, Y. L. K. (2019). Ruthenium arene complexes with mono–carbonyl analogues of curcumin as pendant or bridging ligands: Synthesis, anti–cancer activity and interaction with quadruplex DNA. *Polyhedron, 171*, 396–402.

Blakeley, B. D., DePorter, S. M., Mohan, U., Burai, R., Tolbert, B. S., & McNaughton, B. R. (2012). Methods for identifying and characterizing interactions involving RNA. *Tetrahedron, 68*, 8837–8855.

Brabec, V., & Kasparkova, J. (2018). Ruthenium coordination compounds of biological and biomedical significance. DNA binding agents. *Coordination Chemistry Reviews, 376*, 75–94.

Buldurun, K., & Özdemir, M. (2020). Ruthenium(II) complexes with pyridine–based Schiff base ligands: Synthesis, structural characterization and catalytic hydrogenation of ketones. *Journal of Molecular Structure, 1202*, 127266.

Carvalho, D. E. L., Oliveira, K. M., Bomfim, L. M., Soares, M. B. P., Bezerra, D. P., Batista, A. A., & Correa, R. S. (2020). Nucleobase derivatives as building blocks to form Ru(II)−Based complexes with high cytotoxicity. *ACS Omega, 5*(1), 122−130.

Chaves, O. A., Menezes, L. B., & Iglesias, B. A. (2019). Multiple spectroscopic and theoretical investigation of meso−tetra−(4−pyridyl)porphyrin ruthenium(II) complexes in HSA−binding studies. Effect of Zn(II) in protein binding. *Journal of Molecular Liquids, 294*, 111581−111591.

Chen, G., Fan, M., Liu, Y., Sun, B., Liu, M., Wu, J., Li, N., & Guo, M. (2019). Advances in MS based strategies for probing ligand−target interactions: Focus on soft ionization mass spectrometric techniques. *Frontiers in Chemistry*, 7. https://doi.org/10.3389/fchem.2019.00703

Chen, A., & Shapiro, M. J. (2000). NOE Pumping. 2. A high−throughput method to determine compounds with binding affinity to macromolecules by NMR. *Journal of American Chemical Society, 122*, 414−415.

Chowdhury, R. S., & Majumder, H. K. (2019). DNA topoisomerases in unicellular pathogens: Structure, function, and druggability. *Trends in Biochemical Sciences, 44*, 415−432.

Cuya, S. M., Bjornsti, M. A., & Waardenburg, R. C. A. M. (2017). DNA topoisomerase−targeting chemotherapeutics: what's new? *Cancer Chemotherapy and Pharmacology, 80*(1), 1−14.

Dagenais, P., Girard, N., Bonneau, E., & Legault, P. (2017). Insights into RNA structure and dynamics from recent NMR and X−ray studies of the Neurospora Varkud satellite ribozyme. *Wiley Interdisciplinary Reviews RNA, 8*, e1421.

Daxiong, H., Haiyan, W., & Nailin, R. (2004). Molecular modelling of B−DNA site recognition by Ru intercalators: Molecular shape selection. *Journal of Molecular Modeling, 10*, 216−222.

De, S., Chaudhuri, S. R., Panda, Jadhav G. R., Kumar, R. S., Manohar, P., Ramesh, N., Mondal, A., Moorthy, A., Banerjee, S., Paira, P., & Kumar, S. K. A. (2019). Synthesis, characterisation, molecular docking, biomolecular interaction and cytotoxicity studies of novel ruthenium(II)−arene−2−heteroarylbenzoxazole complexes. *New Journal of Chemistry, 43*, 3291−3302.

Delgado, J. L., Hsieh, C. M., Chan, N. L., & Hiasa, H. (2018). Topoisomerases as anticancer targets. *The Biochemical Journal, 475*(2), 373−398, 23.

Devagi, G., Dallemer, F., Kalaivani, P., & Prabhakaran, R. (2018). Organometallic ruthenium(II) complexes containing NS donor Schiff bases: Synthesis, structure, electrochemistry, DNA/BSA binding, DNA cleavage, radical scavenging and antibacterial activities. *Journal of Organometallic Chemistry, 854*, 1−14.

Dominguez, D., Freese, P., Alexis, M. S., Su, A., Hochman, M., Palden, T., Bazile, C., Lambert, N. J., Nostrand, E. L. V., Pratt, G. A., Yeo, G. W., Graveley, B. R., & Burge, C. B. (2018). Sequence, structure, and context preferences of human RNA binding proteins. *Molecular Cell, 70*, 854−867, 8.

Erkan, S., Kaya, S., Sayin, K., & Karakas, D. (2020). Structural, spectral characterization and molecular docking analyses of mer−ruthenium (II) complexes containing the bidentate chelating ligands. *Spectrochimica Acta A: Molecular and Biomolecular Spectroscopy, 224*, 117399.

Eswaran, J., Sankar, N. K., Bhuvanesh, N. S. P., & Velusamy, K. M. (2018). Ruthenium hydrazone complexes with 1:1 and 1:2 metal−ligand stoichiometry: A comparison of biomolecular interactions and in vitro cytotoxicities. *Transition Metal Chemistry, 44*(4), 369−382.

Foley, F. M., Keene, F. R., & Collins, J. G. (2001). The DNA binding of the ΔΔ−, ΔΛ− and ΛΛ−stereoisomers of $[\{Ru(Me_2bpy)_2\}_2(\mu-bpm)]^{4+}$. *Dalton Transactions*, 2968−2974.

Franklin, R. E., & Gosling, R. G. (1953). Molecular configuration in sodium thymonucleate. *Nature, 171*, 740–741.

Frasca, D., Ciampa, J., Emerson, J., Umans, R. S., & Clarke, M. J. (1996). Effects of hypoxia and transferrin on toxicity and DNA binding of ruthenium antitumor agents in HeLa cells. *Metal–Based Drugs, 3*, 197–209.

Ganeshpandian, M., Palaniandavar, M., Muruganantham, A., Ghosh, S. K., Riyasdeen, A., & Akbarsha, M. A. (2017). Ruthenium(II)–arene complexes of diimines: Effect of diimine intercalation and hydrophobicity on DNA and protein binding and cytotoxicity. *Applied Organometallic Chemistry*, e4154.

Garman, E. F. (2014). Developments in x–ray crystallographic structure determination of biological macromolecules. *Science, 343*, 1102–1108.

Ghosh, B. K., & Chakravorty, A. (1989). Electrochemical studies of ruthenium compounds part I. Ligand oxidation levels. *Coordination Chemistry Reviews, 95*, 239–294.

Guedes, I. A., de Magalhães, C. S., & Dardenne, L. E. (2014). Receptor–ligand molecular docking. *Biophysical Reviews, 6*(1), 75–87.

Gunanathan, C., & Milstein, D. (2014). Bond activation and catalysis by ruthenium pincer complexes. *Chemical Reviews, 114*, 12024–12087.

Helliwell, J. R., & Mitchell, E. P. (2015). Synchrotron radiation macromolecular crystallography: Science and spin–offs. *International Union of Crystallography Journals, 2*, 283–291.

Hong, W. X., Huang, F., Huan, T., Xu, X., Han, Q., Wang, G., Xu, H., Duan, S., Duan, Y., Long, X., Liu, Y., & Hu, Z. (2017). Comparative studies on DNA–binding and *in vitro* antitumor activity of enantiomeric ruthenium(II) complexes. *Journal of Inorganic Biochemistry, 180*, 54–60.

Hoyuelos, F. J., García, B., Leal, J. M., Busto, N., Biver, T., Secco, F., & Venturinib, M. (2014). RNA triplex–to–duplex and duplex–to–triplex conversion induced by coralyne. *Physical Chemistry Chemical Physics, 16*, 6012–6018.

Huang, H. L., Tang, B., Yi, Q. Y., Wan, D., Yang, L. L., & Liu, Y. J. (2019). Synthesis, DNA-binding, molecular docking and cytotoxic activity in vitro evaluation of ruthenium(II) complexes. *Transition Metal Chemistry, 44*, 11–24.

Jeyalakshmi, K., Haribabu, J., Balachandran, C., Swaminathan, S., Bhuvanesh, N. S. P., & Karvembu, R. (2019). Coordination behavior of N,N′,N″–Trisubstituted guanidine ligands in their Ru–arene complexes: Synthetic, DNA/protein binding, and cytotoxic studies. *Organometallics, 38*(4), 753–770.

Jiang, G.–B., Zhang, W.–Y., He, M., Gu, Y.–Y., Bai, L., Wang, Y.–J., Yi, Q.–Y., & Du, F. (2019). New ruthenium polypyridyl complexes functionalized with fluorine atom or furan: Synthesis, DNA binding, cytotoxicity and antitumor mechanism studies. *Spectrochimica Acta Part A: Molecular and Biomolecular Spectroscopy, 227*, 117534.

Kellett, A., Molphy, Z., Slator, C., McKee, V., & Farrell, N. P. (2019). Molecular methods for assessment of non–covalent metallodrug–DNA interactions. *Chemical Society Reviews, 48*(4), 971–988.

Ketron, A. C., & Osheroff, N. (2014). In E. Bell (Ed.), *DNA topology and topoisomerases in molecular life sciences:* An encyclopedia reference (pp. 1–9). New York: Springer.

Khan, R. A., Al–Lohedan, H. A., Farah, M. A., Ali, M. S., Alsalme, A., Al–Anazi, K. M., & Tabassum, S. (2018). Evaluation of (η^6–pcymene)Ruthenium diclofenac complex as anticancer chemotherapeutic agent: Interaction with biomolecules, cytotoxicity assays. *Journal of Biomolecular Structure and Dynamics*. https://doi.org/10.1080/07391102.2018.1528180

Khan, T. A., Bhar, K., Thirumoorthi, R., Roy, T. K., & Sharma, A. K. (2020). Design, synthesis, characterization and evaluation of the anticancer activity of water–soluble half–sandwich ruthenium(II) arene halido complexes. *New Journal in Chemistry, 44*, 239–257.

Kohler, L., Nease, L., Vo, P., Garofolo, J., Heidary, D. K., Thummel, R. P., & Glazer, E. C. (2017). Photochemical and photobiological activity of Ru(II) homoleptic and heteroleptic complexes containing methylated bipyridyl–type ligands. *Inorganic Chemistry, 56*, 12214–12223.

Krebs. (2006). *The history and use of our earth's chemical elements: A reference guide*. Greenwood Press.

Kumar, S. V., Scottwell, S. O., Waugh, E., McAdam, C. J., Hanton, L. R., Brooks, H. J. L., & Crowley, J. D. (2016). Antimicrobial properties of tris(homoleptic) ruthenium(II) 2-Pyridyl–1,2,3–triazole "click" complexes against pathogenic bacteria, including methicillin–resistant *Staphylococcus aureus* (MRSA). *Inorganic Chemistry, 55*(19), 9767–9777.

Lee, R. F. S., Theiner, S., Meibom, A., Koellensperger, G., Keppler, B. K., & Dyson, P. J. (2017). Application of imaging mass spectrometry approaches to facilitate metal–based anticancer drug research. *Metallomics, 9*, 365–381.

Liao, G., Chen, X., Wu, J., Qian, C., Wang, Y., Ji, L., & Chao, H. (2015). Ruthenium(II) polypyridyl complexes as dual inhibitors of telomerase and topoisomerase. *Dalton Transanctions, 44*(34), 15145–15156, 14.

Lin, C. T., Bottcher, W., Chou, M., Creutz, C., & Sutin, N. (1976). Mechanism of the quenching of the emission of substituted polypyridineruthenium(II) complexes by iron(III), chromium(III), and europium(III) ions. *Journal of American Chemical Society, 98*(21), 6536–6544.

Li, J., Sun, Y., Zhu, Z., Zhao, H., & Tan, L. (2016). Binding properties of ruthenium(II) complexes $Ru(bpy)_2(ppn)]^{2+}$ and $Ru(phen)_2(ppn)]^{2+}$ with triplex RNA: As molecular "light switches" and stabilizers for poly(U)·poly(A)*poly(U) triplex. *Journal of Inorganic Biochemistry, 161*, 128–133.

Liu, X. W., Tang, Y. C., Liu, N. Y., Deng, Y. Q., Wang, S., Liu, T., Chen, Y. D., & Lu, J. L. (2019). Topo I inhibition, DNA photocleavage, Molecular docking and cytotoxicities of two new phenanthroline–based ruthenium complexes. *Applied Organometallic Chemistry*, e5312.

Lowery, K. A. S., Drader, J. J., Griffey, R. H., & Hofstadler, S. A. (2000). Fourier transform ion cyclotron resonance mass spectrometry as a high throughput affinity screen to identify RNA binding ligands. *Trends in Analytical Chemistry, 19*, 481–491.

Magnieto, J. R., Kajouj, S., Di Meo, F., Fossepre, M., Trouillas, P., Norman, P., Linares, M., Moucheron, C., & Surin, M. (2018). Binding modes and selectivity of ruthenium complexes to human telomeric DNA G–quadruplexes. *Chemistry, A European Journal, 24*, 1–13.

Ma, S., Wang, F., Feng, Y., Liu, X., & Tan, L. (2019). Binding properties of ruthenium(II) complexes $[Ru(phen)_2(dicnq)]^{2+}$ and $[Ru(bpy)_2(dicnq)]^{2+}$ with the RNA triplex poly(U)·poly(A)*poly(U). *Polyhedron, 162*, 277–284.

Miyada, T., Kwan, E. H., & Yamashita, M. (2014). Synthesis, structure, and bonding properties of ruthenium complexes possessing a boron–based PBP pincer ligand and their application for catalytic hydrogenation. *Organometallics, 33*, 6760–6770.

Molphy, Z., Prisecaru, A., Slator, C., Barron, N., McCann, M., Colleran, J., Chandran, D., Gathergood, N., & Kellett, A. (2014). Copper phenanthrene oxidative chemical nucleases. *Inorganic Chemistry, 53*, 5392–5404.

Muralisankar, M., Dheepika, R., Haribabu, J., Balachandran, C., Aoki, S., Bhuvanesh, N. S. P., & Nagarajan, S. (2019). Design, synthesis, DNA/HSA binding, and cytotoxic activity of half–sandwich Ru(II)–Arene complexes containing triarylamine–thiosemicarbazone hybrids. *ACS Omega, 4*(7), 11712–11723.

Neethu, K. S., Eswaran, J., Theetharappan, M., Nattamai, S. P. B., Neelakantan, M. A., & Velusamy, K. M. (2019). Organoruthenium (II) complexes featuring pyrazole-linked Schiff base ligands: Crystal structure, DNA/BSA interactions, cytotoxicity and molecular docking. *Applied Organometallic Chemistry*, e4751.

Oliver, C. G., Reinharz, V., & Waldispühl, J. (2019). On the emergence of structural complexity in RNA replicators. *RNA, 25*, 1579−1592.

Pages, B. J., Ang, D. L., Wright, E. P., & Aldrich−Wright, J. R. (2015). Metal complex interactions with DNA. *Dalton Transanctions, 44*, 3505−3526.

Peng, M. N., Zhu, Z. Y., & Tan, L. F. (2017). Binding differences of two homochiral $[Ru(bpy)_2dppz]^{2+}$ complexes with poly(U)·poly(A)*poly(U) triplex RNA. *Inorganic Chemistry, 56*, 7312−7315.

Pernara, M., Kokanb, Z., Kralja, J., Glasovacc, Z., Tumirc, L.−M., Piantanidac, I., Eljugad, D., Turele, I., Brozovica, A., & Kirin, S. I. (2019). Organometallic ruthenium(II)−arene complexes with triphenylphosphine amino acid bioconjugates: Synthesis, characterization and biological properties. *Bioorganic Chemistry, 87*, 432−446.

Pieper, T., Borsky, K., & Keppler, B. K. (1999). Non−platinum antitumor compounds. *Topics in Biological Inorganic Chemistry, 1*, 171−199.

Pieter, C. A., Bruijnincx, & Sadler, P. J. (2008). New trends for metal complexes with anticancer activity. *Current Opinion in Chemical Biology, 12*, 197−206.

Pommier, Y. (2013). Drugging topoisomerases: Lessons and challenges. *ACS Chemical Biology, 8*, 82−95.

Qian, C., Wu, J., Ji, L., & Chao, H. (2016). Topoisomerase IIα poisoning and DNA double−stand breaking by chiral ruthenium(II) complexes containing 2−furanyl−imidazo[4,5−f][1,10]phenanthroline derivatives. *Dalton Transanctions, 45*(26), 10546−10555, 28.

Ramanathan, M., Porter, D. F., & Khavari, P. A. (2019). Methods to study RNA−protein interactions. *Nature Methods, 16*(3), 225−234.

Rist, M. J., & Marino, J. P. (2001). Association of an RNA kissing complex analyzed using 2−aminopurine fluorescence. *Nucleic Acids Research, 2*, 2401−2408.

Roy, K. (2019). *In silico drug design: Repurposing techniques and methodologies*. Academic Press, Elsevier.

Sava, G., Alessio, E., Bergamo, A., & Mestroni, G. (1999). Sulfoxide ruthenium complexes. *Topics in Biological Inorganic Chemistry, 1*, 143−169.

Schluga, P., Hartinger, C. G., Egger, A., Reisner, E., Galanski, M., Jakupec, M. A., & Keppler, B. K. (2006). Redox behavior of tumor−inhibiting ruthenium(III) complexes and effects of physiological reductants on their binding to GMP. *Dalton Transanctions, 14*, 1796−1802.

Silva, M. M., Camargo, M. S., Correa, R. S., Castelli, S., Grandis, R. A. D., Takarada, J. E., Varanda, E. A., Castelano, E. E., Deflon, V. M., Cominetti, M. R., Desideri, A., & Batist, A. A. (2019). Non−mutagenic Ru(II) complexes: Cytotoxicity, topoisomerase IB inhibition, DNA and HSA binding. *Dalton Transanctions, 48*, 14885−14897.

Singh, S. K., & Pandey, D. S. (2014). Multifaceted half−sandwich arene−ruthenium complexes: Interactions with biomolecules, photoactivation, and multinuclearity approach. *RSC Advances, 4*, 1819−1840.

Skok, Z., Zidar, N., Kikelj, D., & Ilaš, J. (2019). Dual inhibitors of human DNA topoisomerase II and other cancer−related targets. *Journal of Medicinal Chemistry, 63*(3), 884−904. https://doi.org/10.1021/acs.jmedchem.9b00726

Sliwinska, N. P., van Beijnum, J. R., Casini, A., Nazarov, A. A., Wagnieres, G., van den Bergh, H., Dyson, P. J., & Griffioen, A. W. (2011). Organometallic ruthenium(II) arene compounds with antiangiogenic activity. *Journal of Medicinal Chemistry, 54*, 3895−3902.

Smith, C. A., Sunderl, Smith, A. J., Keppler, B. K., Kratz, F., & Baker, E. N. (1996). Binding of ruthenium(III) antitumor drugs to human lactoferrin probed by high

resolution X−ray crystallographic structure analyses. *Journal of Biological Inorganic Chemistry, 1*, 424−431.
Song, X. Q., Wang, Z. G., Wang, Y., Huang, Y. Y., Sun, Y. X., Ouyang, Y., Xie, C. Z., & Xu, J. Y. (2019). Syntheses, characterization, DNA/HSA binding ability and antitumor activities of a family of isostructural binuclear lanthanide complexes containing hydrazine Schiff base. *Journal of Biomolecular Structure and Dynamics, 38*(3), 733−743. https://doi.org/10.1080/07391102.2019.1587511
Spillane, C. B., Smith, J. A., Buck, D. P., Collins, J. G., & Keene, F. R. (2007). Dinuclear ruthenium(II) complexes as potential probes for RNA bulge sites. *Dalton Transanctions, 7*, 5290−5296.
Srivastava, P., Mishra, R., Verma, M., Sivakumar, S., & Patra, A. K. (2020). Cytotoxic ruthenium(II) polypyridyl complexes with naproxen as NSAID: Synthesis, biological interactions and antioxidant activity. *Polyhedron, 172*, 132−140.
Subasi, E., Atalay, E. B., Erdogan, D., Sen, B., Pakyapan, B., & Kayali, H. A. (2020). Synthesis and characterization of thiosemicarbazone−functionalized organoruthenium (II)−arene complexes: Investigation of antitumor characteristics in colorectal cancer cell lines. *Materials Science & Engineering C, 106*, 110152.
Sullivan, B. P., Salmon, D. J., & Meyer, T. J. (1978). Mixed phosphine 2,2'−bipyridine complexes of ruthenium. *Inorganic Chemistry, 17*(12), 3335−3341.
Sun, B., Musgrave, I. F., Day, A. I., Heimann, K., Keene, F. R., & Collins, J. G. (2018). Eukaryotic cell toxicity and HSA binding of $[Ru(Me_4phen)(bb_7)]^{2+}$ and the effect of encapsulation in cucurbit[10]uril. *Frontiers in Chemistry, 6*(595), 1−12.
Toma, H. E., & Araki, K. (2000). Supramolecular assemblies of ruthenium complexes and porphyrins. *Coordination Chemistry Reviews, 196*, 307−329.
Torres, P. H. M., Sodero, A. C. R., Jofily, P., & Silva−Jr, F. P. (2019). Key topics in molecular docking for drug design. *International Journal of Molecular Sciences, 20*, 4574.
Valente, A., & Garcia, M. H. (2014). Synthesis of macromolecular ruthenium compounds: A new approach for the search of anticancer drugs. *Inorganics, 2*, 96−114.
Vyas, K. M., Mandal, P., Singh, R., Mobin, S. M., & Mukhopadhyay, S. (2020). Arene ruthenium(II)−Phosphine complexes: Green catalysts for hydration of nitriles under mild conditions. *Inorganic Chemistry Communications, 112*, 107698.
Wang, J. C. (2002). Cellular roles of DNA topoisomerases: A molecular perspective. *Nature Reviews Molecular Cell Biology, 3*, 430−440.
Weiss, A., Berndsen, B. H., Dubois, M., Müller, M., Schibli, R., Griffioen, A. W., Dyson, P. J., & Sliwinska, N. P. (2014). *In vivo* anti−tumor activity of the organometallic ruthenium(II)−arene complex $[Ru(\eta^6{-}pcymene)Cl_2(pta)]$ (RAPTA−C) in human ovarian and colorectal carcinomas. *Chemical Science, 5*, 4742−4748.
Wenzel, M., & Casini, A. (2017). Mass spectrometry as a powerful tool to study therapeutic metallodrugs speciation mechanisms: Current frontiers and perspectives. *Coordination Chemistry Reviews, 352*, 432−460.
Wolfe, A., Shimer, G. H., Jr., & Meehan, T. (1987). Polycyclic aromatic hydrocarbons physically intercalate into duplex regions of denatured DNA. *Biochemistry, 26*, 6392−6396.
Wumaier, M., Shi, J.−J., Yao, T.−M., Hu, X. C., Gao, R. R., & Shi, S. (2019). G−quadruplex and duplex DNA binding studies of novel Ruthenium(II) complexes containing ascididemin ligands. *Journal of Inorganic Biochemistry, 196*, 110681.
Wu, B., Ong, M. S., Groessl, M., Adhireksan, Z., Hartinger, C. G., Dyson, P. J., & Davey, C. A. (2011). A ruthenium antimetastasis agent forms specific histone protein adducts in the nucleosome core. *Chemistry, A European Journal, 17*, 3562−3566.
Xi, H. J., Davis, E., Ranjan, N., Xue, L., Hyde−Volpe, D., & Arya, D. P. (2011). Thermodynamics of nucleic acid 'shape readout' by an aminosugar. *Biochemistry, 50*, 9088−9113.

Xu, L., Zhong, N. J., Xie, Y. Y., Huang, H. L., Jiang, G. B., & Liu, Y. J. (2014). Synthesis, characterization, *In vitro* cytotoxicity, and apoptosis–inducing properties of ruthenium(II) complexes. *PLoS ONE, 9*(5), e96082.

Zelonka, R. A., & Baird, M. C. (1972). Benzene complexes of ruthenium(II). *Canadian Journal of Chemistry, 50*, 3063–3072.

Zhang, X., Ma, X., Jing, S., Zhang, S., & Zhang, Y. (2018). Non–coding RNAs and retroviruses. *Retrovirology, 15*, 20.

Zhao, X. L., Han, M. J., Zhang, A. G., & Wang, K. Z. (2012). DNA– and RNA–binding and enhanced DNA–photocleavage properties of a ferrocenyl–containing ruthenium(II) complex. *Journal of Inorganic Biochemistry, 107*, 104–110.

Zhu, Z., Peng, M., Zhang, J., & Tan, L. (2017). Interaction of octahedral ruthenium(II) polypyridyl complex $[Ru(bpy)_2(PIP)]^{2+}$ with poly(U)·poly(A)*poly(U) triplex: Increasing third–strand stabilization of the triplex without affecting the stability of the duplex. *Journal of Inorganic Biochemistry, 169*, 44–49.

CHAPTER 3

Nucleic acid interactions of copper complexes

Shazia Parveen
Chemistry Department, Faculty of Science, Taibah University, Yanbu, Saudi Arabia

1. Chemistry of copper

The symbol for copper, Cu, comes from the Latin word cuprum, meaning "from the island of Cyprus" The Romans obtained much of their copper from Cyprus, an early source of copper ore (Massey et al., 1973). The use of Cu dates back far into history. Cu beads have been found in what is now modern Iraq, dating back to 9000 BCE (Rayner, 2007, p. 56). Cu was widely used in the ancient world as bronze, its alloy with tin, which was used to make cutlery, coins, and tools. In China it was used for bells. Early metalsmiths as far back as 3000 BCE learned to combine copper with other metals to produce more durable alloys. Brass (Cu and Zn) and bronze (copper and tin) are two examples. Cu metal does occur naturally, but by far the greatest source is in minerals such as chalcopyrite and bornite. Cu is obtained from these ores and minerals by smelting, leaching, and electrolysis. The major Cu-producing countries are Chile, Peru, and China.

Cu is placed in group 11, period 4 and d block in the periodic table. Cu has an electronic configuration of $[Ar]3d^{10}4s^1$ and not $[Ar]3d^9 4s^2$ because a fully filled 3d subshell has a lower energy and is more stable. There are two naturally occurring isotopes of Cu; ^{63}Cu and ^{65}Cu; with ^{63}Cu being the key isotope. Cu is a reddish metal with a face-centered cubic crystalline structure. It is malleable, ductile, and an extremely good conductor of both heat and electricity (Hammond, 2004; Haynes, 2014). Cu has low chemical reactivity.

The chemistry of Cu is dominated by the +2 oxidation state, e.g., Cu(II) complex ions, but there is a substantial chemistry of the +1 oxidation state, and Cu(I) compounds can be stabilized by particular ligands. The simplest compounds of Cu are binary compounds, i.e., those containing only two elements. Amino acids form very stable chelate complexes with Cu(II).

Nucleic Acids
ISBN 978-0-12-820503-7
https://doi.org/10.1016/B978-0-12-820503-7.00001-6

Cu is an essential trace element (150 mg in an adult human body) and has a role in the formation of hemoglobin. Cu is an essential micronutrient for both plants and animals. It is a constituent and activator of several enzymes (in plants too) such as ascorbic acid oxidase and lactase. The deficiency in Cu leads to Menkes disease, a genetic disorder leading to anemia and bone disorders (Kaler et al., 2010). Cu ions play a vital role in electron transport/transfer reactions in cytochrome chemistry. Cu plays role as a cofactor for numerous enzymes, such as Cu/Zn superoxide dismutase, cytochrome c oxidase, tyrosinase, ceruloplasmin, and other proteins, crucial for respiration, iron transport and metabolism, cell growth, and hemostasis (Angelova et al., 2011; Azuara et al., 2010; Wehbe et al., 2017). Cu redox systems are involved in the catalytic process in the body (Qiao et al., 2011; Zhou et al., 2014). Cu generates reactive oxygen species (ROS), endogenous DNA damage, and nucleobase affinity, and thus favors proliferative activity (Khodade et al., 2012; Palanimuthu et al., 2013; Santini et al., 2014). Current interest in Cu complexes is stemming from their potential use as antimicrobial, antiviral, anti-inflammatory, antitumor agents, enzyme inhibitors, or chemical nucleases. Cu is an essential metal ion and is a cofactor for several enzymatic reactions that are vital for life. Cu-coordinated complexes have engrossed considerable attention owing to their inimitable biologic (Gandin et al., 2014; Gou et al., 2015), spectroscopic (Hofbeck et al., 2015), and catalytic properties (Chen et al., 2014; Ghosh et al., 2015). Cu is believed to play a pivotal role in angiogenesis (Azuara et al., 2010), especially in growth and development, in cell proliferation and tumor metastasis (Finney et al., 2009), and carcinogenesis (Denoyer et al., 2015). In cancer chemotherapy, Cu illustrates a dual role, with the first being the participation in redox reactions in oxidative stress reduction that otherwise interfere with DNA gene expression, mitochondria, and other membrane phospholipids (Valko et al., 2016). Secondly, it is involved in angiogenesis (Antoniades et al., 2013).

2. Methods of synthesis

This section describes the general procedures of synthesis toward the design of Cu(I)/(II) complexes incorporating a plethora of ligands can be broadly classified as Cu-Schiff base complexes and mononuclear and dinuclear complexes.

2.1 Cu(I)/(II)–Schiff base complexes

Schiff base, named after Hugo Schiff, is an azomethine compound with the general formula −CH -= -N− or C = N− depending on whether the condensation has occurred between a primary amine and aldehydic or ketonic group (Maurya et al., 2015). They can be considered a subclass of imines, being either secondary ketimines or secondary aldimines depending on their structure. Schiff bases are usually crystalline solids, and thus primary amines may be characterized by the use of suitable aldehydes and vice versa. However, the identity of the donor can be varied between sulfur, phosphorus, nitrogen, and oxygen to change the donor properties and hence the coordination abilities of the ligand. Schiff bases have been traditionally synthesized by the condensation reaction between a formyl- or carbonyl-containing derivative with primary amine groups in the presence of certain metal ions, such as alkaline earth cations, which act as templating agents (Akhter et al., 2017; Majid et al., 2019).

The synthesis, properties, and structure of the Schiff base complexes depend on the nature of a Schiff base and metal ion. Homoleptic mononuclear binary Schiff base Cu(II) complexes were synthesized by general procedure of adding the methanolic solution of Cu acetates/nitrates/chlorides such as $[Cu(Z)_2 \cdot nH_2O]$ (where $Z = CH_3COO/NO_3/Cl$) to a stirred methanolic solution of a Schiff base ligand, HL, in 1:2 M ratio (Scheme 3.1). The reaction mixture is then refluxed with continuous stirring in an oil bath at 60-70°C. The precipitate formed is filtered off, thoroughly washed with methanol and cold water, and develops good crystals for copper complex. A similar procedure is employed to synthesize heteroleptic Schiff base complexes by two different ligands, and Cu metal salt in 1:1:1 M ratio. A vast literature has been reported for the synthesis of Cu-Schiff base complexes (Adam et al., 2020; Bhunia et al., 2019; Borthakur et al., 2019; Chang et al., 2019; Fattuoni et al., 2020; Haba et al., 2019; Manna et al., 2019; Rambabu et al., 2020; Rigamonti et al., 2019; Sun et al., 2020; Tan et al., 2020; Tripathi et al., 2018; Wua et al., 2019; Zehra et al., 2019).

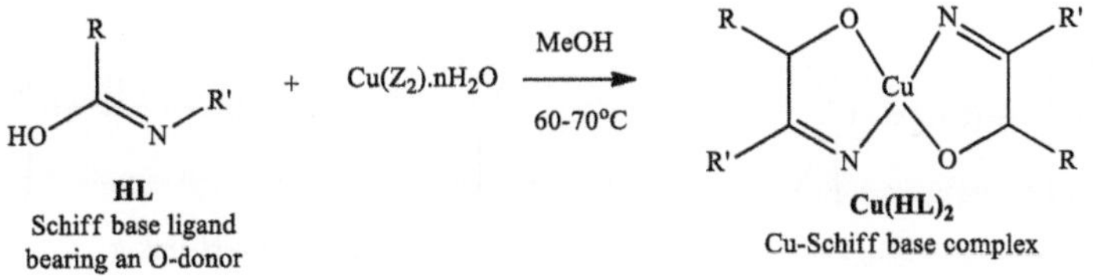

Scheme 3.1 General route to synthesis of Cu-Schiff base homoleptic complex.

2.2 Mononuclear Cu complexes

Mononuclear Cu(I)/(II) complexes are prepared by a general procedure in which the methanolic or ethanolic solution of the desired ligand is added to methanolic/ethanolic solution of [$Cu(Z)_2 \cdot nH_2O$] (where Z = CH_3COO/ NO_3/Cl). The desired Cu(I)/(II) crystals are obtained by proper refluxing, cooling, and drying techniques (Schemes 3.2 and 3.3).

A modification of this synthetic procedure involves carrying out the reactions under dry nitrogen (Chen et al., 2020).

As reported by Saga et al., if the product obtained is amorphous in nature, it can be purified through a column packed with SP-Sephadex C-25. The eluent from the column is concentrated under reduced pressure at room temperature to obtain crystals (Saga et al., 2020).

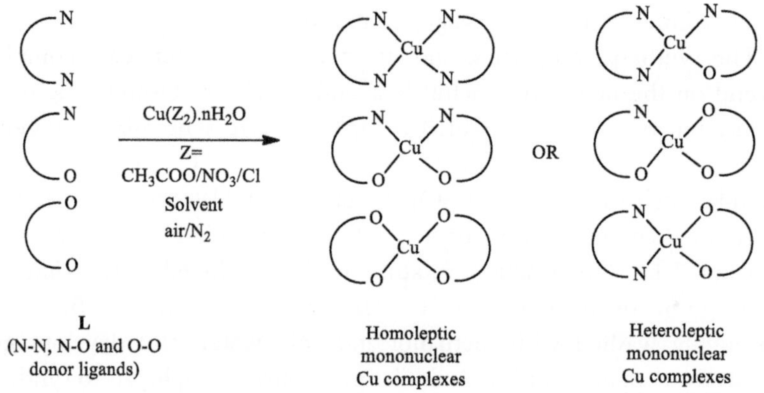

Scheme 3.2 General route to synthesis of mononuclear Cu(I)/(II) complexes.

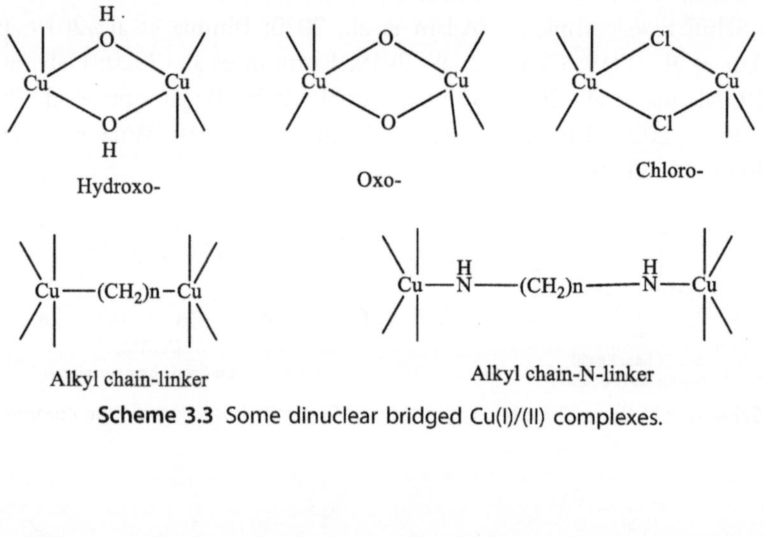

Scheme 3.3 Some dinuclear bridged Cu(I)/(II) complexes.

Liu et al. reported a synthetic method of Cu(I) iodide complex in which a suspension of copper(I) iodide and ligand in CH_2Cl_2 was stirred at room temperature to give a green solution. The Cu(I) complex was crystallized from the solution after slow evaporation at room temperature to give colorless microcrystalline solids. The solid was filtered off and purified by recrystallization from CH_2Cl_2/EtOH to give colorless crystals (Liu et al., 2019).

Another modification was carried out by Ayad et al. using Schlenk line for the synthesis of Cu(II) complex. The procedure involved adding $CuCl_2$ (in THF), the THF solution of ligand in the Schlenk tube and the mixture was stirred at room temperature and then filtered. The resulting solution was concentrated by evaporation of the solvent, and Et_2O was added to precipitate the product, followed by washing with the same solvent and drying in vacuum (Ayad et al., 2019).

A few other recent reports of the synthesis of mononuclear Cu(I)/(II) are available (Afsan et al., 2020; Anitha et al., 2019; Boulsourani et al., 2019; Kacar et al., 2020; Khan et al., 2020; Komarnicka et al., 2020; Roseborough et al., 2020; Sakthikumar et al., 2018; Vailati et al., 2020; Zhang et al., 2019).

2.3 Dinuclear Cu complexes

Dinuclear Cu complexes are those having two Cu centers, usually bridged by a linker, viz., oxo, hydroxo, sulfur, halogen, a carbon chain (including double or triple bonds), an amino terminal, etc., with a variety of ligands, viz., monodentate, bidentate, tridentate, or even tetradentate. Dinuclear copper complexes are synthesized by the reaction of $[Cu(Z)_2 \cdot nH_2O]$ (where $Z = CH_3COO/NO_3/Cl$) and ligand, L, in appropriate solvent, at room temperature with or without protection of inert gas. Then there is stirring/refluxing of the mixture, depending upon the choice of ligands, and the solution is concentrated by evaporation under vacuum and dried to yield crystals.

Numerous literature reports the synthetic aspects of dinuclear Cu(I)/(II) complexes comprising of a plethora of ligands (Bassoli et al., 2019; Bhunia et al., 2019; Cassemiro et al., 2020; Cheng et al., 2019; Kar et al., 2019; Lv et al., 2020; Shirvan et al., 2019; Tanase et al., 2019; Uber et al., 2020; Zhang et al., 2020; Zhao et al., 2019).

3. Methods of analysis

3.1 EPR spectroscopy

Electron paramagnetic (EPR) spectroscopy is an analytical technique that provides information about the coordination and geometry of active spectroscopic moieties containing unpaired electrons. Cu is considered to be an ideal metal for EPR spectroscopy (Andersson et al., 2003; Calle et al., 2006; Farrar et al., 1996). Pulse EPR approaches (electron-nuclear double resonance and hyperfine sublevel correlation spectroscopy) deliver exclusive evidence of the geometry and electronic structure of a Cu-nucleic acid system over an intricate mapping of the hyperfine and nuclear quadrupole interactions of an unpaired electron of the Cu(II) ion with the magnetic nuclei of the nucleotide.

Santangelo et al., in 2006, studied the interaction of Cu(II) with 5′-GMP nucleotide of nucleic acid in solution, employing pulse EPR spectroscopy (Santangelo et al., 2007). The results suggested that Cu coordinated to N7 of the guanine, including five solvent molecules and water. A hydrogen bridge was formed between one of the water molecules and the phosphate group.

In a recent study, Zehra et al. reported the interaction of a Cu(II) complex with DNA and RNA by EPR spectroscopy (Zehra et al., 2019). The EPR parameters are altered upon interaction with DNA/RNA, causing either attenuation or intensification of the EPR signal, which provides the quantitative amount of Cu complex interacting with the nucleic acid. In this case, the complex exhibited shifts in the EPR signal, which demonstrated a deformation of the coordination geometry of Cu(II) (Fig. 3.1). This was attributed to the replacement of one axial oxygen atom of the pentacoordinated Cu(II) by the nitrogen atom from DNA/RNA nucleobases (Facchin et al., 2009). On the other hand, with the RNA interaction, a significant shift was witnessed, suggesting stronger binding with RNA.

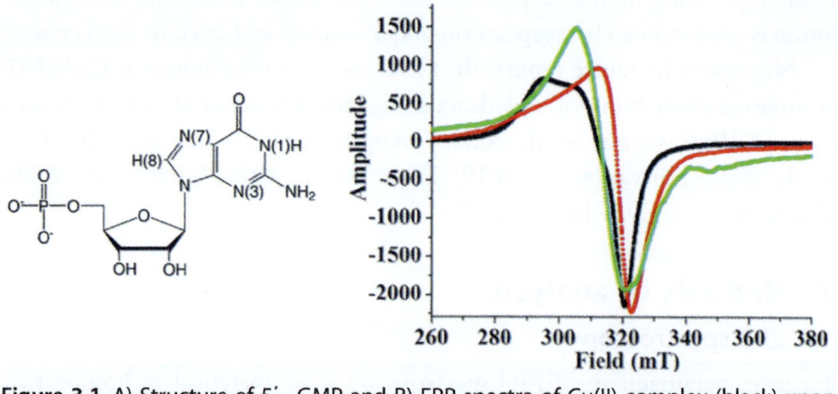

Figure 3.1 A) Structure of 5′–GMP and B) EPR spectra of Cu(II) complex (black) upon binding to DNA (red) and RNA (green). *(Reprinted from Zehra et al. (2019).)*

3.2 X-ray crystallography

Single-crystal X-ray crystallography is a dependable technique to study the structure of nucleic acids and their complexes with drug candidates. The binding modes of complexes with the nucleic acids can be visualized, providing detailed atomic-level structural information. Electron density three-dimensional maps, which are achieved from the experimental results, decide the positions of the atom. After ascertaining these atomic positions, other data including bond lengths and bond angles can be calculated easily. For the first time, single X-ray crystallography was used by Franklin to acquire photographs of B-DNA designating its helical nature (Franklin et al., 1953). These days, crystallographic studies of biomolecules are being carried out at aristocratic research laboratories fulfilling the prerequisite criteria that include the accessibility of tunable high-intensity X-ray sources and sensitive detectors permitting the evaluation of very small crystals with high resolutions (Helliwell et al., 2015). The inability in growing crystals of accurate size and quality, due to shortage of time and inability to analyze appropriate conditions, limits the usage of this technique.

3.3 Molecular docking studies

Molecular docking is such a structure-based drug design technique simulating molecular interaction and predicting the binding mode and affinity between receptors and ligands. A variety of docking programs are available, e.g., HEX, AutoDock, GOLD, GLIDE (Schrödinger), etc., which could be used for calculating the binding mode and affinity of small ligands (Roy, 2019). Docking can be done by two methods: (1) by "lock-and-key model," referring to the rigid docking of receptors and ligands, which highlights the significance of structural complementarity, and (2) "induced fit model," referring to flexible docking, since real models are flexible, in which the receptors and ligands alter their conformation to fit.

Several Cu(I)/(II) complexes have been docked with DNA, RNA, and serum albumin (SA) to ascertain the binding modes with these biomolecules and their affinity (Afsan et al., 2020; Arjmand et al., 2018; Hussain et al., 2019; Khan et al., 2020; Komarnicka et al., 2020; Thakur et al., 2019; Zehra et al., 2019).

3.4 Absorption spectroscopy

The binding mode of the metal complexes to DNA helix is often examined by the electronic absorption spectroscopy, followed by the changes in the absorbance and shift in wavelength. λ_{max} of nucleic acid is in the range of 250-280 nm, depending on the nucleobases concentrations. Whereas, ε_{max} of the nucleic acid depends on the composition of the nucleobase. This technique involves the absorption titrations carried out on a UV-vis spectrophotometer with increasing nucleic acid concentrations, while keeping the complex concentration constant. The variations in the absorbance spectra represent the binding mode. A decrease in absorbance (hypochromism) implicates, in general, intercalative mode of binding due to strong stacking interactions between the planar aromatic chromophore and the base pairs of the DNA, while an increase in the absorption spectra (hyperchromism) infers noncovalent interactions, predominantly electrostatic, groove binding, etc., occurring due to DNA double helix structural damage. The binding constant, K_b, is calculated using the Wolfe-Shimer equation (Eq. 3.1) and Gibb's free energy values for complexes are calculated from Eq. 3.2 (Wolfe et al., 1987).

$$[\text{Biomolecule}]/\ \varepsilon_a\text{-}\varepsilon_f = [\text{Biomolecule}]/\ \varepsilon_b\text{-}\varepsilon_f + 1/K_b\ (\varepsilon_b\text{-}\varepsilon_f) \quad (3.1)$$

Here, [Biomolecule] = concentration of the target biomolecule (nucleic acid/SA); ε_a, ε_f, and ε_b = apparent (A_{abs}/[complex]) and free and bound complex extinction coefficients, respectively. In a plot of [Biomolecule]/ε_a-ε_f vs. [Biomolecule] with a slope of $1/(\varepsilon_b\text{-}\varepsilon_f)$ and intercept of $1/K_b\ (\varepsilon_b\text{-}\varepsilon_f)$, K_b values were obtained by the ratio of slope to intercept.

$$\Delta G = \text{-}RT \ln K_b \quad (3.2)$$

Where, ΔG = Gibb's free energy change, R = 8.314 $JK^{-1}mol^{-1}$ (gas constant), and T = 298 K (temperature).

3.5 Fluorescence spectroscopy

Fluorescence spectroscopy, unlike absorption spectroscopy, is based on emission and is utilized in the identification of nucleic acid-complex interactions. Fluorescence methods have an upper hand owing to their highly sensitive nature, ease of applicability for efficient screening, and comparatively low cost. The preferential biomolecule binding sites can be assessed by fluorescence quenching experiments. The fluorescence study of biomolecules needs extensive fluorescent labeling with a suitable fluorophore, e.g., DAPI, organic dyes, fluorescein, and EtBr (Michel et al., 2020). These experiments require treatment of excess nucleic acid with limited bound fluorophore. The quenching constant, K_{sv}, is obtained by using the Stern-Volmer equation (Eq. 3.3) (Ghosh et al., 1989).

$$Io/I = 1 + Ksv\ [Q] \tag{3.3}$$

Where, Io and I = fluorescence intensities in the absence and presence of complex, respectively, and [Q] = quencher concentration.

This chapter extensively compiles the study of DNA/RNA and SA interactions of Cu(I)/(II) complexes by these two spectroscopic methods (Afsan et al., 2020; Arjmand et al., 2018; Khan et al., 2020; Komarnicka et al., 2020; Kumar et al., 2019; Moradinia et al., 2019; Sakthikumar et al., 2018; Senel et al., 2019; Thakur et al., 2019; Zhang et al., 2019; Zhao et al., 2019; Zehra et al., 2020).

4. Uses of metal complexes

4.1 DNA-interacting copper complexes

Cu complexes and their DNA interactions (both covalent and noncovalent) are the foundation for numerous impending biomedical applications stretching from cancer chemotherapeutics and DNA foot printing agents to gene delivery (Li et al., 2014). The right-handed B-DNA is the most prevalent form of DNA in which the stacking distance between two base pairs is 3.4 Å with 10.5 base pairs residues per full rotation of the helix with a helical diameter of 20 Å (Ramos et al., 2013). This renders the minor groove to be 4.8 Å whereas there is a 10.5Å wide major groove. Cu^{2+} ions are believed to bind to the DNA specifically through the phosphate groups and nucleobases precisely to N7 of G in GC base pairs (Erxleben, 2018). However, A-N7, which is also situated in the major groove like G-N7, can behave as a coordination site for Cu complexes at high concentrations only after other GC sites have been engaged (Andrushchenko et al., 2003). Fig. 3.2 displays the various covalent and noncovalent binding modes of Cu complexes to DNA. Nevertheless, the complexes of Cu, having flexible and wide ranges of coordination geometries and a plethora of different ligands, bearing groups responsible for hydrogen bonding, electrostatic, hydrophobic, or π-π stacking interactions, could bind to DNA via non-covalent interactions (e.g., intercalation, hydrogen bonding, or electrostatic interactions) (Pages et al., 2015).

Sakthikumar et al. reported the DNA interaction of an octahedral Cu complex, **1**, synthesized from 2-(2-morpholinoethylimino)methyl)phenol

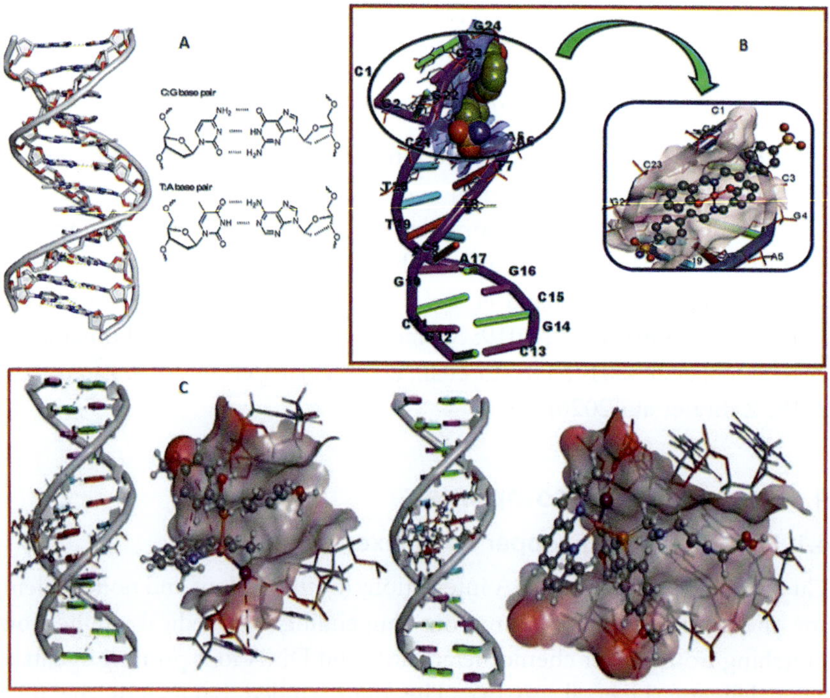

Figure 3.2 (A) X–ray structures of B–DNA (PDB ID: 1BNA), hydrogen bonding between C–G and T–A base Pairs. Adapted from Kellett et al., 2019. (B) Intercalative binding of Cu(II) complex into the DNA. Reprinted with permission from Afsan et al., 2020 and (C) Minor (left) and major (right) groove binding Cu(II) complex. *(Reprinted with permission from Komarnicka et al. (2020).)*

Schiff base ligand (Scheme 3.4) (Sakthikumar et al., 2018). The DNA interaction studies, carried out by electronic absorption titrations, revealed two bands, one corresponding to π-π^* transition of aromatic chromophore and the second to MLCT. Upon increasing concentrations of DNA, a decrease in the absorption intensity, i.e., hypochromism of the IL bands, accompanied with 6 nm bathochromic shift was observed. These results were suggestive of the capability of the Cu complex, **1**, to uncoil the helical structure of DNA and embed between the bases. The K_b value was calculated to be 6.05×10^5 M. In addition, the aromatic moiety could facilitate the deep penetration of complex **1** into a phosphate backbone, allowing the complex to freely intercalate into the DNA base pairs. It could be inferred from these results that complex **1** binds to DNA via intercalation mode.

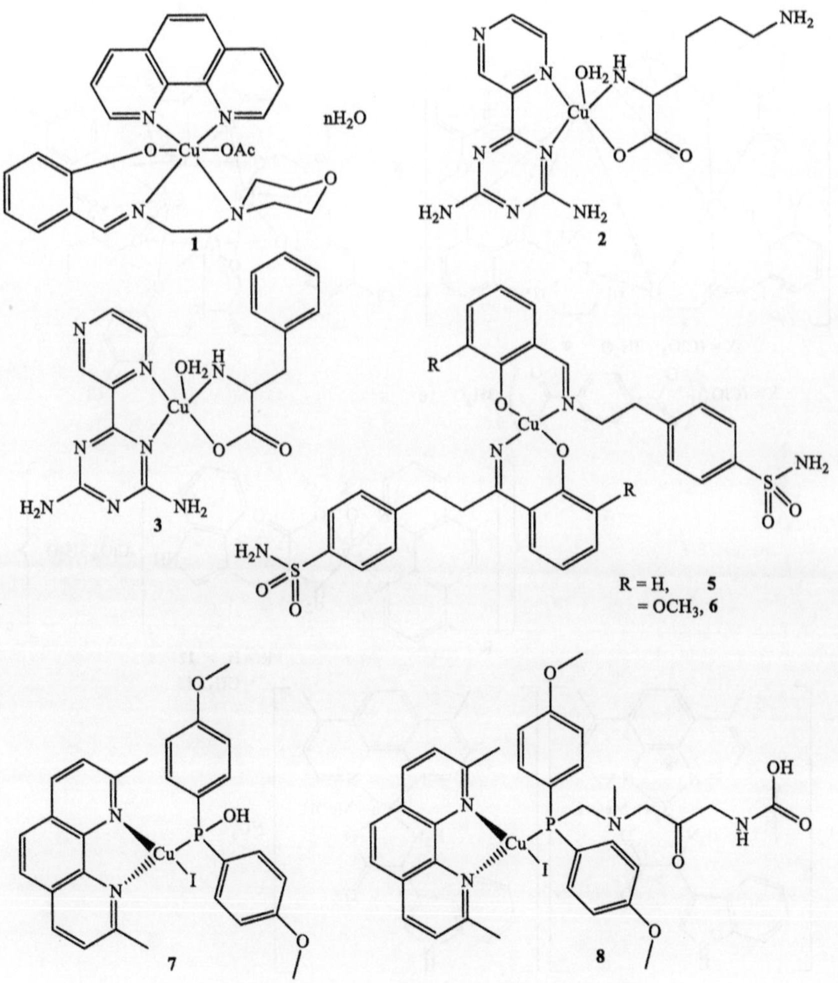

Scheme 3.4 DNA-interacting Cu complexes.

Zhang et al. reported the synthesis and DNA interaction studies of two water-soluble 6-pzta-based Cu(II) complexes, $[Cu(pzta)(LysH)(H_2O)](ClO_4)_2 \cdot H_2O$ (**2**) and $[Cu(pzta)(L\text{-}Phe)(H_2O)]ClO_4 \cdot 0.75H_2O$ (**3**), having distorted square pyramid geometry (Scheme 3.4) (Zhang et al., 2019). Electronic absorption titrations were employed to examine the binding mode between the complexes and DNA. Upon adding incremental amounts of CT DNA to complexes **2** and **3**, hypochromism of the absorption peaks was detected, while the peak positions were not changed. This was indicative of groove binding mode of interaction. This binding to CT DNA involved the surface binding of both complexes to the DNA duplex via hydrogen bonds

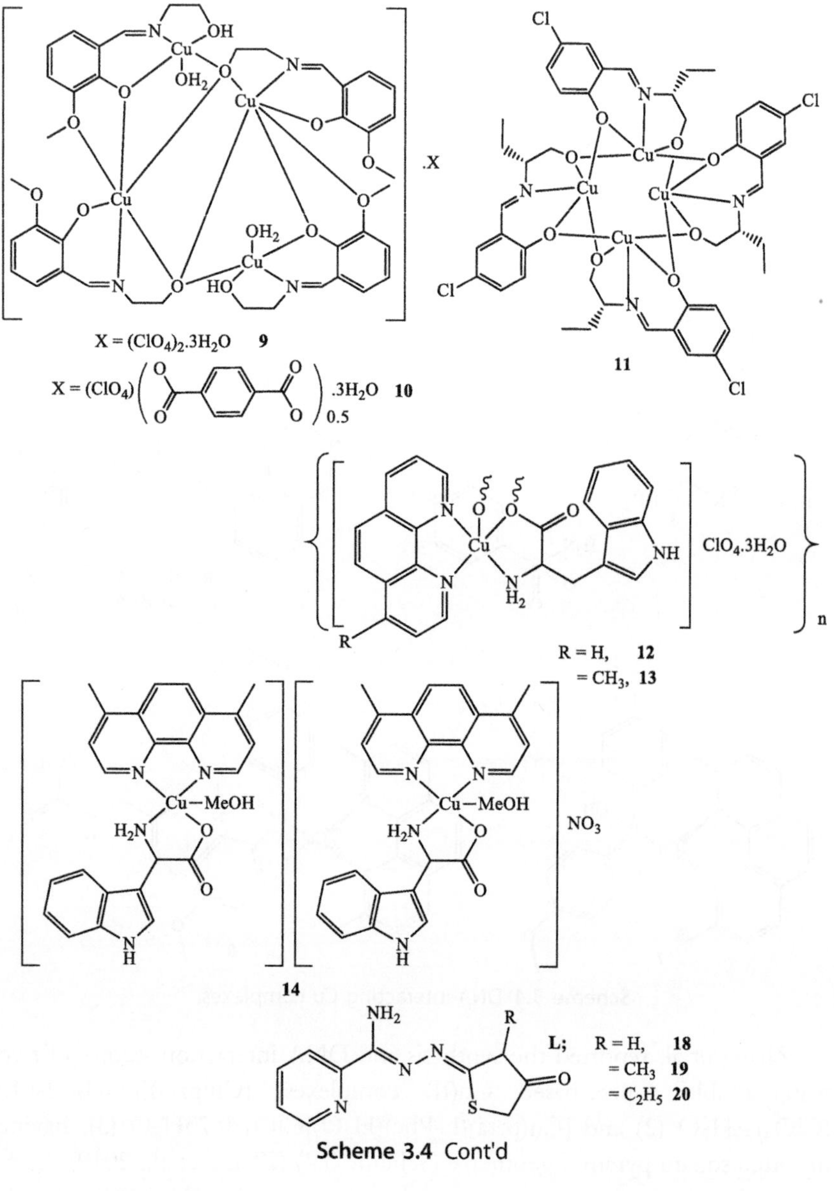

Scheme 3.4 Cont'd

between the amino acid (-NH_2 and -COO-) and pzta (-NH_2) ligands and CT DNA. Furthermore, from the K_b values, it was interpreted that complex **2** exhibited a stronger binding affinity compared with complex **3**, owing to the presence of the protonated amino group (-NH_3^+) in LysH, allowing the scope for additional hydrogen bonds with CT DNA.

Zhao et al. reported the synthesis and DNA binding studies of a water-soluble trinuclear Cu(II) complex, $Cu_3(ppbm)_2(SO_4)_3$, **4** (Zhao et al., 2019). Fig. 3.3 shows a crystal of **4**. The interaction of complex **4** with DNA was carried out by various spectroscopic methods, viz., UV-vis stability studies, EtBr quenching, CD spectroscopy, and molecular docking studies. The CD spectral studies revealed that after the addition of complex **4**, a considerable decrease in the intensity of the positive band of the CD spectra of CT DNA (275 nm) was observed (Fig. 3.4). Moreover, an apparent red shift ~7-8 nm only for the positive band, and no change in negative band (245 nm), was observed, which is an indication that complex **4** interacts with CT DNA encompassing a stacking interaction between the benzimidazole heteroaromatic plane of the complex and the adjacent base pairs of DNA. The results also revealed that complex **4** was unable to unwind the DNA helix, resulting in the loss of helicity. Hence, intercalation was likely owing to strong stacking interactions between the extended planar aromatic phenyl rings and the DNA base pairs.

Afsan et al. reported Cu(II)-Schiff base complexes of the type $[Cu(L^1)_2]$ (**5**) and $[Cu(L^2)_2]$ (**6**) (where HL^1 = (E)-4-(2-((2-hydroxy-3-methoxybenzylidene)amino)ethyl)benzenesulfonamide HL^2 = (E)-4-(2-((2-hydroxybenzylidene)amino)ethyl)benzenesulfonamide (Scheme 3.4) (Afsan et al., 2020). The CT DNA interaction studies of complexes **5** and **6** were carried out by absorption spectroscopy. The results revealed

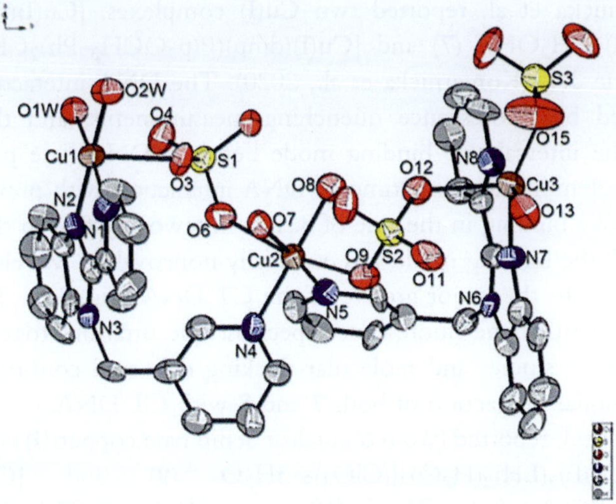

Figure 3.3 Crystal structure of $Cu_3(ppbm)_2(SO_4)_3$, **4.** *(Reprinted with permission from Zhao et al. (2019).)*

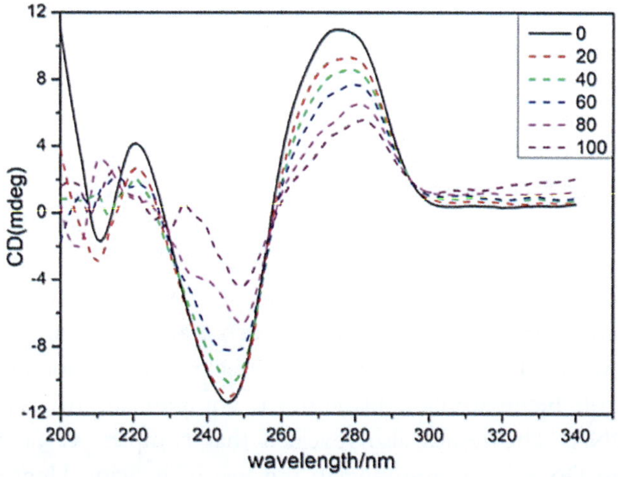

Figure 3.4 The CD spectra of complex **4** upon the titration of CT DNA in Tris–HCl buffer. *(Reprinted with permission from Zhao et al. (2019).)*

hypochromism with a blue shift at the IL band (368-378 nm) (Fig. 3.5). This observation was attributable to the stacking interaction between the aromatic moiety of complexes and the DNA base pairs. Both complexes exhibited intercalation mode of binding. Furthermore, a hyperchromism with blue shift was observed for the band at 265-268 nm, suggesting greater DNA binding and stabilization.

Komarnicka et al. reported two Cu(I) complexes: [Cu(I)(dmp)(P(p-OCH_3-Ph)$_2$$CH_2$OH)] (**7**) and [Cu(I)(dmp)(P(p-OCH_3-Ph)$_2$$CH_2$SarGly] (**8**) (Scheme 3.4) (Komarnicka et al., 2020). The DNA interaction mode was studied by fluorescence quenching measurements, and the results revealed the intercalative binding mode between DNA base pairs. Both complexes demonstrated multimodal DNA interaction with prevalence of minor groove binding in the case of **8**. It is noteworthy that in the case of complex **7**, the binding mode was essentially noncovalent, via electrostatic interactions into the major groove of the CT DNA (Fig. 3.6). This study was indicative that the fluorescence spectroscopic titrations together with DNA cleavage studies and molecular docking delivered confirmation for the multimodal interaction of both **7** and **8** with CT DNA.

Manna et al. reported two tetranuclear Schiff base copper(II) complexes, viz., $[Cu_4(L)_2(LH)_2(H_2O)_2](ClO_4)_2\cdot 3H_2O$ (**9**) and $[Cu_4(L)_2(L\text{-}H)_2(H_2O)_2](ClO_4)$ $(tp)_{0.5}\cdot 3H_2O$ (**10**) (where H_2L = 2-[(2-hydroxy-ethylimino)-methyl]-6-methoxy-phenol) (Scheme 3.4) (Manna et al., 2019).

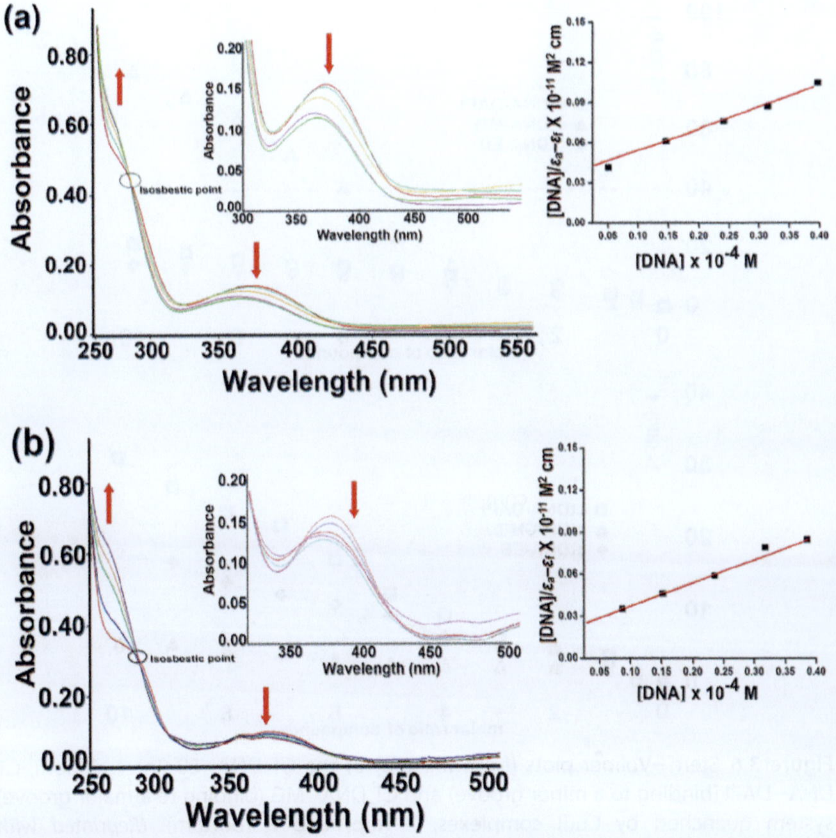

Figure 3.5 Electronic absorption spectra of complexes (A) **5** and (B) **6** with CT DNA. *(Reprinted with permission from Afsan et al. (2020).)*

Both complexes possessed a similar tetranuclear cationic $[Cu_4(L)_2(L\text{-}H)_2(H_2O)_2]^{2+}$ moiety in a double open cubane, where two Cu centers are in a square pyramidal geometry, while the other two revealed a slightly distorted octahedral geometry. The interaction of complexes **9** and **10** with CT DNA was explored via spectroscopic methods (electronic absorption and fluorescence titrations). The results revealed that upon increasing the concentrations of CT DNA, both complexes revealed hyperchromism with a blue shift with three isosbestic points at 229, 241, and 348 nm in revealing the presence of more than two species in solution (Fig. 3.7). This hyperchromism is suggestive of electrostatic noncovalent interactions.

Chang et al. reported a five-coordinate tetranuclear copper complex with the central Cu atoms adopting distorted square pyramidal geometry:

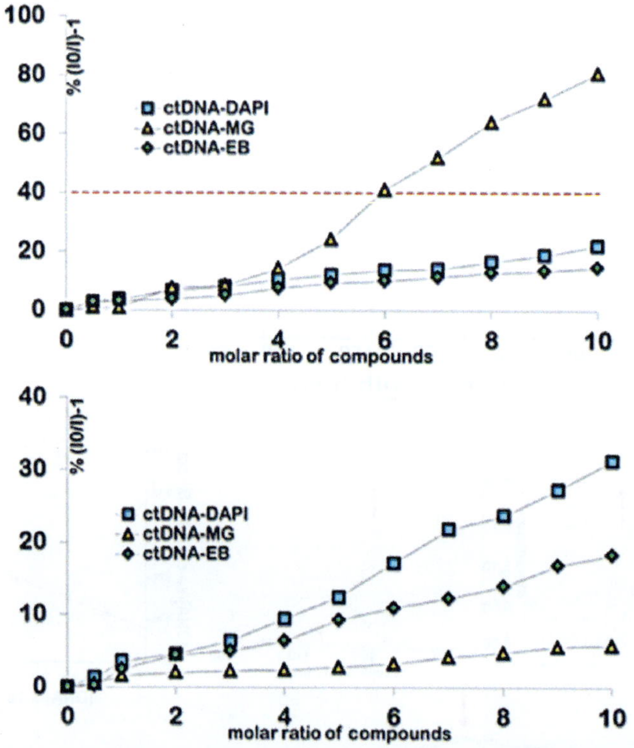

Figure 3.6 Stern–Volmer plots (from the top) of the CT DNA–EB (intercalation), CT DNA–DAPI (binding to a minor groove) and CT DNA–MG (binding to a major groove) system quenched by Cu(I) complexes, **7** (top) and **8** (bottom). *(Reprinted with permission from Komarnicka et al. (2020).)*

$[Cu(ONO)L_2)]_4 \cdot 2CH_3OH$ (**11**), where L= (R)-2-(2-hydroxy-5-chlorobenzylideneamino)butane-1-ol (Scheme 3.4) (Chang et al., 2019). Upon increasing concentrations of DNA, the absorption spectra of **11** displayed substantial hypochromism with a slight red shift, suggestive of the groove-binding and electrostatic mode of interaction. The K_b value was calculated to be 3.38 x 10^4 $M\text{-}^1$, which was small, owing to the fact that complex **11** has a large volume due to multinuclear geometry, thereby decreasing the planarity of the molecule, making its intercalation into DNA base pairs more difficult. Hence, it can be inferred from the above results that the volume/size and planarity of the complex are determinant factors for the mode of binding.

Senel et al. reported two one-dimensional water-soluble coordination polymeric Cu(II) complexes,$\{[Cu(phen)(trp)]ClO_4 \cdot 3H_2O\}n$ (**12**) and

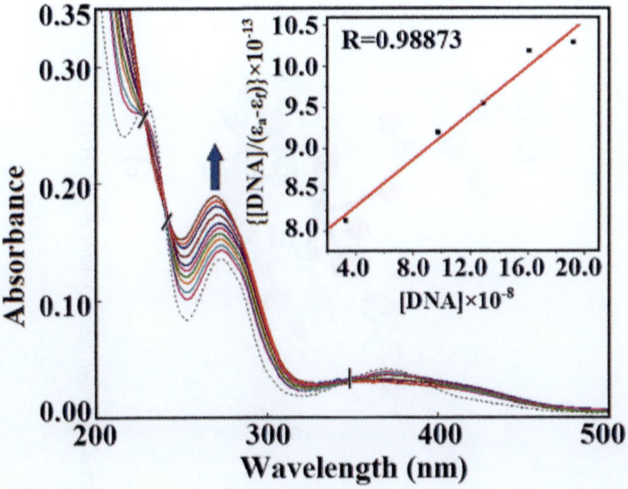

Figure 3.7 Change of the electronic absorption spectra of complex **9** upon the gradual addition of CT DNA. *(Reprinted with permission from Manna et al. (2019).)*

{[Cu(4-mphen)(trp)]$ClO_4 \cdot 3H_2O$}n (**13**), and one dimeric complex containing two discrete Cu(II) complexes, [[Cu(dmphen)(trp)(MeOH)] [Cu(dmphen)(trp)(NO_3)]]NO_3 (**14**) (Scheme 3.4) (Senel et al., 2019). The DNA interaction was investigated by absorption spectral experiments, and binding constants (K_b) were calculated. When the concentration of CT DNA was increased, all three complexes exhibited a hypochromism of 21.2, 28.8, and 23.0%, respectively, suggestive of moderate intercalation mode of binding. Furthermore, the binding activity of the complexes to CT DNA follows the order **14** > **13** > **12**. Dimeric complex **14** displayed the greatest DNA binding affinity owing to the presence of two methyl groups on the phen ring facilitating their involvement in hydrophobic interaction with the hydrophobic CT DNA surface, thereby enhancing the binding affinity.

Boulsourani et al. reported mononuclear Cu(II) complexes, [Cu(L)$_2$(-bipy)] (**15**), [Cu(L)$_2$(bipy)(H_2O)] (**16**), and [Cu(L)$_2$(phen)(H_2O)] (**17**), where L = 2-thiophene carboxylate (Boulsourani et al., 2019). Complex **15** displays pseudo-six-coordinated complex with a square-based distorted octahedral geometry, and complex **16** is on the borderline between five- and six-coordinated geometry, whereas complex **17** has a five-coordinated geometry (Fig. 3.8). The DNA interaction mode of complexes **15**–**17** was carried out by electronic absorption spectral titrations. With the addition of increasing amounts of CT DNA to complexes **15**–**17**, a hypochromism

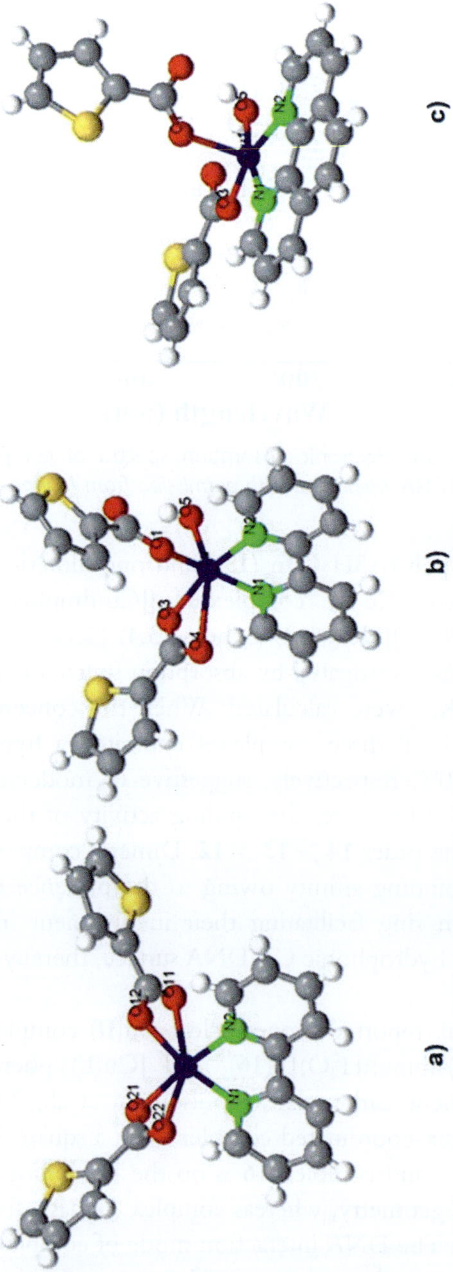

Figure 3.8 Partially labeled plot of **15** (a), **16** (b) and **17** (c). *(Reprinted with permission from Boulsourani et al. (2019).)*

with slight blue shift or no change in absorption bands was observed, attributable to bipy or phen ligand absorption bands. On the other hand, the thiophene ligand absorption bands displayed hyperchromism, with no red shift, creating isosbestic points (Fig. 3.9). These results suggested that the complexes **15–17** were found to bind preferably to CT DNA via a minor groove. Moreover, from the fluorescence studies, it was inferred that complexes **16** and **17** in aqua behave like "DNA light switches". Regarding the increase in intensity, with the increase in concentration of DNA, the luminescence reached about three times for **16** and 10 times for **17**.

Alzuet et al. reported the interaction with DNA of copper(II) complexes, viz., $[Cu(Am4DHotaz)(H_2O)_2](ClO_4)$ (**18**), $[Cu(Am4DHotaz)(NO_3)(MeOH)]\cdot H_2O$ (**19**), $[Cu(Am4Motaz)_2(H_2O)](ClO_4)2\cdot 0.83H_2O$ (**20**), $[Cu(Am4Motaz)_2(NO_3)]NO_3\cdot MeOH$ (**21**), $[Cu(Am4Eotaz)_2(NO_3)]_3(NO_3)3\cdot 2H_2O$ (**22**), and $Cu(Am4Eotaz)_2(ClO_4)](ClO_4)$ (**23**) (Scheme 3.4) (Alzuet et al., 2020). Complexes **18–20** were found to be in a square pyramidal to distorted square pyramidal geometry; however **21–23** exhibited an intermediate between square pyramidal and trigonal bipyramidal (Fig. 3.10). Interaction of complex **20** with CT DNA was studied by thermal denaturation and viscometry measurements. Upon increasing concentrations of complex **20**, to CT DNA, an increase in the melting temperature (Tm) was observed (Fig. 3.11). Tm is illustrative of the transition of double-stranded DNA to a single-stranded DNA. This increase in Tm was suggestive of strong stabilization of duplex DNA and an intercalative and/or an electrostatic binding of the complex to DNA.

Table 3.1 summarizes the geometries, characterization techniques, and the binding modes of Cu(I)/(II) complexes to DNA.

4.2 RNA interacting copper complexes

RNA is an indispensable biopolymer of the human genome (~ 90%) and drug target (Gasser et al., 2011), regulating several crucial cellular functions, especially transcription/translation, splicing processes, and retroviral replication (Arjmand et al., 2019). RNA has a unique structural diversity in terms of binding pockets (very shallow and wide minor groove and narrow major groove pulled deeply into the interior of the molecule) enabling it to be used as a target for noncovalent interactions with metal-based drugs (Guan et al., 2012). RNAs can fold into intricate three-dimensional 2- and 3-degree structures that provide recognition domains to a large variety of

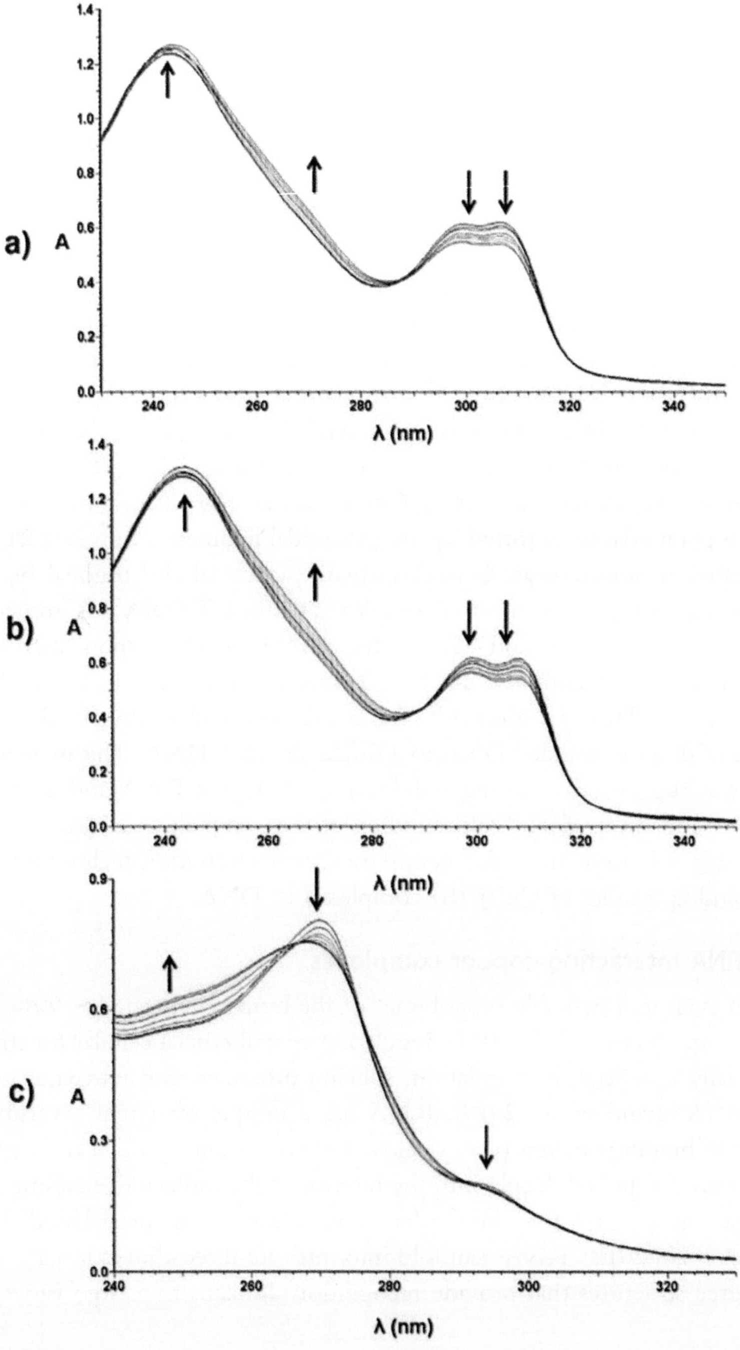

Figure 3.9 UV spectra in the absence and presence of increasing amounts of CT DNA in tris–HCl buffer to (a) **15**, (b) **16**, (c) **17**. *(Reprinted with permission from Boulsourani et al. (2019).)*

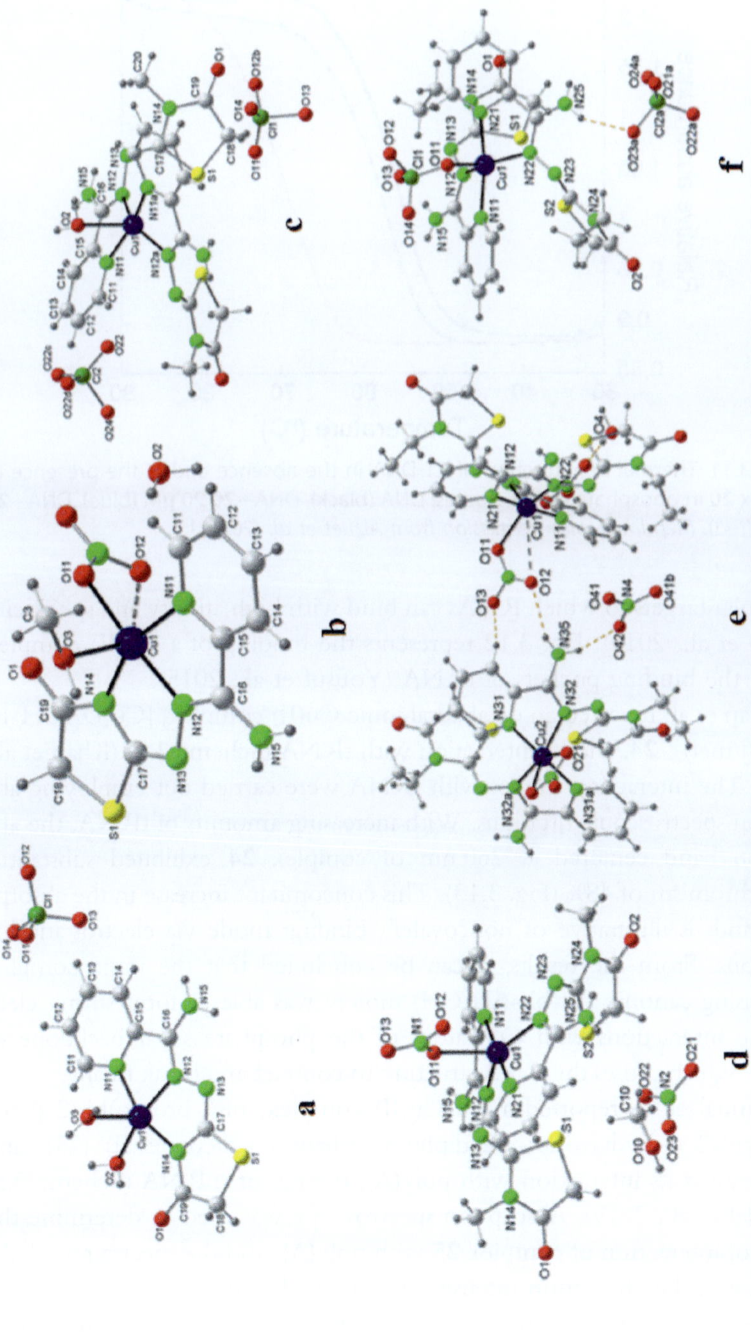

Figure 3.10 Perspective view of (a) **18**, (b) **19**, (c) **20**, (d) **21**, (e) **22**, and (f) **23** showing the asymmetrical unit and the atom-numbering scheme. *(Reprinted with permission from Alzuet et al. (2020).)*

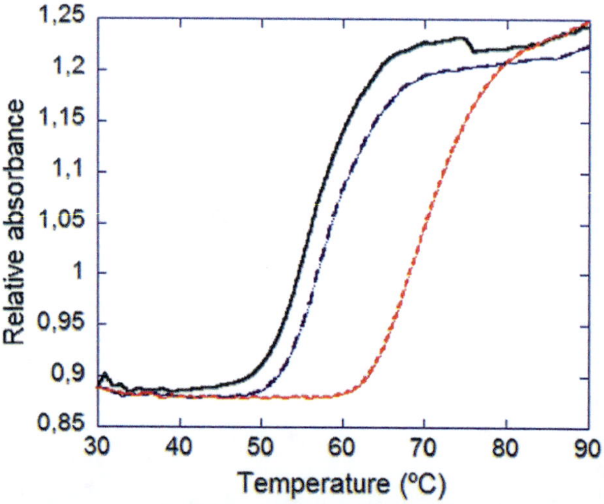

Figure 3.11 Thermal denaturation of CT DNA in the absence and in the presence of complex **20** in phosphate buffer. Curves: DNA (black), DNA+**20** 20 μM (blue), DNA+**20** 50 μM (red). *(Reprinted with permission from Alzuet et al. (2020).)*

molecular targets to which RNAs can bind with high affinity and specificity (Zehra et al., 2019). Fig. 3.12 represents the binding of a Cu(II) complex within the binding pockets of tRNA (Yousuf et al., 2015).

Khan et al. reported an octahedral ionic Cu(II) complex, [Cu(DACH)$_2$(-H$_2$O)$_2$](mef)$_2$, **24**, and its interaction with tRNA (Scheme 3.5) (Khan et al., 2020). The interaction studies with tRNA were carried out employing absorption spectroscopic titrations. With increasing amounts of tRNA, the absorption band centered at 260 nm of complex **24** exhibited substantial hyperchromism of 48% (Fig. 3.13). This concomitant increase in the absorption bands is illustrative of noncovalent binding mode via electrostatic interactions. From the results, it can be concluded that the ionic complex comprising cationic Cu-bis-(DACH) moiety was able to form strong electrostatic interactions with O^2- atom of the phosphate sugar backbone of tRNA, which causes the RNA structure to contract and break finally.

Mandal et al. reported a red Cu(II) complex, bis(l-bromo)bis(2-(benzothiazol-2-yl-hydrazono)-1,2-diphenyl-ethanone)-dicopper(II) (**25**), and they studied its interaction with poly(A), the tail of mRNA (Scheme 3.5) (Mandal et al., 2019). Absorption spectroscopy was used to determine the mode of interaction of complex **25** with poly(A), and the spectra revealed a decrease in the absorption intensity, i.e., hypochromism, upon progressive addition of poly(A). The hypochromic effect revealed strong intermolecular

Table 3.1 Summary of the modes of DNA interaction of Cu complexes.

Complex	Geometry	Target	Characterization techniques	Mode of interaction	References
1	Octahedral	CT DNA	FTIR, ESI-MS, elemental analysis	Intercalation mode	Sakthikumar et al. (2018)
2, 3	Distorted square pyramidal	CT DNA	Single X-ray crystal diffraction, IR, UV-vis, elemental analysis	Groove binding mode	Zhang et al. (2019)
4	Tetragonal pyramid/ octahedral	CT DNA	Single X-ray crystal diffraction, IR, UV-vis, ESI-MS	Intercalation	Zhao et al. (2019)
5, 6	Square planar geometry	CT DNA	Single X-ray crystal diffraction, ESI-MS, FTIR, UV-vis, EPR	Intercalation	Afsan et al., 2020
7, 8	Distorted tetrahedral geometry	CT DNA	Single X-ray crystal diffraction, UV-vis, elemental analysis, IR, ESI-MS	Minor groove binding (**7**) noncovalent via electrostatic interactions into major groove (**8**)	Komarnicka et al. (2020)
9, 10	Square pyramidal/ distorted octahedral	CT DNA	IR, ESI-MS, UV-vis, elemental analysis	Electrostatic noncovalent interactions	Manna et al. (2019)

Continued

Table 3.1 Summary of the modes of DNA interaction of Cu complexes.—cont'd

Complex	Geometry	Target	Characterization techniques	Mode of interaction	References
11	Distorted square pyramidal	CT DNA	Single X-ray crystal diffraction, UV-vis, elemental analysis, IR, ESI-MS	Intercalation	Chang et al. (2019)
12, 13 **14**	One-dimensional water-soluble coordination polymer Dimeric complex	CT DNA	Single X-ray crystal diffraction, UV-vis, elemental analysis, IR, ESI-MS	Intercalation	Senel et al. (2019)
15 **16** **17**	Pseudo-six-coordinated complex with a square based Distorted octahedral Borderline between five- and Six-coordinated five-coordinated	CT DNA	Single X-ray crystal diffraction, UV-vis, elemental analysis, IR, ESI-MS	Interfacial region of minor groove and intercalation site	Boulsourani et al. (2019)
18–20 **21–23**	Square pyramidal to distorted square pyramidal between square pyramidal and trigonal bipyramidal	CT DNA	Single X-ray crystal diffraction, UV-vis, elemental analysis, IR, ESI-MS	Intercalative and/or an electrostatic binding of the complex to DNA	Alzuet et al. (2020)

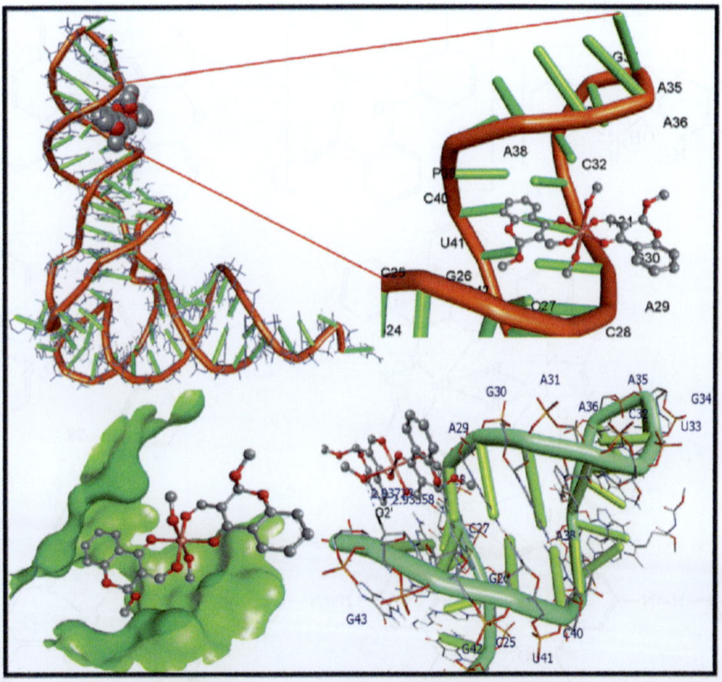

Figure 3.12 Molecular docked model of Cu(II) complex docked into the active pocket of the anticodon arm of tRNA (PDB ID: 6TNA) along with the possible hydrogen bonding interactions. *(Reprinted with permission from Yousuf et al. (2015).)*

interaction comprising effective overlap of the π-electron cloud of **25** with the RNA base pairs.

Tripathi et al. reported two Cu(II) complexes **26** and **27** of the type $[Cu(L^1/L^2)_2]$ where L^1 = 2-hydroxy-5(phenyldiazenyl)benzaldehyde and L^2 = 1-(2-hydroxy-5-(phenyldiazenyl)phenyl)ethanone (Scheme 3.5) (Tripathi et al., 2018). UV-vis absorption spectroscopy was employed to determine the bonding mode of complexes **26** and **27** to tRNA. Upon concomitant increase in the amounts of tRNA, hyperchromism was observed, which indicated that the both complexes bind with tRNA, possibly by electrostatic interaction between Cu(II) complexes and the negative phosphate backbone of the tRNA (Terenzi et al., 2014). While the yeast tRNA helix provides several hydrogen bonding sites in both the minor and major grooves, it is expected that the aromatic groups of Cu(II) complex are probably capable of hydrogen bond formation with tRNA, contributing to the observed hyperchromic effect (Campbell et al., 2011).

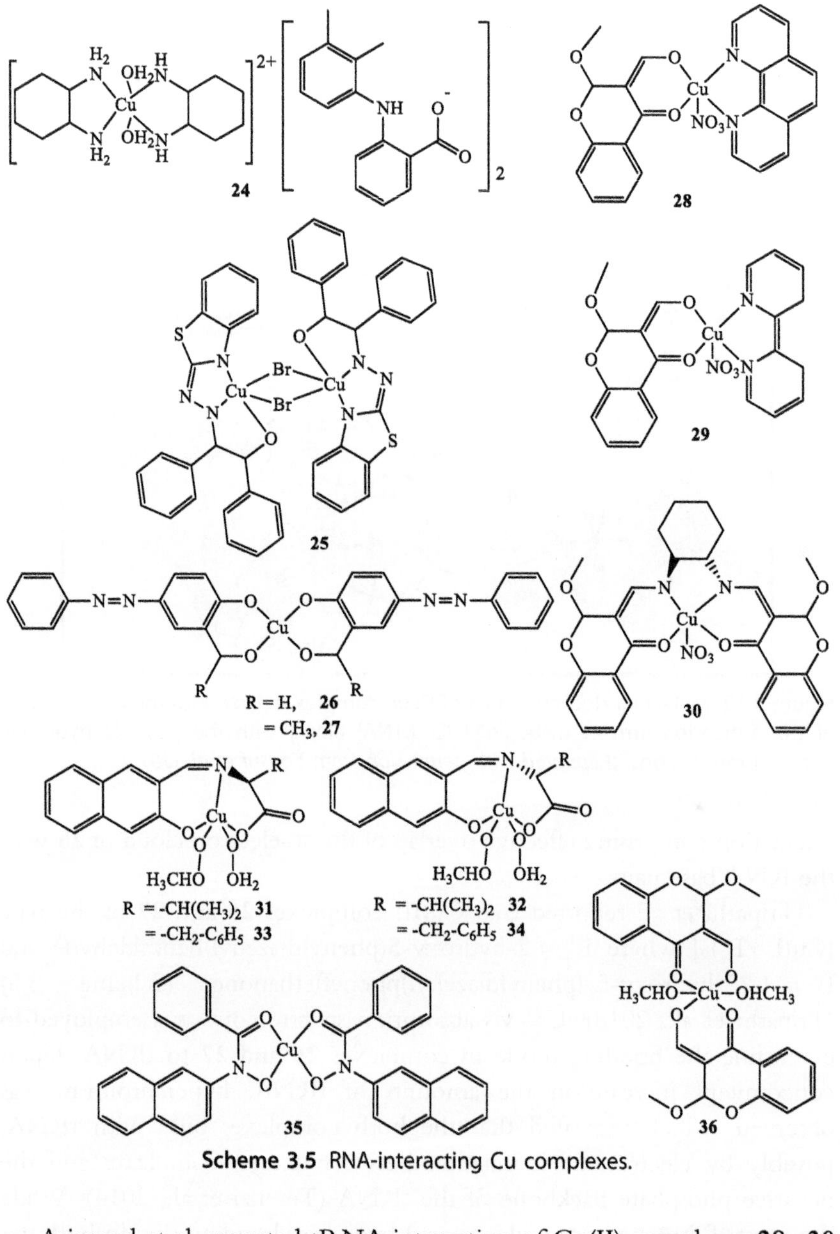

Scheme 3.5 RNA-interacting Cu complexes.

Arjmand et al. reported tRNA interaction of Cu(II) complexes **28–30** derived from bioactive pharmacophore, 3-formylchromone, and phen/bpy and 1R,2R-DACH (Scheme 3.5) (Arjmand et al., 2018). Interaction studies with tRNA were carried out by absorption and emission titrations.

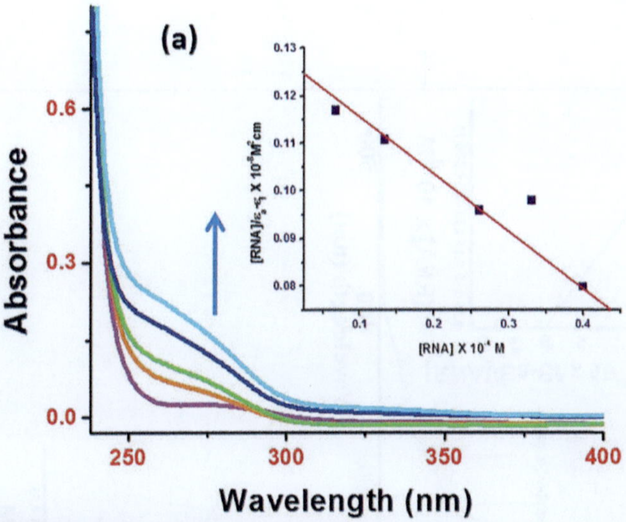

Figure 3.13 Absorption spectra of complex **24** in presence of increasing tRNA concentration. *(Reprinted from Khan et al. (2020).)*

Upon incremental amounts of tRNA to the fixed concentration of complexes **28−30**, hypochromic effect with a red shift of 2-4 nm was observed in LMCT absorption band at 325-400 nm, which was indicative of intercalative mode of binding. In addition, the band at 265-290 nm displayed an increase in absorption intensity, i.e., hyperchromism, together with a blue shift of 5-7 nm suggesting tRNA stabilization. All three complexes displayed an isosbestic point at 295-298 nm associated with existence of the equilibrium between the free and bound-tRNA (Fig. 3.14). These results could give a clear indication of the intercalative binding mode, involving π-π stacking interaction of aromatic planar chromophore of chromone and N,N-donor ligand scaffolds with tRNA base pairs.

Zehra et al. reported interaction with DNA of chiral enantiomeric Schiff base N-(2-hydroxy-1-naphthylidene)-amino acid Cu(II) complexes **31−34** (where amino acids are L/D-valine and phenylalanine) (Scheme 3.5) (Zehra et al., 2019). Complexes **31−34** were explored as RNA-targeting drug candidates with enhanced pharmacologic properties. The binding experiments carried out via absorption titrations revealed a hypochromic effect with red or no shift at the IL band centered at 316 nm and CT bands at 381 nm with tRNA, validating that complexes **31−34** interact via intercalation binding mode with tRNA (Fig. 3.15, Table 3.2). Furthermore, the L-enantiomers (**31** and **33**) were found to exhibit greater

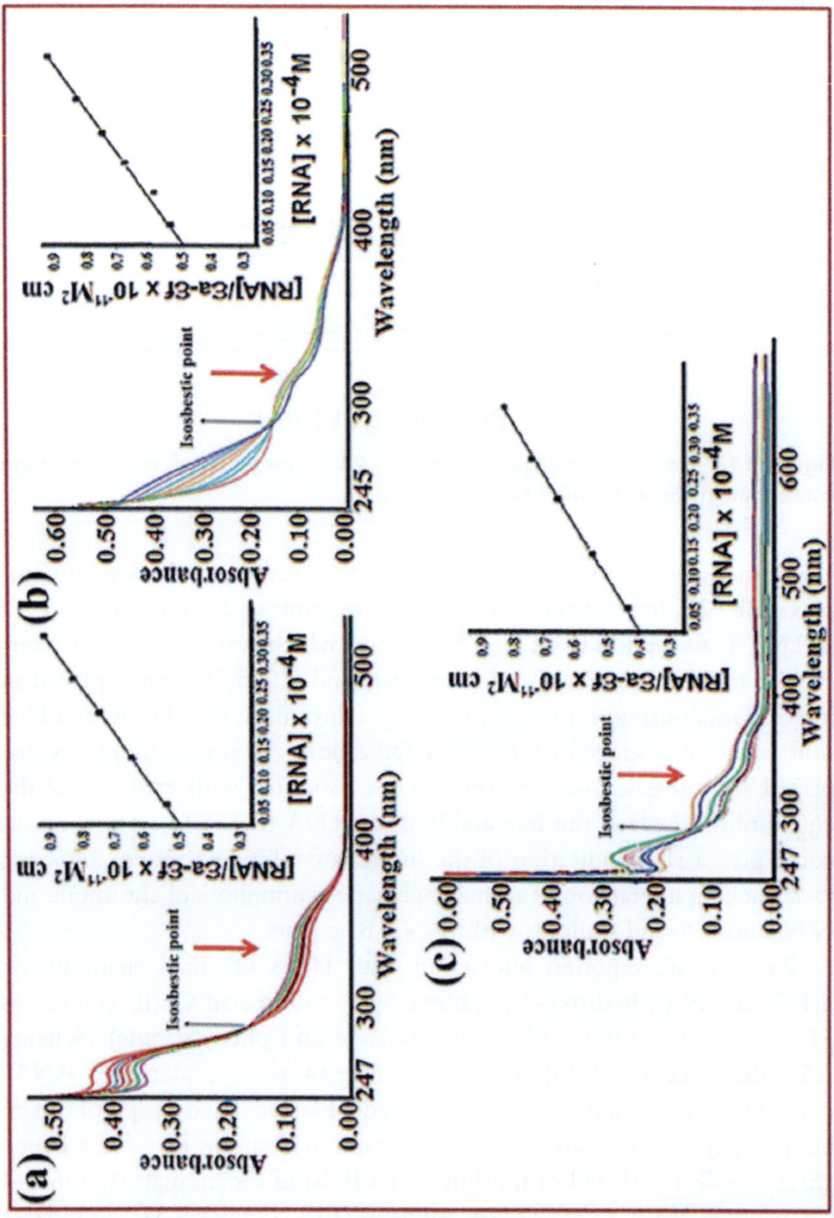

Figure 3.14 Absorption spectra of complexes **28** (a), **29** (b), and **30** (c) in absence and presence of increasing concentrations of tRNA in Tris–HCl buffer (pH 7.2). *(Reprinted from Arjmand et al. (2018).)*

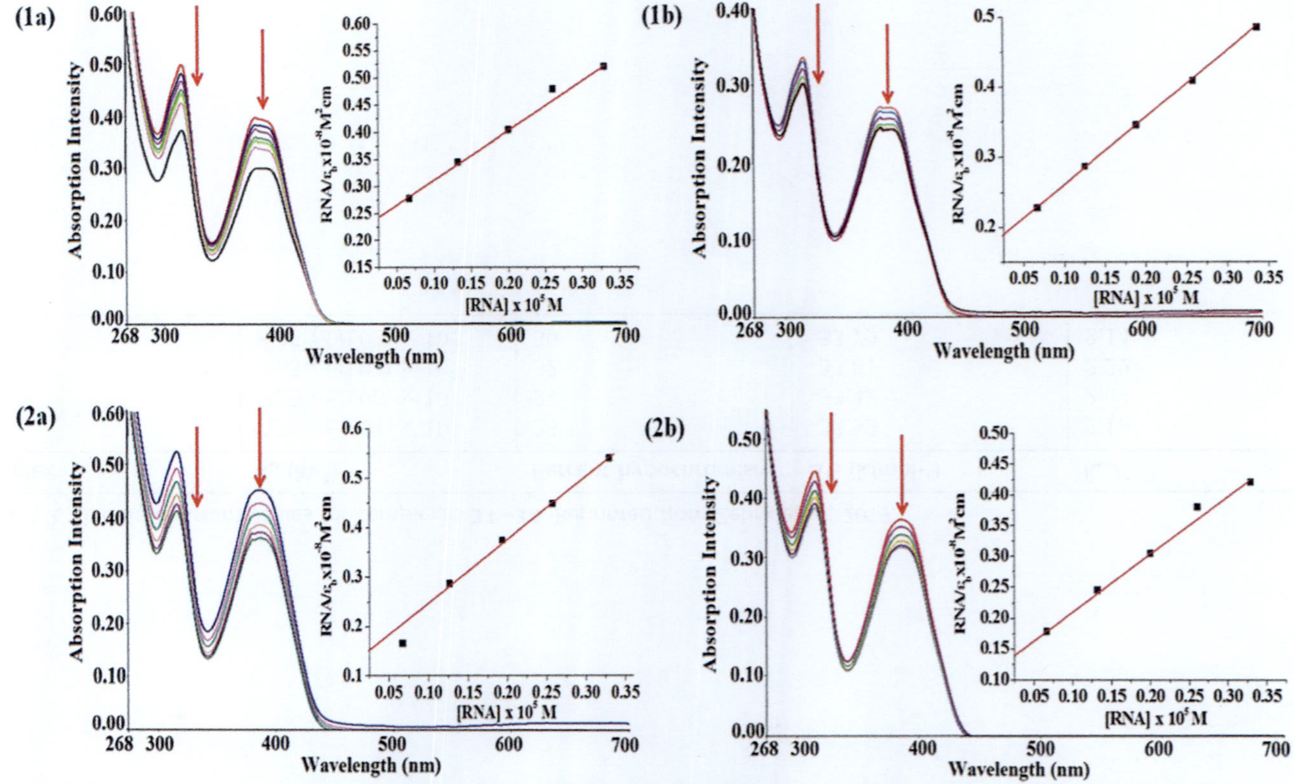

Figure 3.15 Absorption spectra of complexes **31**–**34** in the presence of increasing tRNA concentration. *(Reprinted from Zehra et al. (2019).)*

Table 3.2 Binding constant values for complexes **31–34.** Reprinted from Zehra et al., 2019.

Complex	K_b (M^{-1})	Percent hypochromism	ΔG ($kJmol^{-1}$)	K_{sv}
31	7.55 (±0.04) x 10^5	25	-33.52	2.10
32	7.25 (±0.06) x 10^5	24	-33.42	2.04
33	8.55 (±0.04) x 10^5	32	-33.81	2.29
34	8.45 (±0.02) x 10^5	30	-33.79	2.14

binding propensity due to the presence of a rigid aromatic group in the amino acid moiety.

Thakur et al. explored the interaction of [bis(N-p-NBHA)Cu(II)], **35**, with poly(A), the tail of mRNA that is responsible for its role in initiation of the translation, maturation, and stability of mRNA (Scheme 3.5) (Thakur et al., 2019). The absorption spectroscopic titration experiments were carried out to evaluate the binding parameters involved in the interaction of N-p-NBHA-Cu(II) complex with a poly(A) solution. With cumulative addition of poly(A) to **35**, a hyperchromic effect accompanied with a red shift was observed, which was indicative of partial intercalation due to the effective overlap of the π-electron cloud of the complex and the poly(A) bases.

Yousuf et al. reported a chromone-appended Cu(II) complex **36** and its interaction studies with tRNA carried out by absorption titrations (Scheme 3.5) (Yousuf et al., 2015). Upon increasing concentrations of tRNA to a constant complex concentration, a hypochromism of 46% along with a red shift of 2−4 nm in the absorption intensity at the IL bands centered at 252 and 307 nm was obtained. This decrease in absorption intensity was due to the stacking interaction between the aromatic moiety of ligand of the complex and the base pairs of tRNA. In addition to stacking interactions, the substituted methoxy groups of chromone formed hydrophobic interactions with the helical tRNA. The following inference was withdrawn by these results of interaction studies of **36** with tRNA, where the suggested binding mode is intercalation.

The geometries, characterization techniques, and the modes of binding of Cu(I)/(II) complexes to RNA are summarized in Table 3.3.

4.3 Interaction with other biomolecules

The efficiency of a drug is significantly influenced by the degree to which it binds to proteins in the blood plasma (Fanali et al., 2012; Merlot et al., 2014; Roy et al., 2018). SAs are most abundant protein in the circulatory system, playing a crucial role in the transfer of several kinds of drugs, metal complexes, and metal ions through the bloodstream in the disease sites (Yamasaki et al., 2013). Hence, the binding of the complex to SAs may lead to loss or enhancement of the various types of biologic activities of the original drugs. SAs contain two types of protein, namely, human serum albumin (HSA) and bovine serum albumin (BSA). HSA contains only one tryptophan residue at position 214, and it is structurally a homolog to BSA.

Table 3.3 Summary of the modes of RNA interaction of Cu complexes.

Complex	Geometry	Target	Characterization techniques	Mode of interaction	References
24	Octahedral	tRNA	Single X-ray crystal diffraction, ESI-MS, elemental analysis, thermogravimetric analysis	Noncovalent binding mode, via electrostatic interactions	Khan et al. (2020)
25	Square pyramidal	poly(A)- tail of mRNA	Single X-ray crystal diffraction, FTIR, UV-vis (both in solid state and in solution), elemental analysis, FTIR, room temperature magnetic susceptibility, conductivity measurements	Intermolecular interaction comprising effective overlap of the π-electron	Mandal et al. (2019)
26, 27	Four coordinate	tRNA	IR, UV-vis, ESI-MS	Electrostatic interaction	Tripathi et al. (2018)
28–30	Square pyramidal (**29**)	tRNA	Single X-ray crystal diffraction, IR, UV-vis, ESI-MS	Intercalative binding mode, involving π–π stacking interaction	Arjmand et al. (2018)

31–34	Distorted square pyramidal	tRNA	Single X-ray crystal diffraction, UV-vis, elemental analysis, FTIR, ESI-MS, EPR	Intercalation	Zehra et al. (2019)
35	Square pyramidal/ distorted octahedral	poly(A)	IR, ESI-MS, UV-vis, elemental analysis	Partial intercalation due to the effective overlap of the π-electron cloud	Thakur et al. (2019)
36	Distorted octahedral	tRNA	Single X-ray crystal diffraction, UV-vis, elemental analysis, FTIR, ESI-MS, EPR.	Intercalation involving π-π stacking interaction	Yousuf et al. (2015)

It is the most extensively studied and contains two types of tryptophan residues at position 134 and 212 (Zhang et al., 2012). Fig. 3.16 shows the binding of a Cu(II) complex to HSA (Hussain et al., 2019).

Moradinia et al. reported the synthesis and HSA interaction studies of Cu(II) complex, **37**, of tridentate Schiff base ligand derived from 9,10-phenanthrenequinone and p-toluic hydrazide (Scheme 3.6) (Moradinia et al., 2019). Various spectroscopic and molecular modeling techniques were used to determine the mode of interaction with HSA. The results of UV-vis absorption titrations revealed complex **37** exhibited hypochromism accompanied with no shift with increasing concentrations of HSA, which was clear confirmation of the complex formation between HSA and **37** (Aseman et al., 2019). The results were indicative of nonintercalative binding, probably groove binding mode between the HSA and complex. This minor groove binding mode was further confirmed by molecular docking studies, which showed that **37** exhibited suitable binding energy of −10.53 kcal/Mol and fit in subdomain IB (site III) of HSA by hydrophobic forces between **37** and HSA residues in the binding site.

Kumar et al. reported a Cu(II) complex, [Cu(II)(bipyam)$_2$Cl], **38**, and studied its interaction with HSA by fluorescence spectroscopy (Scheme 3.6) (Kumar et al., 2019). Fig. 3.17 shows the HSA fluorescence spectra, where the fluorescence intensity is decreased upon concomitant addition of complex **38** in a fixed HSA concentrations at different r values. The complex **38** is responsible for the quenching of intrinsic fluorescence of the tryptophan residue of HSA (Wang et al., 2007). From the results the following inference can be drawn: only one binding site is available in complex to interact with HSA. To further evaluate the HSA interaction,

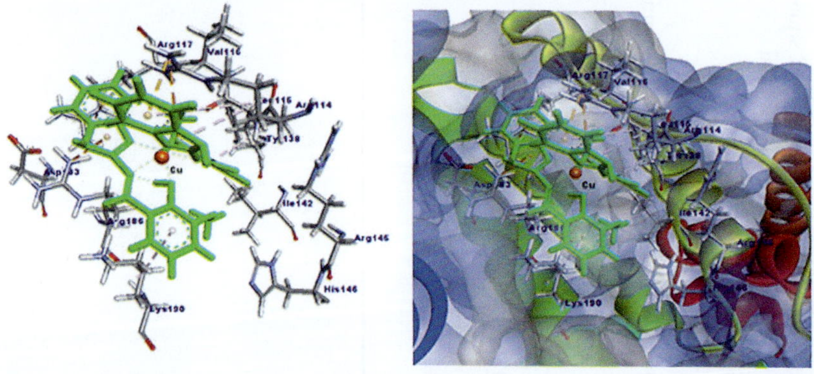

Figure 3.16 Binding of Cu(II) complex to HSA. *(Reprinted from Hussain et al. (2019).)*

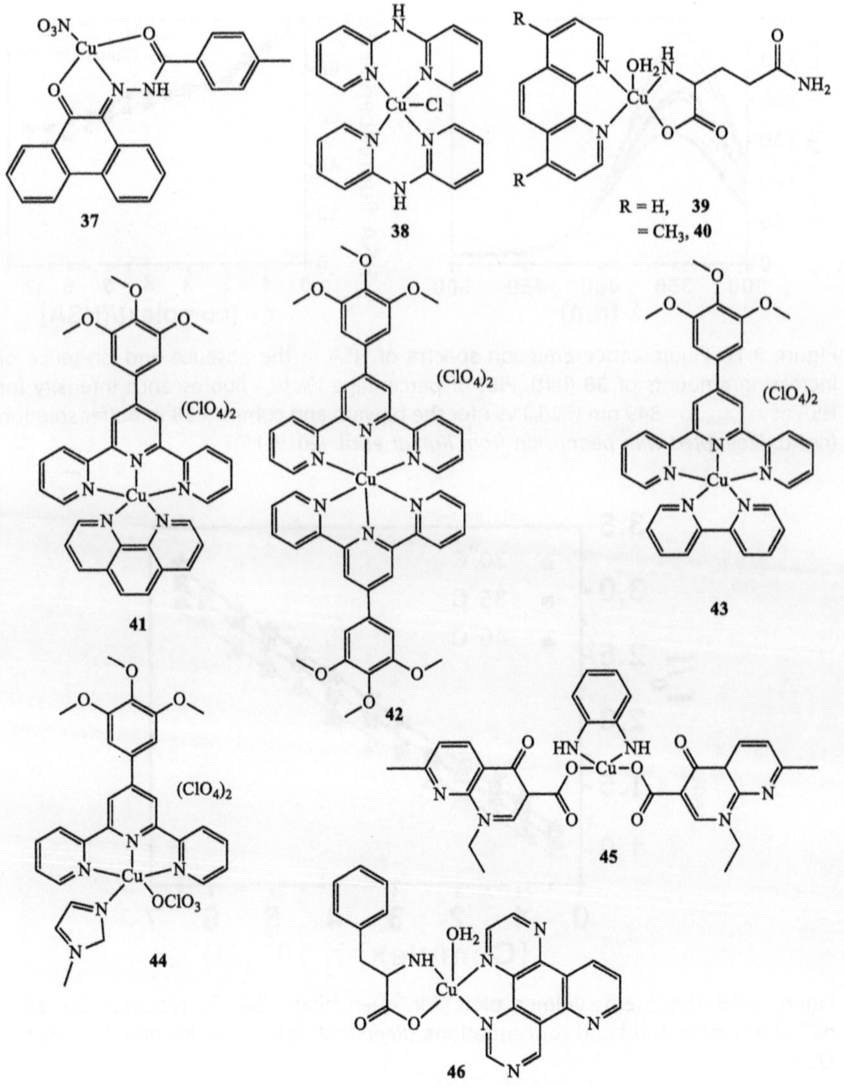

Scheme 3.6 SA-interacting Cu complexes.

temperature-dependent fluorescence quenching mechanisms were evaluated. Fig. 3.18 shows the Stern-Volmer plot of **38** with HSA. The values of n are nearly equal to one at all temperatures, further proving that only one binding site is available at complex **38** to bind to HSA.

Kiraz et al. synthesized water-soluble Cu(II) complexes, $[Cu(phen)(gln)(H_2O)]NO_3 \cdot H_2O$ (**39**) and $[Cu(dmphen)(gln)(H_2O)]ClO_4$

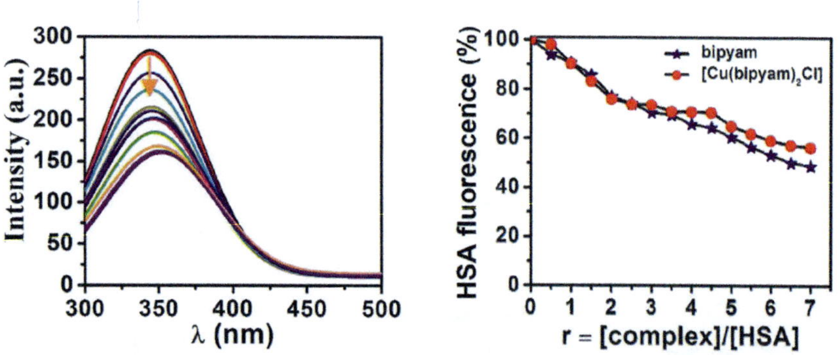

Figure 3.17 Fluorescence emission spectra of HSA in the absence and presence of increasing amounts of **38** (left). Plot of percentage (% I/I_0) fluorescence intensity for HSA at $\lambda_{emission} = 349$ nm (%I/I_0) vs r for the bipyam and complex **38** in buffer solution (right). *(Reprinted with permission from Kumar et al. (2019).)*

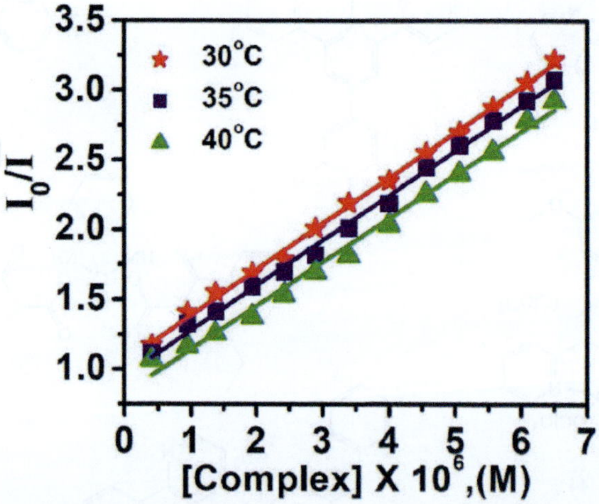

Figure 3.18 The Stern–Volmer plots for quenching HSA fluorescence by **38** at different temperatures and concentrations. *(Reprinted with permission from Kumar et al. (2019).)*

(**40**) (Scheme 3.6) (Kiraz et al., 2019). Fig. 3.19 shows the absorption spectra of BSA in the absence and presence of complexes **39** and **40**. Upon addition of the complexes, an increase in the electronic absorption of BSA was observed. Tryptophan emission quenching experiments were carried out to validate the static formation of complex between BSA and **39** and **40** (Fig. 3.18). The results were supportive of the fact that complexes **39** and **40** bind to BSA and are accountable for the tryptophan fluorescence

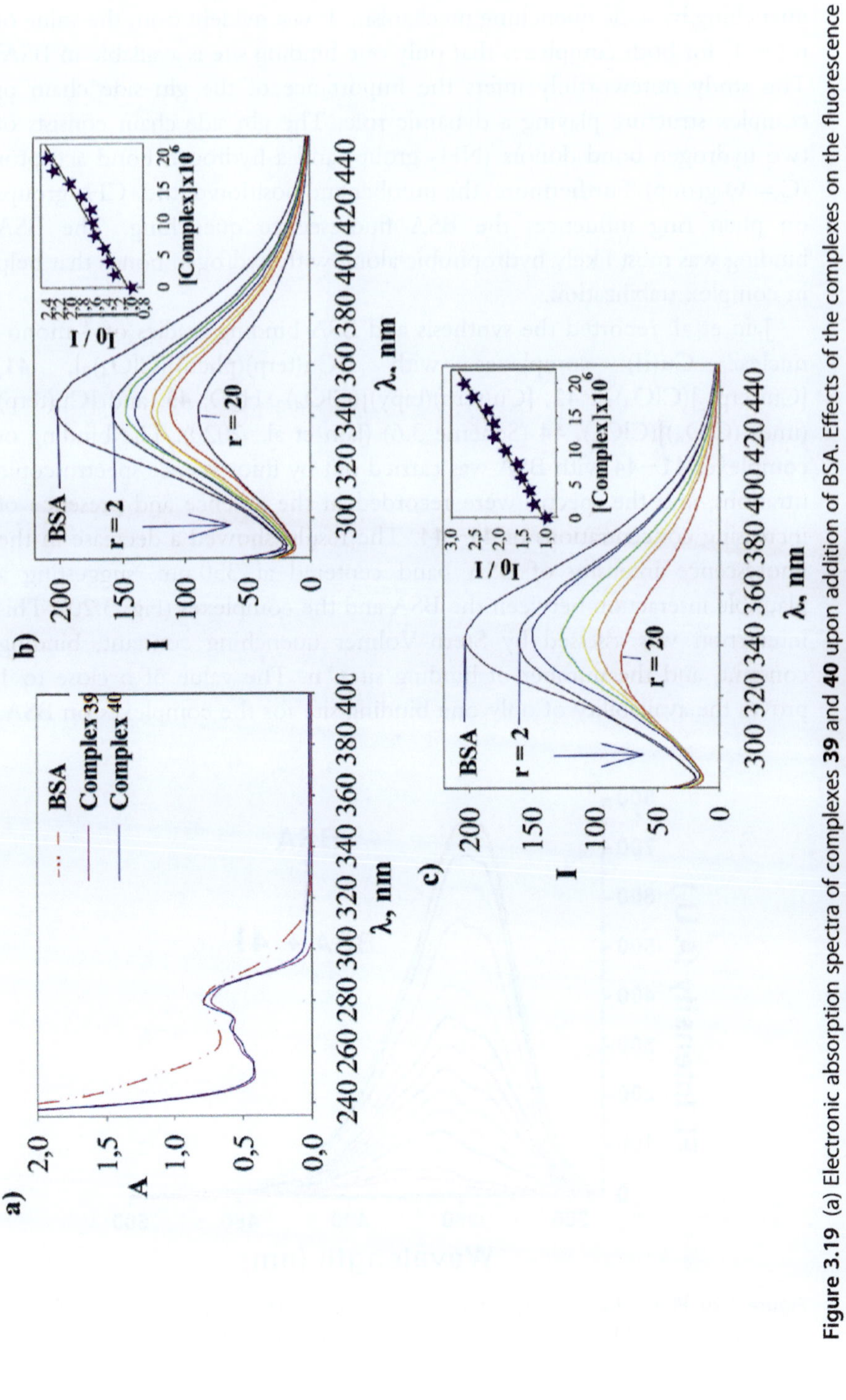

Figure 3.19 (a) Electronic absorption spectra of complexes **39** and **40** upon addition of BSA. Effects of the complexes on the fluorescence spectra of BSA: (b) **39** and (c) **40**. *(Reprinted with permission from Kiraz et al. (2019).)*

quenching by static quenching mechanism. It was evident from the value of n (~ 1) for both complexes that only one binding site is available in BSA. This study noteworthily infers the importance of the gln side chain of complex structure playing a dynamic role. The gln side chain consists of two hydrogen bond donors (NH_2 group) and a hydrogen bond acceptor (C = O group). Furthermore, the number and position of the -CH_3 groups on phen ring influences the BSA fluorescence quenching. The BSA binding was most likely hydrophobic along with hydrogen bonds that help in complex stabilization.

Jain et al. reported the synthesis and BSA binding studies of 4 mononuclear Cu(II) complexes with ([Cu(terp)(phen)]$(ClO_4)_2$], **41**, [Cu$(terp)_2$]$(ClO_4)_2$], **42**, [Cu(terp)(bipy)]$(ClO_4)_2 \cdot H_2O$, **43**, and [Cu(terp)(imd) (ClO_4)](ClO_4), **44** (Scheme 3.6) (Jain et al., 2020). The binding of complexes **41–44** with BSA was carried out by fluorescence spectroscopic titrations, and the spectra were recorded in the absence and presence of increasing concentrations of **41–44**. The results showed a decrease in the fluorescence intensity of BSA band centered at 350 nm, suggesting a plausible interaction between the BSA and the complexes (Fig. 3.20). This interaction was assessed by Stern-Volmer quenching constant, binding constant, and the number of binding sites, n. The value of n close to 1 proves the availability of only one binding site for the complexes on BSA.

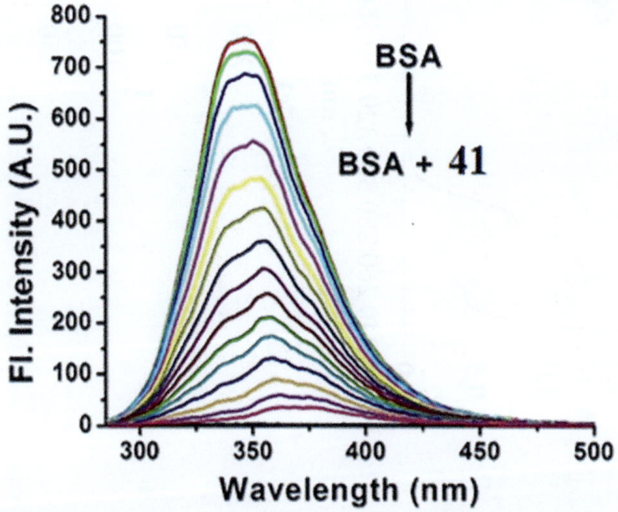

Figure 3.20 Plot of fluorescence emission intensity vs wavelength for BSA at different concentrations of **41.** *(Reprinted with permission from Jain et al. (2020).)*

Yousuf et al. reported Cu(II)-nalidixic acid-DACH complex, **45**, and employed various spectroscopic techniques to determine the interaction with SAs (Scheme 3.6) (Yousuf et al., 2019). Electronic absorption spectroscopy was employed to devise the interaction between **45** and SAs. Upon concomitant increase in the concentrations of complex **45**, keeping SA concentration constant, a hyperchromic effect of the band centered at 279 nm was detected. This was a clear indication that complex **45** interacted with SAs via noncovalent interactions, probably electrostatic hydrophobic contacts. Hydrogen bonding due to the presence of hydrogen bond donors and acceptors in nalidixic acid moiety (pyridone and C=O atoms) and amino group of DACH of the complex further helped in stabilization of the binding. Nevertheless, the K_b values suggested a greater binding propensity with HSA in comparison with BSA.

Inci et al. reported the synthesis and BSA interaction of water-soluble ternary Cu(II) complex, $[Cu(py\text{-}phen)(phe)(H_2O)]NO_3 \cdot H_2O$, **46,** and its BSA binding potential was explored by tryptophan emission quenching experiments (fluorescence spectroscopy) (Fig. 3.21) (Scheme 3.6) (Inci et al., 2019). The Stern–Volmer quenching constants, log K_{sv} and log K_q, were calculated for complex **46** and found to be 4.91 ± 0.02 and 12.91 ± 0.02, respectively, suggesting a tryptophan fluorescence quenching via static quenching mechanism.

Table 3.4 summarizes the geometries, characterization techniques, and the modes of binding of Cu(I)/(II) complexes to HSA/BSA.

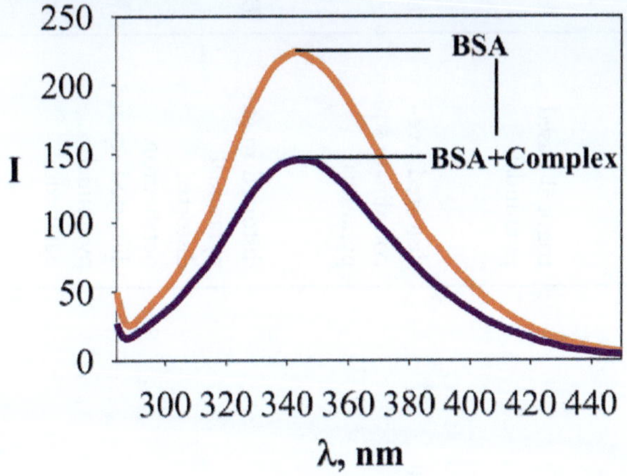

Figure 3.21 The effects of complex **46** on the fluorescence spectra of BSA. *(Reprinted with permission from Inci et al. (2019).)*

Table 3.4 Summary of the modes of Cu complexes interacting with other biomolecules.

Complex	Geometry	Target	Characterization techniques	Mode of interaction	References
37	four coordinate	HSA	ESI-MS, elemental analysis, electrical conductometry, FTIR, UV-vis	Groove binding mode	Moradinia et al. (2019)
38	trigonal-based pyramidal	HSA	single X-ray crystal diffraction, UV-vis, elemental analysis, ESI-MS	Stronger binding in domains of HSA	Kumar et al. (2019)
39, 40	distorted five-coordinate square pyramidal	BSA	single X-ray crystal diffraction, UV-vis, elemental analysis, ESI-MS, ATR-FT-MIR	Hydrophobic along with hydrogen bonds	Kiraz et al. (2019)
41 **42** **44**	distorted square pyramidal distorted octahedron distorted square pyramidal	BSA	single X-ray crystal diffraction, UV-vis, elemental analysis, ESI-MS, EPR	Stronger binding in domains of BSA	Jain et al. (2020)
45	octahedral	HSA and BSA	Single X-ray crystal diffraction, elemental analysis, ESI-MS, EPR	Noncovalent interactions (electrostatic hydrophobic contacts)	Yousuf et al. (2019)
46	distorted five-coordinate square pyramidal geometry	BSA	Single X-ray crystal diffraction, ESI-MS, elemental analysis, FTIR, UV-vis	Binding in domains of BSA	Inci et al. (2019)

5. Limitations

Even though Cu complexes are known to exhibit superior binding affinities to the nucleic acids and other biomolecules, their toxicity has been postulated to originate due to their ability to produce ROS, to displace other metal ions, induction of lipid peroxidation, and/or direct cleavage of nucleic acids. Numerous Cu complexes are biologically active, which is attributed to their binding to either DNA or RNA. On the other hand, in several cases, merely the interaction with isolated DNA has been studied. The experimental data revealed that Cu(I)/(II) complexes interacted with the DNA directly via coordination, yet the detailed molecular interactions and binding modes are not evidently recognized. Moreover, a Cu complex could effectively bind to the biomolecule, in vitro, and its cellular target could be different, and also the mode of action could be more complex.

With the advanced knowledge of comprehensive genome and the rapid growth investigated by epigenetics, nucleic acids have become principle targets with the aim to develop new nucleic acid-interacting Cu complexes. Although there are vast benefits delivered by the use of d-block metals, especially Cu due to its 3D geometrical variations, and the vital role played by the intercalating ligands, which afford a reversible interaction with nucleic acid, the basic factors of such interactions still retain paramount holes in the experimental protocols. These protocols lack the involvement of expensive schemes, methods, and equipment, hence the identification of specific interactions due the lower energetic changes involved, making clear the use of methodologies such as computational chemistry to help solve these problems.

6. Future prospects

There has been an enormous literature on nucleic acid–interacting Cu complexes having a variety of different ligands, often exhibiting specific base-selectivity, complex structural motif, viz., bulge or hairpin loop, and good binding affinities. Nonetheless, the advancement of prognostic binding modes for a more sensible design of Cu-based metallo-drugs has lingered to be challenging. This characteristic binding arises due to the flexibility of Cu^{2+} in its coordination number, geometry, and donor atoms. The DNA conversion into a stable condensed form by metal complexes is an evolving methodology in gene delivery. Numerous Cu complexes are known to induce DNA condensation, even though there are not enough studies. Whereas, noncovalent DNA interactions of Cu have been used in asymmetric catalysis and building sequence- or structure-specific interactions into the design of Cu complex-DNA hybrid catalysts.

This area of research is a hot and current topic considering the improved experimental and analytical techniques available to synthesize novel Cu complexes that are designed to accomplish a determined task, such as direct and specific interaction with a particular region of nucleic acids, DNA, and RNA. It is hoped that the future will see more studies on RNA binding modes. Cu complexes offer a platform for the design of novel therapeutic drugs. The careful selection of ligands could be fruitful in developing the structure and function of Cu complexes with advanced functions and highly specific targeting capabilities, facilitating the identification of action mechanisms of therapeutic leads.

7. Conclusions

In recent years, Cu complexes were found to exhibit prominent anticancer activity by inducing apoptosis, binding strongly to DNA. Cu has high affinity for the nucleic acids, and Cu complexes possess biologically accessible redox properties. Also, many Cu complexes have been reported to efficiently cleave DNA by an oxidative or hydrolytic mechanism. Among the essential metal ions in the human body, Cu^{2+} is third in abundance after Fe^{3+} and Zn^{2+}, and it plays very important roles in several biologic processes. Meanwhile, a large number of conventional chemotherapeutic drugs target DNA, and medicinal chemists have shifted their interest toward targeting RNA, which is able to substantiate a more prolific and favorable therapeutic target. It was found that cisplatin formed RNA-adducts by direct coordination to guanine bases often resulting in distortions that interfere with the functioning of RNA. RNAs can be exploited as drug targets due to the absence of the cellular repair mechanism, their unique structural polymorphism, and their capability to "switch" between single-stranded and double-stranded forms. Cu complexes interact with the nucleic acids via variety of interactions, broadly divided into two categories: (1) covalent interactions via direct coordination of the metal center to nucleic acids' base and (2) noncovalent interactions, viz., intercalation, hydrogen bonding, or electrostatic interactions. Intercalators are complexes containing ligands that are able to π-stack between the stacked base pairs of DNA, thus unwinding DNA. Whereas, a number of octahedral Cu(II) complexes with the ability to display supramolecular interactions, such as hydrogen bonding and π-π stacking interactions, have been reported as DNA groove binders (major or minor). These binding modes of Cu complexes can be specifically distinguished based upon the choice of ligands used. For example, chelating ligands bind to nucleic acids, though intercalation and groove binding modes, enhancing the binding affinity and/or selectivity. Elusive changes to the ligand or complex geometry can have dramatic effects, especially when DNA binding is followed by oxidative DNA cleavage. Whereas, alternatively, RNA-targeted complexes composed of heterocyclic frameworks along with planar aromatic scaffolds could bind through intercalation through π-π stacking in between the RNA bases, specifically in the minor groove.

This chapter provides a general scope about experimental and theoretical approaches that are used in synthesis and nucleic acid binding studies of Cu complexes with advantages and limitations. The various modes, viz., covalent and noncovalent, of interaction of Cu complexes with DNA, RNA, and SAs have been discussed. DNA is the molecular target for many anticancer drugs, and the ability of metal complexes that interact with DNA is dependent on their structural effects on DNA. Hence, DNA is expected to be a clinically important target for many years to come.

References

Adam, M. S. S., Abdel-Rahman, L. H., AbuDief, A. M., & Hashem, N. A. (2020). Synthesis, catalysis, antimicrobial activity, and DNA interactions of new Cu(II)-Schiff base complexes. *Inorganic and Nano-Metal Chemistry, 50*, 136–150.

Afsan, Z., Roisnel, T., Tabassum, S., & Arjmand, F. (2020). Structure elucidation {spectroscopic, single crystal X-ray diffraction and computational DFT studies} of new tailored benzenesulfonamide derived Schiff base copper(II) intercalating complexes: Comprehensive biological profile {DNA binding, pBR322 DNA cleavage, Topo I inhibition and cytotoxic activity. *Bioorganic Chemistry, 94*, 103427.

Akhter, S., Zaman, H. U., Mir, S., Dar, A. Y., & Shrivastava, S. (2017). Synthesis of Schiff base metal complexes: A concise review. *European Chemical Bulletin, 6*(10), 475–483.

Alzuet, G., Castiñeiras, A., Cores, I., Santos, I. G., Álvarez, M. G., & Saa, M. (2020). Structural basis and effect of copper(II) complexes with 4-oxo-thiazolidine ligands on DNA binding and nuclease activity. *Journal of Inorganic Biochemistry, 203*, 110902.

Andersson, K. K., Schmidt, P. P., Katterle, B., Strand, K. R., Palmer, A. E., Lee, S. K., Solomon, E. I., Graslund, A., & Barra, A. L. (2003). Examples of high-frequency EPR studies in bioinorganic chemistry. *Journal of Biological Inorganic Chemistry, 8*, 235–247.

Andrushchenko, V., Van De Sande, J. H., & Wieser, H. (2003). Vibrational circular dichroism and IR absorption of DNA complexes with Cu^{2+} ions. *Biopolymers, 72*, 374–390.

Angelova, M., Asenova, S., Nedkova, V., & Kolarova, R. K. (2011). Copper in the human organism. *Trakia Journal of Sciences, 9*(1), 88–98.

Anitha, N., Saravanan, N., Ajaykamal, T., Suresh, E., & Palaniandavar, M. (2019). Catecholase activity of mononuclear copper(II) complexes of tridentate 3N ligands in aqueous and aqueous micellar media: Influence of stereoelectronic factors on catalytic activity. *Inorganica Chimica Acta, 485*, 98–111.

Antoniades, V., Sioga, A., Dietrich, E. M., Meditskou, S., Ekonomou, L., & Antoniades, K. (2013). Is copper chelation an effective anti-angiogenic strategy for cancer treatment? *Medical Hypotheses, 81*, 1159–1163.

Arjmand, F., Afsan, Z., & Roisnel, T. (2018). Design, synthesis and characterization of novel chromone based-copper(II) antitumor agents with N,N-donor ligands: Comparative DNA/RNA binding profile and cytotoxicity. *RSC Advances, 8*, 37375.

Arjmand, F., Afsan, Z., Sharma, S., Parveen, S., Yousuf, I., Sartaj, S., Siddique, S. R., & Tabassum, S. (2019). Recent advances in metallodrug-like molecules targeting non-coding RNAs in cancer chemotherapy. *Coordination Chemistry Reviews, 387*, 47–59.

Aseman, M. D., Aryamanesh, S., Shojaeifard, Z., Hemmateenejad, B., & Nabavizadeh, S. M. (2019). Cycloplatinated(II) derivatives of mercaptopurine capable of binding interactions with HSA/DNA. *Inorganic Chemistry, 58*(23), 16154–16170.

Ayad, M., Schollhammer, P., Mest, Y. L., Wojcik, L., Pétillon, F. Y., Poul, N. L., & Mandon, D. (2019). Mononuclear copper(II) complexes containing a macrocyclic ditopic ligand: Synthesis, structures and properties. *Inorganica Chimica Acta, 497*, 119081.

Azuara, L. R., & Gomez, M. E. N. (2010). Antineoplastic evaluation of two mixed chelate copper complexes (Casiopeínas®) in HCT-15 xenograft model. *Current Medical Chemistry, 17*, 3606–3615.

Bassoli, S., Ardizzoia, G. A., Therrien, B., & Brenna, S. (2019). Phosphorescence enhancement by close metal-metal interaction in T1 excited state in a dinuclear copper(I) complex. *Dalton Transactions, 48*, 9276.

Bhunia, A., Vojtísek, P., Bertolasi, V., & Manna, S. C. (2019). Tridentate Schiff base coordinated trigonal bipyramidal/square pyramidal copper(II) complexes: Synthesis, crystal structure, DFT/TD-DFT calculation, catecholase activity and DNA binding. *Journal of Molecular Structure, 1189*, 94–101.

Borthakur, R., Kumar, A., De, A. K., & Lal, R. A. (2019). Synthesis, characterization and electrochemical properties of copper(II) complexes derived from succinoyldihydrazine Schiff base ligands. *Arabian Journal of Chemistry, 12*, 2192–2205.

Boulsourani, Z., Geromichalos, G. D., Katsamakas, S., Psycharis, V., Raptopoulou, C. P., Litina, D. H., Sahpazidou, D., & Samara, C. D. (2019). Mononuclear copper(II) complexes with 2-thiophene carboxylate and N-N donors, DNA interaction, antioxidant/anti-inflammatory and antitumor activity. *Materials Science and Engineering C, 94*, 493–508.

Calle, C., Sreekanth, A., Fedin, M. V., Forrer, J., Garcia-Rubio, I., Gromov, I. A., Hinderberger, D., Kasumaj, B., Leger, P., Mancosu, B., Mitrikas, G., Santangelo, M. G., Stoll, S., Schweiger, A., Tschaggelar, R., & Harmer, J. (2006). Pulse EPR methods for studying chemical and biological samples containing transition metals. *Helvetica Chimica Acta, 89*, 2495–2521.

Campbell, N. H., Karim, N. H., Parkinson, G. N., Gunaratnam, M., Petrucci, V., Todd, A. K., Vilar, R., & Neidle, S. (2011). Molecular basis of structure-activity relationships between salphen metal complexes and human telomeric DNA quadruplexes. *Journal of Medicinal Chemistry, 55*, 209.

Cassemiro, B. G., Santos, J. S., Oliveira, W. X. C., Maia, E. C. P., Galvao, B. R. L., do Pim, W. D., & Caldeira, P. P. S. (2020). Dinuclear copper(II) complex with a benzimidazole derivative: Crystal structure, theoretical calculations, and cytotoxic activity. *Applied Organometallic Chemistry, 2020*, e5425.

Chang, G. L., Li, Z., Niu, M. J., & Wang, S. N. (2019). Studies on the manganese and copper complexes derived from chiral schiff base: Synthesis, structure, cytotoxicity and DNA/BSA interaction. *Journal of Coordination Chemistry, 72*, 2422–2436.

Chen, C., Xu, X. H., Yang, B., & Qing, F. L. (2014). Copper-catalyzed direct trifluoromethylthiolation of benzylic C-H bonds via nondirected oxidative C(sp^3)-H activation. *Organic Letters, 16*, 3372–3375.

Chen, H., Xu, L. X., Yan, L. J., Liu, X. F., Xu, D. D., Yu, X. C., Fan, J. X., Wu, Q. A., & Luo, S. P. (2020). Mononuclear Copper(I) complexes based on phenanthroline derivatives PNNP tetradentate ligands: Syntheses, crystal structure, photochemical properties. *Dyes and Pigments, 173*, 108000.

Denoyer, D., Masaldan, S., Fontaine, S. L., & Cater, M. A. (2015). Targeting copper in cancer therapy:'Copper that Cancer. *Metallomics, 7*, 1459–1476.

Erxleben, A. (2018). Interactions of copper complexes with nucleic acids. *Coordination Chemistry Reviews, 360*, 92–121.

Facchin, G., Kremer, E., Barrio, D. A., Etcheverry, S. B., CostaFilho, A. J., & Torre, M. H. (2009). Interaction of Cu-dipeptide complexes with Calf Thymus DNA and antiproliferative activity of [Cu(ala-phe)] in osteosarcoma-derived cells. *Polyhedron, 28*, 2329–2334.

Fanali, G., Trezza, V., Marino, M., Fasano, M., & Ascenzi, P. (2012). Human serum albumin: From bench to bedside. *Molecular Aspects of Medicine, 33*, 209–290.

Farrar, J. A., Neese, F., Lappalainen, P., Kroneck, P. M. H., Saraste, M., Zumft, W. G., & Thomson, A. J. (1996). The electronic structure of Cu_A: A novel mixed-valence dinuclear copper electron-transfer center. *Journal of American Chemical Society, 118*, 11501–11514.

Fattuoni, C., Vascellari, S., & Pivetta, T. (2020). Synthesis, protonation constants and biological activity determination of amino acid-salicylaldehyde-derived Schif bases. *Amino Acids, 52*, 397–407.

Finney, L., Vogt, S., Fukai, T., & Glesne, D. (2009). Copper and angiogenesis: Unravelling a relationship key to cancer progression. *Clinical and Experimental Pharmacology and Physiology, 36*, 88–94.

Franklin, R. E., & Gosling, R. G. (1953). Molecular configuration in sodium thymonucleate. *Nature, 171*, 740–741.

Gandin, V., Tisato, F., Dolmella, A., Pellei, M., Santini, C., Giorgetti, M., Marzano, C., & Porchia, M. (2014). In vitro and in vivo anticancer activity of copper(I) complexes with homoscorpionate tridentate tris(pyrazolyl)borate and auxiliary monodentate phosphine ligands. *Journal of Medicinal Chemistry, 57*, 4745–4760.

Gasser, G., Ott, I., & Nolte, N. M. (2011). Organometallic anticancer compounds. *Journal of Medicinal Chemistry, 54*, 3–25.

Ghosh, B. K., & Chakravorty, A. (1989). Electrochemical studies of ruthenium compounds part I. Ligand oxidation levels. *Coordination Chemistry Reviews, 95*, 239–294.

Ghosh, B. K., Hazra, S., Naik, B., & Ghosh, N. N. (2015). Preparation of Cu nanoparticle loaded SBA-15 and their excellent catalytic activity in reduction of variety of dyes. *Powder Technology, 269*, 371–378.

Gou, Y., Qi, J., Ajayi, J. P., Zhang, Y., Zhou, Z., Wu, X., Yang, F., & Liang, H. (2015). Developing anticancer copper (II) pro-drugs based on the nature of cancer cells and the human serum albumin carrier IIA subdomain. *Molecular Pharmaceutics, 12*, 3597–3609.

Guan, L., & Disney, M. D. (2012). Recent advances in developing small molecules targeting RNA. *ACS Chemical Biology, 7*, 73–86.

Haba, P., Sy, A., Tamboura, F. B., Sarr, M., Thiam, I. E., Barry, A. H., Sall, M. L., Gaye, M., & Retailleau, P. (2019). Synthesis, spectroscopic studies and X-ray structure determination of two mononuclear copper complexes derived from the Schiff base ligand

N,N-dimethyl-N'-((5-methyl-1H-imidazole-4-yl)methylene)ethane-1,2-diamine. *European Journal of Chemistry, 10*(3), 201–208.

Hammond, C. R. (2004). The elements. In *Handbook of chemistry and physics* (81st ed.). Boca Raton: CRC Press.

Haynes, W. M. (2014). *CRC handbook of chemistry and physics, internet version 2015* (95th ed.). Boca Raton, FL: CRC Press/Taylor and Francis.

Helliwell, J. R., & Mitchell, E. P. (2015). Synchrotron radiation macromolecular crystallography: Science and spin-offs. *International Union of Crystallography Journals, 2*, 283–291.

Hofbeck, T., Monkowius, U., & Yersin, H. (2015). Highly efficient luminescence of Cu(I) compounds: Thermally activated delayed fluorescence combined with short-lived phosphorescence. *Journal of American Chemical Society, 137*, 99–404.

Hussain, A., AlAjmi, M. F., Rehman, M. T., Amir, S., Husain, F. M., Alsalme, A., Siddiqui, M. A., AlKhedhairy, A. A., & Khan, R. A. (2019). Copper(II) complexes as potential anticancer and nonsteroidal antiinfammatory agents: In vitro and in vivo studies. *Scientific Reports, 9*, 5237.

Inci, D., Koseler, A., Zeytünlüoglu, A., Aydın, R., & Zorlu, Y. (2019). Interaction of a new copper(II) complex by bovine serum albumin and dipeptidyl peptidase-IV. *Journal of Molecular Structure, 1177*, 317–322.

Jain, S., Bhar, K., Kumar, S., Bandyopadhyaya, S., Tapryal, S., Mandal, C. C., & Sharma, A. K. (2020). Homo- and heteroleptic trimethoxy terpyridine-Cu(II) complexes: Synthesis, characterization, DNA/BSA binding, DNA cleavage and cytotoxicity studies. *Dalton Transactions, 49*, 4100–4113.

Kacar, S., Unver, H., & Sahinturk, V. (2020). A mononuclear copper(II) complex containing benzimidazole and pyridyl ligands: Synthesis, characterization, and antiproliferative activity against human cancer cells. *Arabian Journal of Chemistry, 13*, 4310–4323.

Kar, P., Franconetti, A., Frontera, A., & Ghosh, A. (2019). Chloranilate bridged dinuclear copper(II) complexes: syn-anti geometry tuned by the steric factor and supramolecular interactions. *CrystEngComm, 21*, 6886.

Kaler, S. G., Liew, C. J., Donsante, A., Hicks, J. D., Sato, S., & Greenfeld, J. C. (2010). Molecular correlates of epilepsy in early diagnosed and treated Menkes disease. *Journal of International Medicine and Dentistry, 33*(5), 583–589.

Kellett, A., Molphy, Z., Slator, C., McKee, V., & Farrell, N. P. (2019). Molecular methods for assessment of non-covalent metallodrug-DNA interactions. *Chemical Society Reviews, 48*, 971–988.

Khan, H. Y., Tabassum, S., & Arjmand, F. (2020). Evaluation of cytotoxic potential of structurally well-characterized RNA targeted ionic nonsteroidal anti-inflammatory (NSAID) Cu(II) and Zn(II) DACH-mefenamato drug conjugates against human cancer cell lines. *RSC Advances, 10*, 166.

Khodade, V. S., Dharmaraja, A. T., & Chakrapani, H. (2012). Synthesis, reactive oxygen species generation and copper-mediated nuclease activity profiles of 2-aryl-3-amino-1, 4-naphthoquinones. Bioorg. *Medicinal Chemistry Letters, 22*, 3766–3769.

Kiraz, S., Inci, D., Aydın, R., Vatan, O., Zorlu, Y., & Cavas, T. (2019). Antiproliferative activity of copper(II) glutamine complexes with N,Ndonor ligands: Synthesis, characterization, potentiometric studies and DNA/BSA interactions. *Journal of Molecular Structure, 1194*, 245–255.

Komarnicka, U. K., Kozieł, S., Zabierowski, P., Kruszyński, R., Lesiów, M. K., Tisato, F., Porchia, M., & Kyzioł, A. (2020). Copper(I) complexes with phosphines P(p-OCH_3-Ph)$_2$$CH_2$OH and P(p-$OCH_3$-Ph)$_2$$CH_2$SarGly. Synthesis, multimodal DNA interactions, and prooxidative and in vitro antiproliferative activity. *Journal of Inorganic Biochemistry, 203*, 110926.

Kumar, M., & Masram, D. T. (2019). Evaluation of DNA, BSA, and HSA binding propensity of Copper(II) complex with N-donor ligand 2,2′-dipyridylamine. *Polyhedron, 157*, 511–520.

Li, G. Y., Guan, R. L., Ji, L. N., & Chao, H. (2014). DNA condensation induced by metal complexes. *Coordination Chemistry Reviews, 281*, 100–113.

Liu, L., Liu, L. P., Zhang, R., Zhong, X., Li, F., Wang, L., Wong, W. R., Li, G., Cong, H., Alharbi, N. S., & Zhao, Y. (2019). A new strategy to synthesize three-coordinate mononuclear copper(i) halide complexes containing a bulky terphenyl bidentate phosphine ligand and their luminescent properties. *New Journal of Chemistry, 43*, 3390–3399.

Lv, L., Yuan, K., Si, C., Zuo, G., & Wang, Y. (2020). Mechanism study of TADF and phosphorescence in dinuclear copper (I) molecular crystal using QM/MM combined with an optimally tuned range-separated hybrid functional. *Organic Electronics, 81*, 105667.

Majid, S. A., Mir, J. M., Paul, S., Akhter, M., Parray, H., Ayoub, R., & Shalla, A. H. (2019). Experimental and molecular topology-based biological implications of Schiff base complexes: A concise review. *Reviews in Inorganic Chemistry, 39*. https://doi.org/10.1515/revic-2018-0023

Mandal, N. K., Guhathakurta, B., Basu, P., Pradhan, A. B., Purohit, C. S., Chowdhury, S., & Naskara, J. P. (2019). DNA and RNA binding studies on a novel bromobridged dimeric copper(II) complex stabilized from a Schiff base ligand. *Journal of Coordination Chemistry, 72*, 3625–3644.

Manna, S., Zangrando, E., Puschmann, H., & Manna, S. C. (2019). Tetranuclear Schiff base copper(II) complexes: Syntheses, crystal structure, DNA/protein binding and catecholase-like activity. *Polyhedron, 162*, 285–292.

Massey, A. G., Thompson, N. R., & Johnson, B. F. G. (1973). *The chemistry of copper, silver and gold: Pergamon texts in inorganic chemistry*. Pergamon Press.

Maurya, R. C., Malik, B. A., Mir, J. M., Vishwakarma, P. K., Rajak, D. K., & Jain, N. (2015). Nickel(II) complexes of ONS donor schiff base ligands: Synthesis, combined DFT- experimental characterization, redox, thermal, and *in vitro* biological investigation. *Journal of Coordination Chemistry, 68*, 2902–2922.

Merlot, A. M., Kalinowski, D. S., & Richardson, D. R. (2014). Unraveling the mysteries of serum albumin-more than just a serum protein. *Frontiers in Physiology, 5*, 1–7.

Michel, B. Y., Dziuba, D., Benhida, R., Demchenko, A. P., & Burger, A. (2020). Probing of nucleic acid structures, dynamics, and interactions with environment-sensitive fluorescent labels. *Frontiers in Chemistry, 8*, 112.

Moradinia, E., Mansourni, M., Boroujeni, Z. A., & Bordbar, A. K. (2019). New transition metal complexes of 9,10-phenanthrenequinone p-toluyl hydrazone Schiff base: Synthesis, spectroscopy, DNA and HSA interactions, antimicrobial, DFT and docking studies. *Applied Organometallic Chemistry, 2019*, e4893.

Pages, B. J., Ang, D. L., Wright, E. P., & Aldrich-Wright, J. R. (2015). Metal complex interactions with DNA. *Dalton Transactions, 44*, 3505–3526.

Palanimuthu, D., Shinde, S. V., Somasundaram, K., & Samuelson, A. G. (2013). In vitro and in vivo anticancer activity of copper bis(thiosemicarbazone) complexes. *Journal of Medicinal Chemistry, 56*, 722–734.

Qiao, X., Ma, Z. Y., Xie, C. Z., Xue, F., Zhang, Y. W., Xua, J. Y., Qiang, Z. Y., Lou, J. S., Chen, G. J., & Yan, S. P. (2011). Study on potential antitumor mechanism of a novel Schiff Base copper(II) complex: Synthesis, crystal structure, DNA binding, cytotoxicity and apoptosis induction activity. *Journal of Inorganic Biochemistry, 105*, 728–737.

Rambabu, A., Ganji, N., Daravath, S., Venkateswarlu, K., Rangan, K., & Shivaraj. (2020). Mononuclear Co(II), Ni(II) and Cu(II) complexes of the Schiff base, 2-(((4-trifluoromethoxy)phenylimino)methyl)-6-tert-butylphenol: Synthesis, spectroscopic characterization, X-ray study and biological Evaluation. *Journal of Molecular Structure, 1199*, 127006.

Ramos, J. C. G., Murillo, R. G., Guzmán, F. C., & Azuara, L. R. (2013). Metal-based drug-DNA interactions. *Journal of Mexican Chemical Society, 57*(3), 245–259.

Rayner, W. H. (2007). *Jewelry making through history: An encyclopedia* (p. p56). Westport, CT: Greenwood Publishing Group.

Rigamonti, L., Forni, A., Cariati, E., Malavasi, G., & Pasini, A. (2019). Solid-state nonlinear optical properties of mononuclear copper(II) complexes with chiral tridentate and tetradentate schiff base ligands. *Materials, 12*, 3595.

Roseborough, A., Wheeler, K. A., Hołyńska, M., & Stoian, S. A. (2020). Synthesis and electronic structure of a mononuclear copper(II) complex supported by tris(2-hydroxyliminopropyl)amine. *Polyhedron, 177*, 114306.

Roy, K. (2019). *In silico drug design: Repurposing techniques and methodologies*. Academic Press, Elsevier.

Roy, A., Seal, P., Sikdar, J., Banerjee, S., & Haldar, R. (2018). Underlying molecular interaction of bovine serum albumin and linezolid: A biophysical outlook. *Journal of Biomolecular and Structural Dynamics, 36*, 387–397.

Saga, M., Sakane, G., Yamazaki, S., & Saito, K. (2020). Fluorescent ligand design for mononuclear copper(I) complex fluorescence in aqueous solution. *Inorganica Chimica Acta, 502*, 119368.

Sakthikumar, K., Raja, J. D., Solomon, R. V., & Sankarganesh, M. (2018). Density functional theory molecular modelling, DNA interactions, antioxidant, antimicrobial, anticancer and biothermodynamic studies of bioactive water soluble mixed ligand complexes. *Journal of Biomolecular Structure and Dynamics, 37*(10), 2498–2514. https://doi.org/10.1080/07391102.2018.1492970

Santangelo, M. G., Molner, A. M., Schweiger, A., Mitrikas, G., & Spingler, B. (2007). Structural analysis of Cu(II) ligation to the 5'-GMP nucleotide by pulse EPR spectroscopy. *Journal of Biological Inorganic Chemistry, 12*, 767–775.

Santini, C., Pellei, M., Gandin, V., Porchia, M., Tisato, F., & Marzano, C. (2014). Advances in copper complexes as anticancer agents. *Chemical Reviews, 114*, 815–862.

Senel, P., İnci, D., Aydın, R., Huriyet, H., Zorlu, Y., & Çinkılıç, N. (2019). Methyl substituent effect on one-dimensional copper(II) coordination polymers containing biologically active ligands: Synthesis, characterization, DNA interactions and cytotoxicities. *Applied Organometallic Chemistry, 2019*, e5122.

Shirvan, A., Golchoubian, H., & Bouwman, E. (2019). Syntheses and chromotropic behavior of two halo bridged dinuclear copper(II) complexes containing pyridine-based bidentate ligand. *Journal of Molecular Structure, 1195*, 769–777.

Sun, L. Z., Kuang, X. N., Lin, S., Zhao, L., Yu, X., Li, Z. F., Liu, M., Xin, X. L., Yang, Y. P., & Jin, Q. H. (2020). Nine heteroleptic copper(I)/silver(I) complexes prepared from phosphine and diimine ligands: Syntheses, structures and terahertz spectra. *Polyhedron, 175*, 114177.

Tanase, T., Otaki, R., Okue, A., Nakamae, K., & Nakajima, T. (2019). Dinuclear copper complexes triply bridged by a tetraphosphane, rac-$Ph_2PCH_2P(Ph)CH_2P(Ph)CH_2PPh_2$. *European Journal of Inorganic Chemistry*, 3993–4005.

Tan, Y., Huang, J., Lu, H., Chi, T., & Sun, J. (2020). Synthesis, structure and magnetic property of a copper(II)-cobalt(II) heteronuclear complex with Schiff base ligand. *Inorganic and Nano-Metal Chemistry, 50*, 110–113.

Terenzi, A., Bonsignore, R., Spinello, A., Gentile, C., Martorana, A., Ducani, C., Hogberg, B., Almerico, A. M., Lauria, A., & Barone, G. (2014). Selective G-quadruplex stabilizers: Schiff-base metal complexes with anticancer activity. *RSC Advances, 4*, 33245.

Thakur, Y., Tripathi, M., Verma, B., Khilari, R., Agrawal, R., Likheshwari, Siddiqi, M. K., Pande, R., Mohapatra, E., & Khan, R. H. (2019). Interaction of cobalt(II) and copper(II) hydroxamates with polyriboadenylic acid: An insight into RNA based drug designing. *Nucleosides, Nucleotides and Nucleic Acids, 38*, 481–508.

Tripathi, M., Giri, G. C., Das, D., Pande, R., Sarkar, S., Giri, S., Roymahapatra, G., & Sarkar, A. (2018). Synthesis, characterization and nucleic acid binding studies of mononuclear copper(II) complexes derived from azo containing O, O donor ligands. *Nucleosides, Nucleotides and Nucleic Acids, 37*, 563–584.

Uber, J. S., Barrios, L. A., Estrader, M., Roubeau, O., & Aromí, G. (2020). Dinuclear Cu(II) molecules exhibiting reversible photochromism. *European Journal of Inorganic Chemistry, 14*, 561–567.

Vailati, A. F., Huelsmann, R. D., de Souza, E. M. D., Bortoluzzi, A. J., Xavier, F. R., & Peralta, R. (2020). Multivariate analysis applied to oxidation of cyclohexane and benzyl alcohol promoted by mononuclear iron and copper complexes. *New Journal of Chemistry, 44*, 2514–2526.

Valko, M., Jomova, K., Rhodes, C. J., Kuča, K., & Musílek, K. (2016). Redox-and non-redox-metal-induced formation of free radicals and their role in human disease. *Archives of Toxicology, 90*, 1–37.

Wang, Y., Zhang, H., Zhang, G., Tao, W., & Tang, S. (2007). Interaction of the flavonoid hesperidin with bovine serum albumin: A fluorescence quenching study. *Journal of Luminescence, 126*, 211–218.

Wehbe, M., Leung, A. W. Y., Abrams, M. J., Orvig, C., & Ballya, M. B. (2017). A Perspective-can copper complexes be developed as a novel class of therapeutics? *Dalton Transactions, 46*, 10758–10773.

Wolfe, A., Shimer, G. H., Jr., & Meehan, T. (1987). Polycyclic aromatic hydrocarbons physically intercalate into duplex regions of denatured DNA. *Biochemistry, 26*, 6392–6396.

Wua, Q., Zia, Q., & Qiao, Y. (2019). Copper(II) coordination complex constructed from halogenated tetradentate schiff base ligand: Synthesis, crystal structure, and hirshfeld surface analysis. *Crystallography Reports, 64*(6), 905–909.

Yamasaki, K., Chuang, V. T. G., Maruyama, T., & Otagiri, M. (2013). Albumin-drug interaction and its clinical implication. *Biochimica et Biophysica Acta, 1830*, 5435–5443.

Yousuf, I., Arjmand, F., Tabassum, S., Toupet, L., Khan, R. A., & Siddiqui, M. A. (2015). Mechanistic insights into a novel chromoneappended Cu(II) anticancer drug entity: In vitro binding profile with DNA/RNA substrates and cytotoxic activity against MCF-7 and HepG2 cancer cells. *Dalton Transactions, 44*, 10330–10342.

Yousuf, I., Bashir, M., Arjmand, F., & Tabassum, S. (2019). Multispectroscopic insight, morphological analysis and molecular docking studies of CuII based chemotherapeutic drug entity with Human Serum Albumin (HSA) and Bovine Serum Albumin (BSA). *Journal of Biomolecular Structure and Dynamics, 37*, 3290–3304.

Zehra, S., Roisnel, T., & Arjmand, F. (2019). Enantiomeric amino acid schiff base copper(II) complexes as a new class of RNA-targeted metallo-intercalators: Single X-ray crystal structural details, comparative in vitro DNA/RNA binding profile, cleavage, and cytotoxicity. *ACS Omega, 4*, 7691–7705.

Zhang, C. L., Cai, D. H., Chen, S., Liu, W., Xiong, Y. H., & Le, X. Y. (2019). Synthesis, DNA interaction and SOD-like activities of copper(II) complexes: Investigation of their DNA-interaction mechanism. *Transition Metal Chemistry, 44*, 603–613.

Zhang, X., Li, Y. Y., Jiang, J., Zhang, R., Liao, R. Z., & Wang, M. (2020). A dinuclear copper complex featuring a flexible linker as water oxidation catalyst with an activity far superior to its mononuclear counterpart. *Inorganic Chemistry, 59*(8), 5424–5432. https://doi.org/10.1021/acs.inorgchem.9b03783

Zhang, G., Wang, L., & Pan, J. (2012). Probing the binding of the flavonoid diosmetin to human serum albumin by multispectroscopic techniques. *Journal of Agricultural and Food Chemistry, 60*, 2721–2729.
Zhao, Z., Zhang, J., Zhi, S. C., Song, W., & Zhao, J. (2019). Novel binuclear and trinuclear metal (II) complexes: DNA interactions and in vitro anticancer activity through apoptosis. *Journal of Inorganic Biochemistry, 197*, 110696.
Zhou, W., Wang, X. Y., Hu, M., Zhu, C. C., & Guo, Z. J. (2014). A mitochondrion-targeting copper complex exhibits potent cytotoxicity against cisplatin-resistant tumor cells through a multiple mechanism of action. *Chemical Science, 5*, 2761–2770.

CHAPTER 4

Recent advances in iron complexes and their interaction with nucleic acids

Shazia Parveen
Chemistry Department, Faculty of Science, Taibah University, Yanbu, Saudi Arabia

1. Chemistry of iron

Iron, acquired its name from old Anglo-Saxon (iren) and its symbol Fe from Ferrum in Latin, was recognized and used in prehistoric times around 3500 BCE in Egypt. René Antoine Ferchault de Réaumur in 1722 first explained the different types of iron in his book. This subject enlightened how steel, wrought iron, and cast iron were distinguished by the amount of carbon content in the form of charcoal. The Industrial Revolution that began in the 18th century depended extensively on iron metal. Earth's crust contains 5% of iron by mass and is the second most abundant metal to aluminum and fourth abundant after oxygen, silicon, and aluminum among the elements (Kosik-Bogacka et al., 2019). The Earth's core is supposed to be chiefly composed of iron along with nickel and sulfur. Iron in its pure form is a silvery-white metal, distinguished by its capability in taking and retaining a magnetic field. Iron is also capable of dissolving minor amounts of carbon in the molten state. The commercial production of iron is done in a blast furnace by heating iron ores (especially hematite or magnetite) with coke (i.e., carbon) and limestone. This then produces pig iron that contains ~3% carbon and other impurities, which is used in the production of steel. Yearly, almost 1.3 billion tons of crude steel are produced worldwide.

Fe is a metal belonging to the first transition series and eighth group of the periodic table, comprising 26 electrons with the configuration of [Ar] $3d^6 4s^2$, among which 3d and 4s electrons are comparatively of similar energy, so it can lose a variable number of electrons. Iron's chemistry is based on the existence of two oxidation states, oxidation states +2 (iron(II), "ferrous") and +3 (iron(III), "ferric"). This rich coordination chemistry along with the electron-donating and accepting ability makes

Nucleic Acids
ISBN 978-0-12-820503-7
https://doi.org/10.1016/B978-0-12-820503-7.00005-3

this metal exceptional for numerous physiologic and metabolic pathways in the living body (Fairweather-Tait, 2004; Sánchez et al., 2017). Both Fe(II) and Fe(III) are thermodynamically stable and kinetically reactive and can adapt diverse coordination modes through full or empty coordination sites. The Fe(II)-Fe(III) redox potential and the sizes of the complexes can be controlled depending on the nature of the coordinated atoms of the various ligands.

Iron is an indispensable element for nearly all living organisms. The average quantity of iron in the human body is around 4.5 g (~0.004%), of which nearly 65% is in the form of hemoglobin, which carries oxygen from our lungs to the cells that need it for tissue respiration (Wani et al., 2016); 1% is in the numerous enzymes controlling intracellular oxidation; the majority of the rest is stored in the body specifically in liver, spleen, and bone marrow for future conversion to hemoglobin (Saito, 2014). Other vital biochemical activities such as electron transport in several iron-sulfur proteins, energy production, or cellular proliferation are dependent upon iron-containing cofactors (Crichton, and Boelaert, 2001; Gkouvatsos et al., 2012; Sánchez et al., 2017).

The deficiency of iron in humans causes anemia (Camaschella, 2015). A large number of iron complexes have been in use to treat hypochromic anemias. The diet including red meat, egg yolk, carrots, fruits, whole wheat, and green vegetables contribute most of the 10-20 mg of iron required each day by an average adult.

2. Methods of synthesis

This section describes the general procedures of synthesis involved in designing Fe(II)/(III) complexes incorporating a variety of ligands and that can be broadly classified as mononuclear, dinuclear, tetranuclear, heterobimetallic, and Schiff base complexes.

2.1 Mononuclear Fe complexes

Recently, many mononuclear Fe(II)/(III) complexes bearing a variety of ligands such as polypyridine (Karges et al., 2019; Wang et al., 2020), N,N′-phenylenebis-(salicylideneiminato) (Ibrahim et al., 2020), diamine (Obaleye et al., 2019), NNN-donor ligands (Carvalho et al., 2019), SNS-pincer type ligands (Sogukomerogullari et al., 2019), terpy-type boratriazine chelates (Savard et al., 2019), $B(Ph)_4$ (Hijazi et al., 2017), etc., (Vailati et al., 2020) have been synthesized.

The general procedure followed for the synthesis of mononuclear Fe(II)/(III) complexes involves the reaction between the corresponding ligand and respective iron salt ($FeCl_3 \cdot 6H_2O$, $Fe(ClO_4)_2 \cdot 6H_2O$, $FeCl_3$), in suitable solvent, viz., DMF/MeCN/MeOH/THF, under mild stirring conditions or refluxing. Inert conditions (N_2 atmosphere) with and without the presence of catalysts have also been reported. The structures and crystal structures of some of the representative Fe(II)/(III) mononuclear complexes are shown in Fig. 4.1 and Scheme 1.

2.2 Dinuclear Fe complexes

The general procedure for the synthesis of dinuclear Fe(II)/(III) complexes involves the reaction of Fe ($FeBr_2$/$FeCl_2 \cdot 4H_2O$/$Fe(NO_3)_3 \cdot 9H_2O$/$FeCl_3 \cdot 6H_2O$) with ligand in 2:1 M ratio in the desired solvent (CH_2Cl_2/MeOH/EtOH/THF) under magnetic stirring/refluxing conditions. Generally, a dry box or Schlenk techniques under a nitrogen atmosphere were used. Some of the recently synthesized Fe complexes are included in Fig. 4.2 with bis(phenolate) (Emami et al., 2019), terpyridine (Bocian et al., 2019), 1,3-oxazolidine-based ligands (Bikas et al., 2019), N′-(3-chlorobenzoyl)isonicotinohydrazide (Mardianingrum et al., 2019),

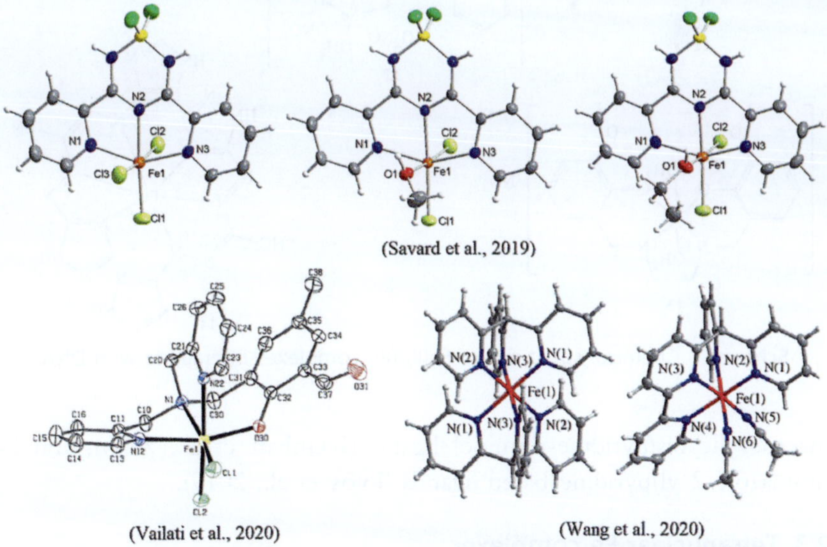

Figure 4.1 Crystal structures of mononuclear Fe(II)/(III) complexes. *(Reprinted from Savard et al. (2019) and Wang et al. (2020) with permission from Elsevier and Vailati et al. (2020) with permission from The Royal Society of Chemistry.)*

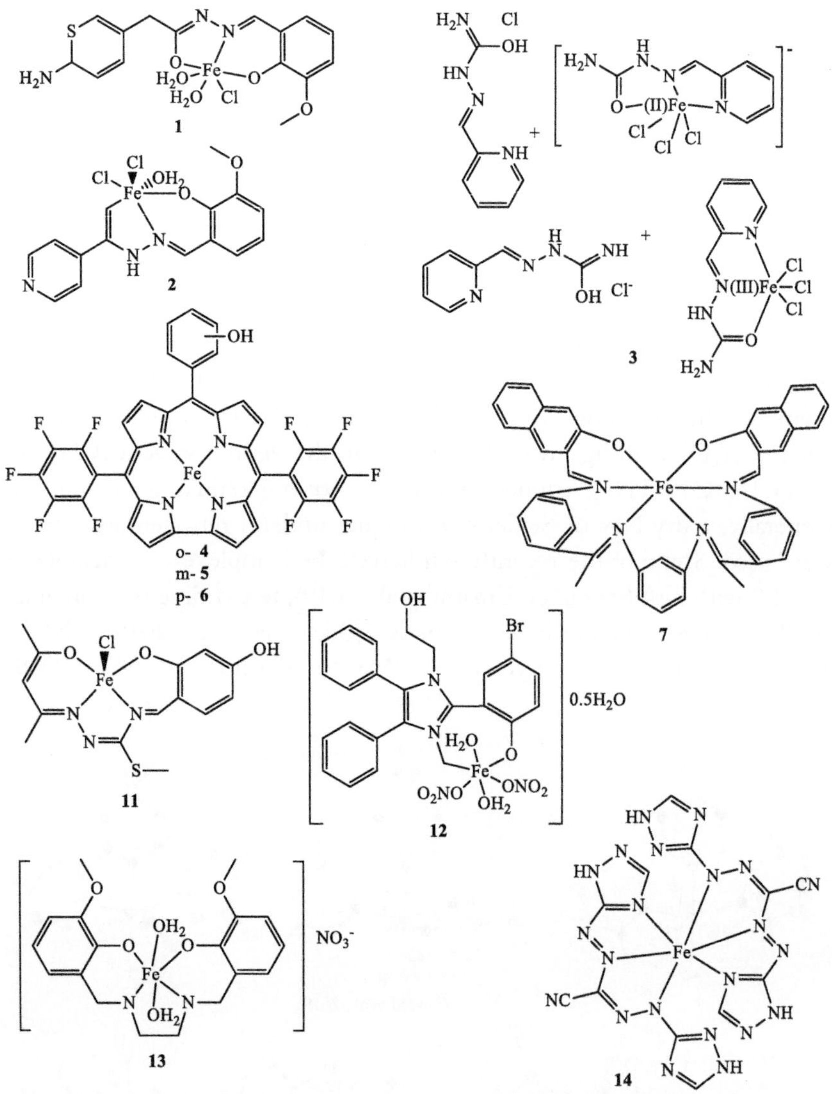

Scheme 1 Chemical structures of Fe(II)/(III) complexes interacting with DNA.

macrocyclic bis(pyridine-diimine) ligand (Reinhart et al., 2020), and 2-(imidazole-2-yl)pyridine-based ligands (Lvov et al., 2019).

2.3 Tetranuclear Fe complexes

Tetranuclear Fe complex involving N-2-pyrimidylimidoyl-2-pyrimidylamidine ligand framework in bidentate and tridentate

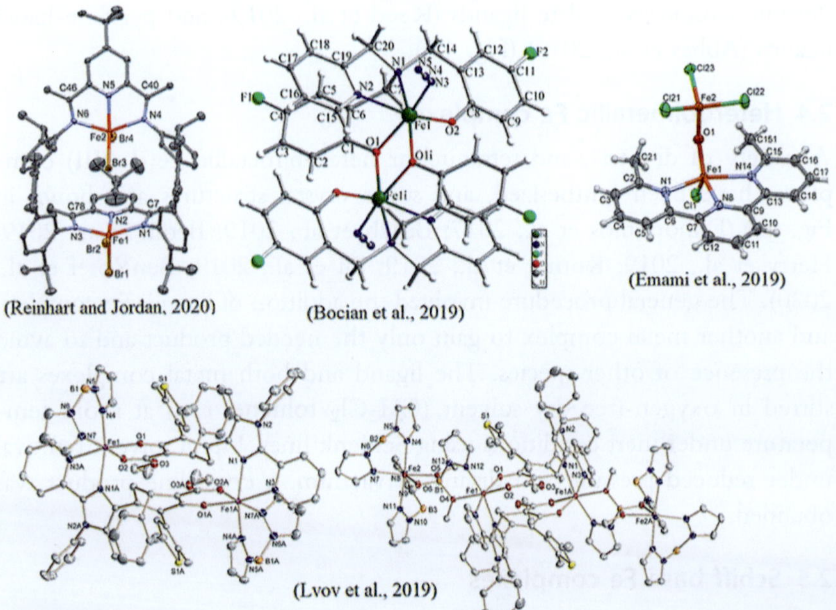

Figure 4.2 Crystal structures of dinuclear Fe(II)/(III) complexes. *(Reprinted from Lvov et al. (2019), BioMed Central; Emami et al. (2019) with permission from Elsevier; Bocian et al. (2019) with permission from The Royal Society of Chemistry; Reinhart and Jordan (2020) with permission from The American Chemical Society.)*

coordination sites with the N-imidoylamidine ligands was recently synthesized by Castañeda (Castañeda et al., 2019). The synthetic procedure involved stirring a solution of $FeCl_4$ in DMSO, layered on top of a solution of ligand[2] in chloroform (metal and ligand in 2:1 M ratio) yielding black needle-like crystals, which were filtered, washed with $CHCl_3$, and dried in vacuo.

In another procedure, the ligand was refluxed in acetonitrile, then iron(II) perchlorate hexahydrate was added, and the resultant mixture was stirred overnight. To this, toluene was added by the vapor diffusion method, yielding the crude product as a precipitate, which was recrystallized in nitromethane and vapor diffusion of toluene (Tanaka et al., 2020). Shiga et al. developed a simpler method by heating a solution of ligand, $Fe(BF_4)_2 \cdot 6H_2O$, and trimethylamine in acetonitrile yielding the crystals of tetranuclear Fe complex upon o-xylene diffusion (Shiga et al., 2019). Other recent synthetic complexes include complexes bearing 1,10-phenanthroline (phen) and 2,2′-bipyridine (bpy) ligands (Lutsenko et al., 2019), (tertbutylamino)pyrazolate ligands (Reed et al., 2019), and pyridine-based ligands (Abbas et al., 2019) (Fig. 4.3).

2.4 Heterobimetallic Fe complexes

A variety of di-, tri-, and tetranuclear heterobimetallic Fe(II)/(III) complexes have been synthesized, and some crystal structures are shown in Fig. 4.4 (Danopoulos et al., 2017; Beach et al., 2019; Bedin et al., 2019; Herry et al., 2019; Kumar et al., 2019; Sil et al., 2019; BenYosef et al., 2020). The general procedure involved the addition of ligand, Fe complex, and another metal complex to gain only the needed product and to avoid the presence of other species. The ligand and both metal complexes are stirred in oxygen-free dry solvent (CH_2Cl_2/toluene, etc.) at room temperature under inert conditions using Schlenk lines. Upon solvent removal under reduced pressure and drying in vacuum, a crystalline product was obtained.

2.5 Schiff base Fe complexes

The Schiff bases are largely used as ligands with multifaceted applications in the area of coordination chemistry as they coordinate to the metal via imine nitrogen forming stable complexes. The imine bond is easy to form by condensation of primary/secondary amines with carbonyl groups. The Schiff base ligands have high coordination ability and very strong biologic properties (Shahraki et al., 2018). The most common Schiff bases have NO- and N_2O_2 donor atoms. Other mononuclear complexes derived from Schiff bases are reported in the literature (Abdel-Rahman et al., 2017; Anacona et al., 2019; Buldurun et al., 2020; Nemec et al., 2019; Scepaniak et al., 2019; Sen et al., 2020; Senthil Kumar et al., 2019).

The general synthetic procedure involved in the synthesis of Fe-Schiff base complexes involves in situ reaction of freshly synthesized Schiff base and $FeCl_3 \cdot 6H_2O$. Firstly, a methanol solution of the corresponding carbaldehyde is refluxed for approximately 30 min; to this, the methanolic solution of $FeCl_3 \cdot 6H_2O$ (1:1 M ratio) is added in situ, affording the desired Fe complex.

3. Methods of analysis

3.1 Absorption spectroscopy

The electronic absorption spectroscopy is a versatile technique to study the binding mode of the metal complexes to DNA helix or other proteins,

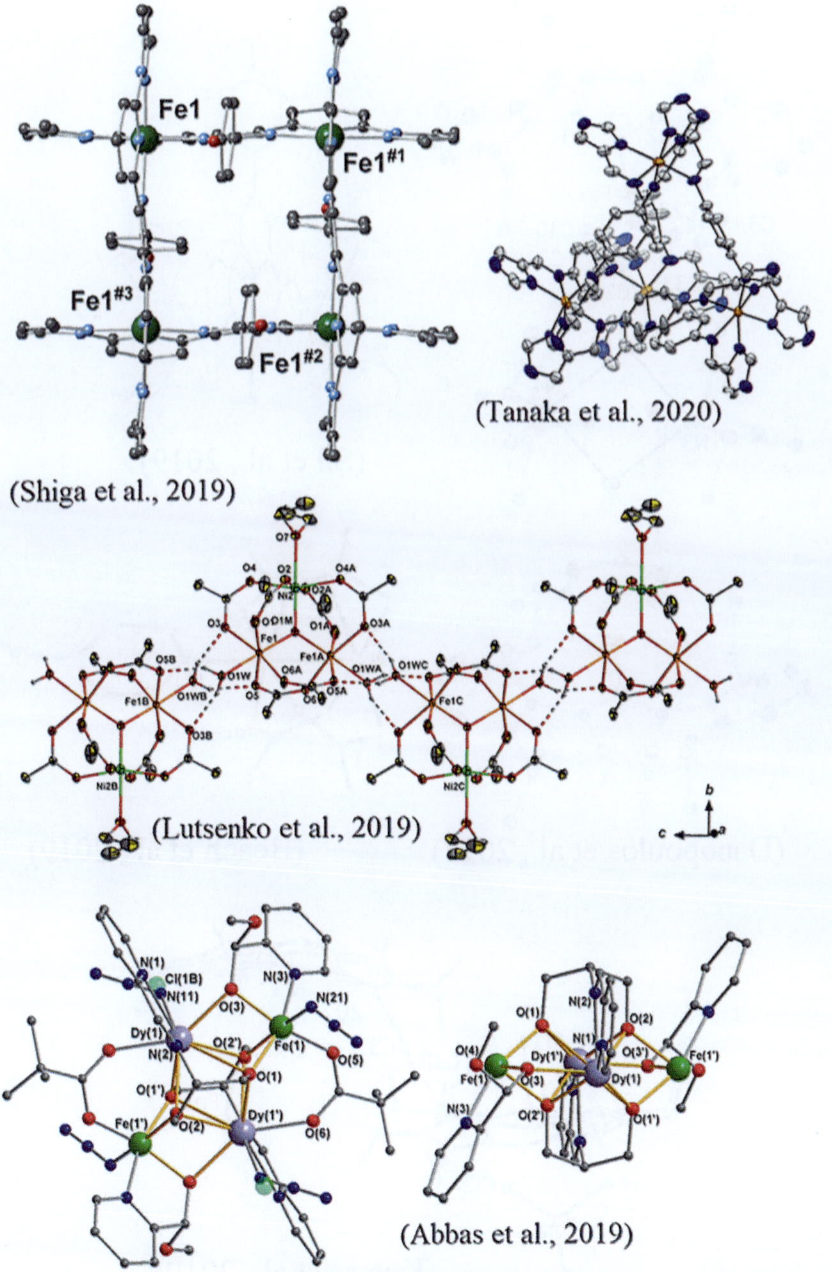

Figure 4.3 Crystal structures of tetranuclear Fe(II)/(III) complexes. *(Reprinted from Abbas et al. (2019); Lutsenko et al. (2019); Shiga et al. (2019); Tanaka et al. (2020) with permission from Elsevier.)*

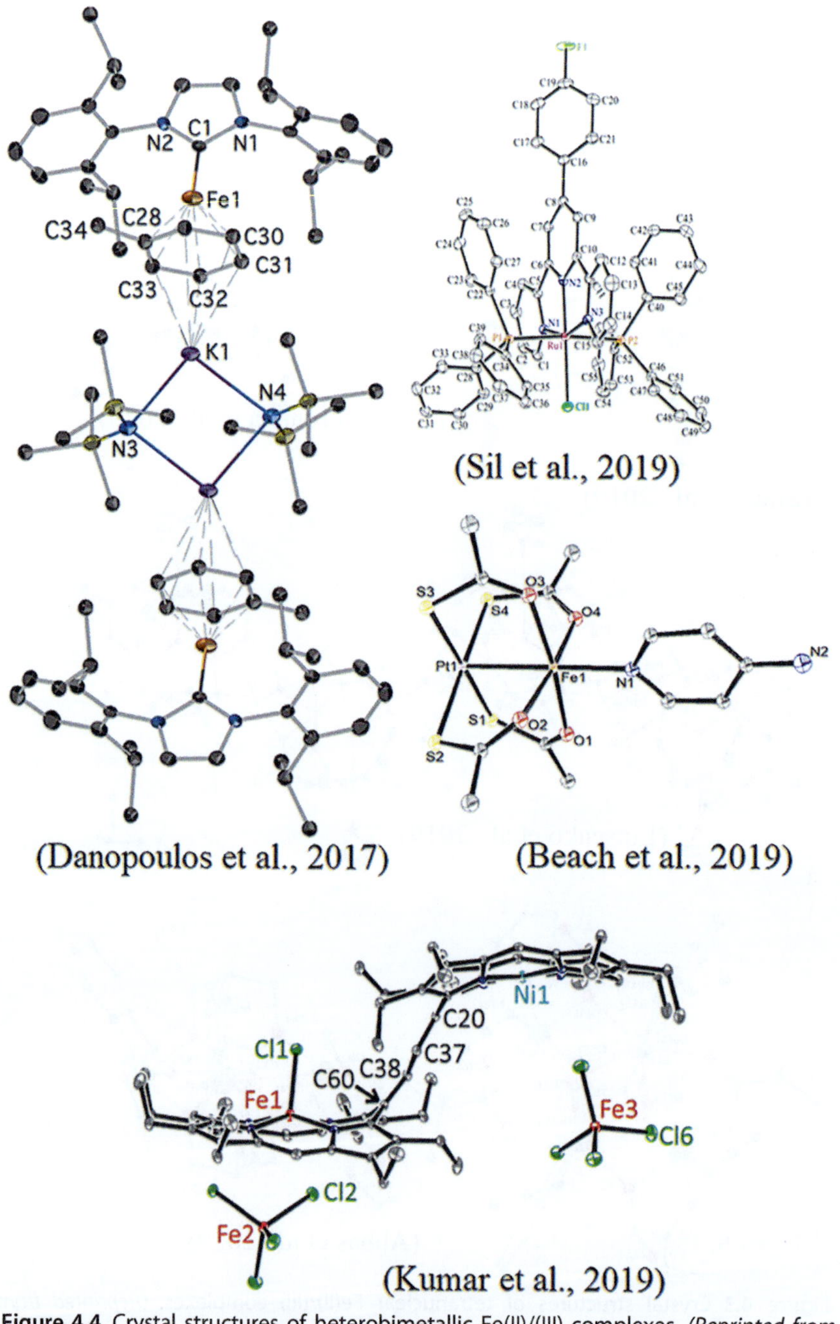

Figure 4.4 Crystal structures of heterobimetallic Fe(II)/(III) complexes. *(Reprinted from Kumar et al. (2019) with permission from The Royal Society of Chemistry; Danopoulos et al. (2017), The Royal Society of Chemistry Sil et al. (2019) with permission from The American Chemical Society; Beach et al. (2019) with permission from Elsevier.)*

accompanied by the absorbance changes and shifts in wavelength. λ_{max} of nucleic acid is in the range of 250-280 nm, depending on the nucleobases concentrations. Whereas, ε_{max} of the nucleic acid depends on the composition of the nucleobase. On the other hand, in proteins, the electronic absorption bands are due to the discrimination of many internal chromophoric groups. The aromatic amino acids accord to bands in the range of 255-300 nm. Human serum albumin (HSA) concentration was determined from absorption spectra, taking the absorbance of a solution of 1 mg/mL at λ_{max} 280 nm (Trp214). Binding of metal complexes to HSA can ascertain the properties of metal-complex protein complexes, by providing beneficial information on the structural features that in turn help in to elucidate the therapeutic effectiveness of metal-based drug candidates (Ascenzi et al., 2010). However, absorption of bovine serum albumin (BSA) at ~280 nm, arises as a result of all types of chromophores (Phe, Tyr, and Trp) (Naveenraj et al., 2010).

This technique involves the absorption titrations carried out on a UV-vis spectrophotometer with increasing nucleic acid concentrations while keeping the complex concentration constant. The variations in the absorbance spectra represent the binding mode. Hypochromism (decrease in absorbance) associates in common, intercalation binding mode attributable to strong stacking interactions between planar aromatic chromophore and DNA base pairs, whereas hyperchromism (increase in absorption) infers noncovalent interactions, predominantly electrostatic, groove binding, etc., occurring due to DNA double helix structural damage. The binding constant, K_b, is calculated using the Wolfe-Shimer Eq. (4.1), and Gibb's free energy values for complexes are calculated from Eq. (4.2) (Wolfe et al., 1987).

$$[B]/\varepsilon_a - \varepsilon_f = [B]/\varepsilon_b - \varepsilon_f + 1/K_b\ (\varepsilon_b - \varepsilon_f) \tag{4.1}$$

Where, [B] is the concentration of the target biomolecule (DNA or serum albumin [SA]); ε_a, ε_f, and ε_b are apparent (A_{abs}/[complex]) and free and bound complex extinction coefficients, respectively. In a plot of $[B]/\varepsilon_a - \varepsilon_f$ vs. [B] with a slope of $1/(\varepsilon_b - \varepsilon_f)$ and intercept of $1/K_b\ (\varepsilon_b - \varepsilon_f)$, K_b values were obtained by the ratio of slope to intercept.

$$\Delta G = -RT \ln K_b \tag{4.2}$$

Where, ΔG is Gibb's free energy change, R is 8.314 $Jmol^{-1}K^{-1}$ (gas constant), and T is the temperature, 298 K.

3.2 Fluorescence spectroscopy

Fluorescence spectroscopy, unlike absorption spectroscopy, is based on emission, and it is utilized in the identification of nucleic acid-complex interactions. Fluorescence methods have an upper hand owing to their highly sensitive nature, ease of applicability for efficient screening, and being comparatively inexpensive. The preferential biomolecule binding sites can be assessed by fluorescence quenching experiments. The fluorescence study of biomolecules needs extensive fluorescent labeling with a suitable fluorophore, e.g., DAPI, organic dyes, fluorescein, and EtBr (Michel et al., 2020). Tryptophan is the chief residue in SA proteins that gives rise to an emission spectrum upon excitation at 295 nm.

These experiments require the treatment of excess nucleic acid with a limited bound fluorophore. The quenching constant, K_{sv}, is obtained by using the Stern-Volmer Eq. (4.3) (Lakowicz et al., 1973).

$$Io / I = 1 + K_{sv} [Q] \tag{4.3}$$

Where, Io and I are the fluorescence intensities in the absence and presence of complex, respectively, and [Q] is the concentration of the quencher.

One of the most appropriate techniques for determining the interaction between metal-based drug candidates and nucleic acids and proteins is fluorescence spectroscopy (Zolfagharzadeh et al., 2014). This chapter extensively compiles the study of DNA and SA interactions of Fe(II)/(III) complexes by these two spectroscopic methods (Dávila−Rodríguez et al., 2018; Ghosh et al., 2019; Hu et al., 2019; Li et al., 2019; Sun et al., 2019; U-Wang et al., 2019; Wu et al., 2019; Carmona-Negrón et al., 2020; El-Shamy et al., 2020; Kongot et al., 2020).

3.3 Circular dichorism spectroscopy

Circular dichroism (CD) plays an important role in the study of biologic macromolecules secondary structure as it is a very sensitive technique, often used for monitoring even slight changes in the conformation of the protein upon binding to ligands (Yadav et al., 2019). The secondary structure of DNA could be altered upon the binding of the complex to DNA.

The CD spectrum of CT-DNA exhibits two bands—a positive band at 270 nm arising due to the base stacking interactions and a negative band at 245 nm attributed to the double-helical suprastructure of the polynucleotide; in a way that affords asymmetric environments for the nucleobases produced by the DNA double-helical structure, which is characteristic of B-DNA (Chatterjee et al., 2017). The DNA's secondary structure is altered upon binding to the metal-complex. In the CD spectrum, after the addition of the complex, little or no effect on the CD peak of DNA signifies simple electrostatic and groove-binding modes; however, the classical intercalative mode of binding enhances both positive and negative peaks additionally stabilizing the structure of B-DNA (Shahabadi et al., 2014).

The CD spectrum of native HSA exhibits two negative bands at 208 and 222 nm, which are characteristic of π-π^* and n-π^* transfer of the peptide bond in the α-helical structure of the protein (Rabbani et al., 2017). Besides, the change observed in the secondary structure of HSA after drug binding may be attributable to the destabilization of diverse interactive forces leading to disruption of interactive bonds that results in modification of secondary structure (Sudlow et al., 1976).

The intensity of the signal from the CD spectra is expressed as mean residue ellipticity (MRE) in degcm^2/dmol, defined according to Eq. (4.4) (Zaidi et al., 2013).

$$\mathrm{MRE} = \theta/(10 \cdot \mathrm{n} \cdot \mathrm{l} \cdot \mathrm{C_p}) \tag{4.4}$$

Where θ, n, l, and C_p are the observed CD (in millidegrees), number of amino acid residues (585 for HSA) (Wardell et al., 2002), optical path length of the cell (1 cm), and molar concentration of HSA, respectively. To calculate quantitative information on the percentage of changes in the α-helix content upon drug binding, the resulting MRE at 208 nm is then analyzed according to Eq. (4.5) (Chaves et al., 2018).

$$\alpha\text{-helix\%} = (-\mathrm{MRE}_{208} - 4000)/(33{,}000 - 4000) \times 100 \tag{4.5}$$

3.4 Molecular docking studies

The field of computer-aided drug design and discovery is a rapidly growing area that has seen many successes in the last few years (Jaiteh et al., 2018; Kumar and Kumar, 2019). Molecular docking is a kind of in silico modeling, which enables the documentation of novel therapeutic compounds by predicting the preferred binding orientation of ligand molecule to the receptor, ligand-target interactions at a molecular level, or describing structure-activity relationships (SARs) by using shape and electrostatic interactions to quantify it (Pagadala et al., 2017; Pinzi et al., 2019). It is a reliable method for ascertaining the position and affinity of a ligand at a receptor, generally a bio-macromolecule binding site (Roche et al., 2015). There are precisely two methodologies that are used for molecular docking: first is the shape complementarity approach and, second, the simulation approach (Tao et al., 2020). The shape complementarity approach utilizes the surface complementarity of the ligand and protein, while in the simulation approach, a simulation process calculates protein-ligand pair-binding energies (Li et al., 2013). This binding energy, also called docking score, obtained is generally in Kcal/mol and is associated with the free energies of binding, so the binding constant can be calculated from Eq. (4.6),

$$\Delta G = -R \times T \times \ln K_b \tag{4.6}$$

where R is the ideal gas constant (0.001986 kcal/mol/K), and T is the temperature in K.

These interaction forces are in general a combination of the flowing categories: (i) electrostatic forces (dipole-dipole, charge-dipole and charge-charge); (ii) van der Waals forces; (iii) steric forces arising due to entropy; and (iv) solvent-related forces, i.e., hydrogen bonding and hydrophobic interactions (Kumar et al., 2019). While working on the nucleic acids, rigid docking is suitable (Yan et al., 2013). In rigid docking the ligand and receptor conformation do not change. Fig. 4.5 displays different interaction

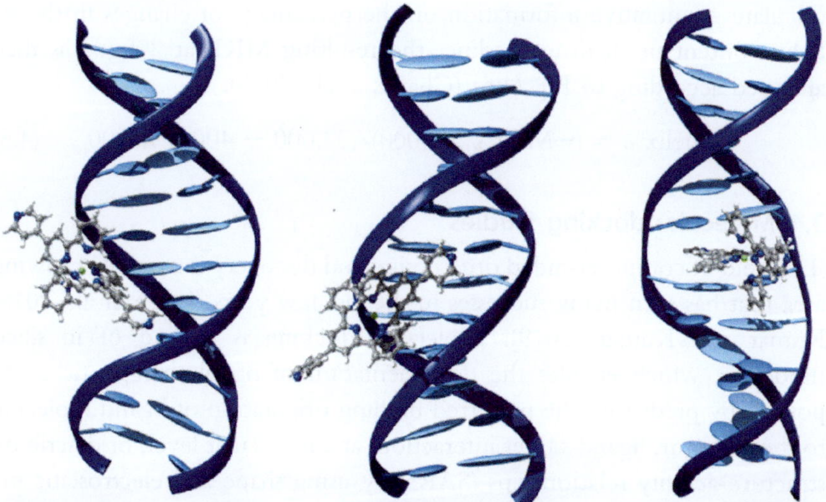

Figure 4.5 Different interaction modes of iron complexes. *(Reprinted from Gattuso et al. (2015).)*

modes of iron complexes to DNA, calculated by molecular docking (Gattuso et al., 2015). More extensive virtual screening methodologies have been developed that improved the docking-based ligand-target complex predictions (Genheden et al., 2015; Rastelli et al., 2019).

Several Fe(II)/(III) complexes have been docked with DNA and SAs to ascertain the mode of binding mode and binding propensity with the targets (Abu-Dief et al., 2020; Carmona-Negrón et al., 2020; El-Gammal et al., 2019; Hu et al., 2019; Kovalska et al., 2019; Kurt et al., 2020; Li et al., 2019; Martins et al., 2017; Rajaretnam et al., 2019; Rudolf et al., 2016).

4. Uses of metal complexes

4.1 DNA interacting iron complexes

Nucleic acids are considered a main class of biopolymers playing a crucial role in the central dogma; viz., DNA contains genetic information that can be transcribed into mRNA and consequently translated to form proteins (Yu et al., 2018). Fe is an element that has variable valences, and it is found in two chief oxidation states: ferrous form [Fe(II)], which is an essential constituent of hemoglobin used for oxygen transport, and ferric form [Fe(III)]. The interconversion of these two valences, i.e., capability of serving both as an electron donor and electron acceptor, executed through the gain or loss of an electron, respectively, renders this metal exclusive for many distinctive physiologic and metabolic pathways that aid in numerous biologic functions (Jia et al., 2017; Matos et al., 2019). Owing to the close proximity of iron complexes with some cellular biochemical pathways, they have been studied for their use as anticancer therapeutic agents. Fe salens can act as oxidation catalysts and thus can also cause oxidative damage and strand breaks in DNA (Herchel et al., 2009). Most Fe salens display a high propensity for DNA that can be further enhanced by introducing DNA recognition entities or positively charged substituents for additional electrostatic interaction with the phosphate groups in the DNA backbone (Erxleben, 2018). Keeping this in view, the study of DNA binding interactions of Fe(II)/(III) complexes becomes a basis for several forthcoming biomedical applications, including cancer chemotherapeutics. In right-handed double-helical B-DNA, the most common form found in nature, the stacking distance is about 10.5 base pairs per turn. This double-helix structure contains a major groove and minor groove. In B-DNA the major groove is wider than the minor groove (Barone et al., 2013). Fig. 4.6

displays different binding modes of ligands toward double-stranded DNA (Guo et al., 2016).

Gammal et al. reported the DNA interaction of a Schiff base hydrazone ligand, (Z)-2-(2-aminothiazol-4-yl)-N′-(2-hydroxy-3-methoxybenzylidene) acetohydrazide (L), and its Fe(III) chelate $[Fe(L)Cl(H_2O)_2]\cdot 3H_2O$ **1** (Scheme 1) (El-Gammal et al., 2019). The method used to study the DNA interaction of ligand and **1** was DNA methyl green colorimetric assay. The results revealed that the ligand ($IC_{50} = 41.5 \pm 2.4$ μg/mL) exhibited the highest DNA-binding potential compared with Fe (III) complex **1** ($IC_{50} = 63.0 \pm 3.5$ μg/mL).

Li et al. reported the interaction of Fe(III) polymer $(FeLCl_2\cdot H_2O)_n$ **2** derived from tridentate Schiff base ligand o-vanillin salicylhydrazone with herring sperm DNA (HS-DNA) by absorption and emission titration methods (Scheme 1) (Li et al., 2019). The results of which revealed that the complex interacted with HS-DNA through an intercalation mode. Fig. 4.7 displays the absorption spectra of the Fe(III) complex **2** in the absence and

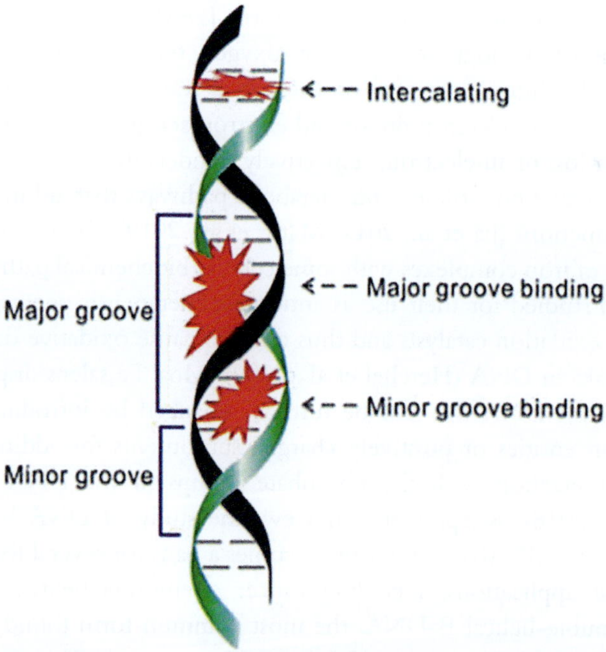

Figure 4.6 Different noncovalent binding modes of ligands toward double-stranded DNA. *(Reprinted from Guo et al. (2016) with permission from with permission from The Royal Society of Chemistry.)*

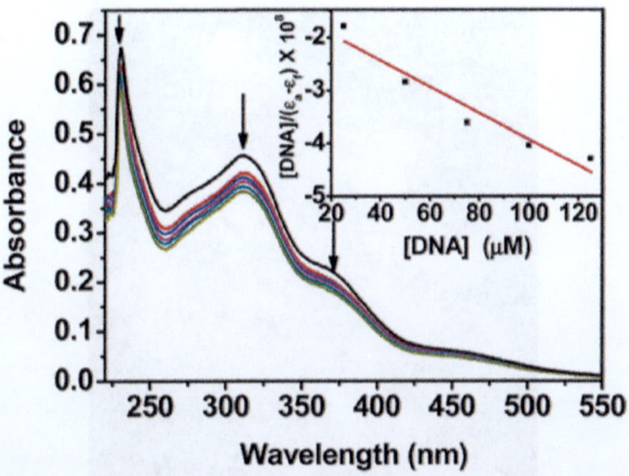

Figure 4.7 Electronic absorption spectra of **2** in the absence and presence of increasing amounts of HS-DNA. *(Reprinted from Li et al. (2019) with permission from The Royal Society of Chemistry.)*

presence of HS-DNA. The results revealed a hypochromism of 15.8% of the absorption band at 312 nm with a slight red shift (~3 nm) suggesting an intercalation mode involving π-π stacking interactions between the hydrazone moiety and DNA base pairs.

U-Wang et al. reported the DNA binding interaction of iron complex, $[(H_2PCS)\cdot Cl]^+[Fe(II)(PCS)Cl_3]^-\cdot[Fe(III)(PCS)Cl_3]\cdot(HPCS)\cdot(Cl)$, **3,** where PCS is pyridine-2-carboxaldehyde-semicarbazone (Scheme 1) (U-Wang et al., 2019). The absorption spectra of **3** in the presence of CT-DNA (0-52 μM) exhibited hypochromism at 307 nm and hyperchromism at 262 nm with an isosbestic point indicating the presence of two absorbing species in solution. The K_b value was calculated at 307 nm. These results were indicative of nonintercalative and groove or surface mode of binding (Devi et al., 2014; Nandy et al., 2014).

Sun et al. reported the CT-DNA binding of Fe(III) complexes, **4-6** derived from o-, m-, and p-monohydroxyl corrole (Scheme 1) (Sun et al., 2019). The absorption spectra **4-6** at a constant concentration with increasing concentrations of CT-DNA exhibited weak hypochromism and negligible bathochromic shift in the Soret bands, which is suggestive of external binding mode to CT-DNA.

Kurt et al. reported the DNA interaction mode of Fe(II) complex derived from Schiff base ligand, [1-(4-{[(3-hydroxynaphthalen-2-yl) methylidene]amino}phenyl)ethan-1-one, **7** (Scheme 1) (Kurt et al., 2020). The DNA binding nature of **7** was investigated by molecular docking

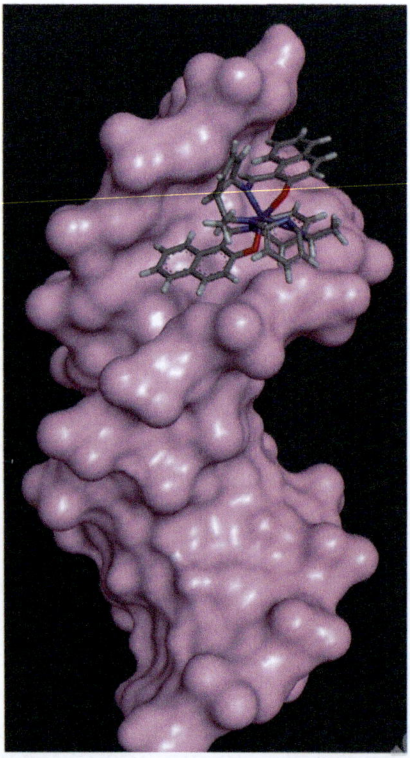

Figure 4.8 Binding mode of complex **4**. DNA is displayed as surface, and complex **4** is displayed as stick ($\Delta G = -6.67$ kcal/mol). *(Reprinted from Kurt et al. (2020) with permission from Elsevier.)*

studies. The results suggested that the Fe(II) complex **7** binds to DNA in the minor groove with a binding score of −6.67 kcal/mol (Fig. 4.8).

Wu et al. reported DNA binding propensities of three iron(III) complexes, namely, $[Fe(L^1)_2]Cl$ (**8**), $[Fe(L^2)_2]\bullet FeCl_4$ (**9**), and $[Fe(L^3)(HL^3)_2]\bullet(FeCl_4)_2\bullet(CH_3OH)$ (**10**) (HL^1 = N′-(4-oxothiazolidin-2-ylidene)picolinohydrazonamide), HL^2 = 2-(2-(1-(Pyridin-2-yl)ethylidene)hydrazono) thiazolidin-4-one, HL^3 = 3-ethyl-2-(2-(1-(Pyridin-2-yl)ethylidene)hydrazono)thiazolidin-4-one (Fig. 4.9) (Table 4.1) (Wu et al., 2019). Fig. 4.10 shows the absorption spectral changes with increasing concentrations of CT-DNA. The results revealed the maximum absorbance at 241-243 nm in the absence of CT-DNA, attributable π-π* electron transition of the aromatic structure of ligands. With incremental amounts of CT-DNA to **10**, the band showed hypochromism with a slight blue shift of 1 nm. The K_b values are represented in Table 4.3. While, on the other hand, two

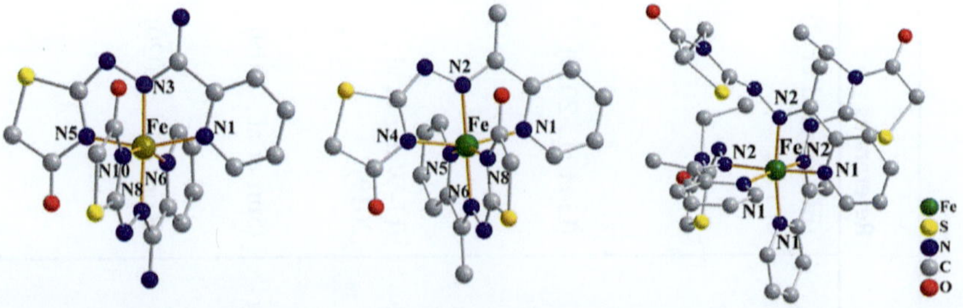

8 9 10

Figure 4.9 Crystal structures of complexes **8-10**. *(Reprinted from Wu et al. (2019) with permission from The Royal Society of Chemistry.)*

Table 4.1 Absorbance spectral changes of complexes **8-10** (Wu et al., 2019).

Complex	Changes in absorptivity	$\Delta\varepsilon$ (%) $M^{-1}cm^{-1}$	K_b 10^4 (M^{-1})
8	Hypochromism	10.4	3.81
9	Hypochromism	10.3	4.32
10	Hypochromism	6.1	4.21

With permission from The Royal Society of Chemistry.

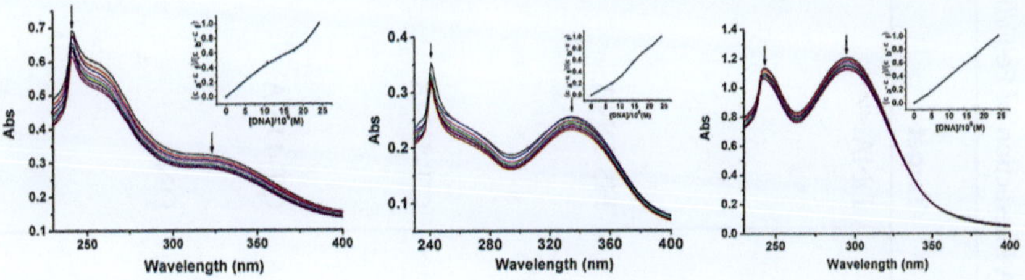

8 9 10

Figure 4.10 Absorption spectra of complexes **8-10** in the absence (*black line*) and presence of increasing amounts of CT-DNA at room temperature in Tris-HCl/NaCl buffer (pH = 7.2). *(Reprinted from Wu et al. (2019) with permission from The Royal Society of Chemistry.)*

bands of **8** and **9** displayed hypochromism without any shift in the absorption bands. The results were indicative of nonintercalation, as intercalation was not possible due to presence of nonplanar ligands.

Kaya et al. reported thiosemicarbazone-derived Fe(III) complex **11** and its binding to CT-DNA (Scheme 1) (Kaya et al., 2019). Upon increasing concentrations of CT-DNA, the absorption intensity of the band at 278.8 nm of complex **11** was increased; i.e., hyperchromism was observed

Table 4.2 Summary of the modes of DNA interaction of Fe(II)/(III) complexes.

Complex	Geometry	Target	Characterization techniques	Mode of interaction	References
1	Octahedral	DNA	Single X-ray crystal diffraction, NMR, IR, elemental analysis, magnetic and UV-vis measurements	–	(El-Gammal et al., 2019)
2	Octahedral	HS-DNA	Single X-ray crystal diffraction, NMR, IR, UV-vis, elemental analysis, ESI-MS	Intercalation mode involving π–π stacking interactions	(Li et al., 2019)
3	Distorted octahedral	CT-DNA	Single X-ray crystal diffraction, IR, UV-vis, magnetic moment	Nonintercalative and groove or surface mode	(U-Wang et al., 2019)
4-6	Square planar geometry	CT-DNA	NMR, HRMS-ESI-MS, FT-IR, UV-vis	External binding mode	(Sun et al., 2019)
7	Octahedral	DNA	^{1}H NMR, FTIR, UV-vis, elemental analysis, thermal analyses, magnetic susceptibility spectral data	Minor groove binding	(Kurt et al., 2020)

8-10	Distorted octahedral	CT-DNA	Single X-ray crystal diffraction, NMR, FTIR, UV-vis, elemental analysis	Nonintercalation	(Wu et al., 2019)
11	Distorted square pyramidal	CT-DNA	NMR, IR, UV-vis, elemental analysis	Intercalation	(Kaya et al., 2019)
12	Distorted octahedral	CT-DNA	NMR, UV-vis, elemental analysis, IR, thermogravimetric analyses, molar conductance, magnetic susceptibility measurements	Intercalation via $\pi \rightarrow \pi^*$ stacking interaction	(Abu-Dief et al., 2020)
13	Octahedral	CT-DNA	Single X-ray crystal diffraction, UV-vis, elemental analysis, FTIR	Intercalation	(Ghosh et al., 2019)
14	Octahedral	CT-DNA	Single X-ray crystal diffraction, NMR, IR, UV-vis, elemental analysis, ESI-MS	Intercalation	(Martins et al., 2017)

Continued

Table 4.2 Summary of the modes of DNA interaction of Fe(II)/(III) complexes.—cont'd

Complex	Geometry	Target	Characterization techniques	Mode of interaction	References
15	-	HS-DNA	Elemental analysis, UV-vis, IR, FAB-mass, EPR, spectral studies, electrochemical studies	Intercalation	(Gubendran et al., 2017)
16-19	Distorted octahedral	CT-DNA	NMR, FTIR, UV-vis, elemental analysis	Nonclassical intercalation or electrostatic interactions	(Dávila-Rodríguez et al., 2018)
20-22	Distorted octahedral	CT-DNA	Single X-ray crystal diffraction, NMR, IR, UV-vis, elemental analysis	Electrostatic interactions	(Takarada et al., 2017)

Table 4.3 Summary of the modes of Fe(II)/(III) complexes interacting with HSA and BSA.

Complex	Geometry	Target	Characterization techniques	Mode of interaction	References
23	Octahedral	BSA	NMR, ESI-MS, elemental analysis, ATR-IR, UV-vis	In one active site of BSA	(Kongot et al., 2019b)
24, 25	Six-coordinated	HSA	NMR, FTIR, UV-vis, elemental analysis, ESI-MS	Stronger binding in domains of HSA	(Matos et al., 2019)
26	Seven-coordinated	BSA	UV-vis, elemental analysis	Electrostatic mode of interaction	El-Shamy et al., 2020
27-29	Six-coordinated	HSA and BSA	-	Site 1 located in protein subdomain IIA	(Kovalska et al., 2019)
30-32	Distorted octahedral geometry	BSA	Single X-ray crystal diffraction, elemental analysis, NMR, FTIR, UV-vis	Static quenching mechanism	(Raj et al., 2019)
33	Distorted four-coordinate square planar geometry	BSA	NMR, IR, elemental analysis, UV-vis	Binding in domains of BSA	(Rudolf et al., 2016)

accompanying a red shift (bathochromism). These results were suggestive of the combination of covalent and noncovalent intercalative binding mode to CT-DNA due to the insertion of the planar moiety of **11** in between the adjacent DNA base pair. This hyperchromism is due to the damage of DNA double helix structure after intercalation with complex **11** involving a strong stacking interaction between chromophore backbone of the ligand and the DNA base pairs (Shahabadi et al., 2011).

Abu-Dief et al. reported Fe(III) complex [Fe(MSEB)$(NO_3)_2(H_2O)_2$], **12**, derived from substituted aryl imidazole ligand (MSEB) and its interaction with CT-DNA via various biophysical methods (Scheme 1) (Abu-Dief et al., 2020). The UV-vis absorption spectra associated with the binding interaction of **12** with CT-DNA revealed hypochromism, which was indicative of the intercalation mode of interaction. This could be attributable to strong π-π^* stacking interaction between the aromatic moiety of the imidazole ligand of **12** and DNA base pairs. The K_b value was calculated to be 4.49×10^5 M^{-1} suggesting a strong interaction with CT-DNA.

Ghosh et al. reported Fe(III) complex **13** derived from N,N′-bis(O-vanillinidene)ethylenediamine (O-VEDH$_2$) Schiff base ligand (Scheme 1) (Ghosh et al., 2019). The absorption spectra of complex **13** exhibited hypochromism with a slight shift in the wavelength, which was indicative of binding to CT-DNA through intercalation owing to strong stacking interaction between ligand moiety of **13** and DNA base pairs (Fig. 4.11). The binding constant, K_b, was determined to be 3.77×10^3 M^{-1} suggesting a strong binding affinity.

Martins et al. reported the binding interaction of previously synthesized Fe(III) complex [Fe(κN3-HL)$_2$] (**14**), where HL = (1E,1E)-N′,2-di(1H-1,2,4-triazol-3-yl)diazenecarbohydrazonoyl cyanide (Scheme 1) (Martins et al., 2016, 2017). Fig. 4.12 displays the changes in the absorption spectra of **14** that revealed hypochromism suggestive of an intercalative mode of binding, as intercalation happens due to π-π stacking between aromatic groups and the base pairs of the DNA ($K_b = 1.98\ [\pm\ 0.26] \times 10^5$/M). The aromatic phenyl rings could stack in between the DNA base pairs, so intercalation binding mode was possible.

Gubendran et al. reported the HS-DNA binding interaction studies by absorption titrations, cyclic voltammetric studies, and CD studies of one Fe(II) complex of the type [Fe(L_2)H_2OCl], **15**, along with other metal complexes where L = 2,2′-(1E,1′E)-(3-(2-hydroxybenzylidene)-pentane-2,4-diylidene)bis(azan-1-yl-1idene)diphenol (Scheme 2) (Gubendran et al.,

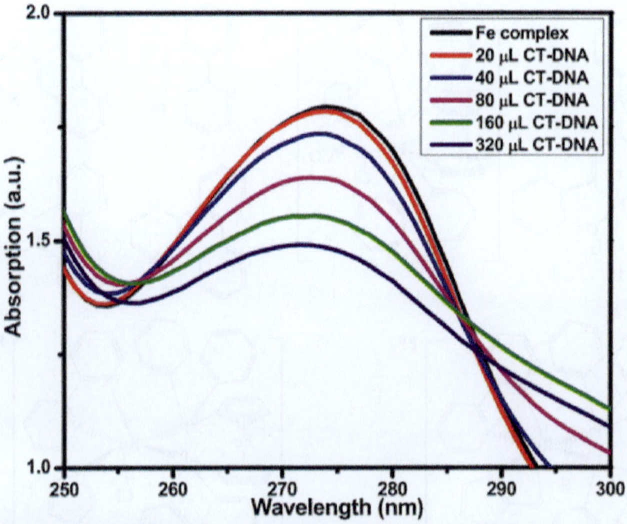

Figure 4.11 Absorption spectra of complex **13** in the absence and presence of CT-DNA. *(Reprinted from Ghosh et al. (2019), American Chemical Society.)*

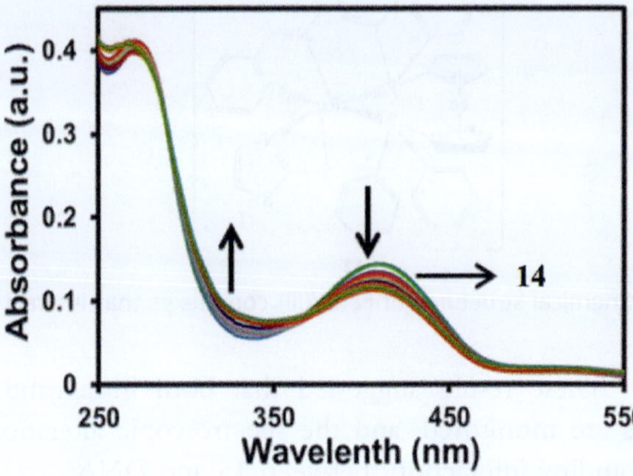

Figure 4.12 Absorption spectra of complex **14** in the absence and presence of increasing amounts of CT-DNA at 25°C in 5 mM Tris-HCl/50 mM NaCl buffer (pH = 7.5). *(Reprinted from Martins et al. (2017) with permission from The Royal Society of Chemistry.)*

2017). The electronic absorption titration of **15** in the presence of increasing amounts of DNA buffer was performed using a fixed metal complex concentration (20 μM) to which increments of the HS-DNA was added (0-160 μM) (Fig. 4.13). The results exhibited a hypochromism of 23% accompanied by a red shift of 8 nm with a binding constant value of

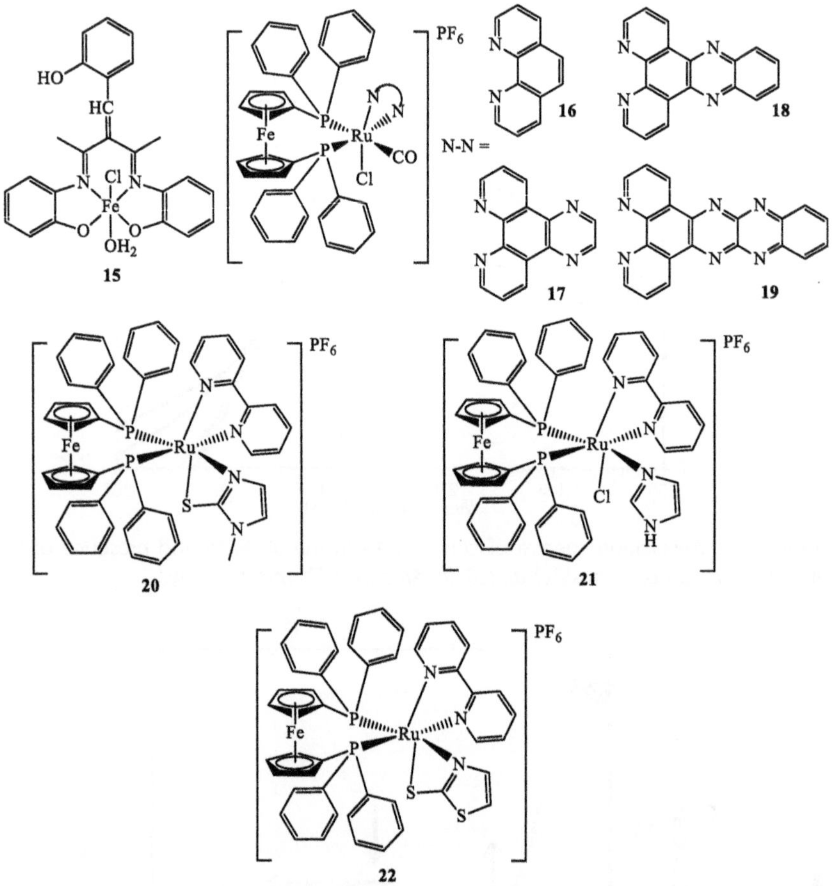

Scheme 2 Chemical structures of Fe(II)/(III) complexes that interact with DNA.

2.1×10^4/M. These results suggested that both intraligand and charge transfer bands are monitored, and the spectroscopic alterations suggested intercalative binding interactions between **15** and DNA.

Dávila-Rodríguez et al. reported the interaction studies of carbonyl heterobimetallic compounds of Ru(II)/Fe(II) containing polypyridyl ligands, with general formula ct-[RuCl(CO)(N-N)(dppf)]PF_6, N-N = phen, **16**; dpq, **17**; dppz, **18**; dpqQX, **19** with CT-DNA (Scheme 2) (Dávila–Rodríguez et al., 2018). The absorption titrations experiments were performed to determine the DNA interaction of complexes **16-19,** but due to the overlapping of the electronic transitions of DNA with those of the complexes, the absorption titrations, at this case study, do not offer useful information. Hence, complex-DNA interactions were studied by

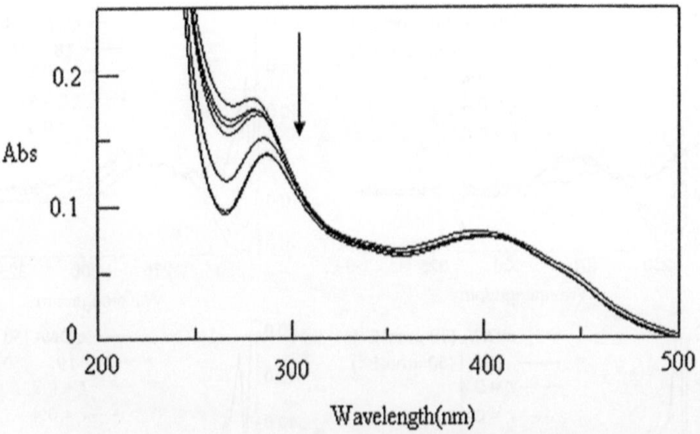

Figure 4.13 Absorption spectra of **15** in the absence and presence of increasing amounts of DNA in Tris-HCl buffer upon addition of DNA. *(Reprinted from Gubendran et al. (2017) with permission from Elsevier.)*

CD and viscosity measurements. CD is a highly sensitive technique that is used to identify the changes in the secondary structure of DNA as the result of drug-DNA interactions (Kelly et al., 2005). A typical CD spectrum of CT-DNA shows a positive base stacking band at 275 nm and a negative right-handed helicity band at 248 nm. Any changes in these two bands are indicative of the mode of binding of complex to B-conformer of DNA. Fig. 4.14 displays the CD spectra of CT-DNA with increasing concentrations of **16-19** up to a molar ratio complex/DNA (r_i): of 0.6. The presence of **16-19** does not have a significant effect on the positive band, and the observed changes in the negative band cannot be interpreted as a conformational change, due to the interference promoted by electronic transitions in this region centered mainly at the polypyridyl ligands (Poulsen et al., 2016). Hence, the type of interactions exhibited by **16-19** are typical for nonclassical intercalation or electrostatic interactions.

Takarada et al. reported the CT-DNA binding studies of three Ru- and Fe-based complexes, viz., [Ru(MIm) (bipy) (dppf)]PF_6, **20**, [RuCl(Im) (bipy) (dppf)]PF_6, **21**, and [Ru(tzdt) (bipy) (dppf)]PF_6, **22** (Scheme 2) (Takarada et al., 2017). The absorption spectral changes upon increasing amounts of CD-DNA with **20-22** revealed that all the complex band changes are at around 301 nm, which could be attributed to an intraligand π - π^* transition, and they showed very weak hypochromism for **20** and **21** but stronger for **22**. These results were suggestive of electrostatic interaction with CT-DNA.

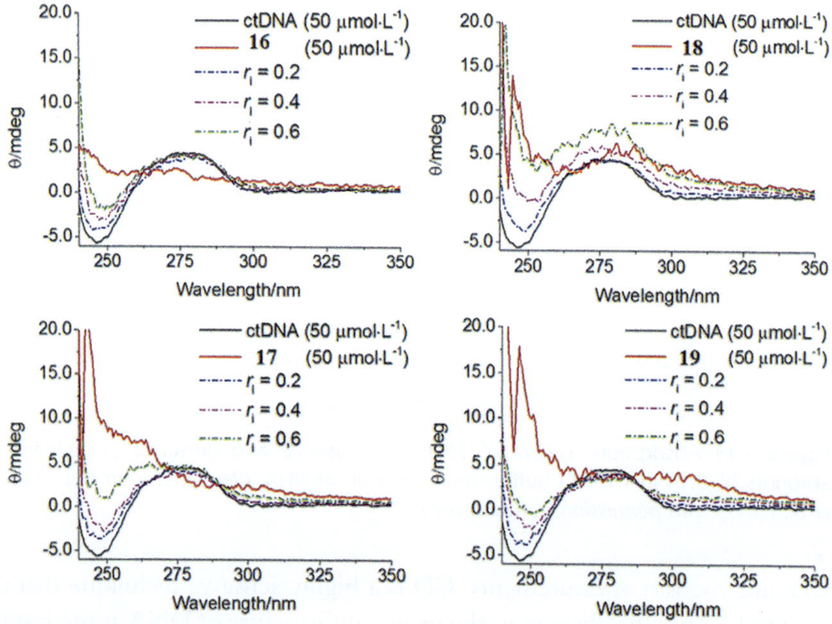

Figure 4.14 Circular dichroism spectra of a solution of CT-DNA in Trizma buffer, pH 7.4, incubated 18 h at 310 K, with complexes **16-19** at different [complex]/[DNA] ratios. *(Reprinted from Dávila–Rodríguez et al. (2018) with permission from Elsevier.)*

The geometries, characterization techniques, and the modes of binding of Fe(II)/(III) complexes to DNA are summarized in Table 4.2.

4.2 RNA-interacting iron complexes

RNA offers a far greater extensive structural diversity compared with DNA. RNA is an exciting molecule, for which several functions are continuously revealed (Cech et al., 2014; Sharp, 2009). It is transcribed as a single strand, and it folds in a complex three-dimensional structure to minimize its total energy. In conjugation with double-helical structures, it forms various nonduplex secondary structures that include bulges, hairpins, and junctions (Fig. 4.15). On the contrary, the interaction of iron complexes with RNA has been much less investigated. Although RNA is less explored as a suitable target for metal complexes, it is rich in noncanonical structures compared with DNA. In addition to the previously discovered messenger RNA, ribosomal RNA, and transfer RNA, permitting the transfer of the genetic information from DNA to proteins, an expansive range of noncoding RNAs have been recognized in the last decades (Alberti

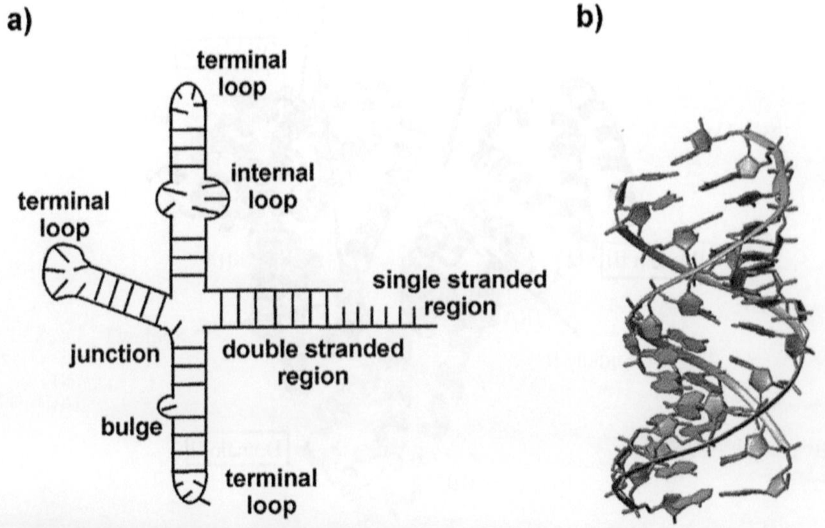

Figure 4.15 (A) Schematic representation of RNA secondary structural elements; (B) A-RNA double helix. *(Reprinted from Alberti et al. (2016) with permission from Elsevier.)*

et al., 2016). In accordance with this, some small molecules have been developed that target RNAs (Disney, 2013; Guan et al., 2012; Velagapudi et al., 2015). Iron complexes, by and large, are remarkably investigated for their DNA-binding ability (Komor et al., 2013; Liu et al., 2011; Pages et al., 2015), but their RNA-binding properties still remain rather unexplored. There is a need to explore the new and existing complexes for their potential to interact with RNA.

4.3 Other biomolecule-interacting iron complexes

Serum proteins play an imperative role in the transport of drug molecules through the blood and membrane barriers to their targeted sites of action (Kongot et al., 2019b; Liu et al., 2019) SAs, viz., human serum albumin and bovine serum albumin, are a chief transport protein of blood plasma, and few definite structural differences could act as markers of many pathologic processes, namely albumin glycation in diabetes (Arasteh et al., 2014), oxidation in liver disease (Ivanov et al., 2002), N-terminal alterations in ischemia, and allosteric alterations by tumor metabolites in cancer (Moergel et al., 2012).

Both BSA and HSA are heart-shaped proteins, having very similar crystal structures (Patel et al., 2015). The HSA molecule is comprised of three helical domains (I, II, and III), each consisting of two subdomains (A

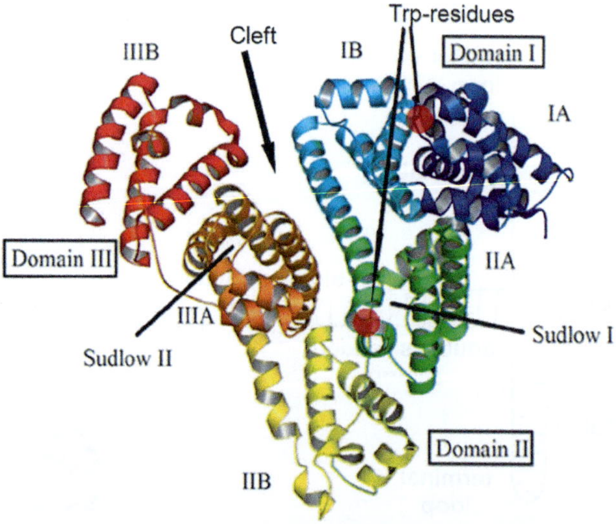

Figure 4.16 Structure of the albumin molecule. *(Reprinted from Kovalska et al. (2019), The Royal Society of Chemistry.)*

and B; Fig. 4.16). The drug-binding site 1, also called Sudlow's I, is a binding pocket within a core in the subdomain IIA. On the other hand, drug binding site 2, also known as Sudlow's II, is situated in subdomain IIIA (Majorek et al., 2012; Sand et al., 2015). Regardless of the structural similarity of these SAs, they own definite regions with significant differences in the sequences of the amino acids, with the BSA molecule being less conformationally flexible compared with the HSA molecule (Akdogan et al., 2012). BSA comprises three types of intrinsic fluorophores containing two residues of tryptophan (trp), which can be quenched (Hu et al., 2019). The mechanistic study of drug interaction with SAs has engrossed the attention of a great number of researchers (Sharif-Barfeh et al., 2017). Any changes in the properties of these amino acid residues can be directly correlated to the dynamics and structure of the protein.

The interaction between drug and protein is the key factor to delineate the pharmacologic properties of drug candidates. This is due to the fact that the delivery and uptake of organic and inorganic metal-based drugs in the body are connected with their interactions with the plasma protein (Hu et al., 2010). The drug efficacy in therapeutic applications may be improved based on its toxicity and deliverances in plasma proteins (Hu et al., 2010). Investigation on the protein-binding activities of drugs is essentially important and helpful in drug design and therapy (Martins et al., 2017; Nicoletti et al., 2008).

Kongot et al. reported the binding of Fe(III) complex [Fe(OH_2) (OMe) L_2], **23**, with BSA (where L = H_2hpdbal-sbdt) (Scheme 3) (Kongot et al., 2019a). Fig. 4.17 represents the fluorescence emission spectra of BSA at 280 nm upon the concomitant addition of **23**. A quenching in the fluorescence was observed, and from the Stern-Volmer's plot, it was confirmed that the quenching mechanism was static as the graph showed an upward

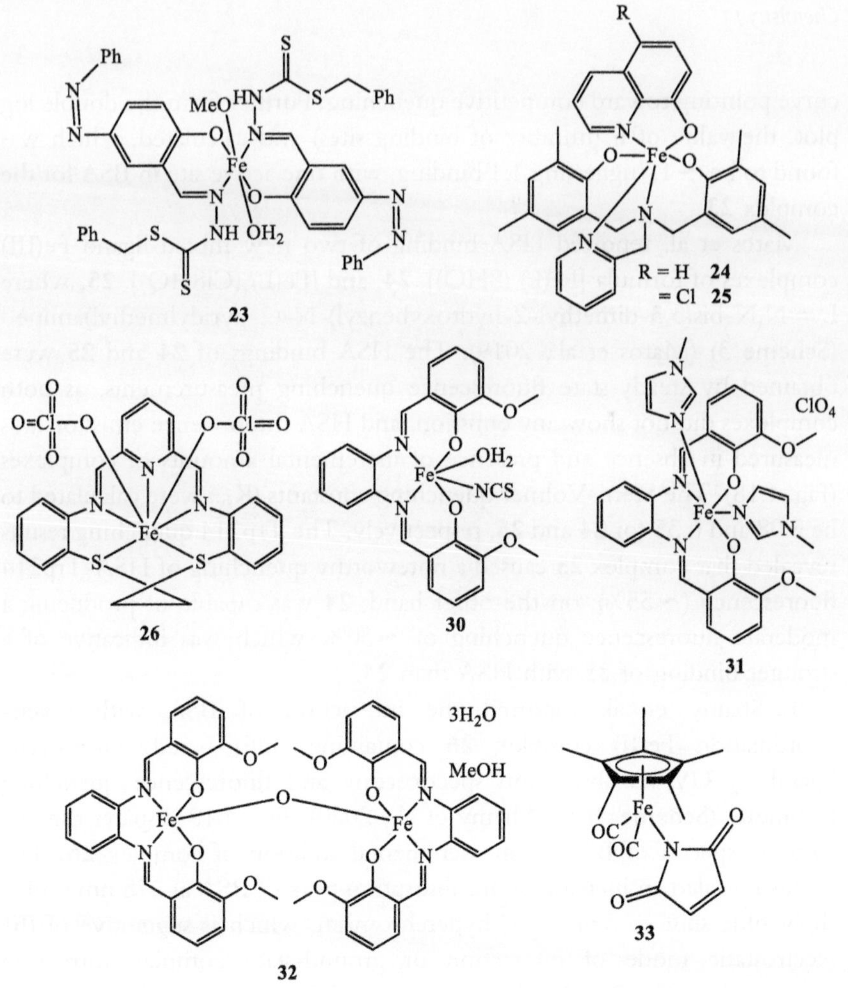

Scheme 3 Chemical structures of Fe(II)/(III) complexes interacting with serum albumins.

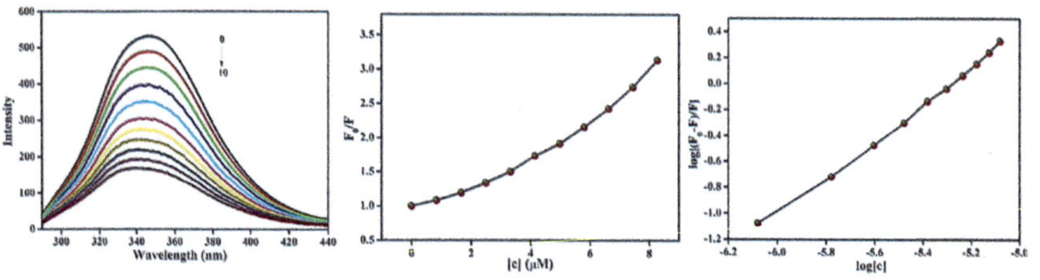

Figure 4.17 Fluorescence profile of BSA with the addition of **23** to visualize the extent of quenching; Stern-Volmer's quenching plot for BSA to calculate the quenching constants; double log graph for BSA to estimate the number of binding sites. *(Reprinted from Kongot et al. (2019b) with permission from The Royal Society of Chemistry.)*

curve pointing toward competitive quenching. Further from the double log plot, the value of n (number of binding sites) was calculated, which was found to be ~1, suggesting 1:1 binding, with one active site in BSA for the complex **23**.

Matos et al. reported HSA binding of two new mixed-ligand Fe(III) complexes of formula [Fe(L) (8HQ)], **24**, and [Fe(L) (Cl8HQ)], **25,** where L = N,N-bis(3,5-dimethyl-2-hydroxybenzyl)-N-(2-pyridylmethyl)amine (Scheme 3) (Matos et al., 2019). The HSA bindings of **24** and **25** were obtained by steady-state fluorescence quenching measurements, as both complexes did not show any emission, and HSA fluorescence emission was measured in absence and presence of incremental amounts of complexes (Fig. 4.18). The Stern-Volmer quenching constants (K_{sv}) were calculated to be 5.08 and 6.35 for **24** and **25**, respectively. The Trp214 quenching results revealed that complex **25** caused a noteworthy quenching of HSA-Trp214 fluorescence (~55%); on the other hand, **24** was capable of producing a moderate fluorescence quenching of ~30%, which was indicative of a stronger binding of **25** with HSA than **24**.

El-Shamy et al. reported the interaction of BSA with seven-coordination Fe(II) complex **26** containing sulfur-based macrocyclic ligand by UV-vis absorption spectroscopy and fluorescence quenching technique (Scheme 3) (El-Shamy et al., 2020). Fig. 4.19 displays the absorption spectra of BSA upon incremental addition of complex **26.** The results revealed an increase in the absorption peak of BSA at 278 nm with a slight blue shift of 5 nm, i.e., hyperchromism, which is suggestive of the electrostatic mode of interaction or ground-state complex formation (Kandagal et al., 2006). This is because BSA gives an absorbance at ~280 nm, due to several chromophores like Phe, Tyr, and Trp (Naveenraj

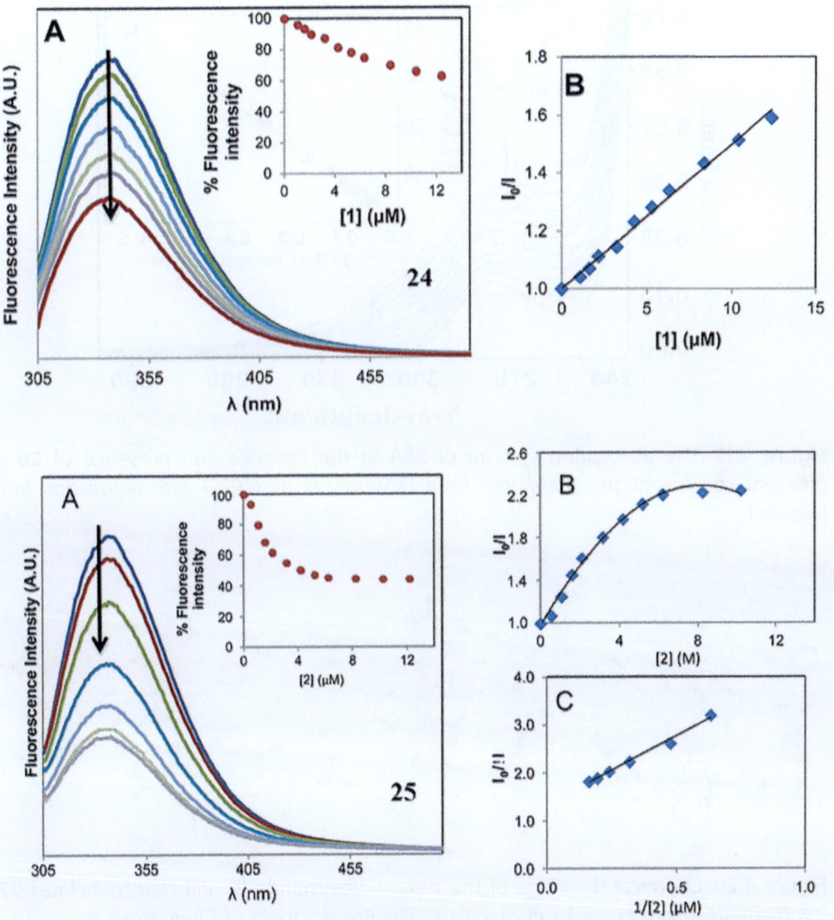

Figure 4.18 (A) Fluorescence emission spectra recorded at room temperature for solutions containing HSA and increasing amounts of **24** and **25**. (B) Stern-Volmer plot at $\lambda_{em} = 340$ nm. (C) Plot for the quenching of HSA in the presence of complex **25** obtained taking into account the accessible fraction of the tryptophan fluorophore. *(Reprinted from Matos et al. (2019) with permission from The Royal Society of Chemistry.)*

et al., 2010). Further, the quenching mechanism is discussed involving energy transfer from BSA to Fe(II) complex. These results were indicative of the interaction of BSA with **26** by mean of ground-state complex formation, and the quenching of the intrinsic fluorescence of BSA is attributed to an energy transfer from BSA to complex involving a static mode of quenching.

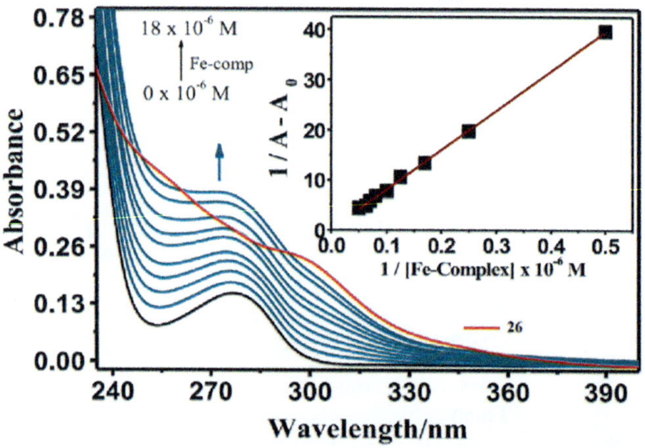

Figure 4.19 The absorption spectra of BSA in the absence and presence of **26** at different concentrations. *(Reprinted from El-Shamy et al. (2020) with permission from Elsevier.)*

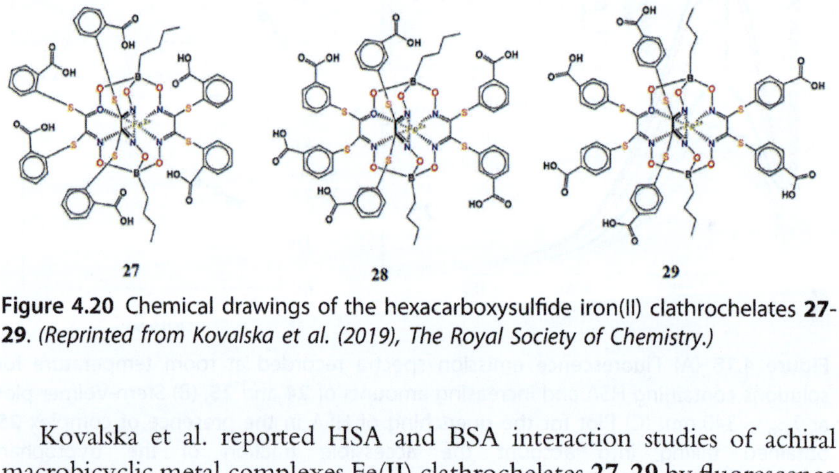

27 28 29

Figure 4.20 Chemical drawings of the hexacarboxysulfide iron(II) clathrochelates **27-29**. *(Reprinted from Kovalska et al. (2019), The Royal Society of Chemistry.)*

Kovalska et al. reported HSA and BSA interaction studies of achiral macrobicyclic metal complexes Fe(II) clathrochelates **27-29** by fluorescence quenching measurements and CD spectroscopy (Fig. 4.20) (Kovalska et al., 2019). Fig. 4.21 represents the Stern-Volmer quenching plots of protein fluorescence quenching intensities versus the clathrochelate-to-protein molar ratio. The results suggested complexes **27** and **28** exhibited similar fluorescence quenching patterns, while with complex **29** (para-substituted analog), the increase was more gradual. On the other hand, for HSA, the quenching patterns for **27-29** exhibited a similar pattern. The reason could be due to multiple quenching of two Trp residues in BSA and single quenching of one Trp residue in HSA. In addition to these results, the

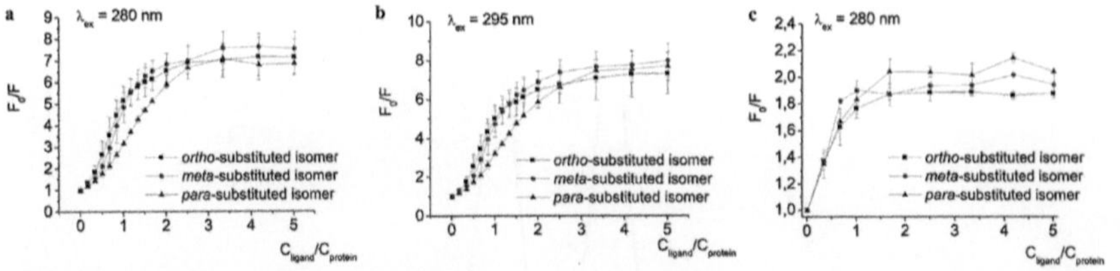

Figure 4.21 Stern-Volmer plots of fluorescence intensity quenching of BSA emission excited at 280 (A) and 295 (B) nm, as well as of HSA emission excited at 280 nm (C), by clathrochelates **27-29**. *(Reprinted from Kovalska et al. (2019), The Royal Society of Chemistry.)*

quenching of HSA and BSA fluorescence was found to be caused by the binding of **27–29** near Trp-213 and Trp-134 of BSA or Trp-214 of HSA, with preference at site 1 located in protein subdomain IIA.

Raj et al. used steady-state fluorescence quenching experiments to investigate the BSA binding of three Fe(III) complexes: [Fe(L) (H_2O) (NCS)], **30**, [Fe(L) (1-methylimidazole)$_2$]ClO_4, **31**, and [(L)Fe(μ-O)Fe(L)]$\cdot$ $3H_2O\cdot$MeOH, **32**, bearing N_2O_2-donor salphen Schiff base, L = N,N′-bis(3-methoxysalicylidene)phenylene-1,2-diamine (Scheme 3) (Raj et al., 2019). The fluorescence intensity of BSA was decreased progressively upon the addition of increasing amounts of **30-32**. The results revealed that all complexes display good binding affinity toward BSA with K_{sv} values of 1.61×10^5, 1.68×10^5, and 3.04×10^5/M for **30-32** respectively with static quenching mechanism.

Rudolf et al. reported the interaction of complex (η^5-Cp*) Fe(CO)$_2$(η^1-N-maleimidato), **33**, with HSA (Rudolf et al., 2016). To validate the binding of **33** with HSA, IR spectroscopy was carried out by spotting a small volume of solution on nitrocellulose discs and drying in the air (Fig. 4.22). It was observed that a set of two υ(CO) bands were observed for the HSA conjugates at 2029 and 1977 cm^{-1}, i.e., at the same position as the starting complex, confirming covalent binding of the complexes to the HSA.

Table 4.3 summarizes the geometries, characterization techniques, and the modes of binding of Fe(II)/(III) complexes to HSA/BSA.

5. Limitations

Although iron is beneficial at normal levels, its excess may be toxic because it is capable of catalyzing free radicals production and could damage several

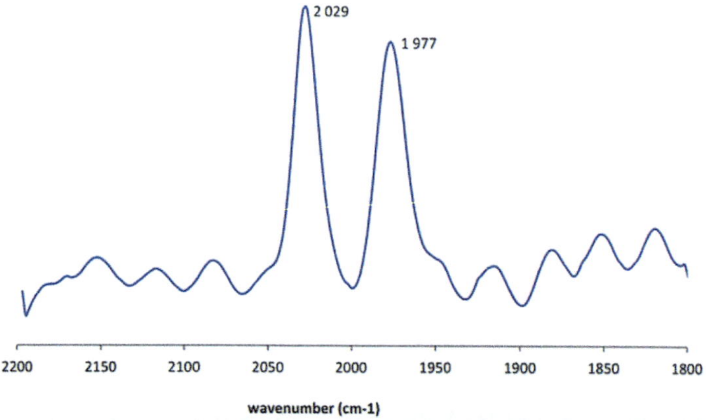

Figure 4.22 IR spectra of conjugates of HSA and **33**. An aqueous solution of conjugate was spotted on a 6-mm-diameter nitrocellulose disc and allowed to dry in the air. *(Reprinted from Rudolf et al. (2016) with permission from Elsevier.)*

cellular macromolecules. Regardless of iron's chemical advantages, it has some serious drawbacks: (i) Fe^{3+} insolubility and (ii) the generation of toxic hydroxyl radicals. Another major drawback is the absence of a common synthetic protocol toward Fe(II)/(III) complexes. Also, some SARs were established in some studies, yet there are no recognized general guidelines.

Reactive oxygen species (ROS) can be generated in reactions that are catalyzed by the presence of iron, and regardless of the complexity of ROS formation, free Fe^{2+} promotes ROS generation via distinct pathways. The hydroxyl radical thus produced has a very short half-life in vivo and high reactivity with almost all types of biomolecules, namely, carbohydrates, nucleic acids, lipids, and amino acids, rendering extreme danger for living organisms. These reactions might cause irreversible cell damage that could lead to organ failure and in due course of time even death. Living organisms cope with this using certain biomolecules to bind to iron making Fe useful in many ways without the risk of ROS generation.

Numerous Fe complexes are found to be biologically active, which is attributed to their binding to either DNA or proteins. It becomes necessary to understand the criteria by which ligands control the reactivity of Fe(II)/(III) ions, as well as the mutual effects that they have on the properties of ligands as both play important roles in target site recognition and the subsequent biologic activity.

6. Future prospects

Iron complexes have substantial potential to act as structure-selective binding agents, and their use in diagnostics could be predictable. However, their use in therapeutics is greatly influenced by their capacity to be transported into human cells and to stimulate an appropriate desirable biologic response. For example, for an efficient chemotherapeutic drug, a slow dissociation rate from DNA is one of the essential properties. This manifests that apart from evaluating the modes of interaction of Fe(II)/(III) complexes with DNA or any other biomolecule, their association or dissociation kinetics are of prodigious diagnostic significance. While the significance of Fe complexes for their interactions with DNA and proteins has long been appreciated, it gives prospects for surpassing the phenomenological fits to a next-generation, correct prognostic understanding of nucleic acid-metal complex interactions. An augmented understanding of DNA structural changes and interactions will simplify the design of drugs possessing ideal physiognomies for a given application. Besides, approaches to site recognition of Fe complex-nucleic acid-binding should not be overlooked.

Even though few nonduplex DNA structures exhibit a critical role in gene regulation, RNA could prove to be a more attractive target for Fe(II)/(III) complexes chiefly in terms of finding greater selectivity in the binding sites. The reason is that RNA is structurally richer than DNA and contains a bigger proportion of nonduplex structures, which allows the formation of intricate three-dimensional structures involving loops, bulges, pseudoknots, and turns. This evidence can be harnessed for future research focused on developing RNA-interacting Fe(II)/(III) complexes with exciting applications. Further, there is a scope of expanding this approach to more complex G-quadruplex metal base-tetrad structures focusing on metal-quadruplex interactions and topology.

7. Conclusions

Nucleic acids are crucial biomolecules that store, transmit, process, and regulate genetic information, aiding as carriers of the genetic code. The evaluation of metal complex-nucleic acid interactions has flourished since the last decade in the field of bioinorganic chemistry. This has gained attention and consequential progress primarily due to the remarkable success that has occurred in nucleic acid technology.

Iron is an essential element for the living body. The human body stores iron in the form of ferritin and hemosiderin in the liver, spleen, marrow, duodenum, skeletal muscle, and other anatomic areas. Iron is utilized by several proteins as a cofactor for major biologic processes. However, iron may also harm cells by catalyzing the generation of free radicals and promoting oxidative stress.

Metal complexes have proven to be potent tools in the diagnosis and treatment of various diseases. DNA-interacting drugs are nowadays currently used in the treatment of many diseases ranging from cancer to chronic inflammation, as well as in the fight against resistant bacterial or viral infections. Metal complex-DNA interactions have been extensively researched. Metal ions coordination to the nucleic acids is critical for their structural properties and function. It has been found that DNA-metal ion interactions could trigger conformational changes. Evidently, metal-DNA interactions are critical to interfere with biologic processes. Fe(II)/(III) complexes bind to DNA and SAs in a multiplicity of ways displaying both strong covalent and weak noncovalent interactions. The main noncovalent binding modes are intercalation, groove binding, and electrostatic binding. Each of these modes is capable of a substantial perturbation in the nucleic acid/protein or could give rise to a site-specific response. The broad range of ligands in Fe(II)/(III) complexes, their oxidation state, their coordination number, and overall size and shape of the complex permits an enhanced selectivity toward the biologic target.

There is a need to understand the functioning and designing of new Fe(II)/(III) complexes bearing specific ligands that interact specifically with nucleic acids, especially RNA. Both the spectroscopy and the chemical reactivity of transition-metal complexes, coupled to biochemical assays, can, therefore, be exploited to obtain a wide range of useful reagents to probe nucleic acids.

Hence interaction studies of Fe(II)/(III) with RNA are another area where future research may advance.

References

Abbas, G., Ibrahim, M., Schmidt, S. F. M., Moreno-Pineda, E., Anson, C. E., & Powell, A. K. (2019). Synthesis of five isostructural tetranuclear Fe_2Ln_2 (Ln = Gd, Tb, Dy, Ho, Er) complexes with an "inverse butterfly" core. *Polyhedron, 158*, 255–261.

Abdel-Rahman, L. H., Ismail, N. M., Ismael, M., Abu-Dief, A. M., & Ahmed, E. A. H. (2017). Synthesis, characterization, DFT calculations and biological studies of Mn(II), Fe(II), Co(II) and Cd(II) complexes based on a tetradentate ONNO donor Schiff base ligand. *Journal of Molecular Structure, 1134*, 851–862.

Abu-Dief, A. M., Abdel-Rahman, L. H., Abdelhamid, A. A., Marzouk, A. A., Shehata, M. R., Bakheet, M. A., Almaghrabi, O. A., & Nafady, A. (2020). Synthesis and characterization of new Cr(III), Fe(III) and Cu(II) complexes incorporating multi-substituted aryl imidazole ligand: Structural, DFT, DNA binding, and biological implications. *Spectrochimica Acta Part A: Molecular and Biomolecular Spectroscopy, 228*, 117700.

Akdogan, Y., Reichenwallner, J., & Hinderberger, D. (2012). Evidence for water-tuned structural differences in proteins: An approach emphasizing variations. In V. N. Uversky (Ed.), *Plos one: Vol. 7. Local hydrophilicity* (p. e45681).

Alberti, E., Zampakou, M., & Donghi, D. (2016). Covalent and non-covalent binding of metal complexes to RNA. *Journal of Inorganic Biochemistry, 163*, 278–291.

Anacona, J. R., Ruiz, K., Loroño, M., & Celis, F. (2019). Antibacterial activity of transition metal complexes containing a tridentate NNO phenoxymethylpenicillin-based Schiff base. An anti-MRSA iron (II) complex. *Applied Organometallic Chemistry, 33*, e4744.

Arasteh, A., Farahi, S., Habibi-Rezaei, M., & Moosavi-Movahedi, A. A. (2014). Glycated albumin: An overview of the *In vitro* models of an *In vivo* potential disease marker. *Journal of Diabetes and Metabolic Disorders, 13*, 49.

Ascenzi, P., & Fasano, M. (2010). Allostery in a monomeric protein: The case of human serum albumin. *Biophysical Chemistry, 148*(1-3), 16–22. https://doi.org/10.1016/j.bpc.2010.03.001

Barone, G., Fonseca Guerra, C., & Bickelhaupt, F. M. (2013). B-DNA structure and stability as function of nucleic acid composition: Dispersion-corrected DFT study of dinucleoside monophosphate single and double strands. *Chemistry Open, 2*, 186–193.

Beach, S. A., Zuckerman, L. A., Portillo, R. I., Shores, M. P., Rheingold, A. L., & Doerrer, L. H. (2019). Heterobimetallic {PtMn} and {PtFe} lantern complexes with exceptionally long metallophilic contacts. *Inorganica Chimica Acta, 493*, 81–90.

Bedin, M., Agarwala, H., Marx, J., Schünemann, V., Ott, S., & Thapper, A. (2019). Synthesis and properties of a heterobimetallic iron-manganese complex and its comparison with homobimetallic analogues. *Inorganica Chimica Acta, 490*, 254–260.

BenYosef, D., Romano, D., Hadiji, M., Dyson, P. J., & Blom, B. (2020). Facile synthesis of heterobimetallic [FeII(μ-diphosphine)RuII] and homobimetallic [FeII(μ-diphosphine) FeII] complexes and their *in vitro* cytotoxic activity on cisplatin-resistant cancer cells. *Inorganica Chimica Acta, 510*, 119731.

Bikas, R., Ajormal, F., Emami, M., Sanchiz, J., Noshiranzadeh, N., & Kozakiewicz, A. (2019). Crystal structure and magneto-structural investigation of alkoxido bridged dinuclear Fe(III) complexes with 1,3-oxazolidine ligands. *Polyhedron, 162*, 20–29.

Bocian, A., Napierała, S., Gorczyński, A., Kubicki, M., Wałesa-Chorab, M., & Patroniak, V. (2019). The first example of an asymmetrical μ-oxo bridged dinuclear iron complex with a terpyridine ligand. *New Journal of Chemistry, 43*, 12650–12656.

Buldurun, K., Turan, N., Bursal, E., Mantarcı, A., Turkan, F., Taslimi, P., & Gülçin, İ. (2020). Synthesis, spectroscopic properties, crystal structures, antioxidant activities and enzyme inhibition determination of Co(II) and Fe(II) complexes of Schiff base. *Research on Chemical Intermediates, 46*, 283–297.

Camaschella, C. (2015). In D. L. Longo (Ed.), *New England Journal of Medicine: Vol. 372. Iron-deficiency anemia* (pp. 1832–1843).

Carmona-Negrón, J. A., Liboy-Lugo, J. M., Santana, A., & Meléndez, E. (2020). Synthesis and structural studies of 16-ferrocenemethyl-estra-1,3,5(10)-triene-3,17β-diol and its interaction with human serum albumin by fluorescence spectroscopy and in silico docking approaches. *Applied Organometallic Chemistry, 34*.

Carvalho, S. S. F., & Carvalho, N. M. F. (2019). Degradation of organic dyes by water soluble iron(III) mononuclear complexes from bis-(2-pyridylmethyl)amine NNN-derivative ligands. *Inorganic Chemistry Communications, 108*, 107507.

Castañeda, R., Harriman, K. L. M., Wong, J. W. L., Gabidullin, B., Murugesu, M., & Brusso, J. L. (2019). Rational design of tetranuclear complexes employing N -imidoylamidine based ligands. *European Journal of Inorganic Chemistry*, 963–972, 2019.

Cech, T. R., & Steitz, J. A. (2014). The noncoding RNA revolution—trashing old rules to forge new ones. *Cell, 157*, 77–94.

Chatterjee, S., & Suresh Kumar, G. (2017). Small molecule induced poly(A) single strand to self-structure conformational switching: Evidence for the prominent role of H-bonding interactions. *Molecular Biosystems, 13*, 1000–1009.

Chaves, O. A., de Lima Santos, M. R., de Oliveira, M. C. C., Sant'Anna, C. M. R., Ferreira, R. C., Echevarria, A., & Netto-Ferreira, J. C. (2018). Synthesis, tyrosinase inhibition and transportation behavior of novel β-enamino thiosemicarbazide derivatives by human serum albumin. *Journal of Molecular Liquids, 254*, 280–290.

Crichton, R., & Boelaert, J. R. (2001). *Inorganic biochemistry of iron metabolism: From molecular mechanisms to clinical consequences*. John Wiley and Sons.

Danopoulos, A. A., Braunstein, P., Monakhov, K. Y., van Leusen, J., Kögerler, P., Clémancey, M., Latour, J. M., Benayad, A., Tromp, M., Rezabal, E., & Frison, G. (2017). Heteroleptic, two-coordinate [M(NHC){N(SiMe 3) 2}] (M = Co, Fe) complexes: Synthesis, reactivity and magnetism rationalized by an unexpected metal oxidation state. *Dalton Transactions, 46*, 1163–1171.

Dávila–Rodríguez, M., Barolli, J. P., de Oliveira, K. M., Colina–Vegas, L., da Silva Miranda, F., Castellano, E. E., Von Poelhsitz, G., & Batista, A. A. (2018). Carbonyl–heterobimetallic Ru(II)/Fe(II)–complexes containing polypyridyl ligands: Synthesis, characterization, cellular viability assays and interactions with biomolecules. *Archives of Biochemistry and Biophysics, 660*, 156–167.

Devi, R. K. B., Devi, S. P., Singh, R. K. B., Singh, R. K. H., Swu, T., Devi, W. R., & Singh, C. B. (2014). Synthesis, spectroscopic, and biological studies on copper(II) complexes containing equatorial–apical chloride bridges: Crystal structure of [Cu_2 (μ-$Cl)_2$ (O-2-butoxyethylpyridine-2-carboximidate) $2Cl_2$]. *Journal of Coordination Chemistry, 67*, 891–909.

Disney, M. D. (2013). Rational design of chemical genetic probes of RNA function and lead therapeutics targeting repeating transcripts. *Drug Discovery Today, 18*, 1228–1236.

El-Shamy, H., Shaban, S. Y., El-Mehasseb, I., El-Kemary, M., & van Eldik, R. (2020). Probing the interaction of iron complex containing N3S2 macrocyclic ligand with bovine serum albumin using spectroscopic techniques. *Spectrochimica Acta - Part A: Molecular and Biomolecular Spectroscopy, 228*, 117811.

El-Gammal, O. A., El-Reash, G. M. A., & Bedier, R. A. (2019). Synthesis, spectroscopic, DFT, biological studies and molecular docking of oxovanadium (IV), copper (II) and iron (III) complexes of a new hydrazone derived from heterocyclic hydrazide. *Applied Organometallic Chemistry, 33*.

Emami, M., Bikas, R., Noshiranzadeh, N., Sanchiz, J., Ślepokura, K., & Lis, T. (2019). Synthesis, characterization and magnetic properties of phenoxido bridged dinuclear iron(III) complex with bis(phenolate) ligand. *Journal of Molecular Structure, 1180*, 392–398.

Erxleben, A. (2018). Transition metal salen complexes in bioinorganic and medicinal chemistry. *Inorganica Chimica Acta, 472*, 40–57.

Fairweather-Tait, S. J. (2004). Iron nutrition in the UK: Getting the balance right. *Proceedings of the Nutrition Society, 63*(4), 519–528. https://doi.org/10.1079/PNS2004394

Gattuso, H., Duchanois, T., Besancenot, V., Barbieux, C., Assfeld, X., Becuwe, P., Gros, P. C., Grandemange, S., & Monari, A. (2015). Interaction of iron II complexes with B-DNA. Insights from molecular modeling, spectroscopy, and cellular biology. *Frontiers in Chemistry, 3*.

Genheden, S., & Ryde, U. (2015). The MM/PBSA and MM/GBSA methods to estimate ligand-binding affinities. *Expert Opinion on Drug Discovery, 10*, 449–461.

Ghosh, M. K., Pathak, S., & Ghorai, T. K. (2019). Synthesis of two mononuclear Schiff base metal (M = Fe, Cu) complexes: MOF structure, dye degradation, H_2O_2 sensing, and DNA binding property. *ACS Omega, 4*, 16068–16079.

Gkouvatsos, K., Papanikolaou, G., & Pantopoulos, K. (2012). Regulation of iron transport and the role of transferrin. *Biochimica et Biophysica Acta (BBA) - General Subjects*, 188–202, 1820.

Guan, L., & Disney, M. D. (2012). Recent advances in developing small molecules targeting RNA. *ACS Chemical Biology*, 7, 73–86.

Gubendran, A., Kesavan, M. P., Ayyanaar, S., Mitu, L., Athappan, P., & Rajesh, J. (2017). Non-enolisable knoevenagel condensate appended Schiff bases-metal (II) complexes: spectral characteristics, DNA-binding and nuclease activities. *Spectrochimica Acta - Part A: Molecular and Biomolecular Spectroscopy, 181*, 39–46.

Guo, Y., Xu, L., Hong, S., Sun, Q., Yao, W., & Pei, R. (2016). Label-free DNA-based biosensors using structure-selective light-up dyes. *The Analyst, 141*, 6481–6489.

Herchel, R., Šindelář, Z., Trávníček, Z., Zbořil, R., & Vančo, J. (2009). Novel 1D chain Fe(III)-salen-like complexes involving anionic heterocyclic N-donor ligands. Synthesis, X-ray structure, magnetic, 57Fe Mössbauer, and biological activity studies. *Dalton Transactions*, 9870.

Herry, B., Batchelor, L. K., Roufosse, B., Romano, D., Baumgartner, J., Borzova, M., Reifenstahl, T., Collins, T., Benamrane, A., Weggelaar, J., Correia, M. C., Dyson, P. J., & Blom, B. (2019). Heterobimetallic Ru(μ-dppm)Fe and homobimetallic Ru(μ-dppm) Ru complexes as potential anti-cancer agents. *Journal of Organometallic Chemistry, 901*, 120934.

Hijazi, A. K., Taha, Z. A., Ajlouni, A. M., Al-Momani, W. M., Ababneh, T. S., Alshare, H. M., & Kuehn, F. E. (2017). Synthesis, catalytic and biological activities and computational study of Fe(III) solvent-ligated complexes having B(Ph) 4 as counter anion. *Applied Organometallic Chemistry, 31*, e3601.

Hu, J., Hernandez Soraiz, E., Johnson, C. N., Demeler, B., & Brancaleon, L. (2019). Novel combinations of experimental and computational analysis tested on the binding of metalloprotoporphyrins to albumin. *International Journal of Biological Macromolecules, 134*, 445–457.

Hu, Y. J., Ou-Yang, Y., Zhang, Y., & Liu, Y. (2010). Affinity and specificity of ciprofloxacin-bovine serum albumin interactions: Spectroscopic approach. *The Protein Journal, 29*, 234–241.

Ibrahim, I., Idris, S. O., Abdulkadir, I., & Onu, A. D. (2020). Redox reaction of N,N′-phenylenebis-(salicylideneiminato)iron(III) with hypophosphorous acid in mixed aqueous medium. *Transition Metal Chemistry, 45*, 211–216.

Ivanov, A. I., Korolenko, E. A., Korolik, E. V., Firsov, S. P., Zhbankov, R. G., Marchewka, M. K., & Ratajczak, H. (2002). Chronic liver and renal diseases differently affect structure of human serum albumin. *Archives of Biochemistry and Biophysics, 408*, 69–77.

Jaiteh, M., Zeifman, A., Saarinen, M., Svenningsson, P., Bréa, J., Loza, M. I., & Carlsson, J. (2018). Docking screens for dual inhibitors of disparate drug targets for Parkinson's disease. *Journal of Medicinal Chemistry, 61*, 5269–5278.

Jia, P., Ouyang, R., Cao, P., Tong, X., Zhou, X., Lei, T., Zhao, Y., Guo, N., Chang, H., Miao, Y., & Zhou, S. (2017). Review: Recent advances and future development of metal complexes as anticancer agents. *Journal of Coordination Chemistry, 70*, 2175–2201.

Kandagal, P. B., Ashoka, S., Seetharamappa, J., Shaikh, S. M. T., Jadegoud, Y., & Ijare, O. B. (2006). Study of the interaction of an anticancer drug with human and bovine serum albumin: Spectroscopic approach. *Journal of Pharmaceutical and Biomedical Analysis, 41*, 393–399.

Karges, J., Goldner, P., & Gasser, G. (2019). Synthesis, characterization, and biological evaluation of red-absorbing Fe(II) polypyridine complexes. *Inorganics,* 7, 4.

Kaya, B., Yılmaz, Z. K., Sahin, O., Aslim, B., Tükenmez, Ü., & Ülküseven, B. (2019). Structural analysis and biological functionalities of iron(III)– and manganese(III)–thiosemicarbazone complexes: *In vitro* anti-proliferative activity on human cancer cells, DNA binding and cleavage studies. *JBIC Journal of Biological Inorganic Chemistry, 24*, 365–376.

Kelly, S. M., Jess, T. J., & Price, N. C. (2005). How to study proteins by circular dichroism. *Biochimica et Biophysica Acta (BBA) - Proteins and Proteomics, 1751*, 119–139.

Komor, A. C., & Barton, J. K. (2013). The path for metal complexes to a DNA target. *Chemical Communications, 49*, 3617.

Kongot, M., Dohare, N., Reddy, D. S., Pereira, N., Patel, R., Subramanian, M., & Kumar, A. (2019a). *In vitro* apoptosis-induction, antiproliferative and BSA binding studies of a oxidovanadium(V) complex. *Journal of Trace Elements in Medicine and Biology, 51*, 176–190.

Kongot, M., Reddy, D. S., Singh, V., Patel, R., Singhal, N. K., & Kumar, A. (2019b). ONS donor entwined iron(iii) and cobalt(iii) complexes with exemplary safety profile as potent anticancer and glucose uptake agents. *New Journal of Chemistry, 43*, 10932–10947.

Kongot, M., Reddy, D. S., Singh, V., Patel, R., Singhal, N. K., & Kumar, A. (2020). Oxidovanadium (IV) and iron (III) complexes with O_2N_2 donor linkage as plausible antidiabetic candidates: Synthesis, structural characterizations, glucose uptake and model biological media studies. *Applied Organometallic Chemistry*, 34.

Kosik-Bogacka, D., Łanocha-Arendarczyk, N., Kalisińska, E., Kot, K., Czernomysy-Furowicz, D., Pilarczyk, B., & Tomza-Marciniak, A. (2019). *Iron, Fe. Mammals and birds as bioindicators of trace element contaminations in terrestrial environments* (pp. 181–212). Cham: Springer International Publishing.

Kovalska, V., Kuperman, M., Losytskyy, M., Vakarov, S., Potocki, S., Yarmoluk, S., Voloshin, Y., Varzatskii, O., & Gumienna-Kontecka, E. (2019). Induced CD of iron(ii) clathrochelates: Sensing of the structural and conformational alterations of serum albumins. *Metallomics, 11*, 338–348.

Kumar, A., Banerjee, S., Sarkar, S., & Rath, S. P. (2019). Stepwise oxidations of a nickel(ii)-iron(iii) heterobimetallic porphyrin dimer: Structure, spectroscopic and theoretical investigation. *Dalton Transactions, 48*, 10089–10103.

Kumar, S., & Kumar, S. (2019). B. Molecular docking: A structure-based approach for drug repurposing. In *Silico drug design* (pp. 161–189). Elsevier.

Kurt, B., Temel, H., Atlan, M., & Kaya, S. (2020). Synthesis, characterization, DNA interaction and docking studies of novel Schiff base ligand derived from 2,6-diaminopyridine and its complexes. *Journal of Molecular Structure, 1209*, 127928.

Lakowicz, J. R., & Weber, G. (1973). Quenching of fluorescence by oxygen. Probe for structural fluctuations in macromolecules. *Biochemistry, 12*, 4161–4170.

Li, Y., Li, Y., Yang, Z., Meng, F., Wang, N., Zhou, M., Xia, Z., Gong, Q., & Gao, Q. (2019). Distinct supramolecular assemblies of Fe(III) and Ni(II) complexes constructed from the o-vanillin salicylhydrazone ligand: Syntheses, crystal structures, DNA/protein interaction, and antioxidant and cytotoxic activity. *New Journal of Chemistry, 43*, 8024–8043.

Liu, H. K., & Sadler, P. J. (2011). Metal complexes as DNA intercalators. *Accounts of Chemical Research, 44*, 349–359.

Liu, F., Zhang, Y., Yu, Q., Shen, Y., Zheng, Z., Cheng, J., Zhang, W., & Ye, Y. (2019). Exploration of the binding between ellagic acid, a potentially risky food additive, and bovine serum albumin. *Food and Chemical Toxicology, 134*, 110867.

Li, Y., Zhang, X., & Cao, D. (2013). The role of shape complementarity in the protein-protein interactions. *Scientific Reports, 3*, 3271.

Lutsenko, I. A., Kiskin, M. A., Nelyubina, Y. V., Efimov, N. N., Maksimov, Y. V., Imshennik, V. K., Zueva, E. M., Goloveshkin, A. S., Khoroshilov, A. V., Rentschler, E., Sidorov, A. A., & Eremenko, I. L. (2019). Tri- and tetranuclear heteropivalate complexes with core {Fe_2Ni O} (x = 1, 2): Synthesis, structure, magnetic and thermal properties. *Polyhedron, 159*, 426–435.

Lvov, A. G., Mörtel, M., Yadykov, A. V., Heinemann, F. W., Shirinian, V. Z., & Khusniyarov, M. M. (2019). Photochromic diarylethene ligands featuring 2-(imidazole-2-yl)pyridine coordination site and their iron(II) complexes. *Beilstein Journal of Organic Chemistry, 15*, 2428–2437.

Majorek, K. A., Porebski, P. J., Dayal, A., Zimmerman, M. D., Jablonska, K., Stewart, A. J., Chruszcz, M., & Minor, W. (2012). Structural and immunologic characterization of bovine, horse, and rabbit serum albumins. *Molecular Immunology, 52*, 174–182.

Mardianingrum, R., Susanti, & Ruswanto, R. (2019). Bis(N′-(3-chlorobenzoyl)isonicotinohydrazide)iron(III) Complex. *Molbank*, M1101, 2020.

Martins, N. M. R., Anbu, S., Mahmudov, K. T., Ravishankaran, R., Guedes da Silva, M. F. C., Martins, L. M. D. R. S., Karande, A. A., & Pombeiro, A. J. L. (2017). DNA, BSA binding and cytotoxic properties of copper(II) and iron(III) complexes with arylhydrazone of ethyl 2-cyanoacetate or formazan ligands. *New Journal of Chemistry, 41*, 4076–4086.

Martins, N. M. R., Mahmudov, K. T., Guedes Da Silva, M. F. C., Martins, L. M. D. R. S., & Pombeiro, A. J. L. (2016). Copper(ii) and iron(iii) complexes with arylhydrazone of ethyl 2-cyanoacetate or formazan ligands as catalysts for oxidation of alcohols. *New Journal of Chemistry, 40*, 10071–10083.

Matos, C. P., Yildizhan, Y., Adiguzel, Z., Pavan, F. R., Campos, D. L., Pessoa, J. C., Ferreira, L. P., Tomaz, A. I., Correia, I., & Acilan, C. (2019). New ternary iron(iii) aminobisphenolate hydroxyquinoline complexes as potential therapeutic agents. *Dalton Transactions, 48*, 8702–8716.

Michel, B. Y., Dziuba, D., Benhida, R., Demchenko, A. P., & Burger, A. (2020). Probing of nucleic acid structures, dynamics, and interactions with environment-sensitive fluorescent labels. *Frontiers in Chemistry, 8*, Article 112. https://doi.org/10.3389/fchem.2020.00112

Moergel, M., Kämmerer, P. W., Schnurr, K., Klein, M. O., & Al-Nawas, B. (2012). Spin electron paramagnetic resonance of albumin for diagnosis of oral squamous cell carcinoma (OSCC). *Clinical Oral Investigations, 16*, 1529–1533.

Nandy, M., Hughes, D. L., Rosair, G. M., Singh, R. K. B., & Mitra, S. (2014). Synthesis, characterization, crystal structure, and DNA binding of two copper(II)–hydrazone complexes. *Journal of Coordination Chemistry, 67*, 3335–3353.

Naveenraj, S., Anandan, S., Kathiravan, A., Renganathan, R., & Ashokkumar, M. (2010). The interaction of sonochemically synthesized gold nanoparticles with serum albumins. *Journal of Pharmaceutical and Biomedical Analysis, 53*, 804–810.

Nemec, I., Svoboda, I., & Herchel, R. (2019). Spin crossover in three mononuclear iron (III) Schiff base complexes. *Metals, 9*, 849.

Nicoletti, F. P., Howes, B. D., Fittipaldi, M., Fanali, G., Fasano, M., Ascenzi, P., & Smulevich, G. (2008). Ibuprofen induces an allosteric conformational transition in the heme complex of human serum albumin with significant effects on heme ligation. *Journal of the American Chemical Society, 130*, 11677–11688.

Obaleye, J. A., & Abosede, O. O. (2019). Fe(III)-doxycycline complexes with diimine ligands: Syntheses, characterization and biological properties. *Macedonian Journal of Chemistry and Chemical Engineering, 38*, 29.

Pagadala, N. S., Syed, K., & Tuszynski, J. (2017). Software for molecular docking: A review. *Biophysical Reviews, 9*, 91–102.

Pages, B. J., Ang, D. L., Wright, E. P., & Aldrich-Wright, J. R. (2015). Metal complex interactions with DNA. *Dalton Transactions, 44*, 3505–3526.

Patel, S., Sharma, K. K., & Datta, A. (2015). Competitive binding of chlorin p6and Dansyl-L-Proline to Sudlow's site II of human serum albumin. *Spectrochimica Acta - Part A: Molecular and Biomolecular Spectroscopy, 138*, 925–931.

Pinzi, L., & Rastelli, G. (2019). Molecular docking: Shifting paradigms in drug discovery. *International Journal of Molecular Sciences, 20*, 4331.

Poulsen, B. C., Estalayo-Adrián, S., Blasco, S., Bright, S. A., Kelly, J. M., Williams, D. C., & Gunnlaugsson, T. (2016). Luminescent ruthenium polypyridyl complexes with extended 'dppz' like ligands as DNA targeting binders and cellular agents. *Dalton Transactions, 45*, 18208–18220.

Rabbani, G., Baig, M. H., Lee, E. J., Cho, W. K., Ma, J. Y., & Choi, I. (2017). Biophysical study on the interaction between eperisone hydrochloride and human serum albumin using spectroscopic, calorimetric, and molecular docking analyses. *Molecular Pharmaceutics, 14*, 1656–1665.

Rajaretnam, B. B., Chellappa, J., Solomon, D. A., Subramanian, I. P., & Selvanayagam, T. D. M. (2019). Evaluation of DNA/BSA binding and chemical nuclease activity of L-tyrosine-based Mn(III) and Fe(III) metallo-intercalators. *Acta Chimica Slovenica*, 196–207.

Raj, M. V. N., Bhar, K., Jain, S., Rana, M., Khan, T. A., & Sharma, A. K. (2019). Syntheses, X-ray structures, electrochemical properties and biological evaluation of mono- and dinuclear N_2O_2-donor ligand-Fe systems. *Transition Metal Chemistry, 44*, 615–626.

Rastelli, G., & Pinzi, L. (2019). Refinement and rescoring of virtual screening results. *Frontiers in Chemistry, 7*.

Reed, C. J., & Agapie, T. (2019). A terminal Fe III –oxo in a tetranuclear cluster: Effects of distal metal centers on structure and reactivity. *Journal of the American Chemical Society, 141*, 9479–9484.

Reinhart, E. D., & Jordan, R. F. (2020). Synthesis and ethylene reactivity of dinuclear iron and cobalt complexes supported by macrocyclic bis(pyridine-diimine) ligands containing o -terphenyl linkers. *Organometallics., acs.Organomet*, 000211.

Roche, D., Brackenridge, D., & McGuffin, L. (2015). Proteins and their interacting partners: An introduction to protein–ligand binding site prediction methods. *International Journal of Molecular Sciences, 16*, 29829–29842.

Rudolf, B., Kubicka, A., Salmain, M., Palusiak, M., Rybarczyk-Pirek, A. J., & Wojtulewski, S. (2016). Synthesis and characterization of new M(II) carbonyl complexes (M = Fe or Ru) including an η1-N-maleimidato ligand. Reactivity studies with biological thiols. *Journal of Organometallic Chemistry, 801*, 101–110.

Saito, H. (2014). Metabolism of iron stores. *Nagoya Journal of Medical Science, 76*(3-4), 235–254.

Sánchez, M., Sabio, L., Gálvez, N., Capdevila, M., & Dominguez-Vera, J. M. (2017). Iron chemistry at the service of life. *IUBMB Life, 69*, 382–388.

Sand, K. M. K., Bern, M., Nilsen, J., Noordzij, H. T., Sandlie, I., & Andersen, J. T. (2015). Unraveling the interaction between FcRn and albumin: Opportunities for design of albumin-based therapeutics. *Frontiers in Immunology*, 5.

Savard, J. M., Castañeda, R., Gabidullin, B., & Brusso, J. L. (2019). Exploring the coordination chemistry of terpy-type boratriazine chelates through a series of mononuclear iron(III) complexes. *Polyhedron, 162*, 8–13.

Scepaniak, J. J., Kang, E. B., John, M., Kaminsky, W., Dechert, S., & Meyer, F. (2019). Non-macrocyclic Schiff base complexes of iron(II) as ParaCEST agents for MRI. *European Journal of Inorganic Chemistry*, 2404–2411, 2019.

Sen, P., Akagunduz, D., Aghdam, A. S., Cebeci, F.Ç., Nyokong, T., & Catal, T. (2020). Synthesis of novel Schiff base cobalt (II) and iron (III) complexes as cathode catalysts for microbial fuel cell applications. *Journal of Inorganic and Organometallic Polymers and Materials, 30*, 1110–1120.

Senthil Kumar, K., Bayeh, Y., Gebretsadik, T., Elemo, F., Gebrezgiabher, M., Thomas, M., & Ruben, M. (2019). Spin-crossover in iron(ii)-Schiff base complexes. *Dalton Transactions, 48*, 15321–15337.

Shahabadi, N., Kashanian, S., & Fatahi, A. (2011). Identification of binding mode of a platinum (II) complex, (DIP), and calf thymus DNA. *Bioinorganic Chemistry and Applications*, 1–7, 2011.

Shahabadi, N., & Maghsudi, M. (2014). Multi-spectroscopic and molecular modeling studies on the interaction of antihypertensive drug; Methyldopa with calf thymus DNA. *Molecular Biosystems, 10*, 338–347. https://doi.org/10.1039/C3MB70340A

Shahraki, S., Shiri, F., & Saeidifar, M. (2018). Synthesis, characterization, in silico ADMET prediction, and protein binding analysis of a novel zinc(II) Schiff-base complex: Application of multi-spectroscopic and computational techniques. *Journal of Biomolecular Structure and Dynamics, 36*, 1666–1680.

Sharif-Barfeh, Z., Beigoli, S., Marouzi, S., Rad, A. S., Asoodeh, A., & Chamani, J. (2017). Multi-spectroscopic and HPLC studies of the interaction between estradiol and cyclophosphamide with human serum albumin: Binary and ternary systems. *Journal of Solution Chemistry, 46*, 488–504.

Sharp, P. A. (2009). The centrality of RNA. *Cell, 136*, 577–580.

Shiga, T., Ishikawa, D., Tachibana, M., Saiki, R., Newton, G. N., & Oshio, H. (2019). Spin crossover behavior of a tetranuclear iron(II) grid complex with a hydroxyl-group functionalized multidentate ligand. *Journal of Magnetism and Magnetic Materials, 485*, 16–20.

Sil, A., Ghosh, U., Mishra, V. K., Mishra, S., & Patra, S. K. (2019). Synthesis, structure, electrochemical, and spectroscopic properties of hetero-bimetallic Ru(II)/Fe(II)-Alkynyl organometallic complexes. *Inorganic Chemistry, 58*, 1155–1166.

Sogukomerogullari, H. G., Yalçin, S. P., Ceylan, Ü., Aytar, E., Aygün, M., Richeson, D. S., & Sönmez, M. (2019). Synthesis of Fe and Cu metal complexes derived from 'SNS' Pincer type ligands and their efficient catalyst precursors for the chemical fixation of $$\hbox {CO}_{2}$$ CO 2. *Journal of Chemical Sciences, 131*, 32.

Sudlow, G., Birkett, D. J., & Wade, D. N. (1976). Further characterization of specific drug binding sites on human serum albumin. *Molecular Pharmacology, 12*, 1052–1061.

Sun, Y. M., Akram, W., Cheng, F., Liu, Z. Y., Liao, Y. H., Ye, Y., & Liu, H. Y. (2019). DNA interaction and photodynamic antitumor activity of transition metal monohydroxyl corrole. *Bioorganic Chemistry, 90*, 103085.

Takarada, J. E., Guedes, A. P. M., Correa, R. S., Silveira-Lacerda, E. de P., Castelli, S., Iacovelli, F., Deflon, V. M., Batista, A. A., & Desideri, A. (2017). Ru/Fe bimetallic complexes: Synthesis, characterization, cytotoxicity and study of their interactions with DNA/HSA and human topoisomerase IB. *Archives of Biochemistry and Biophysics, 636*, 28–41.

Tanaka, T., Sunatsuki, Y., & Suzuki, T. (2020). Synthesis and magnetic properties of tetrahedral tetranuclear iron(II) complexes with bis(bidentate)-type Schiff bases containing imidazole groups. *Inorganica Chimica Acta, 502*, 119373.

Tao, X., Huang, Y., Wang, C., Chen, F., Yang, L., Ling, L., Che, Z., & Chen, X. (2020). Recent developments in molecular docking technology applied in food science: A review. *International Journal of Food Science and Technology, 55*, 33–45.

U-Wang, O., Singh, R. B., Devi, W. B., Singh, U. I., Devi, R. B., Devi, O. B., Shahani, R., & Swu, T. (2019). New dinuclear Schiff base complexes of iron(II/III) and copper(II) ions: Synthesis, crystal structure, and DNA-binding studies. *Inorganic and Nano-Metal Chemistry, 49*, 363–374.

Vailati, A. F., Huelsmann, R. D., Martendal, E., Bortoluzzi, A. J., Xavier, F. R., & Peralta, R. A. (2020). Multivariate analysis applied to oxidation of cyclohexane and benzyl alcohol promoted by mononuclear iron and copper complexes. *New Journal of Chemistry, 44*, 2514–2526.

Velagapudi, S. P., Vummidi, B. R., & Disney, M. D. (2015). Small molecule chemical probes of microRNA function. *Current Opinion in Chemical Biology, 24*, 97–103.

Wang, H., Wu, N., Zheng, J., Zheng, C., & Wang, D. (2020). Synthesis and structures of two mononuclear iron(ii) complexes derived from polypyridine ligands. *Mendeleev Communications, 30*, 100–102.

Wani, W. A., Baig, U., Shreaz, S., Shiekh, R. A., Iqbal, P. F., Jameel, E., Ahmad, A., Mohd-Setapar, S. H., Mushtaque, M., & Ting Hun, L. (2016). Recent advances in iron complexes as potential anticancer agents. *New Journal of Chemistry, 40*, 1063–1090.

Wardell, M., Wang, Z., Ho, J. X., Robert, J., Ruker, F., Ruble, J., & Carter, D. C. (2002). The atomic structure of human methemalbumin at 1.9 Å. *Biochemical and Biophysical Research Communications, 291*, 813–819.

Wolfe, A., Shimer, G. H., & Meehan, T. (1987). Polycyclic aromatic hydrocarbons physically intercalate into duplex regions of denatured DNA. *Biochemistry, 26*(20), 6392–6396. https://doi.org/10.1021/bi00394a013

Wu, Y. G., Wang, D. B., Hu, J. J., Song, X. Q., Xie, C. Z., Ma, Z. Y., & Xu, J. Y. (2019). An iron(III) complex selectively mediated cancer cell death: Crystal structure, DNA targeting and *in vitro* antitumor activities. *Inorganic Chemistry Frontiers, 6*, 1040–1049.

Yadav, P., Kumar Yadav, J., Dixit, A. K., Agarwal, A., & Kumar Awasthi, S. (2019). Insight into the interaction of benzothiazole tethered triazole analogues with human serum albumin: Spectroscopy and molecular docking approaches. *Luminescence, 34*, 812–822.

Yan, Z., & Wang, J. (2013). Optimizing scoring function of protein-nucleic acid interactions with both affinity and specificity. In F. Salsbury (Ed.), *Plos one* (Vol. 8, p. e74443).

Yu, Z., & Cowan, J. (2018). Metal complexes promoting catalytic cleavage of nucleic acids — biochemical tools and therapeutics. *Current Opinion in Chemical Biology, 43*, 37–42.

Zaidi, N., Ajmal, M. R., Rabbani, G., Ahmad, E., & Khan, R. H. (2013). A comprehensive insight into binding of hippuric acid to human serum albumin: A study to uncover its impaired elimination through hemodialysis. In R. Subramanyam (Ed.), *Plos one* (Vol. 8, p. e71422).

Zolfagharzadeh, M., Pirouzi, M., Asoodeh, A., Saberi, M. R., & Chamani, J. (2014). A comparison investigation of DNP-binding effects to HSA and HTF by spectroscopic and molecular modeling techniques. *Journal of Biomolecular Structure and Dynamics, 32*, 1936–1952.

CHAPTER 5

Manganese complexes: Their interaction studies with nucleic acids and biomolecules

Sayyed Jaheera Anwar[1], Irshad Ul Haq Bhat[2] and Hanis Mohd Yusoff[3]
[1]Faculty of Science and Marine Environment, Universiti Malaysia Terengganu, Kuala Nerus, Terengganu, Malaysia; [2]University of Bahrain, Bahrain; [3]Advance Nano Materials (ANoMa) Research Group, Faculty of Science and Marine Environment, Universiti Malaysia Terengganu, Kuala Nerus, Terengganu, Malaysia

1. Chemistry of manganese

Manganese (Mn) is extensively found in Earth's crust and is regarded as one of the five essential trace elements for almost all organisms (Aliff et al., 2020). It is the best mediator for the formation of alloy with steel because it improves the ability to hot-work steel and boosts impact resistance. Manganese was named after the Latin word "magnes," meaning magnet. Mn was revealed by Swedish chemist Scheele in 1771, and later in 1774, it was first isolated by J.G. Gahn by reducing the compound of manganese dioxide. Mn in its pure form is a brittle, hard, gray-white metal and a part of the first-row transition metals with electronic configuration [Ar] $3d^5 4s^2$ (Chemistry of Manganese, 2020). It is a redox-active metal, thus able to participate in Fenton-like chemistry reactions (Chen et al., 2018; Lemire et al., 2013). The element Mn shows a huge difference in probable oxidation states between Mn^0 and Mn^{7+} based on reaction conditions and associates. Except for Mn^{1+} and Mn^{5+}, it exhibits all positive oxidation at ordinary temperature and pressure in a simple manganese/water reaction system (Kurz, 2014). The electropositive nature of Mn is found to be greater than that of its neighboring elements in the periodic table. For this reason, it is often reactive, particularly in the presence of slight impurity. On treatment with dilute aqueous acids, Mn is mixed with water and liberates hydrogen, and it forms Mn^{2+} salts. It does not react readily with nonmetals at room temperature but vigorously reacts on heating. Therefore, it forms Mn_3N_2, Mn_3O_4, MnF^{2+}, MnF_3, and $MnCl_2$ in reaction with N, O, F, and Cl, respectively. It readily

Nucleic Acids
ISBN 978-0-12-820503-7
https://doi.org/10.1016/B978-0-12-820503-7.00006-5

associates with B, C, Si, P, S, and As (Greenwood & Earnshaw, 1997). Mn metal is paramagnetic and capable of existing in 11 dissimilar oxidation states, but only Mn^{2+} and Mn^{3+} states are considered biologically significant (Avila et al., 2013; Bouabid et al., 2016; Dusek et al., 2015; Oulhote et al., 2015). Metal complex magnetic susceptibility values can reveal information on the metal ion oxidation states, electronic structure, stereochemistry, and metal complex binding nature. According to Sennappan et al. (2018), the magnetic susceptibility (μeff) of the complex $Mn(C_{14}H_{14}N_3O)_2Cl_2$ was found to be 5.33 BM, which is slightly lower than the spin-only value of 5.92 BM at room temperature; this means that the manganese is in the bivalent state Mn^{2+} and is similar to a characteristic high-spin octahedral Mn^{2+} complex (El-Tabi et al., 2011). At normal temperatures, the magnetic susceptibility of Mn polymer complexes ($[Mn(HL)_2(OCOCH_2)_2]_n$) is in the paramagnetic region (Diab et al., 2018). The intrinsic binding constant value is affected by factors like complex structure, metal, ligand nature, and the number of ligands in the complex (Sennappan et al., 2018). Due to the presence of high electron spin number, a long electron relaxation period, and the formation of manganese complexes with various ligands, they are crucial in medical applications and capable to serve as carriers for medication targeting in antitumor and antibacterial therapy (Zheng et al., 2022).

2. Methods of synthesis

2.1 Synthesis of neutral di- and trinuclear Mn^{2+} complexes

The manganese complexes with two centers with +2, +3, or +4 oxidation states linked via water-derived ligands (WDLs) are the most commonly studied systems. The WDLs' solid bonding with higher oxidation Mn plays a significant role in water oxidation as well as being quite useful for Mn^{2+} complexes synthesis. The binuclear manganese complexes, particularly of type $[Mn_2(\mu\text{-}O)_2]$, can be synthesized by the general method of synthesis for μ-oxido dimanganese coordination compounds as follows:

(a) One method is the generation of Mn^{2+} or Mn^{3+} ions in a polar solvent like H_2O, MeOH, MeCN, etc., along with weakly coordinating anions (X) like halides and acetates.

(b) Another method is the addition of the chelating ligands to the mixture for coordination with the manganese centers.

(c) Finally, oxidation of the manganese centers with water produces Mn^{2+} and the oxidation states $\geq +3$, while the +3 units mostly contain a minimum of one μ-WLD linkage between the manganese ions (Mukhopadhyay et al., 2004).

Bordbar et al. (2018) synthesized completely air-stable Mn complexes by the means of neutralized ligand (L) condensation with 2,6-diacetylpyridine in the presence of Mn(II) metal ions. Nano-sized divalent and tetravalent Mn^{2+} complexes can be synthesized based on the well-known reflux-precipitation method (Alaghaz & Aldulmani, 2019). The neutral di and trinuclear Mn^{2+} complexes with the nonsteroidal antiinflammatory drugs (NSAIDs), oxaprozin, and flufenamic acid, respectively were synthesized in larger amounts by employing aerobic reaction of a solution of the matching deprotonated NSAID oxaprozin or flufenamic acid with $MnCl_2.4H_2O$ in presence of the respective N,N′-donor ligand (phen or bipy) (Dimiza et al., 2020).

2.2 Synthesis of manganese corroles

Cyclization of the tetrapyrrolic precursor using manganese salt (Liu et al., 2013), freebase corrosion's reaction with manganese salt (Liu et al., 2013), use of manganese salt with bilane via tough C−C bond formations (Yadav et al., 2017), condensation of dipyrromethane (DPM) with an aromatic aldehyde (Kumar et al., 2020), the Rothemund reaction (Paolesse et al., 1999), reductive demetalation of Mn corroles gives highly electron-deficient and perhalogenated free-base corroles (Bröring et al., 2001). for synthesis of Mn complexes were reported.

2.3 Manganese halide complexes

Commercially available anhydrous Mn salts MnX_2 represent the simplest Mn-containing starting materials, of which $MnCl_2$ and $MnBr_2$ are very stable, whereas MnI_2 is light sensitive and is often considered too impure for given synthetic applications. Normally this compound was easily prepared by reacting Mn powder with iodine in ether (Grineva et al., 2021). The manganese fluoride complexes of type A_2MnF_4 (A = alkali metal) are generally prepared by mixing the molten Mn-difluoride and alkali metal fluorides. Whereas, $AMnF_3$-type complexes are commonly prepared either by mixing the solutions of Mn-difluoride and alkali metal fluorides or by fusing the constituents in a melt (Colton & Canterford, 1969). The inorganic metal halide complexes like Cs_3MnI_5 and Cs_3MnBr_5 were synthesized using the lyophilization-aided recrystallization method by Kwon et al. (2020).

2.4 Synthesis of manganese carbonyl and manganese carbonyl halide complexes

Mn, Mn-iodide, and carbon monoxide were combined to create Mn-carbonyl $Mn_2(CO)_{10}$. Brimm et al. (1954) reported the preparation of Mn-carbonyl by reducing Mn-iodide at normal temperature using Mn in diethyl ether under 1000–3000 psig. pressure of carbon monoxide. Mn-iodide was the only Mn-halide that produced Mn-carbonyl, and there was even no alternative found for diethyl ether. The binary carbonyl compounds of Mn were prepared by reducing MnI_2 with $L1AIH_4$ and CO under pressure. Synthesis of Mn-carbonyl halide complexes $[Mn(Cl)(CO)_5]$ were synthesized by the reaction of $[Mn_2(CO)_{10}]$ with SO_2C1_2 (Eq. 5.1).

$$[Mn_2(CO)_{10}] + SO_2C1_2 \rightarrow 2\ [Mn(Cl)(CO)_5] + SO_2 \qquad (5.1)$$

Several synthesis procedures for both $[Mn(X)(CO)_5]$ and $[Mn_2(u\text{-}X)_2(CO)_8]$ complexes (where X = Cl, Br, I) have been reported. Na $[Mn(CO)_5]$ on reaction with diiodoacetylene gives the dimer $[Mn_2(ji\text{-}I)_2(CO)_8]$ as one of the two products. The chief product formed in the reaction of $Na[Mn(CO)_5]$ and $[C1_2C{=}S$ was $[Mn(Cl)_2(CO)_4]\sim$ complex. Almost all the species of $[Mn(Br)(CO)_5\ n(L)_J]$ ($n = 1–5$) were possible to be prepared by monitoring the reaction conditions, stoichiometry, and the cationic complexes $[Mn(CO)(L)_5]Br$ and $[Mn(L)_6]Br$. Novel Mn complexes $[Mn(X)(CO)_5\ M(L)_n]$ were synthesized by substitution of carbonyl in the parent species (Treichel, 2004).

2.5 Synthesis of mixed-Mn complexes

The photolytic or thermal disproportionation of $[Mn_2(CO)_{10}]$ and $[Re_2(CO)_{10}]$ gives $[MnRe(CO)_{10}]$. Reaction of $[MnRe(CO)_{10}]$ and PPh_3 at 130°C forms the $[MnRe(CO)_9(PPh_3)]$ complex. Another synthetic method takes in the displacement of halide ions in $[Re(X)(CO)_5]$ by $[Mn(CO)_5]$ to give $[MnRe(CO)_{10}]$. Reaction of $[Re(O_3SCF_3)(CO)_5]$ with CO provides $[(OC)_5MnRe(13CO)_5]$. Further development of this method led to the formation of quite a lot of phosphine-substituted complexes, $[(OC)_5Mn\text{-}Re(CO)_4(L)]$ (Treichel et al., 2004). Nesterova et al. (2015) prepared $[Fe_4(\mu^{4-O})_4Mn_4(L)_6(DMF)_4]$ 2DMF complex by single-pot open-air reaction method. Recently, the mechano-chemical path or direct synthesis route has become a global spotlight due to its beneficial aspects like simplicity, reaction speed, high yield, eco-friendliness (due to limited or even no use of solvent), and affordability. Moreover, good scale-up is readily accomplished in many cases, and with easy storage and availability of metals in nearly any required degree of purity, this type of synthesis is feasible for both laboratory and commercial production methods (Chandrashekhar et al., 2018). This process involves carbon—carbon and carbon—heteroatom covalent interactions, breaking of hydrogen bonds, and formation of metal—ligand coordination bonds (or rearrangement of bonds) (Friscic, 2012; Kaupp, 2009; Kaupp, 2011; Lazuen-Garay et al., 2007). Beznischenko et al. (2009) reported the synthesis of the complex $[CoL][Mn(OX)_2]Cl\ 3H_2O[L\text{-}N(CH_2NHC_2H_4NH_2)_3]$ via the direct synthesis method. $Mn{:}NH_4[Cr(NCS)_4(NH_3)_2]H_2O$ and $Mn[M_2Mn(OAc)_6L_2]$ (where M = Cd (1), Cu (2)) were synthesized by single-step direct synthesis method with 44% and 77% yield respectively (Nahorn et al., 2013; Semenaka et al., 2010).

3. Methods of analysis

Several reports have been published to learn the metal complexes' interaction with biomolecules. Some of the important practices are described below.

3.1 Electronic absorption titrations

One of the most often used techniques for determining how strongly a chemical binds to DNA is absorption titration. At 25°C, absorption titration tests were carried out with the ligand and its metal complexes at fixed concentrations while the DNA concentration was steadily raised. The steady rise in DNA concentration shows the interaction between the DNA and the compound, which can be monitored using UV-vis spectrometry (Gupta et al., 2013; Kalaivani et al., 2012; Ramachandran et al., 2013). According to Pyle et al. (1989) and Shi et al. (2009), because of the firm stacking relationship flanked by the aromatic chromophore and the DNA base pairs, hypochromism and bathochromism normally result from the intercalation of metal complex interacting with DNA. Because of the ligand's large surface area and the presence of a planar aromatic chromophore, which promotes a strong binding interaction between the ligands and the DNA, the "hyperchromic effect" can also be explained in terms of two additional phenomena. This gives the complex ample opportunity to bind with the DNA through the partial insertion of the aromatic moiety between the stacking base pair (El-Bindary et al., 2017). The extent of hypochromism can be calculated using Eq. (5.2) as follows.

$$H\% = [(A_{Free} - A_{bounded})/A_{Free}] \times 100 \quad (5.2)$$

The intrinsic binding constant (K_b) is a key tool to define the magnitude of the binding strength of compounds with DNA as determined in previous chapters.

3.2 Fluorescence emission spectroscopy

Fluorescence emission spectroscopy (FES) is one of the most suitable and excellent methods built on emission spectra to analyze the macromolecule—ligand interactions in a very short period (Duman et al., 2013; Tunç et al., 2013, 2014). This technique is considered simple, sensitive, and comparatively inexpensive. It is possible to get a high-throughput screening of biomolecules, like lipids, proteins, DNA, RNA, and membranes, but it needs elaborate fluorescent labeling procedures. The most common approach for detecting the interaction of either RNA—protein or RNA—ligand involves labeling the RNA or the ligand with a proper fluorophore such as green fluorescent protein, fluorescein, organic dyes, and quantum dots. The fluorophore fused into RNA is often quenched, and the lowering of quenching on the degradation of the RNA with a ribonuclease forms the basis of an assay in the experiment carried out (Rist & Marino, 2001). According to Liu et al. (2022), the fluorescence experiments revealed that when RNA is bound to the complex, there is an increase in fluorescence intensity as well as a significant redshift, with both peaks redshifted from about 450 to 550 nm (Fig. 5.1). This highlights the potential role that these complexes may play in cellular RNA imaging (Liu et al., 2022). In the case of DNA interaction studies using fluorescence titration, the constant amounts of metal complexes were titrated with an increasing amount of DNA at specific wavelengths, which shows an increase in emission intensity with an increase in molar ratio and a decrease at higher molar ratios. Owing to some free bases in the complex stacking up on the DNA surface, the emission intensity reduces as the DNA concentration rises (Nyarko et al., 2004). Usually, emission enhancement results from increased molecule planarity and a decrease in the frequency of solvent molecules colliding with complexes (Satyanarayana et al., 1992). Bordbar et al. (2018) studied the binding of the Mn complex to calf thymus DNA (CT-DNA) and confirmed that the complex might have been intercalated into adjacent CT-DNA base pairs.

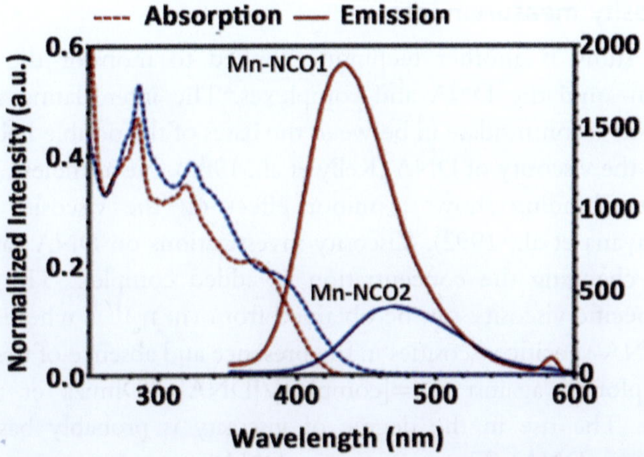

Figure 5.1 UV-vis and FES spectra of Mn complexes. *(Reprinted with permission from Liu et al. (2022).)*

3.3 Electrospray ionization–mass spectrometry and tandem mass spectrometry

The soft ionization technique known as electrospray ionization (ESI) creates multiply charged molecules from a solution under benign circumstances. Electrospray ionization–mass spectrometry (ESI–MS) attains mass spectra straight away from the samples that occur in solution form. Besides, ESI can convert the phase of biomolecules and their complexes (noncovalent and covalent) solution into a gaseous form. It can also monitor the binding of metal ions to proteins or peptides. However, the desolvation process can help in the maintenance of the metal ions bound to a biomolecule to be in the solution form. The solution phase bindings are normally specific bindings that consist of highly complex formation constants and involve high energy to be fragmented during the analysis. Whereas, in MS examination, some ions that cannot bind in the solution phase can bind each other in the gaseous form during the desolvation process of droplets. These interactions are generally nonspecific binding and entail low energy to be fragmented. In a study, the complexes of Mn^{2+}–insulin were investigated using ESI–MS and tandem mass spectrometry (MS/MS) techniques and were identified that form the specific bindings of Mn^{2+} ions to insulin molecules (Gülfen et al., 2018). According to Arjmand et al. (2019), the ESI–MS screening technique can also be utilized to detect RNA–ligand, RNA–complex, or RNA–drug interactions.

3.4 Viscosity measurements

Viscosity study is another technique applied to monitor the mode of interaction amid the DNA and complexes. The intercalating agents are predicted to accommodate in between the bases of the double helix causing a surge in the viscosity of DNA (Kelly et al., 1985). Nevertheless, groove or electrostatic binding shows a minor effect on the viscosity of DNA (Satyanarayana et al., 1992). Viscosity investigations on DNA can be achieved by changing the concentration of added complex. The values of relative specific viscosity can be obtained from $(\eta/\eta_o)^{1/3}$, where η and η_o are the DNA-specific viscosities in the presence and absence of the complex and are plotted against r (=[complex]/[DNA]) (Dimiza et al., 2020) (Fig. 5.2). The rise in the degree of viscosity is probably based on its attraction to DNA. The increase in DNA viscosity suggests that the complex dramatically raises the hydrodynamic length of DNA as a consequence of the untwisting of the base pairs and helical backbone of DNA desired to lodge the intercalators (Chan et al., 2002).

3.5 Circular dichroism spectroscopy

Circular dichroism (CD) spectroscopy is an influential way to monitor conformational changes in DNA as a result of binding between drug and metal complexes. By using this technique, we can identify the fluctuations

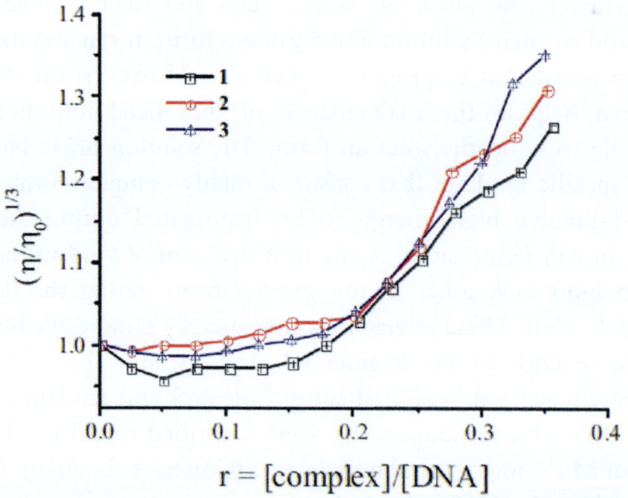

Figure 5.2 The relative viscosity of CT-DNA $(\eta/\eta_o)^{1/3}$ in presence of different complexes (**1**–**3**) at increasing amounts (r = [complex]/[DNA]). *(Reprinted with permission from Dimiza et al. (2020).)*

in the conformation of the DNA throughout a drug–DNA interaction by observing the positive bands at 275 nm and a negative band near 240 nm with a zero-crossover around 258 nm (Lincoln et al., 1997). These two bands indicate the clear outcome of bases' excitation coupling interactions of the bases that is based on the skewed orientation of the DNA backbone (Rodger, 2006). On adding of the complex to the DNA solution, if a drop in intensity for the negative band at ~245 nm and positive band at ~275 nm without shift is observed, it shows that the DNA would have interacted with these complexes and might be changed into other conformations (Maheswari & Palaniandavar, 2004). Whereas, the phenomenon where a much larger decline in intensity for the positive band at ~275 nm with a small blue shift indicates the disturbance of stacking mode and the orientation of base pairs in DNA. However, if the intensity of the positive band at 275 nm decreases significantly, it might be due to a transition from the extended right-handed double helix of nucleic acid to a more compact form (Jmdan et al., 1972). As a result of the interaction between these complexes and DNA during their binding, DNA's conformation is slightly altered. CD spectroscopy is also used as a tool to track any conformational changes that RNA might experience after binding with Mn–NCO1 at room temperature. Bands at (+)240 and (+)300 nm on the RNA itself can be attributed to the helicity of z-RNA and base pair stacking, respectively (Miyahara et al., 2016) (Fig. 5.3). The CD spectrum will display a disrupted base packing band and helicity if the interaction between RNA and small

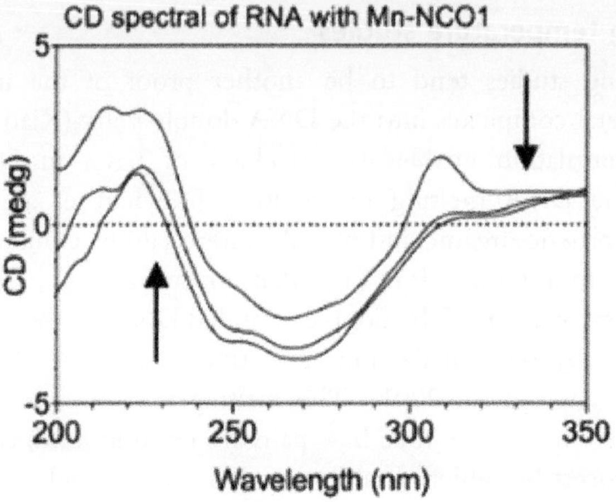

Figure 5.3 CD spectra of RNA with Mn complexes. *(Reprinted with permission from Liu et al. (2022).)*

molecules occurs by intercalated binding, but if not, it occurs through a groove or electrostatic binding (Liu et al., 2022).

3.6 Cyclic voltammetry

Cyclic voltammetry is an electochemical technique that provides additional information regarding the metal complexes and DNA interaction (Mahadevan & Palaniandavar, 1998). The interaction of the molecule into a DNA double helix can be proved by observing the molecule's electrochemical potential. If the complex or molecule shows a positive E_{pa} shift, this indicates the intercalation of the molecule into a DNA double helix, while a negative E_{pc} shift indicates the electrostatic interaction between the molecule and DNA (Carter et al., 1989; Zhang et al., 2005). Additionally, the potentials of over one show both a positive E_{pa} shift and a negative E_{pc} shift, which suggests that the molecule can bind to DNA by intercalation and electrostatic interactions (Jiao et al., 2005). However, the drug diffusion into double-helical DNA causes the development of supramolecular complexes, which results in a decrease in current and a change in the formal potential that may be caused by the drug and DNA's interaction mode (Shah et al., 2010). The inclusion of DNA appears to have reduced the complex's peak currents. The diffusion of the metal complex attached to the massive, slowly diffusing DNA molecule may be the cause of the decrease in voltammetry currents observed in the presence of CT-DNA. The CV of the Mn^{2+} complex in interaction with Fish-DNA (FS-DNA) is shown in Fig. 5.4 (Asadi et al., 2019).

3.7 Melting temperature studies

DNA melting studies tend to be another proof of the interaction of transition metal complexes into the DNA double helix (Xiao et al., 2001). Usually, intercalation enables the stacking of bases in DNA thereby increasing the DNA melting temperature (Neyhart et al., 1993). The natural or synthetic organic and metallo-intercalations exhibit a significant rise in the melting temperature (T_m) (Satyanarayana et al., 1992; Xi et al., 2008). The stabilization of the double-stranded DNA by the complexes can be confirmed by thermal denaturation studies of DNA (Tselepi-Kalouli et al., 1989; Xiao et al., 2001). The melting temperature T_m (the temperature where half of the total base pairs are left unbound) can be used to study the process by which double-stranded nucleic acids become single-stranded on raising the temperature of the solution, which causes a hyperchromic impact on the absorption spectra of DNA bases

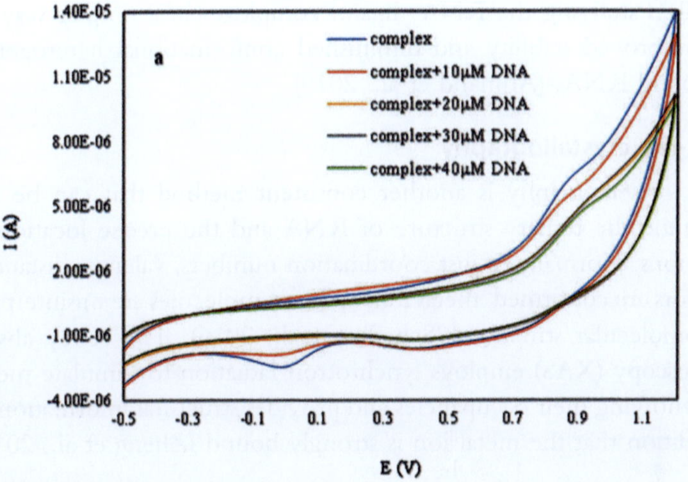

Figure 5.4 Cyclic voltammograms of the complex Mn(II) in presence of FS-DNA. *(Reprinted with permission from Asadi et al. (2019).)*

(λmax = 260 nm) (Cory et al., 1985; Kumar et al., 1993). As a result, the interaction of the complexes with DNA can be roughly inferred from the thermal behavior of DNA in the presence of the complexes.

3.8 NMR spectroscopy

One of the most consistent methods to find RNA-targeted drugs is based on chemical shifts in nuclear magnetic resonance (NMR) spectroscopy. The basis of NMR technology includes either the detection of small molecules with free ligands or bound to RNA macromolecules (Blakeley et al., 2012) or the recognition of alterations in chemical shift (functional environment on binding with RNA target) for the screening of newfangled RNA-targeted drug aspirants. A lot of literature has been published on the utilization of NMR techniques for the screening of RNA-targeted drug candidates (Bartova et al., 2016; Chen et al., 2000; Dagenais et al., 2017). However, recent developments in this area produced subtler NMR cryo-probes that give a fourfold growth in the sensitivity of the compound compared to traditional probes. Even for tiny compounds which interact with RNA, unlike fluorescence, NMR provides very quantitative ligand binding data without any specific knowledge of the biological function of the RNA-targeted molecules. NMR spectroscopy proved to be a successful technology to determine the structure of minor RNA provinces and discovering their intramolecular forces at work and interaction with ligands as well as studying the RNA–ligand complexes in a simpler way due to their improved stability and diminished conformational heterogeneity of the bound RNAs (Arjmand et al., 2019).

3.9 X-ray crystallography

X-ray crystallography is another consistent method that can be used to determine the ternary structure of RNA and the precise location of the metal ions. Normally, if just coordination numbers, valence, distances, and B-factors are confirmed, metal ions and tiny molecules are misinterpreted in macromolecular structures (Schaffer et al., 2016). The X-ray absorption spectroscopy (XAS) employs synchrotron radiation to stimulate metal ions for identifying their occupancies and provides structural information, but in a condition that the metal ion is strongly bound (Zheng et al., 2014).

3.10 Molecular docking

The studies on molecular docking were held to identify the binding nature of the complex with the help of the binding energy of the complex DNA. Initially, both the binding energies, one obtained from the docking imitation and the experimental binding free energy from the UV-vis absorption studies, were obtained. Later the binding constant attained by the UV-vis method was correlated with that of the docked model. The matching of the calculated and experimental binding constants concludes whether the complex–DNA docked model was found to be in correlation with the experimental results. However, the binding constant using Gibbs free energy can be calculated using a basic formula, $\Delta G = -RTLK$ (Shahabadi et al., 2019). The binding mode of RNA can be evaluated through molecular docking simulation by calculating the binding energy of the complex with RNA (Delgado Blanco et al., 2019; Liu et al., 2022; Si et al., 2015).

4. Applications of manganese complexes

Mn complexes have been widely studied compared to other metal complexes in the series of transition metals due to the following advantages.

(1) They are biocompatible, less toxic nature, and they can easily be excreted via kidneys. Mn is one of the crucial trace elements in a healthy organism, being involved in tissue development, growth, and the metabolism of many chemicals (Aschner & Aschner, 2005; Erikson et al., 2005; Keen et al., 1999).

(2) Mn^{2+} and Mn^{3+} may be used as contrast agents because they exhibit enhanced paramagnetic behavior due to having more unpaired electrons in their 5 d orbitals.
(3) Strong redox activity in Mn organic frameworks allows for the use of oxidation potential and pH to activate the imaging to produce a specific retort to the cancer microenvironment, enhancing and helping in its treatment (García-Hevia et al., 2018).

There is vast literature regarding a huge number of different Mn complexes with a variety of applications, as given in Table 5.1. However, some of the important uses of Mn complexes that several studies have reported are the binding nature of Mn complexes to DNA, RNA, and other biomolecules that cause protein transcription and translation disorders (Gunter et al., 2010). They are described as follows.

4.1 Manganese complexes as DNA-interacting agents

Being a popular target for pharmaceuticals and susceptible to many dangerous compounds, research on interactions of DNA with complex molecules is quite interesting (Gills et al., 2008; Ling et al., 2008). The significance of DNA is that it can carry all genetic information of cellular life and finds various uses in molecular biology; therefore, research interest has grown toward the contact of metal complexes with DNA (Abdel-Rahman et al., 2015; Chaviara et al., 2008; Mahalakshmi & Rajavel, 2010). Nowadays, the binding properties of metal complexes with DNA are trending for their varied offerings in nucleic acid chemistry (Asadi et al., 2019). DNA is known to be the main biologic target for several pathologies, so the interaction studies of metal complexes with nucleic acids help in evolving new components for biotechnological and pharmaceutical uses (Alaghaz & Aldulmani, 2019). Raja et al. (2011) stated that the intricate interaction with the DNA base pairs causes the connection of the intercalated ligand's $\pi*$ orbital with the base pairs' π orbitals, in turn lowering the transition energy of $\pi-\pi*$, hence leading to hypochromism. Additionally, a significant "hyperchromic" effect was also observed escorted by a moderate redshift that indicates the DNA helix stabilization. This type of spectral characteristic recommends binding of the ligands and complexes either via electrostatic binding or to the major and minor grooves of DNA (Asadi et al., 2019). The nature of the ligand and the geometry of the complex show impact on the DNA interaction of metal complexes. And the complexes should be steady, indolent in the biologic ecosystem, and water-soluble. Normally, the metal complexes' solubility in water can be

Table 5.1 Important uses of Mn complexes, their interaction with the biomolecules and method of analysis.

S. no.	Mn complex	Interaction/mode of binding	Analysis	Uses	References
1.	Mn (II)—insulin	Specific protein—metal ion interactions	ESI—MS	Insulin drug delivery studies	(Gülfen et al., 2018)
2.	**(i)** SC-52608, superoxide 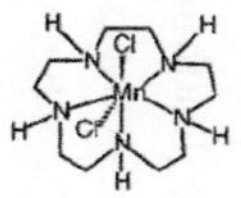 **(ii)** MnTBAP **(iii)** Teslasca 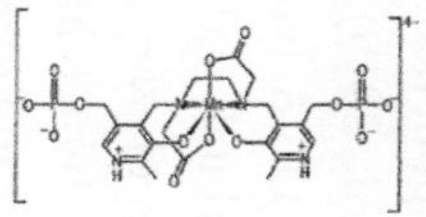	—	—	**(i)** Protect the regionally ischemic and reperfused myocardium from injury **(ii)** Parkinson and Alzheimer diseases **(iii)** Detection of hepatocellular carcinomas	(Guo & Sadler, 1999)
3.		Intercalation (CT-DNA)			(Dimiza et al., 2020)

	Mn(II)–NSAID (oxaprozin or flufenamic acid)	reversible binding (serum albumins)	UV–vis, fluorescence emission spectra	Active free radical scavengers against DDPH radical	
4.	Mn^{2+} methaniminium hydrazone (Schiff base ligand) complex	Intercalation (CT-DNA)	Electronic spectra, magnetic susceptibility, single crystal X-ray diffraction studies, photolumine scence spectra	Potential fluorescent probe for the metal determination	(Sennappan et al., 2018)
5.	$Mn(CH_3COO)_2$	b-cyclodextrin (changes in folding)	TG–DSC measurements	Soil cementation, depressants in the flotation of complex metal ores, as binders and plasticizers in metal oxide–based ceramics, and heavy metal collector	(Ciesielski & Girek, 2011)
6.	Mn complexes (planar hydrophobic ligands) preorganize the metal complex	Noncovalent (Aβ-peptides) covalent binding	NMR, EPR, MS, light scattering or turbidity thioflavin T	Alter peptide aggregation, catalytic antioxidant activity, photoinduced oxidation, peptidase	(Gomes et al., 2020)

Continued

Table 5.1 Important uses of Mn complexes, their interaction with the biomolecules and method of analysis.—cont'd

S. no.	Mn complex	Interaction/mode of binding	Analysis	Uses	References
			fluorescence, gel electrophoresis/ Western blotting, dot blotting, AFM, TEM, XAS, molecular dynamics	activity, toxicity in cells and animal model	
7.	Mn(II)—sparfloxacinato complexes	CT-DNA HSA BSA	UV spectroscopy, DNA viscosity measurements	Antimicrobial activity	(Zampakou, Balala, et al., 2015)
8.	$[Mn(dicl)(bipy)(H_2O)_2](dicl)$ $[Mn(dicl)_2(py)_2(H_2O)_2]$ $[Mn(dicl)_2(bipyam)]$ $[Mn_3(dicl)_6(phen)_2(MeOH)]$	Interchelation (CT-DNA) noncovalent interactions (SA)	CV, UV-vis, FES	Antiinflammatory activity and antiproliferative activity	(Zampakou, Hatzidimitriou, et al., 2015)
9.	$[Mn(erx)_2(phen)]$, quinolone, antimicrobial agents, oxolinic acid, and enrofloxacin	CT-DNA (intercalation) HSA BSA	UV spectroscopy, viscosity measurements, cyclic voltammetry, fluorescence spectra	Antimicrobial	(Zampakou et al., 2013)

10.	$[Mn(C_{18}H_{14}N_{10}S_2)(OAc)](OAc)_2$	Chelation of lipoid layer of the membrane		Antibacterial	(Singh et al., 2010)
11.	Manganese (II)-NSAID (tolfenamic acid)	CT-DNA (interchelation) HSA BSA	DNA viscosity measurements, UV-vis, fluorescence experiments	Scavenging activity against superoxide and hydroxyl radicals. soybean lipoxygenase inhibitor	(Zampakou et al., 2014)
12.	Mn^{2+} interaction with liposomes	Phosphatidyl ethanolamine			(Stollery & Vail, 1977)
13.	$[Mn^{II}(L)]^+$ (Mn^{II}-SOD mimic)	Amyloid-β (Aβ) peptide	UV-vis, EPR, X-ray crystallography, CV	Alzheimer disease and oxidative stress	(Conte-Daban et al., 2018)
14.	Mn(IIII) N-substituted alkyl- and alkoxy alkyl pyridylporphyrins **i)** MnTnBuOE-2-PyP^{5+} **ii)** MnTE-2-PyP^{5+}	Protein S-glutathionylation	Spectro photometric methods	**(i)** Radio protect normal tissue with cancer patients **(ii)** Atopical dermatitis	(Batinic-Haberle & Tome, 2019)

amplified by functionalizing the ligand by polar or charged groups (Ansari et al., 2009; Woldemariam & Mandal, 2008). DNA interaction with many manganese complexes with different functionalized *salen* and *salophen* derivatives has been investigated (Doctrow et al., 2002; Moreno et al., 2010). According to Gravert and Griffin, (1996), the *salen* moiety's ability to bind to and cleave DNA may be affected by the presence of substituents with differing steric and electronic properties. Few chiral and achiral manganese complexes are reported to exhibit different DNA binding/cleavage activities (Niu et al., 2015). Asadi et al. (2019) explored the binding properties of the Mn^{2+} complexes to the FS-DNA that occurred using groove binding mechanism intercalation. The planar structure of the metal complex and the binding of the metal and ligand to the DNA backbone caused the complexes to intercalate with the DNA. The CT-DNA binding of the Mn complexes with different ligands through intercalation has been stated by several researchers. The interaction of Schiff base with DNA has been focused on as Schiff base complexes can cleave DNA on irradiation with visible light (Patra et al., 2009). The coordination chemistry of macrocyclic Schiff base complexes of manganese was found to be attractive research due to their structural, electronic, magnetic, biologic, and catalytic properties (Patel & Thaker, 1999; Wang et al., 2017; Zhang et al., 2017). Abdel-Rahman et al. (2017) revealed that a tetradentate ONNO Schiff base ligand (1,10- (pyridine-2,3-dimethylamino methyl)naphthalene-2,20-diol)-based Mn^{2+} complex disclosed a positive interaction with CT-DNA through intercalation mode and tested for the anticancer property against colon carcinoma cells (HCT-116 cell line) and hepatocellular carcinoma (Hep-G2) cell lines. The binding studies reveal that the Mn^{3+} complexes displayed more robust binding of metal complexes to CT-DNA than the free ligand itself (Keypour et al., 2020). The aforementioned studies confirm that the interaction of the ligand, as well as complexes with DNA, occurs via intercalation and electrostatic force groove binding. However, the interaction of Mn complexes with DNA via a non-intercalation mode of binding has also been reported. According to Sakthi and Ramu (2017) the salicylaldehyde derived 2,4-diiodo-6-((2-phenylaminoethylimino)methyl)phenol Schiff base (L) ligand-based Mn^{2+} complexes interact in a nonintercalation way with herring sperm DNA (HS- DNA). In addition, these complexes are able to cleave the circular plasmid pUC19 DNA competently by using an activator H_2O_2. Mn^{2+} complexes using 3-ethoxy-6-(phenyl azo)-7-hydroxy coumarin (HL) with antitumor activity against human cancer MCF-7 (breast cancer) have been found to bind with CT-DNA by hydrogen bonding (El-Bindary et al., 2017). Researchers are interested in improving the activity of the drug and decreasing its ramification by formulating diverse complexes with metal ions like Mn^{2+}. Many NSAID ligand-based metal complexes are more potent than the parent NSAID ligands as well as the uncomplexed metal salts (Kovala-Demertzi et al., 2009; Shahabadi et al., 2019). The Mn^{2+} NSAID complexes are reported to be one of the most active free radical scavengers against DDPH radical, among all the metal—NSAID complexes, so far reported as well as potent binders of albumins and DNA (Dimiza et al., 2020). In a nutshell, it could be stated that Mn complexes bind to double-stranded DNA through covalent bonding (DNA nitrogen base replaces the complex's labile ligand), groove binding laterally at the major or minor groove of the DNA helix (occurrence of van der Waals interaction/hydrophobic bonding/hydrogen bonding), Coulomb forces amid metal complexes and the phosphate groups on the DNA surface (external or electrostatic interactions), and noncovalent interactions inside the DNA helix (via complex's $\pi \rightarrow \pi^*$ stacking interaction and necleobases of DNA) (Zampakou, Balala, et al., 2015).

4.2 Manganese complexes as RNA-interacting agents

Like DNA, RNA has a dominant function in cell and molecular biology as a genetic information messenger. Apart from that, it involves protein synthesis, translational regulation, and mRNA splicing. Besides, RNA possesses numerous varied secondary and tertiary folded structures like bulges, pseudoknots, mismatched hairpin loops, etc., but it lacks a cellular repair mechanism, due to which it is considered a capable feasible drug target for the pharmaceutical industry. RNA-binding metallodrug therapeutics is an emerging field of study these days. However, there are far fewer findings on RNA-binding metallodrug therapies. Arjmand et al. (2019) stated that there are some reports related to inorganic complexes showing structural, biochemical, and targeting benefits that lead to the binding or cleaving of the RNA tertiary structures used for direct mapping of their binding sites. The transition metal complexes with bioactive pharmacophores could target RNA structures more explicitly and keenly as they closely mimic the endogenous biologic environment with fewer toxic effects. There are uncountable ways for the metal complexes to interact with RNA; the first one is by covalent and noncovalent (electrostatic, groove, surface binding, intercalation, Van der Waals interactions, hydrogen bonding, etc.) and secondly by alteration of conformation of

RNA-binding sites (recognition and selectivity). Wrzesinski et al. (1995) divided RNA hydrolysis induced by the metal ion reaction into three ways: (1) to probe strong metal binding sites in solution with natural tRNAs, (2) to monitor proper tertiary folding of tRNA mutants as a sensitive probe, and (3) to structure probing of other RNAs and RNA—protein complexes. The tRNA hydrolysis reactions induced by Mn^{+2} ions in yeast $tRNA^{Phe}$, in a pair of methionine-specific tRNAs, in yeast glutamic acid accepting tRNA, and in tRNA fragments containing the yeast $tRNA^{Glu}$ anticodon arm have been investigated and are strongly cleaved in the anticodon loop. Ramesh et al. (2011) also confirmed that Mn^{2+} ions can occupy the specific sites in RNA through an outer-sphere interaction that eventually stabilizes tertiary contacts and folding of the RNA. It was also stated that the overall binding affinity of Mn^{2+} is comparatively greater than Mg^{2+} and Ca^{2+}. Semancik and Szychowski (1983) utilized divalent metal cations like Mn^{2+} for the extraction of the viroid RNA as well as for the treatment of purified nucleic acid preparations to improve the detection of these rare and smaller pathogenic RNA molecules. Based upon this concept, Friday et al. (2018) explained the idea of enrichment of specific RNAs using $MnCl_2$. Whereas $MnCl_2$ was able to enrich single-stranded and structured RNAs of 450 nm and below from a total RNA preparation, this method was used to map the transcription start sites of a PSTVd transcript from yeast total RNA under circumstances where the RNA was previously undetectable. When Liu et al. (2022) examined how Mn—NCO1 interacted with various biomolecules, they discovered that RNA was one of the biomolecules where Mn—NCO1 had the most pronounced selectivity. They have further carried out the interaction studies using fluorescence spectroscopy, CD spectroscopy, and molecular docking simulation that exposed that RNA is bound to the Mn—NCO1 through an intercalative binding mode via $\pi-\pi$ interaction between the terpyridine and the RNA residues.

4.3 Manganese complexes as other biomolecule-interacting agents

4.3.1 DNA topoisomerases (Topo I/Topo II)

DNA topoisomerases (Topos) are the enzymes that are involved in controlling DNA topology. They are divided into two types: type I topoisomerase (Topo I), which reversibly breaks a solo strand, and type II topoisomerase (Topo II), which catalyzes strand transfer through the double-strand port of DNA. DNA—Topo complexes are stabilized by drugs that inhibit Topo, which cause fatal DNA damage during replication;

hence, they are well-characterized targets for cancer therapy (Chen et al., 2013; Gaikwad et al., 2022; Kathiravan et al., 2013; Khadka et al., 2013). Molecular docking studies of Mn^{2+} complexes disclose that the complexes express the highest binding capability toward human-DNA-Topo I complex (1SC7) and crystal structure of *Escherichia coli* (3 T88) and are found to be antibacterial and antifungal (Mahmoud et al., 2017). Potocnak et al. (2016) illustrate a 5-chloro-quinoline-8-ol (ClQ)-based Mn complex ($[Mn(ClQ)_2]$) that revealed that complexes can interact with CT-DNA through intercalation and can even inhibit the catalytic activity of Topo I. Because of their high binding affinities, considerable cleavage activities, and excellent Topo I inhibition, [2-(2-morpholin-4-ylethoxy)ethoxy] group substituted Mn^{3+} phthalocyanines as potential anticancer agents (Barut et al., 2016). All of the catalytic activities of Topo II depend on its capacity to cleave and ligate DNA. Divalent metal ions like Mg^{2+}, Mn^{2+}, and Ca^{2+} are frequently used by enzymes that cleave nucleic acids to stabilize both attacking (i.e., amino acids and/or water) as well as leaving groups (i.e., DNA backbone oxygen atoms). The coordination of the divalent metal ions employed in polymerization, ligation, and cleavage reactions of nucleic acids has been linked to a specific conserved area known as the topoisomerase-primase (TOPRIM) domain (shared by a lot of type 1 and type 2 topoisomerases). Soft (or type B) metals, like Mn^{2+}, which are bigger and more polarizable, frequently favor sulfur over oxygen as an inner-sphere ligand. This is why manganese is used extensively in experiments (Deweese & Osheroff, 2010). As there is limited literature regarding the interaction of Mn complexes with Topo II, future research can be carried out in this area.

4.3.2 Serum proteins (HSA/BSA)

Serum albumins (SAs) are the most prevalent protein that contribute 60% of the total albumin. They are abundantly found in plasma, tissues, and biologic secretions all across the body (Digilio et al., 2014; Dong et al., 2014; Savadkoohi et al., 2014). The most researched SA proteins are human serum albumin (HSA) and bovine serum albumin (BSA). They have a disulfide repeating pattern that is preserved and constitutes almost 76% of homology. SAs are significant plasma proteins as they are involved in the transport of metal ions, metal complexes and drugs to their biological targets via the bloodstream. Thus, it is often obligatory to examine the affinity of potentially bioactive compounds with SAs. Their binding might either induce changes in the potential bioactive compound's properties or offer new transportation pathways (Dimiza et al., 2020). The two are significantly different from one another in terms of the quantity and location of tryptophan residues. HSA contains only one tryptophan residue (Trp-212) in domain II, whereas two tryptophan residues are present in BSA (Trp-134 and Trp-212), which made the spectroscopic analysis of the protein easier (Hooshyar et al., 2015). Many metal binding sites are present in HSA contributing to the removal and transportation of both necessary and harmful metal ions. The binding interactions of Mn^{2+} HSA were investigated by Fanali et al. (2012) using a 1 H-NMR relaxometry study. The study provided detailed knowledge about the Mn^{2+} HSA binding qualities and the involvement of HSA in scavenging mechanisms and competitive or allosteric mechanisms that changed the distribution of vital or harmful bio-factors. In addition, the discovery of both main and secondary Mn^{2+} binding sites and their associated activities lends support to the theory that Mn^{2+} bioavailability is primarily governed by allosteric mechanisms (Fanali et al., 2005). HSA (0.65 mM) serves as a reservoir for numerous metallodrugs that can be used for administration. The HSA conjugates get accumulated in tumor tissue as a result of their heightened permeability and retention impact on clearance (Mjos & Orvig, 2014).

The interaction of a serum protein BSA with Mn complexes was studied to evaluate the solution behavior of the active manganese complex in biologic media. The solution studies with BSA using spectroscopic investigations discovered solid binding and interaction among BSA and Mn^{2+} complexes, which gave rise to a potent antifungal and antidiabetic drug candidate that would be easily transported in the biological fluid and membranes with the aid of biocompatible and majorly available serum proteins. The number of binding sites (n) approximation was done using a double log graph of {log(F0 − F)/F} versus log C using fluorescence spectrometry from which the value of n for manganese complex-BSA binding was found to be 1.5. However, synchronous fluorescence spectra revealed a greater extent of quenching of the tryptophan amino acid residue in BSA than the tyrosine residue. The thermodynamic constraints like change in enthalpy, Gibbs free energy, and entropy for the BSA binding reaction were calculated using Van't Hoff's graph of lnKa versus 1/T, and Gibbs free energy change relation showed the negative value suggesting spontaneous and facile binding reaction between protein and manganese complex as reported by Kongot et al. (2020). The chiral alcohol-amine Schiff base manganese (II/III) complexes that exhibit cytotoxicity against three cancer cell lines (HepG2, MDA-MB-231, and A549) have shown binding ability toward BSA by static mode of interaction (Li et al., 2019). According to Hooshyar et al. (2015), the binding mode between Mn^{2+} DiAmsar and HSA (or BSA) was via hydrogen bonding and weak van der Waals interaction. This concept was proved by the indications of $\Delta H°$ and $\Delta S°$ and the outcomes of molecular modeling. The association constant of Mn^{2+} complex to HSA and BSA (Ka) is defined by (Eqs. 5.3 and 5.4).

$$\text{Protein} + \text{Mn (II) complex} \leftrightarrow \text{Protein} - \text{Mn (II) complex} \quad (5.3)$$

$$\text{Ka} = [\text{Protein} - \text{Mn (II) complex}]/([\text{Protein}][\text{Mn (II) complex}]) \quad (5.4)$$

According to Dimiza et al. (2020), the introduction of complexes **1–3**, ($[Mn_3(fluf)_6(phen)_2]$, $[Mn_3(fluf)_6(bipy)]$, and $[Mn_3(fluf)_6(bipy)_2]$), respectively, to the solution of the corresponding SA quench the relative emission band (343 nm for BSA and 351 nm for HSA) (Fig. 5.5A and B). This proves the binding of each coordination compound to albumins and can be attributed to differences in the SA-tryptophan environment caused by changes in protein secondary structure. The SA-quenching constants of complexes **1–3** were greater than the value of 21,010 M^1 s^1, implying the existence of a static quenching mechanism and validating the complexes' interaction with the SAs (HAS and BSA). The K values were sufficiently high to imply complicated binding and transport by the SAs. However, the K values were quite small compared with the values of the association constant of avidin with various compounds ($K = 1015\ M^{-1}$), which is the strongest known noncovalent interaction. Thereby, recommending the reversible binding of the complexes to albumins.

4.3.3 RNase

RNases are a crucial class of enzymes in cells that differ in the structure of RNA and sequences they cleave. Metal ions are frequently involved in catalysis of RNA by activating a nucleophile for cleavaging. These metals can be inhibitory or activating depending on the metal and the RNase (Jones et al., 2022). In metal-dependent RNases, metal ions like Mg^{2+} and Mn^{3+} act as cofactors (Nowotny & Yang, 2006; Zhao et al., 2015). Ando et al. reported that individual RNases bind to a diverse divalent metal ion (Ando et al., 2021). Therefore, it can be concluded that Mn^{2+} can bind to RNase. According to Lai et al. (2003), the binding ability of Mn^{2+} with *Methanococcus jannaschii* RNase HII is greater than that with other metals like Mg^{2+} and Ca^{2+} and believed to be the existence of an enzyme-substrate-metal ion complex. Cowan et al. (2000) explored that Mn^{2+} had a higher

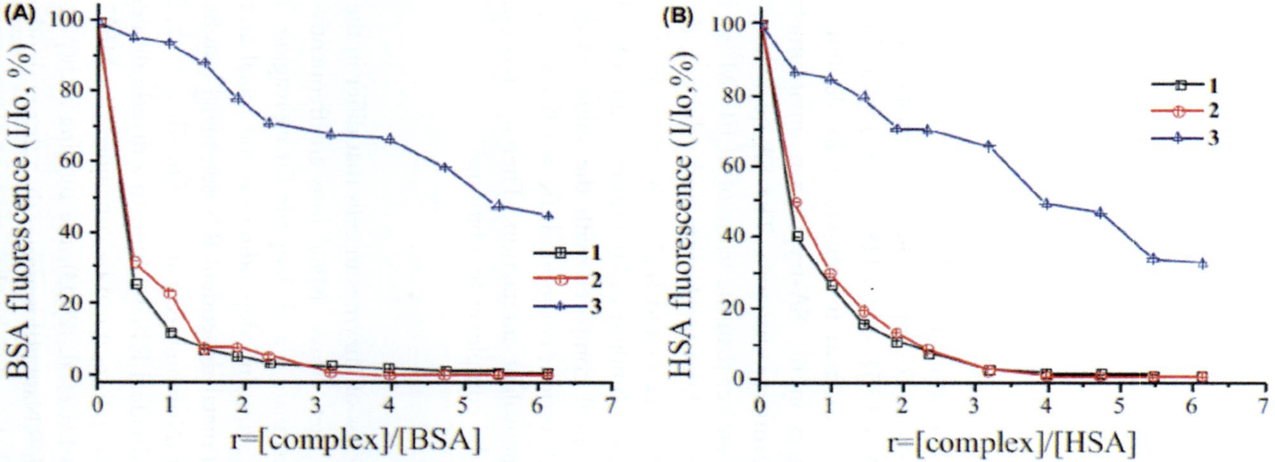

Figure 5.5 Plot of percentage relative fluorescence emission intensity (I/Io, %) for complexes 1–3 of (A) BSA at λem, max = 343 nm versus r (= [complex]/[BSA]) (up to 0.6% of the initial BSA fluorescence for 1, $<$0.5% for 2, 44.5% for 3). (B) HSA at λem, max = 351 nm versus r (= [complex]/[HSA]) for complexes 1–3 (up to 0.8% of the initial HSA fluorescence for 1, 1.0% for 2, 32.7% for 3). *(Reprinted with permission Dimiza et al. (2020).)*

affinity for both *E. coli* RNase HI and HIV-1 reverse transcriptase RNase H domains than Mg^{2+}.

4.3.4 Lipids

The Mn center in the Mn complexes is electron deficient, so it tends to bind an electron-donating ligand (Tovmasyan et al., 2013). It is assumed that the divalent cation Mn^{2+} preferentially interacts with simple negatively charged lipids systems rather than complex, biologic systems (Sule et al., 2020). Mn exhibits stable and specific binding with insulin molecule forming ML and M_2L type complex in majority and M_3L complex in minor quantity. According to Spasojevic et al. (2003), Mn porphyrins interact mostly with anionic moieties. Positively charged metals can interact with the lipid phosphate group, causing membrane dryness and instability (Disalvo, 2015; Mattai et al., 1989). Researchers stated that with Mn^{2+}, because of its small ionic radius, the negative phosphate permits metal lipid binding (Sendecki et al., 2017). It is assumed that the divalent cation Mn^{2+} preferentially interacts with simple negatively charged lipids systems rather than complex, biological systems (Sule et al., 2020).

4.3.5 Peptides

The ligand exchange rates and peptide binding affinity act as significant factors that can be changed by using different oxidation states and metal ions (Barnham & Bush, 2014; Savelieff et al., 2019). Conte-Daban et al. tested the use of a manganese superoxide dismutase mimic to target ROS production and control Aβ aggregation by copper. The Mn complex replaced the Cu^{2+} from Aβ, reduced ROS, and prevented Cu-based peptide aggregation (Conte-Daban et al., 2018). Therefore, the development of metal complexes that specifically target specific protein aggregation could lead to new diagnostic tools and targeted therapeutics. Further studies related to this subject provide more information on the etiology of specific disorders and neurodegeneration such as Alzheimer disease (Gomes et al., 2020), so new opportunities for manganese metal complexes can be explored.

5. Limitations

Though there is an incredible success in the area of manganese-based therapeutics to counter miscellaneous ailments, there are still some limitations to be solved.

1. Poor stability, low solubility, developed cell resistance, side effects, and, biologic activity, and reaction yields (Dimiza et al., 2020).
2. Limited knowledge of the mode of action of metal compounds that do not normally track the drug-like principles of organic compounds and exhibit complex thermodynamic and kinetic reactivities that hinders the drug development process (Xiong et al., 2022).
3. The possibilities of treatment for numerous disorders are still restricted (Zhang et al., 2022).
4. Lack of selectivity confines the effectiveness of current conventional chemotherapeutic treatments (Sun et al., 2022).
5. The therapeutic impact of cancer immunotherapy is hampered by immunogenicity and immunosuppressive deficits (Chen et al., 2022).
6. Low MRI sensitivity and low resolution is hindering its broad clinical applications in diagnostic imaging (Qian et al., 2019).

6. Future prospects

Based on the aforementioned limitations, future studies should be carried out to synthesize novel complexes with improved stability, solubility, and yield. Studies must be done to realize the mode of action. Synthesis of manganese complexes with different ligands should be tried for various therapeutic applications. Development of the formulations of contrast agents mostly include paramagnetic chelates and superparamagnetic nanoparticles (Qian et al., 2019). In addition, nanoparticles have unique biological features that allow for precise targeting, controlled release, and local drug delivery. They can even be utilized as immunological adjuvants to modulate the cancer microenvironment, immunosuppression reliever, potentially improving cancer immunity efficacy (Chen et al., 2022). Therefore, future research must be focused on the use of nano-formulations of Mn for immunotherapy. In this regard, scientists have been attracted to nano-sized Mn complexes with varied oxidation states because of their hold in bioinorganic chemistry and because they may serve as models for active sites of biological systems (Diao & Wang, 2018; Gleiter, 2000; Piri et al., 2019; Stamplecoskie, 2012). Furthermore, employing green synthesis for the preparation of manganese nano-formulations for carrying drugs provides an excellent alternative to traditional medications' clinical limitations and delivers high selectivity for diseased cells while leaving behind unharmed healthy cells. Hence, it can be concluded that nano-formulated manganese-based metallodrugs would be a potential emerging field with improved therapeutic clinical applications for the treatment of many chronic diseases. Laterally, they can also be employed for other applications like diagnosis and catalysis with improved efficiency.

7. Conclusion

Although lot of metal ions are involved in formulation of metallodrugs, manganese-based metallodrugs offer unique opportunities due to having variable oxidation states, being less toxic, being biocompatible, and due to their paramagnetic nature. In this chapter, we have also described the interaction of manganese with DNA, RNA, and other biomolecules like topoisomerases, serum proteins, and lipids. The contact of the manganese complexes with the biomolecules occurs via various binding modes such as covalent, and noncovalent modes like electrostatic, groove, surface binding, intercalation, van der Waals interactions, hydrogen bonding, and sometimes by the alteration of conformation of binding sites, generally termed recognition and selectivity. The ability of manganese to form such huge varieties of complexes led to its enormous applications in the medical field as antimicrobial, antibacterial, anthelminthic, antifungal, anticancer agents. In this chapter, we have reported detailed knowledge of the chemistry of manganese, structures of manganese complexes, synthesis, applications, and its analysis, which will provide a better understanding of Mn-based complexes and help for further advancement of Mn-based therapeutic and investigative agents.

References

Abdel-Rahman, L. H., Abu-Dief, A. M., Hashem, N. A., & Seleem, A. A. (2015). Recent advances in synthesis, characterization and biological activity of nano sized schiff base amino acid M(II) complexes. *International Journal of Nano Chemistry, 1*(2), 79–95.

Abdel-Rahman, L. H., Ismail, N. M., Ismael, M., Abu-Dief, A. M., & Ahmed, E. A. (2017). Synthesis, characterization, DFT calculations and biological studies of Mn(II), Fe(II), Co(II) and Cd(II) complexes based on a tetradentate ONNO donor Schiff base ligand. *Journal of Molecular Structure, 1134*, 851–862, 2017.

Alaghaz, A. M. A., & Aldulmani, S. A. A. (2019). Preparation, Structural characterization and DNA binding/cleavage affinity of new bioactive nano-sized metal (II/IV) complexes with oxazon-Schiff's base ligand. *Applied Organometalogy Chemistry*, 5135.

Aliff, M. N., Reavie, E. D., Post, S. P., & Zanko, L. M. (2020). Metallic elements and oxides and their relevance to Laurentian Great Lakes geochemistry. *PeerJ, 6*(8), e9053. https://doi.org/10.7717/peerj.9053

Ando, T., Jongruja, N., Okumura, N., Morikawa, K., Kanaya, S., & Takao, T. (2021). Identification of the ternary complex of ribonuclease HI: RNA/DNA hybrid:metal ions by ESI mass spectrometry. *Journal of Biological Chemistry, 296*, 100462.

Ansari, K. I., Grant, J. D., Woldemariam, G. A., Kasiri, S., & Mandal, S. S. (2009). Iron (III)-salen complexes with less DNA cleavage activity exhibit more efficient apoptosis in MCF7 cells. *Organic Biomolecular Chemistry, 7*, 926–932.

Arjmand, F., Afsan, Z., Sharma, S., Parveen, S., Yousuf, I., Sartaj, S., Siddique, H. R., & Tabassum, S. (2019). Recent advances in metallodrug-like molecules targeting non-coding RNAs in cancer chemotherapy. *Coordination Chemistry Reviews, 387*, 47–59.

Asadi, Z., Mandegani, Z., Asadi, M., Pakiari, A. H., Salarhaji, M., Manassir, M., Karbalaei-Heidari, H. R., Rastegari, B., & Sedaghat, M. (2019). Substituted effect on some water-soluble Mn(II) salen complexes: DNA binding, cytotoxicity, molecular docking, DFT studies and theoretical IR & UV studies. *Spectrochimica Acta Part A: Molecular and Biomolecular Spectroscopy, 206*, 278–294.

Aschner, J. L., & Aschner, M. (2005). Nutritional aspects of manganese homeostasis. *Molecular Aspects of Medicine, 26*(4–5), 353–362.

Avila, D. S., Puntel, R. L., & Aschner, M. (2013). Manganese in health and disease. *Interrelations Between Essential Metal Ions and Human Diseases, 13*, 199–227.

Barnham, K. J., & Bush, A. I. (2014). Biological metals and metal-targeting compounds in major neurodegenerative diseases. *Chemical and Social Reviews, 43*, 6727–6749.

Bartova, S., Pechlaner, M., Donghi, D., & Sigel, R. K. O. (2016). Studying metal ion binding properties of a three-way junction RNA by heteronuclear NMR. *JBIC Journal of Biological Inorganic Chemistry, 21*, 319–328.

Barut, B., Sofuoğlu, A., Biyiklioglu, Z., & Özel, A. (2016). The water soluble peripherally tetra-substituted zinc(II), manganese(III) and copper(II) phthalocyanines as new potential anticancer agents. *Dalton Transactions, 45*, 14301–14310. https://doi.org/10.1039/c6dt02720b

Batinic-Haberle, I., & Tome, M. E. (2019). Thiol regulation by Mn porphyrins, commonly known as SOD mimics. *Redox Biology, 25*, 101139.

Beznischenko, A. O., Makhankova, V. G., Kokozay, V. N., Dyakonenko, V. V., & Shishkin, O. V. (2009). Direct synthesis of Co/Mn complex with Co-semisepulchrate entity. *Inorganic Chemical Communication, 12*, 473–475.

Blakeley, B. D., DePorter, S. M., Mohan, U., Burai, R., Tolbert, B. S., & McNaughton, B. R. (2012). *Methods for Identifying and Characterizing Interactions Involving RNA Tetrahedron, 68*, 8837.

Bordbar, M., Tavoosi, F., Yeganeh-Faal, A., & Mohammad Hasan Zebarjadian, M. H. (2018). Interaction study of some macrocyclic inorganic schiff base complexes with calf thymus DNA using spectroscopic and voltammetric methods. *Journal of Molecular Structure, 1152*, 128–136.

Bouabid, S., Tinakoua, A., Lakhdar-Ghazal, N., & Benazzouz, A. (2016). Manganese neurotoxicity: Behavioral disorders associated with dysfunctions in the basal ganglia and neurochemical transmission. *Journal of Neurochemistry, 136*, 677–691.

Brimm, E. O., Lynch, M. A., Jr., & Sesny, W. J. (1954). Preparation and properties of manganese carbonyl. *Journal of American Chemical Society, 76*(14), 3831–3835, 1954.

Bröring, M., & Hell, C. (2001). Manganese as a template: A new synthesis of corrole. *Chemical Communications*, 2336–2337.

Carter, M. T., Rodriguez, M., & Bard, A. J. (1989). Voltammetric studies of the interaction of metal chelates with DNA. 2. Tris-chelated complexes of cobalt (III) and iron (II) with 1, 10-phenanthroline and 2, 2'-bipyridine. *Journal of American Chemical Society, 111*, 8901–8911.

Chan, H.-L., Liu, H.-Q., Tzeng, B.-C., You, Y.-S., Peng, S.-M., Yang, M., & Che, C.-M. (2002). Syntheses of ruthenium (II) quinonediimine complexes of cyclam and characterization of their DNA-binding activities and cytotoxicity. *Inorganic Chemistry, 41*, 3161–3171.

Chandrashekhar, V. C., Flores, B. M. M., & Jiménez-Pérez, V. M. (2018). Recent advances in direct synthesis of organometallic and coordination compounds. *Direct Synthesis of Metal Complexes*, 25–85.

Chaviara, A. T., Kioseoglou, E. E., Pantazaki, A. A., Tsipis, A. C., Karipidis, P. A., Kyriakidis, D. A., & Bolos, C. A. (2008). DNA interaction studies and evaluation of biological activity of homo- and hetero-trihalide mononuclear Cu(II) Schiff base complexes. Quantitative structure-activity relationships. *Journal of Inorganic Biochemistry, 102*, 1749–1764.

Chemistry of Manganese - Chemistry LibreTexts. (2020). https://chem.libretexts.org/Bookshelves/Inorganic_Chemistry/Supplemental_Modules_and_Websites_(Inorganic_Chemistry)/Descriptive_Chemistry/Elements_Organized_by_Block/3_d-Block_Elements/Group_07%3A_Transition_Metals/Chemistry_of_Manganese.

Chen, A., & Shapiro, M. J. (2000). NOE pumping. 2. A high-throughput method to determine compounds with binding affinity to macromolecules by NMR. *Journal of American Chemical Society, 122*, 414.

Chen, S. H., Chan, N. L., & Hsieh, T. S. (2013). New mechanistic and functional insights into DNA topoisomerases. *Annual Review of Biochemistry, 82*, 139–170. https://doi.org/10.1146/annurev-biochem-061809-100002

Chen, P., Bornhorst, J., & Aschner, M. (2018). Manganese metabolism in humans. *Frontiers in Bioscience, 23*, 1655–1679.

Chen, X., Gaoa, S., Wanga, X., Guoa, M., Cuid, Y., Chena, Z., Liua, Y., & Wanga, Y. (2022). Advances in the biological mechanism and application of manganese- based nanoformulations for enhanced immunotherapy. *Nano Today, 46*, 101583.

Ciesielski, W., & Girek, T. (2011). Study of thermal stability of b-cyclodextrin/metal complexes in the aspect of their future applications. *Journal of Inclusion Phenomena and Macrocyclic Chemistry, 69*, 461–467.

Colton, R., & Canterford, J. H. (1969). *Halides of the first row transition metals* (p. 212). Wiley.

Conte-Daban, A., Ambike, V., Guillot, R., Delsuc, N., Policar, C., & Hureau, C. (2018). A Metallo pro-drug to target CuII in the context of Alzheimer's disease. *Chemical European Journal, 24*, 5095–5099. https://doi.org/10.1002/chem.201706049

Cory, M., McKee, D. D., Kagan, J., Henry, D., & Miller, J. A. (1985). Design, synthesis, and DNAbinding properties of bifunctional intercalators. Comparison of polymethylene and diphenyl ether chains connecting phenanthridine. *Journal of American Chemical Society, 107*, 2528–2536.

Cowan, J. A., Ohyama, T., Howard, K., Rausch, J. W., Cowan, S. M., & Le Grice, S. F. (2000). Metal-ion stoichiometry of the HIV-1 RT ribonuclease H domain: Evidence for two mutually exclusive sites leads to new mechanistic insights on metal-mediated hydrolysis in nucleic acid biochemistry. *Journal of ABiological Inorganic Chemistry, 5*, 67–74.

Dagenais, P., Girard, N., Bonneau, E., & Legault, P. (2017). Insights into RNA structure and dynamics from recent NMR and X-ray studies of the*Neurospora*Varkud satellite ribozyme. *WIREs RNA, 8*, 1421.

Delgado Blanco, J., Radusky, L. G., Cianferoni, D., & Serrano, L. (2019). Protein-assisted RNA fragment docking (RnaX) for modeling RNA-protein interactions using ModelX. *Proceedings of the National Academy of Sciences United States of America, 116*(49), 24568–24573.

Deweese, J. E., & Osheroff, N. (2010). The use of divalent metal ions by type II topoisomerases. *Metallomics, 2*(7), 450–459. https://doi.org/10.1039/c003759a, 2010 January 1.

Diab, M. A., El-Sonbati, A. Z., Morgan, ShM., & El-Mogazy, M. A. (2018). Polymer complexes. LXXI. Spectroscopic studies, thermal properties, DNA binding and antimicrobial activity of polymer complexes. *Applied Organometalogical Chemistry, 4378*.

Diao, F., & Wang, Y. (2018). Transition metal oxide nanostructures: Premeditated fabrication and applications in electronic and photonic devices. *Journal of Materials Science, 53*, 4334–4359.

Digilio, G., Tuccinardi, T., Casalini, F., Cassino, C., Dias, D. M., Geraldes, C. F. G. C., Catanzaro, V., & Maiocchi, A. (2014). Rossello A. Study of the binding interaction between fluorinated matrix metalloproteinase inhibitors and human serum albumin. *European Journal of Medical Chemistry, 79*, 13–23. https://doi.org/10.1016/j.ejmech.2014.03.064

Dimiza, F., Lazou, M., Papadopoulos, A. N., Hatzidimitriou, A. G., & Psomas, G. (2020). Manganese (II) coordination compounds of carboxylate non-steroidal antiinflammatory drugs. *Journal of Inorganic Biochemistry, 203*, 110906.

Disalvo, E. A. (2015). Membrane hydration: A hint to a new model for biomembranes. *Membrane Hydration: The Role of Water in the Structure and Function of Biological Membranes, 71*, 1–16.

Doctrow, S. R., Huffman, K., Marcus, C. B., Tocco, G., Malfroy, E., Adinolfi, C. A., Kruk, H., Baker, K., Lazarowych, N., & Mascarenhas, J. (2002). Salen-manganese complexes as catalytic scavengers of hydrogen peroxide and cytoprotective agents: Structure-activity relationship studies. *Journal of Medical Chemistry, 45*, 4549–4558.

Dong, S., Li, Z., Shi, L., Huang, G., Chen, S., & Huang, T. (2014). The interaction of plant-growth regulators with serum albumin: Molecular modeling and spectroscopic methods. *Food Cosmetics and Toxicology, 67*, 123–130.

Duman, O., Tunç, S., & Bozoglan, B. K. (2013). Characterization of the binding of metoprolol tartrate and guaifenesin drugs to human serum albumin and human hemoglobin proteins by fluorescence and circular dichroism spectroscopy. *Journal of Fluorescent, 23*, 659–669.

Dusek, P., Roos, P. M., Litwin, T., Schneider, S. A., Flaten, T. P., & Aaseth, J. (2015). The neurotoxicity of iron, copper and manganese in Parkinson's and Wilson's diseases. *Journal of Trace Elements and Medical Biology, 31*, 193–203.

El-Bindary, A. A., Hassan, N., & El-Afify, M. A. (2017). Synthesis and structural characterization of some divalent metal complexes: DNA binding and antitumor activity. *Journal of Molecular Liquids, 242*, 213–228.

El-Tabi, A. S., Shakdofa, M. E., & El-Seidy, A. M. A. (2011). Synthesis and spectroscopic characterizationof Manganese(II), Iron(III) and cobalt(III) complexes of macrocyclic ligand. Potential of cobalt (III) in biological activity. *Journal of Korean Chemical Society, 55*, 919–925.

Erikson, K. M., Syversen, T., Aschner, J. L., & Aschner, M. (2005). Interactions between excessive manganeseexposure and dietary iron-deficiency in neurodegeneration. *Environmental Toxicology and Pharmacology, 19*, 415–421.

Fanali, G., Fesce, R., Agrati, C., Ascenzi, P., & Fasano, M. (2005). Allosteric modulation of myristate and Mn(III)heme binding to human serum albumin. Optical and NMR spectroscopy characterization. *FEBS Journal, 272*, 4672–4683.

Fanali, G., Masi, A. D., Trezza, V., Marino, M., Fasano, M., & Ascenzi, P. (2012). Human serum albumin: From bench to bedside. *Molecular Aspects of Medicine, 33*(3), 209–290. https://doi.org/10.1016/j.mam.2011.12.002

Friday, D., Freidhoff, P., Baumstark, T., & Bruist, M. F. (2018). Enrichment of midsized RNAs with manganese chloride precipitation. *Analytical Biochemistry, 560*, 56–59.

Friscic, T. (2012). Supramolecular concepts and new techniques in mechanochemistry: Cocrystals, cages, rotaxanes, open metal-organic frameworks. *Chemical Society Reviews, 41*, 3493–3510.

Gaikwad, M., Konkimalla, V. B., & Salunke-Gawali, S. (2022). Metal complexes as topoisomerase inhibitors. *Inorganica Chimica Acta, 542*, 121089.

García-Hevia, L., Bañobre-López, M., & Gallo, J. (2018). Recent progress on manganese-based nanostructures as responsive MRI contrast agents. *Chemical European Journal, 25*, 431–441.

Gills, J. J., Lopoiccolo, J., & Dennis, P. A. (2008). Nelfinavir, a new anti-cancer drug with pleiotropic effects and many paths to autophagy. *Autophagy, 4*(1), 107–109.

Gleiter, H. (2000). Nanostructured materials: Basic concepts and microstructure. *Acta Maters, 48*(1), 1–29.

Gomes, M. F., Bataglioli, J. C., & Storr, Tim (2020). Metal complexes that bind to the amyloid-b peptide of relevance to Alzheimer's disease. *Luiza Coordination Chemistry Reviews, 412*, 213255.

Gravert, D. J., & Griffin, J. H. (1996). Steric and electronic effects, enantiospecificity, and reactive orientation in dna binding/cleaving by substituted derivatives of $[SalenMnIII]^+$. *Inorganic Chemistry, 35*, 4837–4847.

Greenwood, N. N., & Earnshaw, A. (1997). *Chemistry of the elements* (2nd ed.). Oxford: Butterworth-Heinemann.

Grineva, A. A., Lugan, N., & Valyaev, D. A. (2021). *Organometallic manganese compounds in organic synthesis. Jean-baptiste sortais manganese catalysis in organic synthesis* (pp. 1–37). Wiley-VCH, 978-3-527-34730-8. ⟨10.1002/9783527826131.ch1⟩. ⟨hal-03376634⟩.

Gülfen, M., Özdemir, A., Lin, J., & Chen, C. (2018). Investigation of manganese (II)-insulin complexes using electrospray ionization mass spectrometry. *International Journal of Biological Macromolecules, 120*, 557–565.

Gunter, T. E., Gerstner, B., Lester, T., Wojtovich, A. P., Malecki, J., Swarts, S. G., Brookes, P. S., Gavin, C. E., & Gunter, K. K. (2010). An analysis of the effects of Mn^{2+} on oxidative phosphorylation in liver, brain, and heart mitochondria using state 3 oxidation rate assays. *Toxicology and Applied Pharmacology, 249*(1), 65–75.

Guo, Z., & Sadler, P. J. (1999). Metals in medicine. *Angewantde Chemie, 38*(11), 1512–1531.

Gupta, R. K., Pandey, R., Sharma, G., Prasad, R., Koch, B., Srikrishna, S., Li, P.-Z., Xu, Q., & Pandey, D. S. (2013). DNA binding and anti-cancer activity of redox-active heteroleptic pianostool Ru (II), Rh (III), and Ir (III) complexes containing 4-(2-methoxypyridyl) phenyldipyrromethene. *Inorganic Chemistry, 52*, 3687–3698.

Hooshyar, Z., Bardajee, G. R., Shafagh, P., Ghiasvand, S., Khanjari, M., & Dianatnejad, N. (2015). In vitro study on the interaction of Mn(II)-DiAmsar with human serum albumin (HSA) and bovine serum albumin (BSA) by spectroscopic and molecular docking methods. *Journal of Iran Chemical Society, 12*, 715–725. https://doi.org/10.1007/s13738-014-0530-7, 2015.

Jiao, K., Wang, Q. X., Sun, W., & Jian, F. F. (2005). *Synthesis, characterization and DNA binding*.

Jmdan, C., Lerman, L., & Venable, J. (1972). Structure and circular dichroism of DNA in concentrated polymer solutions. *Nature, 236*, 67–70.

Jones, S. P., Goossen, C., Lewis, S. D., Delaney, A. M., & Gleghorn, M. L. (2022). Not making the cut: Techniques to prevent RNA cleavage in structural studies of RNase–RNA complexes. *Journal of Structural Biology, 6*, 100066.

Kalaivani, P., Prabhakaran, R., Dallemer, F., Poornima, P., Vaishnavi, E., Ramachandran, E., Padma, V. V., Renganathan, R., & Natarajan, K. (2012). DNA, protein binding, cytotoxicity, cellular uptake and antibacterial activities of new palladium (II) complexes of thiosemicarbazone ligands: Effects of substitution on biological activity. *Metallomics, 4*, 101–113.

Kathiravan, M. K., Khilare, M. M., Nikoomanesh, K., Chothe, A. S., & Jain, K. S. (2013). Topoisomerase as target for antibacterial and anticancer drug discovery. *Journal of Enzyme Inhibitors and Medical Chemistry, 28*, 419–435. https://doi.org/10.3109/14756366.2012.658785

Kaupp, G. (2009). Mechanochemistry: The varied applications of mechanical bond-breaking. *Crystal Engineering Communication, 11*, 388–403.

Kaupp, G. (2011). Reactive milling with metals for environmentally benign sustainable production. *Crystal Engineering Communication, 13*, 3108–3121.

Keen, C. L., Ensunsa, J. L., Watson, M. H., Baly, D. L., Donovan, S. M., Monaco, M. H., & Clegg, M. S. (1999). Nutritional aspects of manganese from experimental studies. *Neurotoxicology, 20*, 213–223.

Kelly, J. M., Tossi, A. B., McConnell, D. J., & Ohuigin, C. (1985). A study of the interactions of some polypyridylruthenium (II) complexes with DNA using fluorescence spectroscopy, topoisomerisation and thermal denaturation. *Nucleic Acids Research, 13*, 6017–6034.

Keypour, H., Azizi, E., Mahmoudabadi, M., Salehzadeh, S., Hajibabaei, F., & Gable, R. W. (2020). Synthesis and crystal structure of manganese(III), zinc(II) and cadmium(II) complexes based on a symmetrical macroacyclic Schiff base ligand containing piperazine moiety, DNA binding studies of complexes. *Transition Metal Chemistry, 45*, 4.

Khadka, D. B., & Cho, W. J. (2013). Topoisomerase inhibitors as anticancer agents: A patent update. *Experts Opinion in Theraputic, 23*, 1033–1056. https://doi.org/10.1517/13543776.2013.790958

Kongot, M., Reddy, D. S., Singh, V., Patel, R., Singhal, N. K., & Kumar, A. (2020). A manganese (II) complex tethered with S-benzyldithiocarbazate Schiff base: Synthesis, characterization, in-vitro therapeutic activity and protein interaction studies Spectrochimica. *Acta Part A: Molecular and Biomolecular Spectroscopy, 231*, 118123.

Kovala-Demertzi, D., Hadjipavlou-Litina, D., Staninska, M., Primikiri, A., Kotoglou, C., & Demertzis, M. A. (2009). Anti-oxidant, in vitro, in vivo anti-inflammatory activity and antiproliferative activity of mefenamic acid and its metal complexes with manganese (II), cobalt (II), Nickel (II), copper (II) and zinc (II). *Journal of Enzyme Inhibitors and Medical Chemistry, 24*, 742–752.

Kumar, C., & Asuncion, E. H. (1993). DNA binding studies and site selective fluorescence sensitization of an anthryl probe. *Journal of American Chemical Society, 115*, 8547–8553.

Kumar, M., Kumar, G., Kant, A., & Masram, D. T. (2020). Role of metallodrugs in medicinal inorganic chemistry Shahid-ul-Islam. In Athar Adil Hashmi, & Salman Ahmad Khan (Eds.), *Advances in metallodrugs: Preparation and applications in medicinal chemistry* (pp. 71–114).

Kurz, P. (2014). In Antoni Llobet (Ed.), *Complexes of first row d-block metals: Manganese. Molecular water oxidation catalysis: A key topic for new sustainable energy conversion schemes* (1st ed.).

Kwon, S. B., Choi, S. H., Yoo, J. H., Kim, B. Y., Kang, B. K., Song, Y. H., & Yoon, D. H. (2020). Organic solvent-free lyophilization assisted recrystallization synthesis of high-purity green emissive Cs3MnX5 (X = I, Br). *Journal of Alloys and Compounds, 845*, 156324.

Lai, B., Li, Y., Cao, A., & Lai, L. (2003). Metal ion binding and enzymatic mechanism of Methanococcus jannaschii RNase HII. *Biochemistry, 42*, 785–791.

Lazuen-Garay, A., Pichon, A., & James, S. L. (2007). Solvent-free synthesis of metal complexes. *Chemical Society Review, 36*, 846–855.

Lemire, J. A., Harrison, J. J., & Turner, R. J. (2013). Antimicrobial activity of metals: Mechanisms, molecular targets and applications. *Nature Review of Microbiology, 11*, 371–383.

Li, Z., Yan, H., Liu, K., Huang, X., & Niu, M. (2019). Syntheses, structures, DNA/BSA binding and cytotoxic activity studies of chiral alcohol-amine Schiff base manganese (II/III) complexes. *Journal of Molecular Structure, 1195*, 470–478.

Lincoln, P., Tuite, E., & Nordén, B. (1997). Short-circuiting the molecular wire: Cooperative binding of Δ-[Ru (phen) 2dppz] 2+ and Δ-[Rh (phi) 2bipy] 3+ to DNA. *Journal of American Chemical Society, 119*, 1454–1455.

Ling, X., Zhong, W. Y., Huang, Q., & Ni, K. Y. (2008). Spectroscopic studies on the interaction of pazufloxacin with calf thymus DNA. *Journal of Photochemical and Photobiology, 93*(3), 172–176.

Liu, H., Mahmood, M. H. R., Qiu, S(Samuel)., & Chang, C. K. (2013). Recent developments in manganese corrole chemistry. *Coordination Chemistry Reviews, 257*, 1306–1333.

Liu, J., Gu, Q., Du, W., Feng, Z., Zhang, Q., Tian, Y., Luo, K., Gong, Q., & Tian, X. (2022). Nucleolar RNA in action: Ultrastructure revealed during protein translation through a terpyridyl manganese (II) complex. *Biosensors and Bioelectronics, 203*, 114058.

Mahadevan, S., & Palaniandavar, M. (1998). Spectroscopic and voltammetric studies on copper complexes of 2, 9-dimethyl-1, 10-phenanthrolines bound to calf thymus DNA. *Inorganic Chemistry, 37*, 693–700.

Mahalakshmi, N., & Rajavel, R. (2010). Binuclear copper (II), Nickel (II) and oxovanadium (IV) schiff base complexes bearing N2O2 donors and their DNA cleavage and antibacterial activity. Inter. *Journal of Pharmaceutical Technology, 2*(4), 1133–1157.

Maheswari, P. U., & Palaniandavar, M. (2004). DNA binding and cleavage properties of certain tetrammine ruthenium(II) complexes of modified 1, 10-phenanthrolines—effect of hydrogen-bonding on DNA-binding affinity. *Journal of Inorgranic Biochemistry, 98*, 219–230.

Mahmoud, W. H., Mahmoud, N. F., & Mohamed, G. G. (2017). Synthesis, physicochemical characterization, geometric structure and molecular docking of new biologically active ferrocene based Schiff base ligand with transition metal ions. *Applied Organometalogical Chemistry, 31*(12), 3858.

Mattai, J., Hauser, H., Demel, R. A., & Shipley, G. G. (1989). Interactions of metal ions with phosphatidylserine bilayer membranes: Effect of hydrocarbon chain unsaturation. *Biochemistry, 28*, 2322–2330.

Miyahara, T., Nakatsuji, H., & Sugiyama, H. (2016). Similarities and differences between RNA and DNA double-helical structures in circular dichroism spectroscopy: A SAC-CI study. *Journal of Physical Chemistry, 120*(45), 9008–9018.

Mjos, K. D., & Orvig, C. (2014). Metallodrugs in medicinal inorganic chemistry, bioinorganic enzymology. *Chemical Review, 114*, 4540–4563, 2014.

Moreno, D., Daier, V., Palopoli, C., Tuchagues, J.-P., & Signorella, S. (2010). Synthesis, characterization and antioxidant activity of water soluble Mn III complexes of sulphonato-substituted Schiff base ligands. *Journal of Inorganic Biochemistry, 104*, 496–502.

Mukhopadhyay, S., Mandal, S. K., Bhaduri, S., & Armstrong, W. H. (2004). Manganese clusters with relevance to photosystem II. *Chemical Review, 104*, 3981–4026.

Nahorn, O. V., Makhankova, V. G., Kokoza, V. N., Omelchenko, I. V., Dyakonenko, V. V., Shishkin, O. V., & Jezierska, J. (2013). Direct synthesis of linear trinuclear MII2MnII complexes with acetate and NAN donor ligands. *Journal of Molecular Structures, 1038*, 211–215.

Nesterova, O. V., Chygorin, E. N., Kokozay, V. N., Omelchenko, IV, Shishkin, O. V., Boča, R., Pombeiro, A. J., et al. (2015). A self-assembled octanuclear complex bearing the uncommon close-packed {Fe4Mn4(μ4-O)}molecular core. *Dalton Transactions, 44*, 14918–14924.

Neyhart, G. A., Grover, N., Smith, S. R., Kalsbeck, W. A., Fairley, T. A., Cory, M., & Thorp, H. H. (1993). Binding and kinetics studies of oxidation of DNA by oxoruthenium (IV). *Journal of American Chemical Society, 115*, 4423–4428.

Niu, M., Hong, M., Chang, G., Li, X., & Li, Z. (2015). A comparative study of cytotoxicity and interaction with DNA/protein of five transition metal complexes with Schiff base ligands. *Journal of Photochemical and Photobiology, 148*, 232–241.

Nowotny, M., & Yang, W. (2006). Stepwise analyses of metal ions in RNase H catalysis from substrate destabilization to product release. *EMBO Journal, 25*(9), 1924–1933. https://doi.org/10.1038/sj.emboj.7601076

Nyarko, E., Hanada, N., Habib, A., & Tabata, M. (2004). Fluorescence and phosphorescence spectra of Au (III), Pt (II) and Pd (II) porphyrins with DNA at room temperature. *Inorganic Chim Acta, 357*, 739–745, 2004.

Oulhote, Y., Mergler, D., Barbeau, B., Bellinger, D. C., Bouffard, T., Brodeur, M. E., Saint-Amour, D., Legrand, M., Sauve, S., & Bouchard, M. F. (2015). Neurobehavioral function in school-age children exposed to manganese in drinking water. *Environmental Health Perspectives, 122*, 1343–1350.

Paolesse, R., Natale, C. D., Macagnano, A., Sagone, F., Scarselli, M. A., Chiaradia, P., Troitsky, V. I., Berzina, T. S., D'Amico, A., et al. (1999). Langmuir-blodgett films of a manganese corrole derivative. *Langmuir, 15*, 1268–1274.

Patel, I. A., & Thaker, B. T. (1999). Manganese(III) complexes with hexadentate schiff-bases derived from heterocyclic β-diketones and triethylene tetramine. *Indian Journal of Chemistry, 38A*, 427–433.

Patra, A. K., Bhowmick, T., Roy, S., Ramakumar, S., & Chakravarty, A. R. (2009). *Inorganic Chemistry, 48*(7), 2932–2943.

Piri, Z., Moradi-Shoeili, Z., & Assoud, A. (2019). Ultrasonic assisted synthesis, crystallographic, spectroscopic studies and biological activity of three new Zn(II), Co(II) and Ni(II) thiosemicarbazone complexes as precursors for nano-metal oxides. *Inorganic Chim. Acta, 484*, 338–346.

Potocnak, I., Vranec, P., Farkasova, V., Sabolova, D., Vatascinova, M., Kudlacova, J.,K., Radojević, I. D., Comic, L. R., Markovic, B. S., Volarevic, V., Arsenijevic, N., & Trifunovic, S. R. (2016). Lowdimensional compounds containing bioactive ligands. Part VI: Synthesis, structures, in vitro DNA binding, antibacterial and anticancer properties of first row transition metals complexes with 5-chloro-quinolin-8-ol. *Journal of Inorganic Biochemistry, 154*, 64–77.

Pyle, A., Rehmann, J., Meshoyrer, R., Kumar, C., Turro, N., & Barton, J. K. (1989). Mixed-ligand complexes of ruthenium (II): Factors governing binding to DNA. *Journal of American Chemical Society, 111*, 3051–3058.

Qian, X., Han, X., Yu, L., Xu, T., & Chen, Y. (2019). Manganese-based functional Nanoplatforms: Nanosynthetic construction, physiochemical property, and theranostic applicability. *Advanced Functional Materials*, 1907066.

Raja, D. S., Bhuvanesh, N. S., & Natarajan, K. (2011). Biological evaluation of a novel water-soluble Sulphur bridged binuclear copper (II) thiosemicarbazone complex. *European Journal of Medical Chemistry, 46*, 4584–4594.

Ramachandran, E., Raja, D. S., Rath, N. P., & Natarajan, K. (2013). Role of substitution at terminal nitrogen of 2-oxo-1, 2-dihydroquinoline-3-carbaldehyde thiosemicarbazones on the coordination behavior and structure and biological properties of their palladium (II) complexes. *Inorganic Chemistry, 52*, 1504–1514.

Ramesh, A., Wakeman, C. A., & Winkler, W. C. (2011). Insights into metalloregulation by M-box riboswitch RNAs via structural analysis of manganese-bound complexes. *Journal of Molecular Biology, 407*(4), 556–570.

Rist, M., & Marino, J. (2001). Association of an RNA kissing complex analyzed using 2-aminopurine fluorescence. *Nucleic Acid Research, 29*(11), 2401.

Rodger, A. (2006). Circular dichroism and linear dichroism. *Encyclopedia of Analytical Chemistry*, 1–34. https://doi.org/10.1002/9780470027318.a5402.pub2

Sakthi, M., & Ramu, A. (2017). Synthesis, structure, DNA/BSA binding and antibacterial studies of NNO tridentate Schiff base metal complexes. *Journal of Molecular Structure, 1149*(5), 727–735.

Satyanarayana, S., Dabrowiak, J. C., & Chaires, J. B. (1992). Neither. DELTA.-nor. LAMBDA.-tris (phenanthroline) ruthenium (II) binds to DNA by classical intercalation. *Biochemistry, 31*, 9319–9324, 1992.

Savadkoohi, S., Bannikova, A., Kasapis, S., & Adhikari, B. (2014). Structural behaviour in condensed bovine serum albumin systems following application of high pressure. *Food Chem, 150*, 469–476.

Savelieff, M. G., Nam, G., Kang, J., Lee, H. J., Lee, M., & Lim, M. H. (2019). Development of multifunctional molecules as potential therapeutic candidates for alzheimer's disease, Parkinson's disease, and amyotrophic lateral sclerosis in the last decade. *Chemical Review, 119*, 1221–1322.

Schaffer, M. F., Peng, G., Spingler, B., Schnabl, J., Wang, M., Olieric, V., & Sigel, R. K. O. (2016). The X-ray structures of six octameric RNA duplexes in the presence of different di- and trivalent cations. *International Journal of Molecular Science, 17*, 988, 2016.

Semancik, J. S., & Szychowski, J. (1983). Enhanced detection of viroid-RNA after selective divalent cation fractionation. *Analytical Biochemistry, 135*, 275–279.

Semenaka, V. V., Shishkin, O. V., Nesterova, O. V., & Volodymyr, R. B. (2010). Direct synthesis of an heterometallic {MnII3CrIII4} wheel by decomposition of Reineckes salt. *Dalton Transactions, 39*, 2344–2349.

Sendecki, A. M., Poyton, M. F., Baxter, A. J., Yang, T., & Cremer, P. S. (2017). Supported lipid bilayers with phosphatidylethanolamine as the major component. *Langmuir, 33*, 13423–13429.

Sennappan, M., Krishna, M. P., Hosamani, A. A., & Krishna, R. H. (2018). Synthesis, characterization, nucleic acids interactions and photoluminescent properties of methaniminium hydrazone Schiff base and its Mn(II), Co(II), Ni(II), Cu(II), Zn(II) and Cd(II) complexes. *Journal of Molecular Structure, 1164*, 271–279. https://doi.org/10.1016/j.molstruc.2018.03.054

Shah, A., Zaheer, M., Qureshi, R., Akhter, Z., & Nazar, M. F. (2010). Voltammetric and spectroscopic investigations of 4-nitrophenylferrocene interacting with DNA. *Spectrochim Acta, A: Molecular and Biomolecular Spectroscopy, 75*, 1082–1087.

Shahabadi, N., jamshidi, Z., Hadidi, S., Shiri, F., & Fatahi, N. (2019). Intercalation of manganese-mefenamic acid complex into double stranded of calf thymus DNA. *Nucleosides, Nucleotides and Nucleic Acids., 38*(11), 901–919.

Shi, S., Yao, T. M., Geng, X. T., Jiang, L. F., Liu, J., Yang, Q. Y., & Ji, L. N. (2009). Synthesis, characterization, and DNA-binding of chiral complexes Δ-and Λ-[Ru (bpy) 2 (pyip)] 2+. *Chirality, 21*, 276–283.

Si, J., Cui, J., Cheng, J., & Wu, R. (2015). Computational prediction of RNA-binding proteins and binding sites. *International Journal of Molecular Science, 16*(11), 26303–26317.

Singh, D. P., Kumar, K., & Sharma, C. (2010). New 14-membered octaazamacrocyclic complexes: Synthesis, spectral, antibacterial and antifungal studies. *European Journal of Medical Chemistry, 45*(3), 1230–1236.

Spasojevic, I., Batinic-Haberle, I., Reboucas, J. S., Idemori, Y. M, & Fridovich, I. (2003). Electrostatic contribution in the catalysis of O2- dismutation by superoxide dismutase mimics. MnIIITE-2- PyP5+ versus MnIIIBr8T-2-Py. *Journal of Biological Chemistry, 278*, 6831–6837.

Stamplecoskie, K. G., & Scaiano, J. C. (2012). Silver as an example of the applications of photochemistry to the synthesis and uses of nanomaterials. *Photochemical and Photobiology, 88*(4), 762–768.

Stollery, J. G., & Vail, W. J. (1977). Interactions of divalent cations or basic proteins with phosphatidylethanolamine vesicles. *Biochim Biophysics Acta Biomembrane, 471*, 372–390.

Sule, K., Umbsaar, J., & Prenner, E. J. (2020). Mechanisms of Co, Ni, and Mn toxicity: From exposure and homeostasis to their interactions with and impact on lipids and biomembranes. *BBA – Biomembranes, 1862*(8), 183250.

Sun, D., Gao, W., Hu, H., & Zhou, S. (2022). Why 90% of clinical drug development fails and how to improve it? *Acta Pharmaceutica Sinica B, 12*, 3049–3062.

Tovmasyan, A., Weitner, T., Sheng, H., Lu, M. M., Rajic, Z., Warner, D. S., Spasojevic, I., Reboucas, J. S., Benov, L., & Batinic-Haberle, I (2013). Differential coordination demands in Fe versus Mn water-soluble cationic metalloporphyrins translate into remarkably different aqueous redox chemistry and biology. *Inorganic Chemistry, 52*, 5677–5691.

Treichel, P. M., et al. (2004). *Manganese carbonyls and manganese carbonyl halides in comprehensive organometallic chemistry* (Vol 6) (Manganese group. X`xCasey, Abel E.W, Wilkinson G. Science).

Tselepi-Kalouli, E., & Katsaros, N. (1989). The interaction of [Ru (NH_3)5Cl]2þ and [Ru$(NH_3)_6$]3þ ions with DNA. *Journal of Inorganic Biochemistry, 37*, 271–282.

Tunç, S., Duman, O., & Bozo-glan, B. K. (2013). Studies on the interactions of chloroquine diphosphate and phenelzine sulfate drugs with human serum albumin and human hemoglobin proteins by spectroscopic techniques. *Journal of Luminescence, 140*, 87–94.

Tunç, S., Duman, O., Soylu, I., & Bozo_glan, B. K. (2014). *Study on the bindings of dichlorprop*.

Wang, S., Li, Y. J., Ju, F. F., Xu, W. T., Kagesawa, K., Li, Y. H., Yamashita, M., & Huang, W. (2017). The molecular and supramolecular aspects in mononuclear manganese (III) Schiff-base spin crossover complexes. *Dalton Transactions, 46*, 11063–11077.

Woldemariam, G. A., & Mandal, S. S. (2008). Iron (III)-salen damages DNA and induces apoptosis in human cell via mitochondrial pathway. *Journal of Inorganic Biochemistry, 102*, 740–747.

Wrzesinski, J., Michatowski, D., Ciesiolka, J., & Krzyzosiak, W. J. (1995). Specific RNA cleavages induced by manganese ions. *FEBS Letters, 374*, 62–68.

Xi, P.-X., Xu, Z.-H., Liu, X.-H., Chen, F.-J., Huang, L., & Zeng, Z.-Z. (2008). Synthesis, characterization, antioxidant activity, and DNA-binding studies of 1-cyclohexyl-3-tosylurea and its Nd (III), Eu (III) complexes. *Chemical Pharmaceutical Bulletin, 56*, 541–546.

Xiao, S., Lin, W., Wang, C., & Yang, M. (2001). Synthesis and biological evaluation of DNA targeting flexible side-chain substituted b-carboline derivatives. *Bioorganic Medical Chemistry Letters, 11*, 437–441.

Xiong, X., Liu, L.-Y., Mao, Z.-W., & Zou, T. (2022). Approaches towards understanding the mechanism-of-action of metallodrugs. *Coordination Chemistry Reviews, 453*, 214311.

Yadav, O., Varshney, A., & Kumar, A. (2017). Manganese(III) mediated synthesis of A2B Mn(III) corroles: A new general and green synthetic approach and characterization. *Inorganic Chemical Communication, 86*, 168–171.

Zampakou, M., Akrivou, M., Andreadou, E. G., Raptopoulou, C. P., Psycharis, V., Pantazaki, A. A., & Psomas, G. (2013). Structure, antimicrobial activity, DNA- and albumin-binding of manganese(II) complexes with the quinolone antimicrobial agents oxolinic acid and enrofloxacin. *Journal of Inorganic Biochemistry, 121*, 88–99.

Zampakou, M., Rizeq, N., Tangoulis, V., A. Papadopoulos, N., Perdih, F., Turel, I., & Psomas, G. (2014). Manganese(II) complexes with the non-steroidal anti-inflammatory drug tolfenamic acid: Structure and biological perspectives. *Inorganic Chemistry, 53*(4), 2040–2052.

Zampakou, M., Balala, S., Perdih, F., Kalogiannis, S., Turel, I., & Psomas, G. (2015). Structure, antimicrobial activity, albumin- and DNA-binding of manganese(II)–sparfloxacinato complexes. *RSC Advances, 5*, 11861–11872.

Zampakou, M., Hatzidimitriou, A. G., Papadopoulos, A. N., & Psomas, G. (2015). Neutral and cationic manganese (II)—diclofenac complexes: Structure and biological evaluation. *Journal of Coordinative Chemistry, 68*, 4355—4372.

Zhang, S.-S., Niu, S.-Y., Qu, B., Jie, G.-F., Xu, H., & Ding, C.-F. (2005). *Studies on the interaction.*

Zhang, N., Fan, Y., Huang, G., Buac, D., Bi, C., Ma, Y., Wang, X., Zhang, Z., Zhang, X., & Dou, P. (2017). l-Tryptophan Schiff base cadmium(II) complexes as a new class of proteasome inhibitors and apoptosis inducers in human breast cancer cells. *Inorganic Chim Acta., 466*, 478—485.

Zhang, Y., Chen, L., Sun, R., Lv, R., Du, T., Li, Y., Zhang, X., Sheng, R., & Qi, Y. (2022). Multienzymatic antioxidant activity of manganese-based nanoparticles for protection against oxidative cell damage. *ACS Biomaterial Science and Engineering, 8*, 638—648.

Zhao, P., Jin, S.-f., Lu, J.-Z., Lv, J.-l., Wu, G.-q., Chen, P.-P., Tan, C.-L., & Chen, D.-W. (2015). *Novel porphyrin—daunomycin hybrids: synthesis and preferential binding to gquadruplexes.*

Zheng, H., Chordia, M. D., Cooper, D. R., Chruszcz, M., Muller, P., Sheldrick, G. M., & Minor, W. (2014). Validation of metal-binding sites in macromolecular structures with the checkmymetal web server. *Nature Protocols, 9*(1), 156—170.

Zheng, R., Guo, J., Cai, X., Bin, L., Lu, C., Singh, A., Trivedi, M., Kumar, A., & Liu, J. (2022). Manganese complexes and manganese-based metal-organic frameworks as contrast agents in MRI and chemotherapeutics agents: Applications and prospects. *Colloids and Surfaces B: Biointerfaces, 213*, 112432.

Index

Note: 'Page numbers followed by "*f*" indicate figures and "*t*" indicate tables.'

CPI Antony Rowe
Eastbourne, UK
August 28, 2023